the
POLITICS of MISTRUST

MANAGING INFORMATION

A Series of Books in Organization Studies and Decision-Making

Edited by **AARON WILDAVSKY**, *University of California, Berkeley*

What impact does the computer have on organizations (both public and private), and the individual decision makers within them?

How can "data" be converted into "information for decision"?

Who produces (and who consumes) such data? with what effects? under which conditions?

What are the sources of error—and the means of overcoming them—in contemporary management information systems (MIS)?

What is the state of the art in MIS theory?

How can we increase our understanding of information and its management, as well as the surrounding organizational environment?

These are critical questions in an era of information overload, coupled with the need for decision-making by managers and policy makers dealing with finite resources. The **Managing Information** series meets the need for timely and careful analysis of these vital questions. Studies from a variety of disciplines and methodological perspectives will be included. The series will analyze information management from both public and private sectors; empirical as well as theoretical materials will be presented.

the POLITICS of MISTRUST

Estimating American Oil and Gas Resources

Aaron Wildavsky
Ellen Tenenbaum

with **PAT ALBIN** and the assistance of
NATALE CIPPOLINA, EHUD LEVY-PASCAL,
and **DAVID VACHON**

SAGE PUBLICATIONS   Beverly Hills   London

Copyright © 1981 by Sage Publications, Inc.

For information address:

SAGE Publications, Inc.
275 South Beverly Drive
Beverly Hills, California 90212

SAGE Publications Ltd
28 Banner Street
London EC1Y 8QE, England

Printed in the United States of America

Library of Congress Cataloging in Publication Data

Wildavsky, Aaron.
   The politics of mistrust.

   (Managing information ; v. 1)
   Includes bibliographical references and index.
   1. Petroleum industry and trade—United States.
2. Gas, Natural—United States.   3. Energy policy—
United States.   4. Power resources—United States.
I. Tenenbaum, Ellen, joint author.   II. Albin, Pat,
joint author.   III. Title.   IV. Series.
HD9566.W48   553.2'8'0973   80-29049
ISBN 0-8039-1582-9
ISBN 0-8039-1583-7 (pbk.)

FIRST PRINTING

CONTENTS

To
RUTH ZEMLIAK
and
EVA WILDAVSKY

ACKNOWLEDGMENTS

This book stems from research made possible through a project funded as a subcontract with the Lawrence Berkeley Laboratory of the University of California in support of the authors of energy information validation in the Energy Information Administration of the U.S. Department of Energy.

The comprehensive character of this book was made possible by a talented group of colleagues who wrote initial drafts of various chapters. Pat Albin did the historical studies in the second, third, and fourth chapters, Natale Cippolina the seventh chapter on reserve reporting, David Vachon the eighth on credibility. Ehud Levy-Pascal contributed to the eleventh chapter's discussion of oil and gas reserve estimation in the U.S. Department of Energy. Presley Pang participated in preparing the tenth chapter, on facts, theory, and relevance.

We wish to thank Edward Cowan, Mary Douglas, Darius Gaskins, Jr., William Hederman, Robert Heine, Mark Horowitz, R. J. Maisonpierre, Richard Mancke, Bart McGuire, Vincent McKelvey, Pietro Nivola, John Schanz, Fred Singer, Bernard Tenenbaum, and Thomas Wander for their helpful comments, which in no way imply agreement.

All concerned admire the splendid way in which LeRoy Graymer, the President of the Institute for Policy and Management Research, facilitated our efforts at every stage. Mappie Seabury provided a close editing of the manuscript. Several secretaries were involved at various stages of the work typing numerous drafts and revisions, but we particularly thank Annette Howard and Doris Patton for their competence and kindness.

INTRODUCTION

We will have done a hell of a disservice [to future generations] if
we do again what we did in 1973.
                                        —*Charles Duncan, Secretary of Energy*
                                        Wall Street Journal, *February 27, 1980*

Energy may be the worst-handled policy problem of the century. Its
history has been one of internal contradiction. On the demand side,
manipulation of prices by the petroleum cartel together with certain
federal and state policies have put the United States in the position of
subsidizing the import of oil. Huge increases in the price of foreign oil
began in 1973, along with a vast outflow of foreign exchange, a steep
decline in the dollar, and enhanced inflation.

Some groups greeted the multiple price increases in foreign oil with a
certain satisfaction. At last, they thought, citizens would have to conserve
by returning to a simpler and more natural way of life. Yet the factors that
led to subsidizing imports kept the price of gasoline low. Fulminations
about gas-guzzling automobiles could not overcome the signals of this
topsy-turvy price system: Use it, it's cheap.

On the supply side, a nation noted for its productivity (one that a
quarter-century earlier had gloried in its wartime ability to produce the
unheard-of number of 50,000 airplanes a year) allowed domestic petroleum production actually to drop. At times this production decline resulted from a conscious decision to preserve resources at home in the long run
by importing more in the short run. But at other times, domestic production efforts that might have been desirable were being stifled. The nuclear
power industry was virtually paralyzed. Challenges to oil and gas exploration and new pipelines led to abandonment or delay. Regulation of
surface- and deep-coal-mining and offshore drilling, as well as opposition

to mining in wilderness areas, restricted production. Except for modestly funded research, which produced the usual answer that help was just over the horizon, no new sources of energy were developed. In short, the nation, with a growing demand for shrinking energy supplies, was caught in a web of contradictory policy signals.

Private producers of oil and gas who earlier had welcomed government intervention to limit their production and protect their profits, now urged the government to lift its price controls. Higher production usually is touted as the way to lower prices. Yet, producers argued, with higher prices they could bring forth great quantities of oil and gas. Not unless, consumer advocates countered, the government first agrees to tax away substantial profits. Not unless, Congress members argued, you can prove that the profit motive acutally will lead to new discoveries or technologies that will increase the supply of oil and gas.

Of course, if everyone knew the answer there would be no reason to ask the question. Since oil and gas resources lie underground (and estimators lack Superman's X-ray vision), the usual way to find out is to drill holes. Proof is impossible without drilling, drilling is not done unless profit will come, and profit will not come without the prospect of higher prices. Out of these arguments came not an increase in production, but only a deadlock of wills.

Government was unable to generate a consistent national energy plan. It was as if Uncle Sam blindfolded himself, stopped his ears, gagged his mouth, tied his legs and feet, and yet wondered why he wasn't getting anywhere. The root of the problem seemed to be that government could neither replace private markets nor agree on how markets should operate.

Energy is more than policy. Energy carries a considerable emotional loading. Energy symbolizes science and technology, the lifeblood of industrial civilization. Shut off that energy and you alter the technology on which that society rests. Our use (misuse, abuse) of energy also galvanizes opposition to industrial society. Those who wish to change the course of modern society, therefore, find energy a powerful fulcrum.

Energy is politics, too. Who has energy has power. The very use of the word to describe a desirable characteristic in people and to name the force that moves machines shows how central energy has become. It is not surprising, then, that the controversies over private versus public power (whether rural electric cooperatives or the Tennessee Valley Authority) refer both to energy in the economy and to power in society.

Energy policy engages passion more than intellect; our irrational handling of energy policy is unmatched by our behavior in any other field. Why have we done this to ourselves? What is it about energy that has provoked the worst aspects of policy thinking?

ENERGY AS A POLARIZING ISSUE

Well-known issues, such as energy, carry their own contexts on their backs. Their history is such, and the number of conflicts so large, that participants tend to develop attitudes and predispositions that are used as a kind of shorthand whenever certain polarizing subject matter impinges on their consciousness. By studying the history of such an issue, we can ascertain the context into which it is likely to be put by a variety of participants.

Some issue-contexts exercise a severe dichotomizing effect by which opinion is polarized into two opposing groups. In some others, all the participants have not chosen sides. And there are still other issue-contexts in which participants are fragmented into many groups that take a variety of positions (Wildavsky, 1962).

Now consider issues on which there is consensus. The values, and hence the desired objective, are agreed upon. All the facts may not be in, or there would be no need for thrashing out a decision, but everyone understands the kinds of facts that will count as evidence. Search is instrumental: What alternatives, with which predicted consequences, will best achieve those accepted objectives? The facts set forth are value-laden in that their relevance and acceptability are predetermined by prior agreement. In this process of instrumental search the pitfall is that indicated actions which dispute existing policies may be disregarded, precisely because current patterns of action are so well established.

In a diffused issue-context, however, search is open: Fact and policy exist, each looking for the other. Since neither ends nor means are evident, the predominant problem is to match resources with objectives. If openness is strength, immobility and indecision are the potential weaknesses of diffusion.

By contrast, within a polarized issue-context, the one thing actors have in common are enemies. Search is simple and subjective: Whatever will discomfort the enemy is wanted. All facts dissolve into policy theories; "facts" do not exist except to justify policies. For example, estimates, not only of recoverable oil and gas resources or reserves (which cannot be seen) but also of holdings above ground (which are visible), are contested if such estimates point in the wrong direction. Estimates are approved if they serve the right side.

Let us look at facts from the standpoint of policies. Only when we agree about policies do we accept factual evidence for what it can tell us about accomplishing objectives. If the context is diffuse, it is hard to certify any facts without knowing to what policies such facts relate. And when the context is polarized, assertions substitute for facts: "I know all I need to know about you mean, ornery. . . ." What this exercise has to tell us is of profound importance for understanding energy policy.

Participants can see eye to eye on policies or can agree to accept the outcomes of institutions and processes, even if not pleased with the outcome. An issue area is settled either when a range of policies is seen as broadly acceptable or when institutions and processes are deemed legitimate, so that their outcomes can be accepted. The stake that participants have in the processes, then, is greater than their stake in specific outcomes. Just the opposite occurs in oil and gas: The participants dispute not only policies but processes as well.

Will a political settlement follow if, at long last, "we the people" agree on the facts about energy? Or is political settlement a prerequisite to agreeing on which facts we are willing to certify as relevant for public policy?

A TRACER ELEMENT:
ESTIMATES OF OIL AND GAS RESOURCES AND RESERVES

Studying energy policy is perplexing precisely because there appears to be so much of it (though critics of the Department of Energy claim the problem is that there is *no* energy policy). But to study the entire history of energy policy, even if possible, could be wearying as well; once we crawled into the thicket, we would never get out—too many trees and too little forest. What we need is a laser beam to search the past, so that energy policy—and the relationship between data and policies involved—would stand out against the background. It would be especially desirable if this concentration on American expeience with energy were one in which the least, rather than the most, conflict ordinarily would be expected to show up.

One would think that estimates of oil and gas reserves and resources—some general agreement on estimates of quantities—surely ought to be one area of energy set firmly in scientific inquiry. Actually, however, this most rational aspect tosses on a sea of irrationality, lost in the fog of mistrust. If reasonable people fail to approach even a reasonable facsimile of agreement over estimates, how could agreement on larger issues be hoped for?

For insight we have looked into resource and reserve estimation from their beginnings at the turn of the century. At the outset, reserves and resources are to be distinguished: Resources refer to the total amount of oil and gas that physically exists in a specified volume of the earth's crust, including the undiscovered. Reserves are only a small portion of total resources. Reserves refer to oil or gas that has been discovered and is producible at the prices and technology existing when the estimate was made. The appendix to this report, written by John J. Schanz, Jr., of the research organization, Resources for the Future, provides an excellent introduction to the estimation of oil and gas reserves and resources.

A few numbers relating to total oil resources of the United States will illustrate the disagreement over estimates:

1908	U.S. Geological Survey	A range was estimated of between 10 billion barrels and 24.5 billion barrels, predicting that the U.S. would run out of oil completely between 1935 and 1943.
1921	U.S. Geological Survey/ American Association of Petroleum Geologists	9 billion barrels
1974	M. King Hubbert (an independent estimator)	72 billion barrels
1974	Vincent McKelvey (U.S. Geological Survey)	A range between 200 billion barrels and 400 billion barrels

The title of the appendix, "Oil and Gas Resources: Welcome to Uncertainty," indicates that a resource estimate, and to some extent a reserve estimate, contains enough uncertainty so that quite possibly either a high or low estimate for the same field—or reservoir within a field—might be reasonable. And sometimes, for different reporting purposes, different estimates for the same area have been prepared. Indeed, the very word "accuracy" is acknowledged to be a misleading notion when one is dealing with underground and unseen oil and gas. As Schanz (1978: 4) points out, the engineer's estimate of reserves "may range from the least amount of oil and gas that appears to have been found to the outer limit of what the reservoir might ultimately produce if the buried structure is entirely filled with oil and gas."

> If estimators are agreed on anything, it is that the definitions of terms must be examined closely and more standard definitions accepted. . . . This is not as easy as it may seem. Even a seemingly simple term "total oil and gas in place" changes in meaning due to changes in information and the economic or technological perception of the analyst. Gas in tight sands or heavy oils would not have been encompassed within the definition of that term a few years ago [1978: 15].

There are no measurements in oil or gas reserve and resource appraisals:

> Even in discovered reservoirs we do not measure the oil in place—it is estimated. Reserves are an estimated value derived from a prior estimate of the oil in place, taking into account economics and technology. If the oil-in-place estimate changes, so will that of the reserves. Reserves and resources are equal to the estimated oil in place multiplied by an assumed recovery factor, substantially less than 100 percent for oil, less the amount of cumulative production. Nothing could be simpler yet so uncertain [1978: 15].

What stands out in the episodes described in our analysis is how strikingly the elements of uncertainty and judgment have fueled mutual mistrust between participants on opposite poles of energy policy issues, to compound the confusion and frustration of all.

DEJA VU IN ENERGY POLICY

Did the United States behave rationally about energy before 1973, so that what is new in the international environment may be deemed responsible for difficulties? No, U.S. behavior always has been irrational (except in wartime), if by that one means that inconsistent policies are followed. What is unusual is the remarkable similarity of the contradictory positions taken; press a button and the years—teens, twenties, thirties, sixties, seventies—sound almost identical in theme. The big difference is that earlier on, the economics of the industry were so favorable that foolish behavior did not matter. Now it does.

We begin at the turn of the century because that is when the trouble began—political trouble so deep and divisive it has prevented Americans from agreeing on where they are now in energy, let alone where they would like to go. The United States Geological Survey (USGS) first estimated the nation's total oil and gas resources in 1908. These estimates came to be used for two purposes: Industrial interests wanted to locate the most promising fuel resources, and conservationists wanted to show how scarce and limited those resources were. Already the lines of policy preference were sketched. Each side seized on USGS estimates to confirm particular stands and advance its own aims. Estimates of the USGS, which came in low, were used to strengthen conservationist suspicions of rampant industry wastefulness; industry rejected those results, purportedly on grounds of methodology.

Conflict over energy was reflected in estimation methods, in categories and definitions, and in reported results. No matter when we tune in, during peacetime—whether 1910 or 1980, 1920 or 1970, 1930 or tomorrow—the cast of characters may differ but the play is the same: One faction claims you have manipulated estimates for your own nefarious purposes; the other retorts that opponents have corrupted estimates for private gain. Only during World Wars I and II did conflict over data Subside, a turn of events we shall examine closely.

The estimates of oil and gas reserves most widely used have been those published annually by the American Petroleum Institute (API) and the American Gas Association (AGA). The process by which these associations estimate oil and gas reserves grew out of their internal structures. From its birth in 1919, the API adopted a decentralized form of organization composed of networks of committees and subcommittees. With this structure the API could contain conflicts among sectors of the industry, respect individual firms' competitive interests and trade secrets, and avoid violating government antitrust law. The API's Committee on Proved Reserves and its regional subcommittees likewise represented a balancing of different interests and concerns. The joint API/AGA estimation system serves as an aid to industry planning. But the purpose of the Committee on Proved Reserves and its subcommittees within the API and AGA is *not* to obtain an accurate estimate of the nation's proved oil and gas reserves; in fact, reserves outside the domain of subcommittee members' responsibility may go unreported. Subcommittee members come from producing companies, universities, consulting firms, or state government agencies. A member who comes from a company usually is responsible for fields in which his company is active; but he is not there (though others may dispute this) as a representative of his company and, indeed, may be denied access to certain of his own company's data. A member may decide to ask, or decide not to ask, for internal records of another company in putting together estimates. If the member asks, the other company may or may not share those records. Thus, total estimates are tempered by mutual respect for the proprietary nature of each company's reserve information. The API and AGA systems try to get estimates of interest to a variety of companies without trespassing on private information. Methods are based on what can be agreed upon among companies in competition, rather than on what would be optimal if one wanted to estimate total reserves. The API and AGA explain that what is lost is a relatively small part of the total, and that its absence is essential to permit the overall operation to continue.

Estimators created new categories and definitions of resources and reserves from time to time, either to counter charges by the government or Congress, or to reduce the likelihood of unwanted policies being enacted. In the early 1920s, for example, government conservationists and geologists (including the USGS) were attacking the oil industry for its wasteful use of oil. The USGS's gloomy oil resource estimates were suggesting that the nation had very little oil left. The Federal Oil Conservation Board (FOCB) was created in 1924 to clamp down on the industry. In reaction, the API worked up a category of estimates to make the resource picture look brighter than the government contended; this new category was "proved reserves." This move was made to put the issue of scarcity and waste into a more optimistic perspective, thus strengthening the industry's position. It was intended also to elevate the professional reputation of the API, to serve a public relations function, and to be a very general aid to planning for exploration.

In 1966 the API and AGA expanded their estimation activities to include new information on productive capacity. This step was intended not only to comply with government requests, but was used also to convince critics in Congress and elsewhere in the government that it was becoming more expensive for companies to find oil and gas in the United States. At that time, many people saw industry's story as an excuse for pushing up regulated prices. The new API and AGA statistics and presentation were used to package their point of declining returns on exploration.

Policies affect estimates. Take the case in which a pipeline company applies to the Federal Energy Regulatory Commission (FERC) for permission to expand its facilities in a certain location. FERC wants to know whether there are enough reserves to justify the new construction. It is in the pipeline's interest—and in the interest of its cooperating producer, which supplies the reserve data the pipeline submits to FERC—that the report be optimistic. For other purposes, a producer's interest might be better served by reporting less. The Federal Power Commission's (FPC)[1] natural gas pricing formula showed a clear inverse relationship between estimated reserves and allowable price: the lower the reserves, the higher the price. Thus, a conflict of interest in data reporting was created. When reserve estimates gathered by the AGA no longer were used in rate-making, the government-induced incentive to report on the low side ended also.

No firm is a monolith when it comes to estimating reserves. Within the same firm several different estimates may exist, all of which involve proved reserves. Though the geologist's report may be lower than the controller's report, each may be legitimate in the context of the purpose at hand and the professional standards of each person reporting. In fact, different officials performing different functions may see reason to file different estimates with the Internal Revenue Service, the Securities and Exchange Commission, and the bank from which a loan is requested. Viewing the industrial firm as a political coalition fits comfortably into academic organization theory, where it is standard stuff; the theory looks quite different to participants in practical politics operating in the federal political arena.

IF WE HAD BETTER ESTIMATES,
WOULD MISTRUST END?

Baffling credibility problems began to plague natural gas reserve estimates in the early and mid-1970s. Natural gas reserve data had not always been important to the government. It was the Federal Power Commission's implementation of price ceilings, during the 1960s, that made the accuracy of gas reserve data become a matter of national concern for pricing purposes. If low reserve estimates imply a higher justifiable price, as the FPC's formula stipulated, there is bound to be concern over possible bias in reporting estimates. Congress therefore proceeded to challenge the accuracy of gas reserve estimations for purposes no one had in mind when the data were originally collected. Federal agencies, Congress, producing companies, trade associations, and consumer groups all began to hurl charges of conspiracies to cook and misuse data. Efforts were launched to have government take over collecting reserve estimates on the grounds that once truly credible estimates existed—independent, accurate, and auditable—then, finally, everyone could agree on a consistent national energy policy. After a number of exhausting separate investigations, all went away as they came—dissatisfied.

All these interests and incentives, when added to the physical and technical uncertainties surrounding estimation, fueled the mutual mistrust of actors on opposite sides of issues. To what extent, we ask, did the collection, reporting, or presentation make a difference in how those gas reserve estimates were received by people who would use the data? Did perception of the data depend on methods of collection? on who was supplying the data? on who was collecting the data? on the results themselves? Two hypotheses are examined. The first says that if estimates are accurate and unbiased, people will not argue over them but will have a solid basis of mutual understanding. The alternative hypothesis is that disagreement over estimates is a *consequence* of conflicting policy preferences.

If the first hypothesis—better data will lead to better policy—is more satisfactory, then what is needed is improved estimation procedures and more emphasis on thorough, independent validation of estimates. Once participants have a data-collection process acceptable as truly professional, they will abide by the results. Such agreement on data will produce agreement on policy direction; i.e., once the size of the shortfall is certain, appropriate measures to reduce the gap will be agreed upon.

This is a tall order. To increase reliability, it would be preferable to have at least two wholly independent estimates. Without entirely replacing the oil industry, however, it is hard to see how government can provide its own original data—data based on the results of drilling—unless government does the drilling. The magnitude of the pool of energy to be estimated explains why government has gone to the edge several times but has never taken the plunge.

Government might try duplicating certain private activities by sampling. When this happened in the past, however, the complaint was that something had been left out (unless, as we found, the conclusions supported one's policy preferences). Even if two independent estimates agreed with one another, widespread acceptance could not be guaranteed. Both might be wrong. But, for oil and gas reserve and resource data, perfection is not for this world. Certainty occurs after the fact (if at all), never before (Schanz, 1978).

The government has put its money behind the first hypothesis. In so doing, estimation has become the house that Jack built. The Department of Energy has biases and policy preferences, so Congress creates the Energy Information Administration (EIA) to get the true, hard facts. The EIA is not trusted, so Congress creates a bureau to validate EIA estimates; this bureau is not trusted, so Congress mandates special teams to carry out annual audits. Got it now? Audit teams watch over the bureau that watches the administration that watches the department that is watched by Congress. Can this series of spies solve the problem of lack of confidence, we ask, or is it rather the very manifestation of that problem? "There is no one left to trust except thee and me," the joke goes, "and I am beginning to wonder about thee."

The first hypothesis, if it could ever be borne out, would seem to give everyone—estimators, data validators, and participants in policy—more cause for optimism than the second. If the second hypothesis appears to be better supported—i.e., disagreement over estimates is not the cause but the consequence of disagreement over basic policy perspective—then what? For estimators and independent data validators this suggests a "damned if you do, damned if you don't" situation. No amount of scientific data collection and validation can assure acceptance. As long as energy issues are polarized, one side will always attack data results, if those data influence their particular policy aim.

We look closely at the policy aims of various participants in the debates over energy estimates. Is the difference between the highest and lowest estimate large enough to determine a given policy decision? We look at a number of proposed policies and pose this question of policy relevance (both for undiscovered, recoverable U.S. resources and for proved reserves): Would a high or low resource estimate dominate a policy decision? And if not—if the proposed policies are not sensitive to high or low estimates—then why so much fighting over these numbers?

What happens, we ask, on the few occasions when experts agree on estimates? The politically polarized pull those estimates apart. What is done with the data on estimates when, at long last, they begin to appear? Not much. Even those who claim they want data the most, do not use them. Why, then, does agreement dissipate into disagreement and demand for data retreat as soon as supply advances?

If disagreement over estimates reflects rather than causes deep political and philosophical dissension, then we need some basic political settlement for the direction of national energy policy. If data-driven theories are untenable—that is, if facts do not determine policies—then we must ask how a structural settlement, involving changes in institutions and processes, might lead to sufficient consensus on policy to permit resolution of disputes over data. If this is our conclusion, agreement on broad perspectives must exist before agreement on the importance of data can come about.

In searching for what it would take to bring adversaries to consensus on energy, and in imagining what a consensus might look like, the political and economic literature has not been able to offer guidance. There is a literature concerned with the economic theory of regulation, which, in George Stigler's (1980) words,

> explains the timing, content and locus of regulatory programs by the interest groups in the society—groups which possess effective political strength and use it to increase their incomes. Industries such as railroads and occupations such as physicians have offered apt examples of such groups. . . . The rent-control laws are tenant dominated, the minimum wage law is AFL-CIO dominated, and much of recent energy policy has been consumer dominated [Stigler, 1980].

But the economic theory of regulation "does not have a well-developed theory on the question of which coalitions will be formed and which will achieve most."

That is precisely what we try to offer by the close of this book. We examine the coalitions that arose, how they came to distrust each other, and how on every issue their positions and their use of data came to be entirely predictable. We then suggest what the future holds for a settlement that could mitigate their mistrust. And if there is no such settlement on the horizon, can any other arrangement be created to preserve (or, if one prefers, create) better energy estimation? We explore a variety of possibilities for sharing more widely the dilemmas that arise when estimation is done without agreement on the policy purpose it is supposed to serve.

By this time we hope the reader has become aware that this book is about more than energy. From the standpoint of the policy analyst, the book is about the sensitive relationship between theories and facts, policies and data. For the political scientist, the book is meant as a contribution to the theory of coalitions in governmental regulation. And for the economist, we hope to have shown that the uses of economic theory depend not on any intrinsic value but on the social perspective of the participants. Decision-making, everyone agrees, is a social activity. The implications of this trite observation, however, have not been thought out. If intelligent choice is not only an intellectual but an interactive process, the quality of social relations is of critical importance for policy-making. If energy policy is schizophrenic, this is because it reflects a long-standing social division.

THE ORIGINS OF MISTRUST: DIVIDED PERSPECTIVES

In this book our aim is to understand why action has been bedeviled by energy policy. Through understanding the history of estimation of reserves and resources, we hope to specify the conditions for agreement. Starting with the dissolution of the Standard Oil Trust, we show that only when a political settlement was reached, as in the great world wars, were estimates accepted. It is easy to blame estimators; it is hard to create an agreed-upon context for public policy in which estimators can do their work to mutual satisfaction.

How come energy estimators never do the job right? Perhaps they are always wrong because their political masters, as the British would say, do not agree on what is right. Estimators may do their work without prejudice. The differences among them may be due entirely to uncertainty and adoption of different assumptions. But these scientists do not control what the political process does to their work, and that is our subject.

Why did estimates encounter such bitter dissension? One clue that enlarged our understanding was the discovery that a given individual, trying to make sense of the confusion over energy, tended to subscribe to one of two philosophies.

The first, a resource-oriented view, sees the world running out of conventional sources of energy: The world cannot produce enough oil to meet ever-growing demands. Unless it becomes self-sufficient in energy, the United States is in peril, dependent on the unpredictable actions of outside forces. To avoid this, the United States must take strong conservation measures and develop an assured domestic energy supply.

The second view looks at the world through an evolutionary or adaptive lens: World oil prices will increase predictably in the future; in response, demand will decrease and more discoveries and new technologies will be developed in new areas of the world. According to this view, prices are the best signal for inducing conservation, and the United States should integrate itself into a world energy marketplace. Striving for domestic self-sufficiency would be foolish, costly, even dangerous.

Throughout the history of American energy policy, these two polarized perspectives have determined the array of policies to be considered. To take a recent example, the appearance of fuel shortages, as our analysis will show, is rooted in an accumulation of policies guided mainly by quantity theory. Because the "energy crisis" of 1973 was initiated by a boycott, and because prices were believed to be better administered than competitive, discussion in Congress revolved about the "gap" or "shortfall" in supply as it related to demand. How to reduce consumption or increase production in order to narrow the shortfall? The quantity-related argument rejected market price as an appropriate mechanism to reduce demand or increase supply, suggesting instead such administrative methods as import quotas, allocation formulas, and rationing. Given this perspective, the demand by many legislators for detailed data on recoverable resources, reserves, and holdings was understandable. Since policy, under a quantity approach, consists of allocating resources to those who are judged to need them, it is essential to know how much oil and gas is above ground, how much is readily available below ground, and how much can be expected in the future.

This concept of a gap or shortfall in energy, on which most of the debate on energy policy has been focused in recent years, is only known under a price theory to refer to expected lead times or lag times. In the structural sense, though, there is not now nor has there been nor could there ever be a shortfall in a market economy—any more than there could be a shortfall in Cadillacs, apart from waiting for the car you ordered. Only if prices were controlled at below-market levels could a real gap exist between what was demanded and what someone was willing to supply.

Our book begins with a theoretical discussion of quantity and price theories because these world views rationalize the positions taken by participants in energy policy from the turn of the century until today. These theories are abstractions, not reifications. Except for a benighted scribbler here or there, we do not claim these theories are necessarily known or advocated as such by anyone. Nor do we believe that these theories provide a proper ground for energy policy under all conceivable conditions. If quantity and price theories are neither descriptive of positions people actually hold nor prescriptive of policy positions they should take, why do we think they are so important as to deserve pride of place?

Let us reemphasize our objectives: This is neither a dictionary nor an encyclopedia of energy estimation; we do not attempt to cover everything, even if that were possible. When the word "analytical" modifies "history," it signifies that we want to be selective so as to aid thought, not exhaustive so as to inhibit it. Thus, we seek to select out of the booming and buzzing confusion of this world those aspects that simplify sufficiently so we can make mental manipulations of the categories concerned. Our aim is to explain why the United States has stultified itself over energy policy, especially in recent times. Our claim, not yet substantiated, is that thinking in terms of quantities and prices affords insight into inability to arrive at satisfactory policies, i.e., policies that would satisfy the participants and the society.

At first blush, the suggestion that there are only a few perspectives on energy policy is surprising. The industry is complex. Companies not only come in many sizes, they exist in different regions and are surrounded by varied economic interests and political prospects. Refiners and pipelines and companies that both use energy and supply equipment to the industry face different situations. Conservationist and consumer groups come in more varieties than ketchup. And what is good for consumers in the Northeast may not be desirable for those in the Southwest. Yet, remarkably, each side reveals a policy perspective—through its identifications, demands, and expectations—that suggests adherence to a price theory or to a quantity theory. Can we prove it? The proof, as the saying goes, is in the pudding. There may be other ways of ordering energy behavior that are more accurate or more parsimonious, but these were the patterns that crystallized before us.

Is it likely that perspectives that congealed early in this century could have survived so long as to continue to stultify energy policy? Obviously, conditions have changed; so have the names and affiliations of the participants in energy policy. We shall show that, instead of changing their views in accord with the evidence, the adherents of these perspectives change their interpretations to fit their preconceptions. For seven decades? Yes, we were surprised too that whenever we poked a proverbial finger into the text, this decade or that, the same story surfaced. Everyone has heard tell of individuals who carry unresolved early childhood conflicts into adult situations, making decisions difficult because they bring with them extraneous material. The American people have been carrying with them unresolved conflicts over the structure of the oil industry and the legitimacy of its prices. If people feel something always seems to be in the way of sensible solutions, they are not far from wrong.

Are these "as if" price and quantity theories predictive? We think so. Yet, like all theories, they have to be fed data on the participants and the conditions they face.

Our task is to introduce sufficient variety to make a model of behavior in oil and gas estimation, but not so much as to continue the confusion that has characterized efforts to gain understanding. Following the rule of parsimony, we divide the oil and gas industrialists into those who would always support free markets (the smallest firms) and those who variously call for controls and for free markets (the largest firms). Those whose outlook is guided by quantity theories are similarly divided into consumerists (who want prices kept down) and preservationists (who call for reduced demand). Conditions are either war or peace; in peacetime, either a period of downward pressure on prices or upward pressure on prices. Many more conditions might be specified. The test is whether there is purchase in proliferating categories. Not, we think, for our purposes. If by classifying the participants and the conditions we can predict whether they will support or attack high or low estimates of reserves or resources, then we have achieved what we set out to do.

The outline below is a prelude to the predictions that unfold in the book.

How Will They Interpret Estimates?

	During war	During peace: periods of downward pressure on prices (1920s and 1930s)	During peace: periods of upward pressure on prices (1970s)
Constant marketers (small firms): a price perspective			
Variable marketers (the majors): a price perspective			
Consumerists: a quantity perspective			
Preservationists: a quantity perspective			

Of course, we are not neutral. But our bias does not consist of favoring price or quantity theories regardless of context. We could support policies based on either perspective (or, preferably, both in parallel), provided they were consonant with the institutions within which they had to function. What we wish to convey is the damage due to inconsistent policy, the insidious effects of conflicting signals. Devising quantity-minded policies in the context of an essentially private domestic industry was responsible for much of the failure we see around us. Unwillingness to think in terms of quantities when faced with price-fixing abroad has led to disregard for appropriate countermeasures. The inability to decide what perspective is appropriate for which institutions is responsible for the dizzyingly contradictory policy signals that have plagued the United States since 1973.

The perspectives of quantity and price have roots deep in Western philosophy. Are things to be valued in and of themselves as quantity theory holds, or are they instruments for other purposes, as price theory has it? Is exchange (prices) or merit (quantities) to be the basis for social value? Without going further into the matter now, it should be apparent that whether they appeal materially or philosophically, these perspectives exert strong sway over their adherents. They help organize the universe, explaining how it works and why it is desirable for things to work that way. Price and quantity theories help us explain the past and predict future behavior because that is also the function they perform for their adherents.

Were there no overarching perspectives, the energy arena undoubtedly would be fragmented. Internal differences among the participants would militate against external coherence. Precisely because there are two main perspectives, the participants come to know where they stand and who are their friends and enemies.

The importance of these perspectives also helps explain the stance we take toward the history of estimation. We go into enough detail for the reader to see how world views are reflected in the otherwise confusing welter of events. Because it is global conceptions we are after, our concern is with the public rationale offered for behavior. For the most part, checking what participants say against what they do, there is reasonable correspondence. No doubt some words are sheer rhetoric, others a plea for public support, still others uttered to establish a bargaining position. Yet, we would maintain that the public positions are never "mere words." They teach the interests involved forms of appropriate discourse. Reiterated on countless occasions, they ultimately carry convinction to those who utter them. Opponents as well as adherents take cues from these utterances, deepening their dismay at how others could be so blind or so foolish. If words did not matter, it would be quite impossible to explain how, as society changes so drastically, lines drawn early in this century have persisted so strong and so long.

It is a mark of an intelligent organism that it discards bad solutions and retains good ones. It is a sign of mental health that energy is devoted to meeting presenting problems, not to battling ghosts of the past. When internal conflicts remain unresolved, so that old quarrels are retained even as new appear, fewer resources remain to cope with contingencies. Immobilism drives away innovation. When there was a super abundance of oil and gas, internal conflicts only exhausted those directly involved. Now inability to come to terms with ourselves over energy may exhaust the country as well. In the end, we will return to the question of whether a political settlement would enable these perspectives to complement rather than compete with one another.

NOTE

1. In 1977 the Federal Power Commission became the Federal Energy Regulatory Commission.

REFERENCES

SCHANZ, J. J., Jr. (1978) "Oil and gas resources: welcome to uncertainty." Resources for the Future 58 (March).

STIGLER, G. J. (1980) "Trying to understand the regulatory leviathan [review of James Q. Wilson, ed., The Politics of Regulation]." Wall Street Journal (August 1).

WILDAVSKY, A. (1962) "The analysis of issue-contexts in the study of decision making." Journal of Politics 24: 717-732.

PART I HISTORY OF MISTRUST

THE FIRST SECTION of the book begins with a conclusion. What patterns, we asked ourselves, emerged so consistently intact through the very different circumstances of the 1900s—the 1920s, the 1930s, and the two world wars? The patterns we discovered that explain this remarkable predictability of behavior are what we call quantity and price perspectives. It is this conclusion that constitutes the first chapter.

The two overarching perspectives help us make sense of energy policy in this country. Chapter 2 shows how mistrust over resource estimates developed from the turn of the century, when what people did with land and oil began to matter. By 1925 the major lines of conflict were drawn, the quantity and price perspectives discernible.

With the dissolution of the Standard Oil Trust, the policy structure that resulted occupied a no man's land. Government was unwilling to let industry operate freely, yet unable to decide how or where to control it. The 1930s saw the inexorable development of partial and contradictory policies. Chapter 3 describes the peculiar arrangements that government and industry put together. These relationships were formed without a consistent price or quantity perspective, without a basis of fundamental philosophical understanding. They accomplished only further and deeper conflict over resource estimates.

Wartime brought peace to energy policy. The two world wars paradoxically produced social harmony among participants; consequently, the bitter differences over resource estimates were forgiven, accepted, disregarded. Chapter 4 shows how wartime smoothed over the conflicts—and how, the moment peace appeared on the horizon, conflict over estimates reared its head once again.

1
QUANTITY OR
PRICE THEORIES

THE PROBLEM BEFORE US is to understand why there has been no agreement about oil and gas reserves and resources from the turn of the century to today. Behind this problem looms a larger one: After the oil embargo and manifold price increases of 1973, why was the government of the United States unable to agree on whether the nation had a problem, and, if so, what were its dimensions and what could be done about it? Why, in the midst of talk of lessening dependence on OPEC oil, was the domestic price kept down by subsidizing imports? A scant six years later, as dependence on oil imports increased markedly, prices had doubled again. If an energy gap or shortfall existed, why was there no agreement on how large it was? And, if the price of oil and gas was too high or too low, why was there no agreement on which, or what to do about either rate? If the foreign price increase raised severe distributional difficulties between economic classes and regions, why were high-priced imports encouraged and lower-cost domestic production discouraged, thus making things worse for everyone?

Imagine the field of energy as a vast and sprawling historical novel, with a confusing cast of characters who take contradictory positions in different periods. The novel is a roman à clef in which the characters refer to real people (or, for us, real perspectives) whose names and activities change over time. This first chapter intends to be a key to that cast of characters whose perspectives (the groups with which these actors identify, the demands they make, and the expectations they have about oil and gas estimates) remain the same, but whose positions vary according to the conditions of the time.

Can a single key unlock so many doors? Our aim is not to replicate the confusion of the real world, which leaves everyone wondering (as in

Abbott and Costello's wonderful old routine) "Who's on first?" What they say in baseball parks is right: "You can't tell the players without a scorecard." What they do not tell you in the energy arena is that the players keep shifting positions. Ours is more like a miniature softball team with but four players who cover all essential bases. The game, as we portray it here, admittedly is oversimplified, but we believe it captures the essence of the activities. Besides, as history takes over from theory, there will be enough complexity about energy for everyone; any American can testify to that.

Basically there are four "characters"—two types of quantity theorists, preservationists and consumerists, and two types of price theorists, constant and variable marketers. These are generalized models only; in no way do we suggest that everyone (or anyone) in the world falls neatly into one type or another. But we believe that certain behavior patterns of the participants in energy policy may be explained as if they fit into these fairly distinct set of characteristics.

Given the four perspectives, we ask: What prescriptions on policy would those theorists make under different historical conditions? Which estimates of resources and reserves would fit each policy position? What would happen if government took on the task of reconciling these proposed policies or getting agreement on supporting estimates? If we are correct, the stasis in energy all of us have observed in recent years is one of the consequences of conflict among actors pursuing these perspectives.

Why, one may well ask, would perspectives originating early in this century operate so strongly decade after decade, emerging in our time with undiminished virulence? Because, given these perspectives through which we interpret events, each decade furnishing additional evidence of the rectitude of those who agree and the disreputability of those who disagree, history only reinforces their initial dispositions. The experiences from which the participants in energy policy learn are artifacts of how they view the world.

It is not our purpose in this chapter to argue in favor of one or another perspective. Rather, we wish to spell out the consequences of looking at energy in a number of ways initially, for each perspective alone, and then by taking them in various combinations. The abstract model of the energy arena thus created does not pretend to say that it represents the exact behavior of each participant. Ours is an "as if" model: It claims that if the participants acted on the perspectives we assign them, they would interact so as to produce patterns of policy that otherwise appear so puzzling.

Quantities and prices are not synonyms for planning and markets. If that was our intention, we would use those terms themselves. Every political and economic system, we believe, uses combinations of the two.

A socialist government, for instance, though it is evidently committed to state direction, may, sometimes, use prices to allocate resources; or, instead of directly providing quantities of resources to industries, it may give them loans, urging them to make the best deals they can within certain constraints. In that sector of industry, then, the interaction and adaptation characteristic of prices replace the single-sided fixity of direct orders we associate with central allocation of quantities. Contrariwise, in a largely market economy, government often intervenes to see that certain quantities of medical care or food or transportation are provided.

In normative terms of policy preferences, the basic issue is not prices versus quantities, but whether one wants to regulate a particular economic activity. Only after this question has been settled in favor of regulation does it become meaningful to ask whether the best form of control is by prices or by quantities (e.g., by pollution prices or by pollution standards) or by some other means. As alternative modes of control, prices and quantities are actually closely related to each other. (They are "dual" to each other.) Given prices, the implicit or explicit rule is to maximize profits at those prices; given quantities, the rule specifies the achievement of the targets at minimum cost. In theory, one control problem is as hard or as easy as the other. What we want to know is why, in the current crisis, the benefits of neither approach have been obtained.

The most deep-seated distinctions between quantity theories and price theories are moral. The moral premises of the two theories diverge over two notions: (1) knowledge of the individual's needs and wants (who knows what is best for the individual?) and (2) the appropriate use of resources for the good of the community. Put differently, quantity theories and price theories disagree fundamentally over what people should have, and how they should get it. The "should have" premise concerns the idea of demand; the "should get" premise has to do with supply.

DEMAND: NEEDS OR WANTS?

A quantity-based theory holds the assumption that what the individual wants and what is best for that individual are two separate things. While people aim to satisfy personal wants, they can be ignoring social needs, to the detriment of all. Building on this separation of want and need, quantity theory stresses the necessity for some other, higher intelligence to know what each citizen needs and to assure he or she has it for the good of the community as a whole. Quantity theory regards material self-interest as self-indulgence, potentially corrosive to the fabric of the common good.

As central controllers, we need not claim to know with precision what people need or want, but we can make estimates and distribute those amounts. Our claim as quantity theorists is that most people (by their own standards) will be better off by the fair distribution of goods and services we would make than under the operation of an efficient market that carried with it a highly inequitable distribution of income.

By contrast, price theory makes no operational distinction between want and need; demand can mean either. The premise of a price theory is that the individual knows best what he or she wants. Whether that want is also a need is the individual's own business. While the individual's awareness of his or her own needs may be imperfect, no other intelligence can better decide what they are. The individual's consciousness may be "false" but no one else's is "true" in the sense of being an acceptable substitute. What the individual does know better than anyone else over the range of circumstances is his or her own situation. Accordingly, under a price system, the spontaneous decisions of innumerable individuals over time will leave most people better off than will any alternative arrangement. Harnessing this self-interest for the welfare of the whole is central to price theory.

We can illustrate these ideas and their implications for collective knowledge by drawing an analogy with two familiar disciplines, quantities belong to engineering, prices to evolution. Engineering designs systems to conform to a previously determined hierarchy of objectives; every action is geared to serve a purpose common to the entire enterprise. Evolution is not designed by anyone; no one determines whose needs are to be satisfied under what priority, or what people's needs are. Each member of every species can have objectives as varied as the number of individuals, and information is contributed by all—all experience is of value—because it reveals something about the special circumstance of each creature.

It follows that such objectives need not be consistent but may well contradict one another. Evolution may generate more total information, information about the inconsistent and opposing interests of creatures, but this is not information that belongs to a human engineer. Nor is this information available before it is used; it is historic, revealing itself with the unfolding of experience. If all the information that evolution generates could be known by one central mind, neither competition nor selection would be necessary.

Evolution is a constantly changing process, and its information is not naturally manifest in the form of fixed quantities; evolution is about relationships over time. Evolution is about competition and adaptation, about relationships to people and to conditions, not about fixed needs and requirements.

Engineering seeks to enclose time; plans have a beginning and an end. The planner, in engineering a system, expects that enough data are known and collectible to produce the information needed to realize that system. Information is about occurrences at fixed points in time. In this simplification, structures do not evolve beyond narrow limits covered creatively by servo-mechanisms and the aptly named control theory. Optimistically, systems are meant to remain what they started out to be.

Quantities describe points; prices reflect relationships. From this fundamental distinction flow fateful consequences. Prices represent relationships between buyers and sellers over time. Neither supply (or suppliers) nor demand (or demanders) can be considered alone, but must always be considered in relation to one other. An unceasing interdependence characterizes a price theory. Harry Johnson (1968: 3) considered this concept of an interdependent system central to understanding the British economy:

> The interdependence of the separate parts of the economy . . . implies that a change in conditions in any part of the system— whether occurring automously or resulting from changes in governmental policy—will set up repercussions that will reverberate to a greater or lesser extent throughout the whole system. Thus, for example, the British policy of protecting coal from the competition of rival fuels not only imposes an international competitive disadvantage on energy-intensive British industries, but it accounts in part for the inadequate standards of heating and lighting to be found in many British homes, and contributes marginally to the misery of the aged poor.

Similarly, in the United States, an inquiry into the poor position of the coal industry in the 1950s and 1960s might trace the repercussions of fixing the price of a substitute fuel, natural gas, at below-market cost. Inefficiencies, misallocations, and damage to lower-income people are all possible under both quantity and price systems.

Quantity theories require targets: Prices search for unknown relationships. The objective in quantity theory is to amass stipulated amounts to meet the predetermined needs of participants. Price theory knows nothing of targets; prices are announcements of the latest round of negotiations. The objective under a price theory is not to arrive at a previously determined target, but to discover what set of prices, for the time being, will bring buyers and sellers together. On the other side, quantities could be tried out to find those optimal levels at which prices offered by demanders just equal prices charged by suppliers. This last procedure would be analogous to searching for market-clearing prices.

In a quantity-oriented model, decisions by those who decide for others are justified on the basis of their presumed merit. In a price model, the basis for justification is agreement among buyers and sellers. The correct quantity is determined by intellectual argument and judgment; the agreed-upon price emerges through sequences of social interactions. Quantities can be "correct" or "incorrect," but prices can only be agreed upon.

The information requirements of a quantity-oriented system are substantial, because it is necessary to determine how much each participant needs for each purpose. Information requirements of price systems are much less: what people want compared to what they can get as reflected in successful and unsuccessful sequences of bids. In a price system no one has the "big picture." The system results from diverse activities; it is not a design. The myriad sequences of relationships in the mind cannot be captured on computers. Thus, decision makers in a quantity system can state information requirements for the whole, but participants in a price system cannot.

SUPPLY: WILL ANY MIX OF RESOURCES DO?

The critical consequence of quantity theories, so far as we are concerned here, is that one is led to thinking in terms of amounts of commodities to be provided and consumed, rather than prices to be paid for desired commodities. Quantity theories are about either supplying a given demand or demanding a given supply, but not both together. Relationships between suppliers and demanders are not evolutionary. Under a quantity theory, a central intelligence can decide accurately what others should have and, also, the optimal way to provide it.

Quantity theory holds some commodities to be intrinsically more valuable than others; price theory does not see any one set of resources as possessing intrinsic worth. Safeguarding a commodity, with the idea that it is intrinsically valuable, is quite different from considering alternative (or opportunity) costs of buying or selling a good. To take the most obvious example for our purposes, quantity theories may consider certain resources to be exhaustible—used up, gone forever. Such a resource—oil, for example—is seen as subject to exploitation by selfish individuals with no regard for the needs of future generations. In order to parcel out consumption over time in the most foresighted way, allocators of quantities must know how much of any given exhaustible resource exists.

Under price theory, by contrast, the world does not "keep kosher." No mix of resources is forbidden for producing a given product or result. Substitutability is more central than exhaustibility. Neither oil nor any other single source of energy possesses intrinsic value. No form of energy is "priceless," to use a common word. Instead, as we gradually use up the better deposits, the costs of extracting additional oil increase. It follows from price theory that other resources will appear on stage to serve the same function.

One may hear the phrase "blind evolution" applied to this process for good reason because, as the creatures involved go about adapting, they cannot say where the system as a whole is going. An act of faith is required. Retrospectively, this act may be reasonable in that, looking back, spontaneity may be seen to have done better than control. Looking forward, however, neither the particular path to be taken nor the successful adaptability of certain individuals can be described. After all, luck or an element of randomness has to play a part; otherwise, everyone would be able to outguess the system and come out ahead. To have winners there have to be losers. This irreducible element of faith applied to exhuastible resources has been well described by Friedrich A. Hayek (1960: 369):

> In a sense, of course, most consumption of irreplaceable resources rests on an act of faith. We are generally confident that, by the time the resource is exhausted, something new will have been discovered which will either satisfy the same need or at least compensate us for what we no longer have. We are constantly using up resources on the basis of the mere probability that our knowledge of available resources will increase indefinitely—and this knowledge does increase in part because we are using up what is available at such a fast rate.

Because quantity theory recognizes certain goods as inherently valuable in an absolute sense, it is crucial to have accurate estimates of the amount of the commodity in the ground; how else orchestrate its preservation? Where price theories answer such questions as "Do we have enough?" by interaction—discovering what can be done by doing as much as anyone will pay for—quantity theories do so by cognition; determination replaces discovery. Hence, quantity theorists have a critical need for data on which to base decisions.

In a price system individuals are supposed to act on the basis of mutual advantage. Self-interest minimizes the need for coercion or exhortation as a means for organizing society. As Charles Schultze (1977: 18) says, "If I want drivers to economize on gasoline usage, advertising appeals to patriotism, warnings about the energy crisis, and 'don't be fuelish' slogans are no match for higher prices at the gas pumps."

But it is precisely such deliberate use of humanity's material self-interest that quantity theory finds morally offensive. The specter of selfish individuals wasting finite natural resources, buying the wrong goods, and ignoring the poor is very compelling.

SHORTAGE: ONLY IN A QUANTITY SYSTEM

Questions such as "Do we have enough? Will we run out? When will we run out? How can we prevent shortages as demand overtakes supply? How can we close the gap between supply and demand?" can be answered only by collecting data, which must be analyzed and interpreted. Someone must say how much is enough for whom; or predict future rates of consumption; or estimate how much of a resource can or should be supplied, and at what rates; or determine a "just" price, or a "fair" profit.

Under a price model there is no such thing as shortage. Supply always is equal to demand, absent price controls or rationing and apart from temporary lead times and lag times to be expected. "How much do we have?" is not considered a useful question, because the amounts of a given commodity that can be brought into use economically depend on the prices people will pay. The conjectural response to "How much will we have?" also depends on what future prices will be, that is, on whether searching for and extracting the resource will be worthwhile. Prices, acting as indicators to producers and consumers, connect supply and demand.

In summary, prices permit any combination of resources to be used so long as the purpose (i.e., manufacture, transportation) is satisfied. Where price is the regulator, it is not oil or gas that matters, but alternative sources of production, whatever they are. The task of the economy is to increase total value by using the full capability of the system to satisfy wants.

Fundamental moral differences separate a quantity from a price perspective. Quantity theory is wary of the powerful motive of material self-interest. If the good of the community is to be served, it is up to a central authority to determine what goods and how much of services individuals should have. Moreover, not just any mix of resources will do in supplying individual needs. Certain resources must be saved from human squandering because they possess intrinsic merit. There is no better or worse mix of resources in a price system. Commodities are substitutes rather than absolutes. The relative notion of opportunity cost (and alternative uses) replaces the absolute idea of merit goods.

SCARCITY: PHYSICAL OR ECONOMIC?

What about the concept of physically limited supplies? "The world will never run out of any nonrenewable resource provided prices are allowed to adjust," says economist Hendrik Houthakker (1976: 10). The logic is straightforward. If the cost of extracting one resource keeps rising as each additional unit is extracted, alternative energy sources will be brought into play as they become profitable. High prices for oil, of course, will set off a chain of reactions throughout the economy as users consider doing with less, going without, or switching to another source of energy. This use of prices to make these countless adjustments attracts advocates; and it is precisely this chameleon-like quality that repels opponents.

Price theory expresses its relationship to human welfare in terms of overall output, productivity, or gross national product. The greater the overall output, the better off the community. In this light, it is not clear that diminution in one resource means reduction in overall productivity. The important question from the standpoint of the economy as a whole is not so much a concern with our natural resource base per se, but with the total capital base, that is, with all the inputs to economic growth (Milliman, 1962).

To economist Jerome Milliman (1962: 202) there is not only no such thing as a free lunch, but also

> no such thing as a fixed, inflexible requirement for individual natural resources that is impossible of variation. That is to say there is *some degree* of substitutability for each and every kind or class of input! It may be helpful, nevertheless, to admit that there are problems of easy substitutability between various kinds of capital but it is difficult to see how this really constitutes an argument for special treatment of natural resources. First of all, it is not a question of "all or none" but a question of a little more versus a little less. . . .

> I know of no important policy decisions that are of this "all-or-none" variety. Even though it is quite true that a particular resource—say water—is necessary to human life and thus has infinite value, the question is never posed in these terms. Rather policy questions are concerned, for the most part, with whether or not a certain incremental supply is justified; this is to ask what is the value and the cost of water at the margin? . . .

> It is also clear, moreover, that so-called "needs" or "requirements" computed purely on the basis of the physical possibilities for substitution are not very meaningful in an economic context. Time and time again we study projections for the future based purely upon crude extrapolations of present usage without any consideration of the possibilities of changes in the combinations of inputs in the light of their changing economic feasibility. Economic demands must consider relative prices and costs; and the degree of substitution of various inputs will reflect these relationships.

But would substitution of energy resources ever be too costly? No more particularly so than for any other input, says Milliman (1962: 202): [T] he fact that the cost of substitution increases the more it is extended is true of all capital inputs and does not appear to be a special attribute of natural resource capital."

Also, Milliman sees little likelihood of a fatal mistake in judgment or estimation: "I know of no examples throughout history where any civilization suddenly 'ran out' of this or that mineral." Arguments that a nonrenewable natural resource has intrinsic value and deserves special attention do not convince Milliman.

Questionable, too, are the premises that an individual acting alone overconsumes and must be induced to save a proper quantity for future generations. In *The Constitution of Liberty,* Hayek (1960) identifies two major preservationist arguments for central control of energy conservation:

(1) The community as a whole is more concerned about the future than is the individual.
(2) Government has greater foreknowledge of the future than does the individual.

As to the first claim, presumably it is not in the individual's interest to take the long view and, therefore, future needs would be valued more highly by the community as a whole. If valid, this contention would justify central direction of most economic activity. But Hayek (1960: 370) sees no substantive justification for it: "There is no more justification in a free society for relieving the individual of responsibility for the future than there is for claiming that past generations ought to have made more provision for us than they did." An argument has been made, indeed, that by following quantity theory, too much might be left for future generations. This reasoning stems from uncertainty as to what is the optimal pattern of future use of a nonrenewable resource. There is no reliable way of taking future demand into account. Except for a few minerals, future markets do not exist. Rather than buy futures, people may buy reserves, which they will withhold from production in expectation of higher prices in the future. Houthakker (1976: 14) develops this argument:

> Speculation of this type cannot prevent an unduly low rate of consumption, which would leave future generations with more reserves than they need—just the opposite of what conservationists worry about! It may be objected that our descendants will appreciate anything useful we save for them, so that it is not possible to leave them too much. This objection overlooks the fact that exhaust-

ible resources are substitutes for labor and capital, so that too much of the former will often mean too little of the latter. Rather than endow our heirs with gold mines (not to mention monetary gold stocks) we should perhaps leave them more productive capital.

Note that Houthakker wants to leave the future with a convertible capability, while quantity theorists want to assure future generations of specific resources.

What about the assertion that the government is more knowledgeable than are separate individuals? Hayek (1960: 371) evaluates this claim by contrasting what the government can know (and individuals cannot) with individual knowledge about which government must remain ignorant. Surely, he acknowledges, the government will know more about some things than do individuals. But "there will always exist . . . an even greater store of knowledge of special circumstances that ought to be taken into account in decisions about specific resources which only the individual owners will possess and which can never be concentrated within a single authority." If we want to bring together all relevant knowledge, Hayek recommends dispersing government's knowledge *downward,* rather than centralizing all the specializing all the special knowledge possessed by individuals.

THE PRESERVATIONIST ATTACK ON PRICE:
IT INDUCES WASTE

A major objection to price on the part of preservationists, who subscribe to a physical view of scarcity, is the wastefulness of oil production. The first half of this century saw continuous charges leveled against oil companies for wasteful practices. With too-rapid extraction, the low prices only signaled that people could consume more. What have been the effects on energy consumption of prices preferred by the major oil companies?

No doubt the majors prefer to maximize income by charging the price that will lead to sales which yield the greatest profit. Since the 1920s, the oil majors have favored free markets when prices were high, and regulation of production to raise prices if prices fell too low. The point of "prorationing" controls instituted in the 1930s for limiting domestic production, and the point of restrictions on importing oil from abroad, was to protect prices at profitable levels. The consequences, then, have been to raise prices and to decrease consumption below what it would have been without controls. Indeed, if one wanted primarily to encourage conservation, prices should have been set much higher.

From a preservationist point of view, from the beginning until the late 1930s the short-run economics of the oil industry had led to far lower prices than justifiable. So preservationists helped raise prices by favoring regulation that would restrict output—the same forms of regulation that the majors and the independent producers favored. Thus, the industry and the preservationists became strange bedfellows. Preservationists castigated the major producers for their reckless, wasteful practices. But when these companies pushed for controls to limit quantities and protect their profits, the preservationists joined in—for their own very different reasons.

In quantity theories that call for preserving as much as possible of a physically irreplaceable resource, price is problematic: The less oil costs, the more is used up. This line of thought suggests that an appropriate calculation of quantities should be the net gain or net loss of energy from an activity. Indeed, today there is a distinct group of professionals known as "net energy analysts" who evaluate physical projects, government programs, and mechanical devices according to the amount of energy spent in the enterprise (Wall Street Journal, 1979).

What we notice in a preservationist framework is an important distinction between physical scarcity—which quantity theorists see as their primary concern—and economic scarcity, the particular concern of price theorists. Economic scarcity is not ultimately physical, but concerns material welfare as command over resources. Physical scarcity refers to the diminution of a finite quantity; this view leads quantity theorists to give the diminishing resource intrinsic value and to try to preserve as much as possible. Cementing this desire is a particular perception of moral responsibility: Since the individual consumes without regard to what his children will be left with, some central rule maker must induce individuals to use less, for the benefit of future generations.

THE CONSUMERIST ATTACK ON PRICE:
THE INDIVIDUAL'S RIGHT TO ENERGY

Preservationists think oil prices are unfair because the intrinsic value of oil is greater than its merely monetary price. Consumerists reject price, but for other reasons:

(1) An uncontrolled price system is impervious to unequal distribution of income among participants and unequal treatment of regions. With world energy prices dramatically on the rise since 1973, the higher prices American consumers must pay seem suspect: These prices give huge windfalls only to domestic producers. The posted price seems unjust because it represents a massive redistribution of money from millions of

small consumers to a handful of large producers. On the surface, the consumerist cry is for cheap and abundant energy, but the objection to price involves a great deal more; it attacks the structure of the energy industry. Consumerists' rejection of price is rooted partly in the belief that competition is being crushed by monopoly forces. If the competitive market worked, price would not be a problem. The ideal market in this view probably would comprise a large number of small firms. Consumerists' mistrust of price begins with bigness in industry. Price is not fair because the structure and behavior of large industry, which sets these prices, is unfair to the millions.

(2) The second problem consumerists have with unregulated price is that they believe major oil companies, like monopolies, have the power to set prices and promote favorable legislation. Hence, there is no workable competition in the energy-producing industry. It follows, not surprisingly, that the income of oil companies is believed too high, after allowing for costs of production plus a fair profit.

And once it is believed that oil companies are monopolies and that competition cannot exist, quantity theories may be justified on the grounds that government will make decisions just as intelligently as a giant monopoly, and perhaps more equitably.

To those who equate national welfare with overall productivity or national product, prices are primary because, under competitive conditions, prices will lead to the largest amount to divide among members of society. To those who equate welfare with preserving the fragile web of nature, and to those who equate welfare with income equality, prices are immoral. Between economic opportunity cost, worth as alternatives sacrificed, and intrinsic merit, worth as correct or "natural" value, there is no meeting place.

TWO APPROACHES TO ENERGY REVISITED

In order to make comparisons between the two underlying perspectives, let us simplify our simplifications so that quantity and price theories stand out in bold relief.

From the standpoint of planning, the paradox is that quantity theorists are apt to adopt a much more materialist, fixed-quantity, fixed-priorities view of reality than would price theorists. This is paradoxical because the responsibilities of planning are a burden assumed in the name of the fight against selfish materialism, and against the impaired vision about society's needs attributed to the price theorists by those quantity theorists.

TABLE 1.1   Two Approaches to the Energy Problem

	Quantity Theory	Price Theory
Demand and Supply	Planned design; individual wants are quite separate from his real needs; needs are known to planners who combat self-interest and materialism by controlling allocation of supplies to community on a moral basis, which corresponds to individual needs; cognition determines allocation.	Hidden design; individual choice sovereign; individual needs add up to community needs. It is not immoral to follow demand; interaction determines allocation.
Other Differences	(a) Quantities are part of a system of moral postulates.	Prices are signals in exchange of information.
	(b) Some commodities are vested with intrinsic worth.	Nothing is priceless.
	(c) Some mixtures are not acceptable.	No mixtures are disallowed.
	(d) Exhaustibility of some resources is relevant to the planning calculus.	Since no resources have intrinsic value, all being substitutable and mixable and none being priceless, exhaustibility is not relevant.

SOURCE: Adapted from letter by anthropologist Mary Douglas to Aaron Wildavsky, after she read the draft of this chapter.

From the whole scope of reality, quantity theorists select certain more real things, which can be precisely labeled by being quantified and evaluated according to a fixed moral order. Quantity theorists have nominalist epistemological leanings: The named valuables in such a universe have the physical properties of being able to be counted, but also of diminishing in absolute quantity. These theorists exert control by inducing others to accept the fear of exhaustibility of those valuables which are not allowed to be priced, substituted for, or mixed. For quantity theorists, preservation becomes the dominant social value.

To plan, quantity theorists need clear information and a lot of it; they need to manipulate it by equations. Quantities must be unambiguous for those mathematical operations to be performed. Their professional resistance to ambiguity is extended to evaluation, so that quantity theorists are thrown by proposals to mix or substitute. Denial of intrinsic worth is anathema because it throws doubt on the value of time spent on calculations.

The scale of values in the back of this planner's mind is just as hidden as the invisible market mechanism and must not be exposed to the light of day. The grand picture quantity theorists want to keep in view is that of an equitable social system. To allow a shifting price structure into that view certainly muddles it. So planners bracket off the most important elements in their planned design (such as life, health, food, energy) by deeming them priceless, that is, things which should be protected from the vagaries of a price system. Quantity theorists solve the dilemma of evaluating the invaluable by concentrating on quantities.

Price theorists, by contrast, are good within a specific context and bad at conceiving the grand vision of society. Their strategy, in argument, is to restrict contexts to those within which their faculty of combination gives good results. Price theorists are bad at selecting equivalents and parallels; by introducing ridiculous examples they appear to give human life a trivial and (what appears to others worse) a monetary value. Price-theory planners are weak on those moral perceptions which depend on the power of analogy and sympathy.

Prices lack moral vision because they are only symbols of whatever societal values hold, in proportion to the ability to participate in markets. To become the servant of one's own desires, critics of price theory charge, is morally monstrous. It is also nerve-wracking. By nature, prices should be unpredictable, in the sense that one seldom can predict them. For with predictability would come control, and with control, the absence of the spontaneity that searches out previously unknown combinations to achieve social satisfaction. Therefore, price theory is accused of gambling with the public interest.

Why should temporary aberration, bad luck, or misfortune be accepted if government can do something about it? Why allow an industry to grow sick if a tax provision or a production limit could provide a cure—at which time markets might operate more successfully? The temptation is hard to resist. There are always losers who can be made winners by adjustments to the structure of the system.

And who is to come down from Sinai and say what that structure should be? What is and is not permissible is fuzzy enough at the edges (Who can compete under what conditions and which rules?) to suggest that following a punctilious form is not necessarily right. The evil done by the structure is evident; the good must remain mysterious. The loss of a national product may be indirect and impalpable; the loss to this industry or that firm is direct and tangible.

Once it is understood that everyone wants to keep parts of life private—outside the cost nexus, outside of explicit exchange, valued in and of themselves (like family and friendship)—quantity theories may be viewed in a different light. Quantities, or intrinsic merits, are not aberrations but, rather, integral parts of human life. Like the sacred and the profane, quantities and prices are not matters of either/or but of more or less. To draw a dividing line is difficult. When the line is drawn too far on one side, creative combination becomes difficult; draw it too far on the other and—treating like things alike—creative combination becomes precarious. Differentials break down amidst confusion among cultural categories. What should be the ultimate ends and what should be the instruments of human life never are trival questions.

IS ENERGY POLICY ROOTED IN PRICE
OR QUANTITY THEORY?

Historically, until about the time of World War I, energy prices in the United States—left to the private market—were the main determinants of the magnitude and composition of the energy sector. Sometimes prices were partially regulated by local or state agencies, sometimes not.

But, as noted already, all controls since then illustrate quantity theory at work. A brief look at our history of planning for energy reveals conflicting patterns of control. State and local governments pushed for supply-restraining policies to protect local private producers. This restricted output resulted in higher prices than would have existed in an unregulated market system. Federal direction, on the other hand, tended to keep prices to consumers down. The first actions on a federal level took place during World War I—the percentage depletion allowance, and favorable tax treatment of intangible drilling and development costs. These measures were quantity-oriented, encouraging increases in supplies. And the greater the supplies available, the lower prices were likely to be.

Most subsequent federal policies have continued this approach of keeping short-run prices down for consumers by encouraging development. There are important exceptions to this cheap-and-abundant motivation for federal policy; the oil import-control program of the 1960s aimed to support oil-producing states in their goal to protect the incomes of domestic producers. In general, federal and state policies have been similar in operation, by physically changing quantities of energy supplied. At the same time, however, these policies have opposed each other in the direction of change; federal policy has encouraged more supplies at low prices, while state policy has restricted supply and pushed for higher prices. In short, policy has given inconsistent signals, and the signals have called for manipulating quantities rather than encouraging markets to operate with their own price signals.

ACTORS IN ENERGY POLICY

Four groups of actors dominated the long history of conflict over oil and gas resource estimation. Out of the Progressive tradition came two of these groups: preservationists and consumerists, far apart in philosophy but both representing quantity theory.

Preservationists considered oil and natural gas to be among nature's finite and irreplaceable natural resources and therefore gifts to be treasured. Thus, for the welfare of future generations, as much oil and gas as possible should be conserved, and used sparingly. Preservationists distrusted competition, for the free market allowed entrepreneurs open season to plunder these precious resources. Because prices did not signal nature's limited supply, prices were perverted. Monopoly, then, might be tolerable or even encouraged if it helped maximize the amount of oil or gas preserved in the ground. Since supply was to be taken as a finite given, the policy aim of preservationists was to control consumption. Shortage, to preservationists, was a physical condition resulting from insatiable demands on dwindling supplies.

While preservationists took supply as the given and sought to control illegitimate demand, consumerists saw demand as given and legitimate, but supply as manipulated by the big companies. The quantities of energy individuals should have were the quantities citizens were used to at the customary low prices. To consumerists, shortage was a political (not physical) phenomenon resulting from the major firms holding back available supplies to millions of needy consumers. The policy aims of consumerists were to break up the structure of the large oil industry, to make competition "workable" once again, to keep wealth and power out of the hands of big industry, and to ensure the people a cheap and abundant supply of energy. Consumerists gave no intrinsic value to oil and natural gas; the value of these energy resources was their political power.

Consumerists believed that small firms and individuals were in ever-increasing danger of being swallowed up by large, integrated corporations. A prime concern of consumerists was to prevent massive redistributions of wealth and power from the many consumers and competitive small firms to the few big corporations. Consumerists rejected prices as manipulated by the powerful oil companies. Because such prices were believed to be illegitimate, it was thought they ought to be controlled by government during a process of going back to old-fashioned competition. If it was impossible to bring this about, prices should be set by government indefinitely. Essentially, government should take over the provision of energy.

Preservationists and consumerists had little in common philosophically, except for a distrust of large private oil companies. On policy preferences, the two groups diverged; preservationists rejected the idea of taking people's demands as a given and pressed for sacrifice and abstinence. Preservationists would control to minimize quantities demanded. Consumerists would control to maximize quantities supplied. But for both the emphasis was on control.

The other two groups of actors very roughly represented "industry"— the majors and the independents. The "majors" usually were vertically integrated oil companies, controlling not only production but also transportation, refining, and marketing. The "independents" mainly were independent producers whose sole activities were to discover, drill, and bring oil and gas to production. Majors could afford to sacrifice some short-term profits to ensure longer-term, gradual increases. Majors would not reject competition, but their free-market principles were not consistent. In times of high demand relative to supply, the majors rejected government price ceilings; but when supplies were extremely plentiful and demand was not as in the 1930s, the majors wanted government to set protective price floors or to establish restrictions on production. To the majors, the notion of shortage generally meant a gap in price—the difference between a high market price and a lower, administered price (regulated by government or set by a group of firms).

Independent producers generally were in a less stable financial position than the majors. With control only over the production end of the process, independents could make profits only by selling oil or gas to pipelines and refiners. The independent producer was less able to sacrifice short-term income, and could not (like the majors) establish cooperative agreements on prices or production levels. To the independent producer there was no such thing as shortage, oversupply, or undersupply, but only a price.

Though independents were reluctant to support direct quantitative limitation of supply, they were happy to accept indirect subsidies to enhance supplies. When there are tax breaks to encourage drilling, for example, this had the effect of increasing supply beyond where profitability would otherwise have carried it. Independents were less variable than the majors, but still were variable marketers.

From these characterizations of the four perspectives it is a relatively straightforward matter to predict the position of each on oil and gas estimates. At the extremes, preservationists believed that the nation was soon to run out. The appearance of less was proof positive; if there seemed to be more, it would only encourage people to consume more. The independents, by contrast, were not interested in U.S. reserve estimates; they would always find more if the price was right.

Consumerists considered the question of estimates to be purely political; it depended on who was publishing the estimates and what interest they wanted to advance using those estimates. If the estimate was high, it strengthened the consumerists' belief that there was indeed enough oil and gas for consumers; if there was a shortage, the majors were deliberately holding back abundant supplies. If the estimate was low, consumerists rejected the estimate on grounds of methodology, or on grounds of bias because industry was the ultimate source of the estimate.

The majors needed prices for competitive purposes, and they needed estimates for planning and public relations. Since their time horizons were longer than those of the independents, the major firms wanted to know the general dimensions of the supply situation. They got this general feel from their own reserve estimation system, the American Petroleum Institute/American Gas Association Reserve Reporting System, conducted nationwide every year starting in the mid-1920s. The impetus for starting their own estimation system was to publish more optimistic (and, at that time, more favorable) estimates than the gloomy ones published by the U.S. Geological Survey. The majors wanted estimates to support stable and profitable prices and to get a feel for where promising future suppliers were located.

The existence of a war to which a country is dedicated is a good example of the lawyer's adage that circumstances alter cases. War reduces the number and range of participants and, increasing their cohesion, makes a political settlement possible. Consumerists get some government control of industry, and industry has a large say in how it is run. Prices are controlled to include profits. And, to mollify preservationists, there is rationing.

During peacetime periods of relative abundance, preservationists would claim vital resources were being used with profligate haste. They would, therefore, press government to limit heavy private production. At the same time, however low prices might be, consumerists would claim they were not low enough—that is, not as low as would result from genuine competition. Thus, consumerists would advocate regulation to limit prices. An evident compromise would be controls over both prices and production.

So long as supplies were ample, the potential conflict in those two positions might not be apparent. But suppose supplies (say, of oil) were straining to keep up with demand? Preservationists then would want severe limits over quantities; consumerists would favor severe limits on price increases. If the two were incompatible—low prices leading to higher consumption and less production leading to lower—what could government do to respond? The difficulty might be alleviated temporarily by importing oil. Consumption would go up and domestic production down.

That was the policy of the 1950s. When it appeared that there might be a glut, depressing the domestic industry, preservationists were pushed out, again on a defense rationale, and imports were restricted in the 1960s. After 1973, however, imports no longer could be used to moderate domestic differences. It was one thing for government to go along with anticorporate critics of oil policy; it was another for government simultaneously to decrease production and increase consumption without raising prices.

The so-called solution was to subsidize imports in order to control prices. Preservationists were pleased because domestic production fell; consumerists were content because prices stayed down; variable marketers still could make money abroad; and only constant marketers had cause for concern. But this misallocation of resources, causing simultaneous underproduction and overconsumption, was bound to catch up with us, leading to a vast outflow of dollars to pay for foreign oil that subsidy made "cheaper" to consumers.

Thus, we have a hint as to why there has been so much disagreement over oil and gas resource estimates, which by nature embody a great deal of physical uncertainty. Participants looked for a high or a low estimate to advance policies they preferred. Their preferred policies in turn were reflections of deeper perspectives oriented to quantity or to price.

Circumstances changed frequently throughout the history of oil and gas resource estimation. Remarkably, however, the positions of the various actors remained consistent and predictable. When one comes to know the participants within the context of price or quantity perspectives, and once one knows the circumstances, positions on energy policy and the way estimates were used are predictable. Sixty years ago all these factors had begun to gel, as the next chapter shows.

REFERENCES

HAYEK, F. A. (1960) The Constitution of Liberty. Chicago: University of Chicago Press.

HOUTHAKKER, H. S. (1976) "The economics of nonrenewable resources," Discussion Paper 493, Harvard Institute of Economic Research.

JOHNSON, H. G. (1968) "The economic approach to social questions." Economica (February): 3.

MILLIMAN, J. W. (1962) "Can people be trusted with natural resources?" Land Economics (August).

SCHULTZE, C. L. (1977) The Public Use of Private Interest. Washington, DC: Brookings.

Wall Street Journal (1979) "Energy-costly energy is wasting resources, some analysts worry." May 3.

2 A LEGACY OF MISTRUST
Disillusionment with
Oil Estimates

ASK ALMOST ANY AMERICAN today what causes the nation's difficulties, and high on his list will be the oil companies, who, he believes, charge too much for oil and pay too little in taxes. Had the same question been asked seventy years ago, the answer would have been remarkably similar—with this exception: He would have said The Oil Company—Standard Oil. The dramatic nature of this identification tended to obscure more complex issues and conflicts and solidify overly simplified polarities. The repetitive cycle of accusation and mistrust began early on and has formed the narrow arena of debate in which, except for two world wars, policy has been confined ever since.

For many Americans, the astonishingly rapid growth of the Standard Oil Company—from one firm among many to the single firm, dominant over an entire industry—symbolized the concentration of economic power that emerged during the last quarter of the nineteenth century. Many considered this to be the ultimate violation of the American values of democratic government, competition, and individual opportunity. A wave of economic consolidation had swept over much of American industry during the 1880s, and continued through the first decade of the twentieth century. The rise of powerful and privileged economic organizations was met, of course, with hostility, which then became linked with such other leading political issues as tariff reform, agricultural problems, and urban poverty. Monopoly and economic privilege became the seminal issue of the Progressive movement.

The oil industry received particular scrutiny. It was one of the newest forms of industry to emerge; the uses of oil were just beginning to be realized at the turn of the century. Coal was still king, but petroleum gained sudden stature when the growing Southwest found oil cheaper to

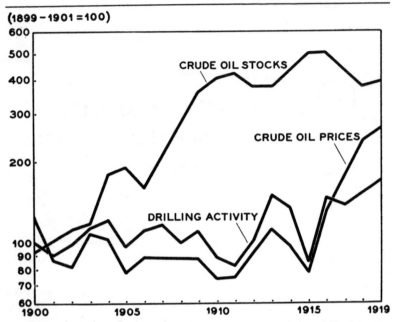

(1899 – 1901 = 100)

SOURCE: Williamson et al. (1863: 40). Reprinted by permission of Northwestern University Press.

Figure 2.1: Indexes for Crude Oil Stocks, Crude Oil Prices, and Drilling Activity, 1900-1919

obtain than coal, and when the Navy converted to oil. Figure 2.1 indicates the growth in crude oil stocks, prices, and drilling activity from 1900 to 1919.

Oil was unique among growing industries, mostly because of the physical nature of the resource and, in turn, due to the way the industry organized itself. The unusual characteristics of oil and of the industry were not fully understood in the early years. Progressives objected intensely to the industry, but to what specific aspects? Conservationists within the Progressive movement protested the rampant and wasteful competition among small businesses as vital to equal opportunity. The attacks thus came from two sides of Progressivism: preservationists, and those against monopoly, who generally reflected the "consumerist" pattern we identified in the first chapter. The two strains of Progressivism posed a united front against Standard Oil, but at heart their interests were not really congruent.

The story of Standard Oil reveals the beginnings of mistrust over energy. The relevant actors and their philosophical and policy preferences had taken shape by the first world war. When the first estimates of the country's oil resources were presented, reactions to the figures were already predictable.

THE GROWTH OF THE INDUSTRY

Perhaps it all began when Colonel Drake struck oil at Titusville, Pennsylvania, in 1859. From that point on the petroleum industry grew, at first haltingly, then by leaps and bounds. Oil first entered the market in the form of kerosene—in lamps to give light and in stoves for heat. In 1900 two out of every three gallons leaving the refinery were kerosene; the rest was a variety of experimental by-products. At that point the emergence of cheap manufactured gas and the spread of the electric light bulb would probably have spelled the end of the petroleum industry. But fuel oil rose to save the day, becoming a potent rival of coal in industrial use and transportation. Between 1900 and 1910 fuel oil production jumped sixfold, the Navy converted to fuel oil, and the petroleum industry was secure.

Petroleum, like other industries, experienced the periodic booms and busts of the late nineteenth century, and shared the expansion and change that marked the shift from an agricultural to an industrial economy. In its own way, however, petroleum fluctuated perhaps more; discovery of new sources was erratic and unpredictable. Oil men read the evidence of seepages, rode hunches, and employed diviners (as for water, following a forked, trembling stick).

Drilling techniques developed quickly. In fact, all the basic production techniques known in the nineteenth century were developed in the first ten years, 1859 to 1869. Once oil was discovered, it was drilled and exploited at a frantic pace, regardless of the apparent demand for the oil. The reason for such desperate competition to exploit lay in a curious provision of property law that came to govern oil and gas ownership—the Rule of Capture. This rule came to the oil industry from a Pennsylvania case of 1843, Acton v. Blundell, which defined the rights to natural gas (see Ely, 1938). Under the Rule of Capture the owner of a well was entitled to everything he could pump out of it, even though the oil may have flowed from his neighbor's land. This rule, together with private ownership of oil-bearing lands, and together with leasing laws which favored the lessor, led to cutthroat competition and tremendous waste. Each competitor raced to drain his neighbor's wealth, and floods of oil sent prices plummeting. This exacerbated the erratic cycles of shortage and glut. Petroleum stocks often greatly exceeded refiners' capacities to process the oil or marketers' ability to distribute it. The Rule of Capture also made for extremely wasteful production practices—recklessly fast drilling, wells placed too close to each other, and even drilling at an angle so as to tap adjacent properties.

By the early 1870s, geologists expressed concern over these wasteful practices. They began to voice the preservationist concept of the imminent exhaustion of a precious resource. Geologist J. F. Carll took the industry to task: "We have reaped this fine harvest of mineral wealth in a most reckless and wasteful manner" (Williamson and Daum, 1959: 376). Within ten years, Carll (n.d.: 23) concluded that the Pennsylvania fields had been "wastefully and excessively depleted," and that production could not continue for another five years. "From this time forward we have no reasonable ground for expecting ... that these oil fields will continue to supply the world with cheap light as they have in the past ... therefore it is wise to pause and consider how best to husband our remaining resources."

Professor J. P. Leslie, addressing the American Institute of Engineers in 1893 (see Williamson and Daum, 1959: 376), predicted extinction of the oil fields within the lifetime of his audience. The abundance of the previous twenty years was "but a temporary phenomenon ... which could not be expected to continue into the future." These predictions about exhaustion of petroleum resources formed the core of the later, larger conservation movement. This movement grew even though the dire predictions repeatedly were shown to be wrong. For the conservation movement also raised persistent controversy over production practices. Concerns about the outcome, resource exhaustion, had no effect in the early years on fiercely competitive exploitation. Producers, for their part, were caught in subservience to the Rule of Capture, operating within legal and institutional arrangements which induced wasteful and destructive practices.

THE RISE AND SUPPOSED FALL OF STANDARD

In its early years the petroleum industry was intensely competitive, not only in drilling and production, but down the line in its refining and distributing phases. By the late 1870s, a second, seemingly contradictory characteristic of the industry became evident: Its domination by a single firm. John D. Rockefeller, Sr., began to fashion the Standard Oil Company in 1862, only three years after Colonel Drake drilled the world's first oil well in Titusville.

By the turn of the century Standard Oil was an established multinational corporation. The vertically integrated company, together with its thirty-seven subsidiaries, owned most of the leases to the oil fields, the drills and pumps, the pipelines and railroad tank cars, the refineries, and the service stations that distributed the finished products.

Standard Oil did not achieve its position entirely through beneficent or even legal means. In an era that was not noted for a high level of business ethics (it was, after all, the age of the robber barons), Rockefeller and his associates were not overly nice. Neither were they any worse than their colleagues in other industries. In fact, Standard Oil exhibited little of the personal brutality that characterized development of the railroad and coal industries, or the consolidation of the steel industry.

Rockefeller understood from the beginning that control of the industry would be based not on oil production but on transportation and refining. In fact, Standard directly owned only 33 percent of total production in 1898, the high point of its ownership of crude supplies. The subsequent development of fields on the Gulf Coast and in the Midcontinental Field marked a shift in the geography of oil, and by 1911 Standard's share of total production was only 11 percent. Ownership of sources of crude oil was not necessary—indeed, crude production itself was relatively risky; far better for others to take the risks and then set one's own price on their product.

Transportation control was achieved first through arrangements with railroads and later through a monopoly of pipelines. Areas of land, or rights of way, were secured across proposed routes of potentially competing lines. Information was gathered by bribing certain strategic employees or officials. In collusion with railroads, new lines were blocked; bogus firms were set up, appealing to antimonopolist buyers. To producers using competing lines, premiums were offered which would draw them into Standard's orbit. The company used its pipeline monopoly to freeze out independent refiners, refusing to provide service to essential points or setting unreasonable requirements on the quantity of crude necessary to qualify as a shipment. Higher rates were charged on petroleum coming from producers outside of Standard's control.

Refineries were bought up rapidly; through various means those unwilling to sell were forced to do so. In a three-month period in 1872, Rockefeller managed to buy up all but three of the twenty-five refining companies in Cleveland. Next he attempted to persuade independent refiners to join him in a voluntary association, stressing the benefits of combination and the uncertainties of competition. The independents refused Rockefeller's offers, and he launched a campaign to force the combination. By using his already considerable Cleveland monopoly to play railroads off against each other, Rockefeller forced them into freight agreements. Thus, Standard's control over freight markets and shippers was increased, to the geographic and financial disadvantage of the independents. The few remaining large refiners finally were persuaded to come together in one large organization. The arrangements were secret, and new members acted as stalking horses for Standard, buying up competition in other areas.

When the smoke cleared, the monopoly was a fait accompli. Before the campaign there had been 15 refineries in New York, 12 in Philadelphia, 22 in Pittsburgh, and 27 in the Oil Regions. By 1877, Standard Oil had absorbed all competition in Philadelphia, Pittsburgh, and the Oil Regions. Only a few scattered independent refiners remained in New York' By 1880 Standard Oil was refining 95 percent of the oil produced in the United States.

The linchpin of the Standard empire was its domination of marketing, and it was its marketing practices which were most dramatically evident to the public. Standard's abuses were chronicled regularly in the press and documented by federal investigators. Prices for refined products, especially kerosene, varied in different parts of the country—lower where competition existed, higher where it did not. Standard indulged in price-cutting to drive out competitors, immediately raising prices when the objective had been achieved. Favored customers got rebates. What struck the public as perhaps most obnoxious, however, was the elaborate system of espionage employed by Standard to obtain information about competitors' sales. (Spies usually were railroad employees.) Standard then would cut prices to their competitors' customers, encouraging them to cancel orders. Standard also set up phony independent retailing firms to create the impression of competition where none existed.

Finally, less apparent to the public, but real enough, Standard used its formidable control over domestic prices of refined products, raising prices in America in order to finance price wars against competitors in Europe. In effect, American consumers financed Standard's quest for new overseas markets.

The creation of the Standard Oil Trust in 1882 was the first and most remarkable consolidation in American industry. Other businesses striving for monopoly looked to Standard as their model. The size, the economic power, and the potential political power of these new entities aroused public concern. As Bruce Bringhurst (1979: 2) states: "Wealth is easily translated into political power, and the effective exercise of democratic government becomes increasingly difficult as control over society's economic resources concentrate in ever fewer hands."

By the turn of the century, waves of antagonism had grown against big business. The Standard Oil Trust was a natural target for attack. In 1890

Congress passed the Sherman Antitrust Act. This act laid the foundation for most federal antitrust policies. Its most famous provisions were Section 1, which prohibited contracts, combinations, and conspiracies in restraint of trade, and Section 2, which prohibited attempts to monopolize. Section 1 focused on the market *conduct* of firms, such as price-fixing or other anticompetitive practices. Section 2 focused on the *structure* of the market that the firm was alleged to monopolize.

Was Standard Oil a monopoly? Testing for monopoly in the economic sense would require asking three questions (Mancke, 1976: 38):

(1) Is market structure more conducive to competition or monopoly? If the industry has many strong companies and it is easy for new firms to enter the market, these are signs of competition.

(2) Do the firms conduct themselves in a way that encourages collusive behavior? Agreements to fix prices or harass competitors suggest a potential for monopoly.

(3) Do the firms consistently enjoy abnormally high profits?

Monopoly, however, turned out to be more than economics, beyond the realm of antitrust law. The public associated with "monopoly" a large absolute size, the specter of a few individuals in a few top oil company positions making vast fortunes on a natural resource vital to all citizens. Hatred of monopoly was based less on a particular vision of the workings of the economy than on an elemental passion for equality. This hatred of monopoly engaged not only the egalitarian mind but also the conservationist mind. The word "conservation" began to be used to mean preservation of equal opportunity, nearly as much as it meant preservation of a natural resource. The passion for equality and the passion for wise use of resources meshed in the emergence of the Progressive movement, and in the Progressives' stand against "monopoly power."

The Progressive movement grew out of the Midwest and spread through the North and Northeast. It was a broad movement of social protest, preservationist thought, and economic reforms. In a sense the movement was a reaction to the previous fifty years, for the second half of the nineteenth century brought tremendous expansion, a remarkable development of industrial capacity, and new organizational and industrial forms. But this growth carried some terrible social costs and destruction of natural resources. These ravages gave impetus to the Progressive movement of the early twentieth century. Progressivism was a confrontation with the tensions of the new century, an attempt to develop the means to remedy what was perceived as the accumulated evils of an exuberant expansion.

The movement was far from monolithic; of necessity, so pervasive a movement encompassed many issues and was divided by diverse perspectives. Progressivism meant different things to urban professional and farmer, to easterner and westerner. Progressives were concerned with issues as diverse as control of the railroads, taxation and tariff policies, political reform, labor conditions, and conservation. The Progressive movement in general was characterized by optimism and a firm belief in the value of education and of publicity for its aims. But how to define and to achieve social progress was not seen uniformly. Out of the many strands of Progressivism, two major lines may be distinguished, tied to notions of the value of competition and of the morality and effectiveness of economic concentration—or monopoly versus competition.

One group held that large business organizations, combining to restrain trade and increase their profits, spelled the death of that natural competition which was necessary to sustain basic political values—the freedom and independence of the individual and small business. This group of Progressives (of the "consumerist" pattern) leaned toward the breakup of large organizations, prevention of combination, and legislative protection of the individual (person or firm) from the power of monopoly capital.

The other Progressive strand saw the terrible costs and destruction of the late nineteenth century as the result of fierce, unregulated competition (though they did not fully realize that competition was wild largely *because* of certain rules, namely the Rule of Capture). They believed large-scale organizations capable of efficiency, and even socially beneficial. Cooperation would ameliorate the fierce destructiveness of competition. Big business, of course, could not be trusted to refrain from abuse without some external supervision; hence the reliance on the regulatory commission. It was within this strand that preservationist thought was at home, for preservation in the sense of removing incentives toward wasteful exploitation meshed with preservation of the natural resource.

Journalists of the "consumerist" progressivist tradition struck the first blows against Standard. Henry D. Lloyd attacked Standard Oil as early as 1881 in an article, "The Story of a Great Monopoly," which attracted so much attention that it went into seven editions. His writings against Standard Oil (and other monopolies) spanned ten years and culminated in an influential book, *Wealth Against Commonwealth*. The journalistic coup de grâce was Ida N. Tarbell's *History of the Standard Oil Company*. Through such journalists, Standard Oil became firmly identified by the American public as "the archetype of predatory monopoly" (McGee, 1958: 137).

Standard was assailed not merely on the economic grounds of concern to the antitrust investigators, but on political and moral grounds. The

preface to Tarbell's *History of Standard Oil Company* (1950: ix) illustrates
how entirely apart from economics was the attack on monopoly:

> The Standard Oil Trust was chosen [for this study] for obvious
> reasons. It was the first in the field, and it has furnished the
> methods, the charter, and the traditions for its followers. It is the
> most perfectly developed trust ideal of entire control of the com-
> modity in which it deals. Its vast profits have led its officers into
> various allied interests, such as railroads, shipping, gas, copper, iron,
> steel, as well as into banks and trust companies, and to the acquiring
> and solidifying of these interests it has applied the methods used in
> building up the Oil Trust. It has led in the struggle against legislation
> directed against combinations. Its power in state and government, in
> the press, in the college, in the pulpit, is generally recognized. The
> perfection of the organization of the Standard, the ability and daring
> with which it has carried out its projects, make it the pre-eminent
> trust of the world—the one whose story is best fitted to illuminate
> the subject of combinations of capital.

The states then launched a series of prosecutions. In 1906 alone, state
governments filed at least thirteen lawsuits against Standard, bringing the
total number of suits from 1904 through 1906 to over twenty.

In 1906 the federal government became involved. The Bureau of Corporations of the Commerce Department issued a highly publicized report on
the entire petroleum industry. This study concluded that the Rockefeller
enterprises dominated the business. The cartel was guilty of anticompetitive conduct: railroad rebates, discriminatory pricing, and non-
competitive distribution of its products.

Based on the evidence the Bureau of Corporations had gathered, the
government sued in the federal district court in St. Louis to break up the
oil empire under the Sherman Antitrust Act. The district court decided
that the Standard Oil Company should be broken up into its component
companies. This decision was eventually sustained by the Supreme Court
in 1911.

It had taken five years, four hundred individual testimonies, and
twenty-one printed volumes before the Supreme Court decided against
Standard Oil. That decree separated the Standard Oil Company of New
Jersey from thrity-seven of its subsidiaries and affiliates. The parent
company was enjoined from collecting dividends on its stock in its subsidiaries, and the Standard Oil Company was divided into a series of
companies, each confined to a particular geographic area.

The public, and the small independent firms hurt by Standard, hoped that the action against the Standard Oil Company would result in real dismemberment of the trust and punishment of its leaders. A restoration of "balance" between the powers of government and industry, a return to natural competition, and relief from perceived abuses were expected. But the dissolution decree proved eventually to be almost ineffectual, even by narrow antitrust standards. Perhaps the main reason was that the ruling followed corporate, not functional lines. Entities were separated, but longtime business practices were not.

Although the total cartel had been vertically integrated in structure, with Standard controlling all four phases of the industry, Standard had actually been controlling numerous separate firms. There were firms in the producing business, other firms in refining, pipeline companies, and still others that were solely distribution companies.

The short-term result was that the four phases, though they were now formally "separated," kept to their old patterns of doing business, thereby foiling much of the purpose of the dissolution. And in the long run, the major successor firms themselves began to integrate vertically. Standard of Indiana and Standard of Ohio, for example, soon acquired wells and pipelines to get crude oil to their refineries. Within a few years, successor firms were to expand and become fully integrated, even as competitors to the parent firm. Apparently what had been proved was the superiority and efficiency of that organizational structure Rockefeller had pioneered. Successful entrants to the industry (except for producers) would be the large, integrated organizations.

Another factor contributing to public uneasiness, and to the image of bogus dissolution, was the way successor corporations were staffed. Previously unimportant employees were rapidly promoted to leadership in the successor firms. As a New York *World* headline of September 7, 1911, read: "Oil Trust Lamp Beats Aladdin's with Its Magic. Humble Clerks, Agents and Mechanics 'Called Upstairs' in No. 26 Broadway, and Lo! They Were Directors!" This was rather an exaggeration, but the fact remains that the leadership of successor companies came from within, often through rapid promotions. These men might continue to treat their former superiors with deference; certainly they were conditioned to the strong emphasis on company loyalty that had long been a feature of Standard management.

After the formal dissolution other events tended to confirm public mistrust. Standard Oil stock rose spectacularly because the dissolution process revealed to investors that the real assets of the companies had been undervalued for years, and because of the rapid expansion of the petroleum industry in the first decade of the century. Standard paid high dividends in the two years following dissolution, while at the same time the price of most petroleum products rose as well.

Ironically, by the time the dissolution went into effect in 1911, the Standard Oil Company was not the monopoly it had been in 1900. Standard Oil remained dominant in the oil industry, but by 1911 external events and autonomous market forces had affected Standard's position. In its own defense at the trial, Standard argued that the conduct of which it was accused was legal. Standard argued in addition that recent stiff competition drove it to its shadier transactions. The competition was stiffening as geographic forces shifted rapidly. At the turn of the century new oil fields opened up, for which Standard could not obtain leases. The most famous one was Spindletop in East Texas, the first Texas gusher. The oil fields of East Texas and the Gulf Coast were rapidly exploited and soon began to run dry. Drillers moved west and struck oil in Oklahoma and Kansas. The midcontinental fields proved to be richer and more stable than the Gulf fields. Then California began producing. Throughout this period, all Standard could monopolize was the Illinois field. The new fields everywhere else spawned the rival companies Texaco, Phillips, Gulf, Union, and Sunoco. By 1910 these competitors had reduced Standard's share of the production market significantly from almost 90 percent in 1880.

Control over refinery capacity declined from a virtual monopoly in 1880 to a still-substantial but certainly not monopolistic 64 percent. Standard's control of marketing also declined. Ironically, dissolution had the eventual effect of forcing managerial change on the old Standard Oil and its successors, and fostering Standard's entry into new fields and into what would become the more important products—fuel oils and gasoline. The oil industry had been breaking up on its own, and with the dissolution the industry regrouped itself from domination by one company to domination by a handful of integrated "majors."

No one was satisfied by the dissolution of Standard Oil. Certainly the antimonopolist Progressives were embittered by what they considered a triumph of evil. And nothing in the dissolution gave encouragement to preservationists; the Rule of Capture remained the guiding light for exploration and field development. Independent producers were dissatisfied, for the power of the large integrated firms to set prices remained unbroken. Finally there was a residue of suspicion of a government that had issued an ineffectual punishment against Standard Oil.

Ultimately, the issues—competition or combination, the relationship between government and industry—were made no clearer. The dissolution served only to reinforce the polarities in the oil arena. Independents resented the majors. The egalitarian Progressives resented the majors and harbored a vague suspicion of the government that failed to break up the industry. Preservationists resented all oil producers for their wasteful and destructive practices, and they were unhappy with a government that failed to regulate drilling or limit production. The Progressive movement itself lost its united front and became fragmented. For in addition to everything else, the Progressive party of 1912 had been the party of Theodore Roosevelt. Once it failed to gain for him the Republican nomination in 1916, the party as a national force began to wither.

CONFLICT OVER RESOURCE ESTIMATES: PREDICTABLE

It was in this fragmented atmosphere of the days just before the United States entered into World War I that the first estimates of the country's remaining oil resources were received. From the beginning, mistrust surrounded oil and gas reserve estimation. Producers of the first estimation data were geologists whose public statements suggested that a finite quantity of petroleum was in danger of exhaustion. These views indicated a path for government involving regulation of the oil industry's exploitation practices and quantities of output. Industry, on the other hand, generally was of the opinion that resources were virtually inexhaustible, and that future discovery and supply would rest on adequate price incentive. Industrialists also understood and bitterly opposed the regulatory implications of low estimates. Evidently, nothing much has changed from that day to this. A history of oil and gas reserve estimation provides a useful focus for analyzing the political environment in which oil policy has been debated and argued but never settled.

The first survey of the nation's petroleum resources was conducted in 1908 by the U.S. Geological Survey. In fact, from 1908 through 1919 the USGS was the dominant producer of data about this country's petroleum resources.

The federal government had first become involved with oil through the USGS in the 1870s. The agency's initial concern was to aid drillers in their search for oil through the application of modern science. At first the oil men were skeptical. But the USGS advanced techniques of locating oil pools by studying their relation to geological features. With markedly increased success in finding oil pools, the operators turned gratefully to the USGS. The role of the USGS was two-pronged: It helped business in locating the most promising fields; at the same time, it urged specific conservation practices to reduce the flagrant waste. The agency in the beginning served both industry and conservationists.

George Otis Smith, director of the USGS when the first oil resource estimates were made, held the opinion that geologic research sponsored by the government should be practical and oriented toward a business policy for public lands (which meant that governmentally sponsored geologic research should be directed toward discovery of mineral-rich properties, which, in turn, should be properly developed). But Smith was also a conservationist in the sense that he was strongly critical of certain industry practices. The two-pronged mission of the USGS fell into a kind of ambivalence. Eventually the petroleum geologists connected with the agency adopted an increasingly preservationist view toward the nation's endowment of oil.

The progressivist administration of Theodore Roosevelt was concerned with the use made of public resources, and the USGS land classification projects were the basis on which public lands bearing minerals were included or withdrawn from exploitation. In the summer of 1907, director Smith led a project that withdrew large amounts of oil-rich land from private exploitation and into public reserves.

Furthermore, it was under Roosevelt's administration that the Standard Oil Trust came under the heaviest criticism. Thus, conservationist and antimonopoly concerns provided the impetus for a nationwide survey of just how much oil the United States had. In 1908 the USGS produced the first survey of this country's petroleum resources, estimating the total quantity of oil (proved reserves plus ultimately recoverable resources) at between 10 and 24.5 billion barrels. While this was more than a twofold range, even the highest bound was extremely low: The survey projected future production upon past rates of increase and predicted the United States would run out between 1935 and 1943.

In 1915 an even more pessimistic estimate was made by West Coast geologist Ralph Arnold, who revised the USGS estimate downward, and put the original supply at about 5.8 billion barrels. Further revisions that year by the USGS raised Arnold's estimates to about 7.6 billion barrels. By 1918 the Geological Survey had settled on 6.9 billion barrels (see Table 2.1). Also, in 1918 Chester G. Gilbert and Joseph E. Pogue of the Division of Mineral Technology of the Smithsonian Institution estimated resources at 7 billion barrles, saying, "There is no hope that new fields, uncounted in our inventory, may be of sufficient magnitude to seriously modify the estimate given" (see Pew, 1945: 3).

Of course, all the estimation efforts of this period were only the roughest of educated guesses. Not until late in this period did geologists systematically begin to analyze subsurface structures by examining well logs and core samples. It was only after 1917 that oil companies used core drilling in connection with exploratory wells, and not until after 1919 that

TABLE 2.1   Domestic Cumulative Production, Estimates
             of Unmined Crude Reserves, and Proved Reserves,
             Selected Years: 1908-1928 (billions of barrels)

Year	Cumulative production	Estimates of unmined reserves	Proved reserves
1908	1.99	8.0 (Day)	
1914	3.34	5.8 (Arnold)	
1915	3.62	7.5 (U.S.G.S.)	
1916	3.92	6.1 (U.S.G.S.)	
1918	4.61	6.9 (U.S.G.S.)	
1926	9.44		8.8
1927	10.34		10.5
1928	11.24		11.0

SOURCE: Williamson et al. (1963: 48). Reprinted by permission of Northwestern
University Press.

the importance of subsurface stratigraphic studies was recognized. The
early estimates were projections of discoveries in known fields only.
Rarely did they include the realm of the undiscovered or postulate about
new basins that might be found in the future. Nevertheless, what all the
estimates by the Geological Survey and the Smithsonian seemed to say
was: We are fast running out.

USGS Director Smith (Petroleum Age, 1924: 51), looking back at the
first years of this century, summed up the prospects for oil conservation:

> The petroleum industry—present and past—is best described as
> frenzy of exploitation. A blind faith that demand will overtake
> supply, that prices will at least equal costs, that profits will reward
> perseverance, is the only trace of sanity underneath the delirium that
> is everywhere seen in the hunt for oil. . . . It is all too evident that
> the oil business is travelling "in high" with the gear shift locked.

A related worry was that the United States would one day have to pay
for its waste by importing oil. Before World War I, USGS geologist I. C.
White had warned about our nation's impending loss of energy self-sufficiency. This worry began to loom large as the United States prepared to
enter the war. Reporting to the Senate, Mark Requa (Pew, 1945: 8), chief
of the Petroleum Division of the U.S. Fuel Administration, suggested that
the United States, on the basis of current estimates, could meet increased
domestic and foreign petroleum demands for only five to ten years, and

thereafter, production may remain stationary for another short period, following which there will be a period of twenty or more years during which the production will decrease from year to year, while consumption increases, causing greater and greater imports from foreign fields and higher prices culminating in acute shortage.

Requa warned that "in the exhaustion of its oil lands and with no assured source of domestic supply in sight, the U.S. is confronted with a crisis of the first magnitude." His statement concluded (Pew, 1945: 8),

We must either plan for the future or we must pass into a condition of commercial vassalage, in time of peace relying upon some foreign country for the petroleum wherewith to lubricate the highways of commerce, in time of war, at the mercy of the enemy who may either control the sources of supply or the means of transportation; in either event our railways and factories will cease operation, our battleships will swing helplessly at anchor, and our country will resound with the martial tread of a triumphant foe.

The immediate concern of the U.S. Geological Survey's research centered upon wasteful drilling and production practices. They were called "flushfield" methods and defined as "rapid, uncontrolled development, with production quickly peaking, declining crude oil prices, and a race between crude production and above ground, storage capacity to handle this output" (Williamson et al., 1963). Some estimators believed more oil was lost in flushfield production than was marketed.

Flushfield methods were the springboard from which USGS conservationists launched their protests. Director Smith, as quoted in the *Mining and Scientific Press,* was moved by the problem to conclude that

future historians will date the end of barbarism from the time generations begin to feel that they rightfully have no more than a life estate in this sphere [oil resources] with no right to squander the inheritance of their kind.

I. C. White said in the same publication:

Just as sure as the sun rises and the sum of two plus two is four, unless this insane riot of destruction and waste of our fuel resources which has characterized this past century shall be speedily ended, our industrial power and supremacy will, after a meteor-like existence, revert before the close of the present century to those nations that conserve and prize at their proper value the priceless treasures of carbon.

In March 1921, at a meeting of the American Association of Petroleum Geologists, White requested the president of the association to cooperate with the USGS in making a new survey. The joint committee included state and company geologists, and consulting specialists. This distinguished group estimated our resources to be about 9 billion barrels of oil. This, their report stated, "was enough to satisfy the present requirements of the United States for only twenty years if the oil could be taken out of the ground as fast as it is wanted." The Geological Survey added that the United States was "already absolutely dependent on foreign countries to eke out her own production, and, if the foreign oil can be produced, this dependence is sure to grow greater as our own fields wane" (Pew, 1945: 9).

INDUSTRY REACTIONS

The oil industry was hostile to predictions of coming scarcity, and the acid lines their criticism would follow soon was apparent. An editorial in *The Oil and Gas Journal* (1916: 2) repudiated preservationist fears and pessimistic estimates:

> The fact that our forefathers were always equal to every emergency does not seem to weigh one particle with them. The suggestion that our children may be perhaps as smart as ourselves and fully as capable of attending to their business does not appeal for a minute to such prophets of disaster as Pinchot and his faction. They want to legislate for all times. They desire to tie the hands of future generations with useless statutes which but hinder the efforts which practical and common sense men are putting forward every day.

Could we trust future generations to be wise, or were we depriving them of the very wherewithal to fend for themselves?

Responding to a prediction by Ralph McKee of the Colorado School of Mines that petroleum production would begin to decline in three years, *The Petroleum Refiner* (1922: 15) said:

> The good professor's declarations are an awful strain upon his intelligence. He is just too reckless with his reputation for anything. Evidently he has not been reading the late news from Arkansas, Oklahoma and Texas. When Ralph is dead and forgotten the "peak of production" will be a petroleum promontory still unscaled.

At the 1922 meeting of the American Petroleum Institute, A. C. Veatch, chief geologist for Sinclair (and formerly of the USGS) spoke of the "exhaustion bogey" raised by those sincere but misguided patriots in his old agency. Veatch said exhaustion should not be expressed in terms of years because that ignored fundamental economic factors. He believed that long before exhaustion occurred prices would approach an economic limit that would curtail certain uses and make production of synthetic liquid fuels feasible.

Resolutions adopted by the Western Petroleum Refiners' Association represented characteristic industry views. Foolish publicity, they said, had led the public to believe that there was a danger of shortage in petroleum products and a possibility of exhaustion of resources in the near future. The truth was that despite the predictions of experts and the drains of the war, demand was being met and the industry was expanding. The Western Petroleum Refiners (1921) expressed confidence in the nearly inexhaustible resources and in the industry's capacity to develop them.[1]

Industry fears that low USGS estimates might encourage government intervention were buttressed by the kinds of statements made by USGS members. As early as 1907, geologists in the field had urged the director of the USGS to take action to safeguard oil development on public lands. As a result, vast stretches of potential oil-bearing lands in California and Wyoming had been withdrawn. In part, the rationale was to ensure adequate supplies for the Navy; the first two naval petroleum reserves were established in 1912. How much more would the government take?

Future events proved the USGS estimates between 1908 and 1922 to be wildly low. Considering the nature of the information available at the time, however, and the complexity involved in attempting to estimate unmined reserves accurately, this is not surprising. Interestingly enough, all erred on the same side. Was it safer to sit on the low side?

We may assume that the USGS made the most accurate survey possible with the knowledge and equipment available to them. Despite the strong preservationist orientation of many members, the survey had a considerable interest in legitimizing the profession of resource estimation and development. One should ask not only "Why were the estimates so low?" but also "How did the estimates of resources and reserves contribute to the miasma of mistrust which had characterized the oil arena for so long?"

The USGS estimates contributed to the desire by the industry to do its own estimates. And given the relatively primitive state of the art, could not higher estimates also seem plausible? Furthermore, the first world war had brought the federal government significantly into energy policy; the government's actions happened to mesh conveniently with industry interests, to supply the needs of war. But now that the war was over and

preservationist concerns arose once again, there were fears that government action would turn to regulating the oil industry. In 1919 the
American Petroleum Institute (API) was established to represent the
industry. The API soon countered the USGS resource estimates with a
series of its own, which predictably painted a brighter picture. By the
mid-1920s, both preservationists and industry had estimates ready to use
in deeper policy disputes.

The stage for mistrust was set sixty years ago. In those early years the
primary emerging actors were the conservationists, led by the professionals
of the USGS; and the major firms of the oil industry, who constituted the
core of the American Petroleum Institute. Less dominant but already
evident were the antimonopolists of the progressive tradition, who today
might be called consumerists; and the smaller, independent firms of the
industry.

Neither the antimonopolists nor the independents produced their own
nationwide resource estimates. The independent firms were not concerned
with the long view of national estimation. Some independents joined the
API, and these firms subscribed to the API's estimates. The antimonopolists who fought for Standard's dissolution and who were ultimately disappointed in the outcome had no overriding interest in seeing either high
or low estimates. Until the dissolution in 1911, they did join the conservationists against Standard and would have subscribed to the earliest USGS
estimates.

By 1925 the major lines of conflict over estimates were drawn. Big oil
finds in the late 1920s and 1930s discredited the low estimates of the
Geological Survey—though, as we shall see, only for a time; and there was
continued fear on the part of the industry that conservationism, supported
by low estimates, was merely a vehicle for regulation or expropriation.
Add to this the physical and technical uncertainties of the data in question, and one has the ingredients for ongoing bitterness and acrimony.

N O T E

1. The text of the resolution advanced by the Western Petroleum Refiners'
Association (1921) reads:

> Whereas, the general public through the public press and periodicals and
> trade journals has been led to believe there is danger of a shortage of

petroleum products and the exhaustion of nature's crude supply within a given period, and

Whereas, this discussion has caused the manufacturers of internal combustion engines and users of fuel oil much concern, deterring many prospective consumers from the adoption of oil as a fuel, and

Whereas, we believe this has proved a serious detriment to the industry, now therefore be it

Resolved, that we, the Western Petroleum Refiners' Association . . . call the attention of the oil consuming world to the fact that the exhaustion of crude petroleum in 15 to 25 years has been constantly predicted by alleged experts for the past 30 years, and that notwithstanding we have just emerged from the greatest war of all times, making enormous demands upon the petroleum industry, that the industry not only met every demand, but today, in spite of the marvellous expansion of the automobile industry, holds in reserve storage larger quantities of gasoline, kerosene and fuel oil than at any other time in its history. . . .

We do not share in the alarming predictions of so-called experts and hereby publicly express our confidence in the ability of the petroleum industry of the world to supply the needs of the world indefinitely. Yet we anticipate there may be periods of temporary shortage, even as there have been in the past, but these have only marked the way for expansion. These periods have always been of short duration, while operators exploited for new fields, and we confidently believe, in view of present prospective future fields, it will prove so in the future.

REFERENCES

ACTON v. BLUNDELL (1843) 12 M&W 325

BRINGHURST, B. (1979) Anti-Trust and the Oil Monopoly: The Standard Oil Cases, 1890-1911. Westport, CT: Greenwood.

CARLL, J. F. (n.d.) Geographic Survey of Pennsylvania: Seventh Report on the Oil and Gas Fields of Western Pennsylvania, for 1887, 1888.

ELY, N. (1938) "The conservation of oil." Harvard Law Review 51: 1209-1244.

LLOYD, H. D. (1881) "The story of a great monopoly." Atlantic Magazine (March).

MANCKE, R. B. (1976) "Competition in the oil industry," in E. Mitchell (ed.) Vertical Integration in the Oil Industry. Washington, DC: American Enterprise Institute.

McGEE, J. S. (1958) "Predatory price cutting: the Standard Oil of New Jersey case." Journal of Law and Economics (October).

Oil and Gas Journal (1916) August 24.

Petroleum Age (1924) October 15.

The Petroleum Refiner (1922) January 5.

PEW, J. E. (1945) "The United States petroleum resources." Testimony before the Special Committee to Investigate Petroleum Resources, June 19.

TARBELL, I. M. (1950) History of the Standard Oil Company. New York: Peter Smith.

Western Petroleum Refiners' Association (1921) Resolution, May 9.

WILLIAMSON, H. F. and A. R. DAUM (1959) The American Petroleum Industry, 1859-1899: The Age of Illumination. Evanston, IL: Northwestern University Press.

WILLIAMSON, H. F., R. P. ANDREANO, A. R. DAUM, and G. C. CLOSE (1963) The American Petroleum Industry. Evanston, IL: Northwestern University Press.

3

DISAGREEMENT ON PERSPECTIVES AND DATA
The 1920s and 1930s

THE BITTER LEGACY of the Progressive era persisted into the 1920s and 1930s; conditions changed but characteristic responses did not; former Progressives remained divided into two confusing camps. Preservationists believed competition was a compact with the devil to exploit God-given resources. Antimonopolist Progressives upheld the notion of free competition among many small firms and believed that the monopolistic behavior of the majors had rendered competition false.

When it came to general castigation of the major integrated oil companies, the progressive factions presented a united front. But when it came to remedies, to public policy, preservationists preferred control of demand, and antimonopolists preferred control of the industry's structure to ensure consumers a plentiful supply. The divergent tendencies under that veil of similarity led each side to blame the oil industry for the policies of the other side—preservationists condemning "unrestrained" competition, and politicians against monopoly criticizing policies that constricted output—as if neither had had anything to do with it.

Industry too was divided. The independents, who could make money only by selling oil, wanted competition. So did the majors, except when it was inconvenient—as when superabundance of supplies made it desirable to ask government to limit production. Both factions in the oil industry feared that government might get overzealous; a government which directly set prices, they thought, might also want to make over the structure of the industry to suit itself.

Government, also involved in contradictions, could try to enforce competition or to control production. It could not do both at the same time, however—though that did not stop it from trying.

POLICY PREFERENCES:
CONGRUENT ONLY WHEN CONVENIENT

"There are a great many people in favor of conservation no matter what it means," said President Taft (Milliman, 1962: 199). Conservation has many definitions. Attitudes toward conservation are prisms through which major conflicts over oil (and, more recently, gas) have been deflected. One view, which we call preservationist, considers oil as a distinct physical property, a fixed quantity, in danger of being wasted. Oil can be burnt off, run off, or used up; when it is gone there is no more. It must be used sparingly, to ensure supplies for future generations. Consumption must therefore be controlled. It is essential to know how much oil is under the ground (hence the critical nature of both resource and reserve estimates in this view), for if fixed physical quantities are to be controlled, one must know their dimensions. This definition of conservation—preservation of a fixed physical quantity—assumes shortage, which is anything less than an infinite and inexhaustible supply.

For a mineral resource such as petroleum, conservation means that consumption must conform to the needs of future generations. Wasteful production practices must be reformed, to save oil in the shortrun for wise use in the longer run. As A. C. Pigou (Milliman, 1962) wrote,

> it is the clear duty of government, which is the trustee for unborn generations as well as for its present citizens, to watch over, and if need be, by legislative enactment, to defend the exhaustible natural resources from rash and reckless exploitation.

Preservation of a precious and finite resource cannot be left either to the working out of supply and demand or to a profit-motivated industry. Thus, a preservationist urges regulation to reduce both consumption and quantities the industry produces. This view is rooted in quantity theory; it stands outside the realm of economics.

A second definition of conservation refers to the efficient development and use of a resource, and thus essentially contradicts the first. The object here is to get the most out of a given resource. This is an economic definition and, as such, a relationship, dealing not with a fixed quantity but with the relationship of supply and demand via price: More oil will be discovered and made available through a proper price. Petroleum use and product substitution, too, will be governed by price, not by the perception of an unalterable, fixed quantity of the resource. We shall call this a "free-market" definition.

A third notion of conservation emerged from desires of variable marketers: Conservation means stabilization of prices at a high enough level to assure steady supplies in the longer run and to protect against boom-bust cycles. This interpretation allowed for planning and government involvement.

The various definitions of conservation were not only justifications of self-interest, but also articles of faith. Thus, the conflicts which followed became deeper and more intractable. Each view of conservation was part of a core system of ideas about the nation and the proper guidance of its future. One's opponents were not only wrong; they were bad. Outcomes of their activities threatened not only the economy but also the society and its future. It followed, then, that opponents could not be trusted; if opponents were not to be destroyed, they must at least be tamed. For preservationists, this meant not only that production must be controlled, but also that power must be broken, through divestiture or other means.

How did such contradictory definitions of a single word, "conservation," arise? A look at how the oil supply situation actually changed between 1918 and 1928 will set the stage for answering this question.

At the close of World War I the industry's main worry was the possibility of long-run shortage. This concern led to an intensive drive by refiners to acquire or expand their holdings of oil-producing properties. It was not until the mid-1920s that worries of shortage receded. For during the same years production was on a steady increase. In fact, from 1918 through 1923 production began to exceed the volume of crude oil runs to stills by an ever-widening margin. During this five-year period, crude oil stocks rose from about 138 million barrles to nearly 377 million barrels. Figure 3.1 depicts the supply trend of the 1920s.

Not surprisingly, as supplies increased over the decade, prices fell. (See Figure 3.2.) Crude oil prices, once removed from wartime restrictions, jumped between 1918 and 1920. But with output exceeding runs to stills, particularly during the brief depression of 1921, prices plummeted through 1923. A slackening in the rate of crude production during 1924-1926 brought a corresponding decline in crude oil stocks and a moderate rise in prices. After 1926 the reverse trend took hold: Supply increased and prices fell again. Between 1920 and 1930 oil went from more than $3.00 a barrel to a little over $1.00.

When the developed supply of the resource is so abundant that it outstrips immediate capacity to use and drives prices below cost for some producers, former free marketers demand control on supply to maintain adequate (i.e., higher) prices. This is what happened in the 1920s; some free marketers became "variable marketers," prepared to abandon the market when it benefited them to do so.

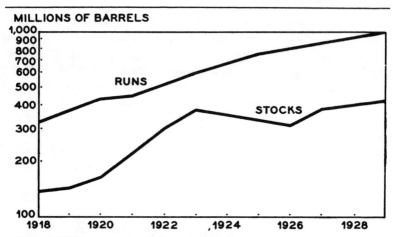

SOURCE: Williamson et al. (1963: 464). Reprinted by permission of Northwestern University Press.

Figure 3.1: Crude Oil Runs To Stills and Crude Oil Stocks, 1918-1929

Early in the 1920s major oil firms and independents feared intervention in the operation and structure of the industry. Some majors, as well as the independents, appeared to be free marketers. While the relationship between government and industry during World War I had been coopera-tive and controls had been voluntary, a precedent had been set for subjection to less voluntary control during future times of emergency. The general climate of public opinion was not wholly unfavorable to controls, as reactions to the Teapot Dome scandal and to the La Follette committee report indicated. Preservationists had plenty of ammunition. Their percep-tions of shortage, supported by low USGS resource estimates, would make strong regulatory policies (affecting all phases of the industry and directed toward reduced consumption) more likely.

Free-marketer behavior receded in the late 1920s, when more than relative superabundance became apparent. Real gluts then started appear-ing regularly, and the positions of major firms and independents began to diverge. Major firms began to consider price stabilization desirable. How-ever, the majors did not control all production and were prevented by law from establishing cartel prices. It was in the interest of the majors, in conditions of overabundance, to restrict delivered supply in order to maintain prices. Therefore, government regulation which approximated the effects of cartel pricing became desirable.

There is no way to demonstrate conclusively that major firms initiated efforts to get government to limit production so as to prevent prices from

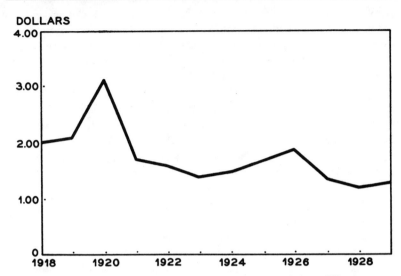

SOURCE: Williamson et al. (1963: 464). Reprinted by permission of Northwestern University Press.

Figure 3.2: Average Price per Barrel of Crude Oil, 1918-1929

falling. But if it were true that major firms were able to control prices, they would not have sought government help. There is enough evidence to cast doubt on the question. What is certain is that when preservationists suggested, even during gluts, that the nation might run out of this vital fluid if it were uncontrolled, the majors were not loath to join preservationists in accepting regulation. In times of plenty, as experienced in the late 1920s, the majors appeared to unite with the preservationists in urging the government to limit output. They called out the word "conservation" in deceptive unison. The majors, as variable marketers, joined with conservationists only so long as government did for the majors what they could not do unaided—raise their income.

Abundant reserves, however, do not necessarily mean developed reserves or supplies that are accessible on the market. Though enormous reserves may exist, they may have yet to be developed. Furthermore, supplies could be limited by "bottlenecks," such as inadequate refining capacity or transportation facilities, demand for specific fractions (i.e., gasoline, lubricating oils), or restricted imports. Major firms desired a situation in which *reserves* ready for development were abundant but in which *delivered supply* was limited in some way so that higher prices could be maintained.

Major firms and independents differed on long-range objectives. Generally, when we refer to independent firms, we mean those who deal entirely in the direct production of crude petroleum, although there are independent refiners, distributors, and marketers. Independent producers developed the raw material of the petroleum industry and obviously were dependent on those who transported, refined, marketed, and distributed their product. The majors integrated all of these control points into one firm. In conditions of oversupply, only the strongest firms would survive, and majors tended to be economically stronger than independents. Moreover, in such conditions majors leaned toward "cooperation" in pricing and toward control of production for independents. Control of production meant independents had less to sell and were thus even more dependent on their more powerful brethren. In short, independent firms dealt mainly in the short run and could not share the same kinds of long-range objectives as the integrated major firms.

Major firms wanted increasing dependence on oil—that is, an annual increase in demand just a little higher than the increase in supply. A large discrepancy between supply and demand would drive prices too high and thus would interfere with the steady growth of demand. Therefore, in the late 1920s and 1930s the majors, though claiming an abundance of resources in order to limit controls on industry structure, tended to accept limited production on a field-by-field basis—"prorationing," as the general policy was called—to keep up prices. Firm structure, price, and exploitation of petroleum thus cannot be treated separately.

Major integrated firms sought an "optimal rate of recovery" for a nonrenewable resource. This optimal rate of recovery is an economic definition of efficiency in a special sense, involving consideration of many factors, including interest rates. The amount of oil to be recovered is a determinant of price, so recovery must be carefully phased. Too-rapid recovery might mean low prices and missed profits. Too-slow recovery could lead to high prices and consequent political obstacles or product substitutions. Hence the major firms' notion of conservation was price stabilization, to help ensure a predictable and "optimal" rate of recovery over the long run.

What was each actor trying to maximize? Preservationists wanted to maximize the quantity of oil remaining in the ground, to keep it for future use. Free marketers did not maximize or minimize the value of oil above or below ground. They held a general belief in prices arrived at through competition. The minor or independent firms most closely approximated free marketers. These firms, lacking both a long-term perspective and diversified organization, wanted to maximize their short-term profits.

Major firms wanted to maximize long-term profits, and were willing, and able, to sacrifice some of their short-run incomes to ensure a greater return over the long term.

What were the actors' attitudes toward regulation? For preservationists, prices should be administratively determined, in accordance with external social goals. Free marketers would rely on the market to determine price. Variable marketers would prefer administered prices when supply appeared high, market prices when it was low.

It is not surprising that attitudes toward regulation varied with perceptions of shortage or oversupply. If there seemed to be an oversupply, major firms wanted the government to protect prices, preservationists wanted the government to protect a resource that would eventually be exhausted, and independents preferred that government control the majors. If there was an apparent undersupply, major firms feared regulation; conservationists wanted the government to harness production and exploitation by industry; and independents wanted no controls at all. Stated simply, oversupply meant low profits (hence welcome of price supports) and undersupply meant high profits (hence rejection of controls). Estimates were important in reinforcing those perceptions, and were accepted or rejected as they were perceived to support or undermine an established position.

The antimonopolist Progressives must be introduced to complete the picture. This group wanted to break up the oil industry, so as to weaken its political power and increase competition. Failing that, these Progressives preferred regulation; for them it was not oil itself that mattered but the political power oil generated. Table 3.1 indicates actors' preferences.

THE EARLY 1920s:
PRESSURE FOR GOVERNMENT TO CONTROL OIL

During the 1920s the greatest scandal to touch the government since the Reconstruction exploded into public consciousness: Teapot Dome. In 1921, Edward Denby, Secretary of the Navy in the Harding Administration, was persuaded to transfer to the Department of the Interior certain parts of the public oil lands (in California, Montana, and Wyoming), which had been part of the Naval Oil Reserve Program. Under a policy of allowing private firms to develop these reserves, Albert B. Fall, Secretary of the Interior, leased these lands to Edward L. Doheny and Harry Sinclair. The contracts were awarded in secrecy and without competitive

TABLE 3.1   Where They Stood: The 1920s and 1930s

	Preservationists	Variable Marketers Majors	Free Marketers Independents	Antimonopolists
Maximize	Quantity of oil, a precious natural resource	Long-term profits	Short-term profits	The kind of healthy competition that will assure plentiful, inexpensive supply
Conservation	Preservation of a fixed physical quantity	Stability of price and quantity to assure longer-term supply and profit	Efficient relative use of all resources as inputs to national product	Not applicable. The nation has a rich endowment.
Attitude toward shortage	Due to excessive consumption and overproduction. Government should control both exploitation and consumption. Favor high administered prices.	Due to government controls. Government should lift controls.	Due to government controls. Desire no government controls.	Due to contrivance by major firms. Break up monopolistic practices and restore healthy competition.
Attitude toward oversupply	Due to wasteful exploitation practices. Government should curb wasteful production. Favor high administered prices.	Due to outside forces, namely the Rule of Capture. Government should protect prices; to accomplish this by limiting production is acceptable.	Due to the Rule of Capture. Government should control the majors, not independents.	Suggests plentiful supplies; weakens large firms' case for raising prices. Government should not act to protect prices.
Importance of resource estimates	Accuracy important. Low estimate strengthens policy objectives.	Approximation sufficient. Rejected low USGS estimates.	Approximation sufficient. Estimates not important.	Accuracy important. Low estimates strengthen evidence of monopolistic practices and deliberate underreporting.

bidding. Subsequent investigation disclosed that Sinclair had "lent" Fall $100,000. Eventually, Fall was convicted of accepting the money as a bribe.

The public perceived the scandal as reaching deeply into the administration; even Harding's innocence was in doubt. The Naval Oil Reserve policy was deeply compromised and the affair served to focus public attention on the oil industry and its relations with the government, which had been given a virtually free hand in working out the necessary wartime system of production and distribution. Teapot Dome exposed the transferring of income from the state to those few citizens privileged to develop publicly owned lands commercially. The public's distaste for this kind of governmentally created privilege was profound. The scandal served to confirm the preservationist, antimonopolist, and public opinion that a rapacious industry was holding captive a corrupt government.

The La Follette Committee investigation of the oil industry added to the repulsion. The La Follette report contended that the pre-1911 pattern of industry control exercised by Standard Oil had not substantially changed by 1923. And to top it all, the USGS in 1920 was predicting that at current rates of use, the "unmined supply" of oil in 1930 would not exceed 3.2 billion barrels (Pogue, 1921: 20, cited in Ely, 1938: 1212).

These events stimulated an already significant public discussion concerning whether the government should impose stronger regulations on the industry. At the same time the oil industry was having its own difficulties. The postwar period of readjustment was characterized by short cycles of economic recession; the industry was plagued with alternating perceptions of shortfall and threats of glut, and petroleum prices fluctuated wildly.

The government needed some way to preserve confidence in itself and investigate conditions in the industry without losing industry cooperation. The solution was to create an agency that could oversee the oil industry without actually controlling it, so the government would be in a position somewhere between those calling for outright government intervention and those who were unalterably opposed. There were models in the recent past: the Petroleum Advisory Committee and its successor, the National Petroleum War Services Committee. Organized in 1917 to advise the government about war-related problems, the Petroleum Advisory Committee was given virtually a free hand to work out the necessary wartime system of production and distribution. The functions of the successor committee remained unchanged during World War I, when it was reconstituted as the National War Service Committee and placed under the supervision of the Oil Division of the Fuel Administration.

In 1924 the Federal Oil Conservation Board (FOCB) was created to investigate the following issues:

(1) the size of crude reserves (Was there a shortage or an oversupply?);
(2) the technical conditions of production (Was production wasteful?);
(3) the economic disruption caused by production (What were the causes of price instability?);
(4) naval reserve policy (In terms of national defense, was there danger in the current situation?); and
(5) potential future resources and alternative energy sources.

The mandate of the FOCB was to explore the proper relationship between government and industry in order to determine if the legal structure was adequate to prevent waste, ensure efficient development, prevent illegal activity (and reassure the public on this score), preserve naval reserves, and, finally, to ensure proper development, allocation, and use of alternate resources.

President Coolidge's letter of December 19, 1924, establishing the Federal Oil Conservation Board, identified as the first problem the legality of common production practices: "It is evident that the *present method* of capturing our oil deposits *is wasteful* to an alarming degree in that it becomes impossible *to conserve oil in the ground* under our present leasing and royalty practice if a neighboring owner or lessee desires to gain possession of his deposit" (FOCB, 1976: viii-ix; emphasis added).

The government's implicit definition of conservation as physical preservation is expressed in those italicized phrases: There is physical waste; petroleum is not being conserved in the ground. "We are not today, however, facing an undersupply of oil. The production of our 300,000 wells is in excess of our immediate requirements. That overproduction in itself encourages cheapness, which in turn leads to wastefulness and disregard of essential values" (FOCB, 1976: ix). Cheap oil was seen as a consequence of overproduction and therefore wastefulness, encouraged by the current system of ownership and leasing. The legal system prevented cooperation or regulation to prevent wasteful practices.

Indeed, the industry seemed locked into the Rule of Capture, which encouraged destructive, exploitative behavior which no one could avoid. Then there were tax policies that encouraged exploration and drilling. In 1926, under Coolidge's own administration, Congress introduced percentage depletion allowance tax treatment for oil and gas production. Just a few years earlier, "quick expensing" had been enacted: The oil and gas industry was allowed to deduct from taxable income any "intangible drilling and development costs." These included almost everything: wages, fuel, repairs, hauling, and so forth, even if one only got dry holes. The effect, indeed the purpose, of these two tax policies was to encourage exploration and production beyond what an unregulated market would have indicated. With production thus stimulated, prices fell, and the tradition of expecting cheap and abundant energy was reinforced. Thus, Coolidge's concern with wasteful production harkened not only to the venerable Rule of Capture, but also required a look at conscious policies made under his own administration.

The next step was inevitable; when in doubt, raise the flag, blow the bugle, and cry national defense. Cheap oil means leaving less oil in the future for uses for which oil is essential, such as fueling ships and planes. "Oil, of which resources are limited," Coolidge continued, "is largely taking the place of coal, the supply of which seems to be unlimited, but coal cannot take the place of oil in most of its higher uses on land or sea or in the air." Here was a dangerous situation indeed. Because of the development of aerial warfare and conversion of naval fleets to petroleum fuels, future military needs depended on petroleum supplies. Again from Coolidge's letter: "It is even probable that the supremacy of nations may be determined by the possession of available petroleum and its products" (FOCB, 1976).

Future shortages would have dire consequences for the economy as well. According to the President's best information, current supply was kept up by heavy annual new drilling. If there were to be a failure of new production for as little a time as two years, a serious depression would result. "The problem of a future shortage in fuel . . . must be avoided or our manufacturing productivity will be curtailed to an extent not easily calculated" (FOCB, 1976). Why uncertainty about future supply would not be reflected in rising prices was never discussed. After all, the government itself was an active participant in its role as lessor of oil lands, and in its guardianship role of lands containing large reserves of petroleum, which remained in the public domain.

Coolidge's administration was favorable to business ("The business of America is business") and to a laissez-faire policy, but in the wake of Teapot Dome and in response to congressional and public pressure, the administration felt itself responsible for the supervision of industry. The uneasy situation was expressed in this equivocal comment by the President:

> I would express the desire that these conferences may be open and exhaustive. The oil industry itself might be permitted to determine its own future. That future might be left to the simple working of the law of supply and demand but for the patent fact that the oil

industry's welfare is so intimately linked with the industrial prosperity and safety of the whole people that the government and
business can well join forces to work out this problem of practical
conservation [FOCB, 1976].

What to do first? The FOCB decided to conduct a survey. The board
sent questionnaires requesting data on "refining, production, distribution,
possible substitutes, manufacture and consumption of petroleum products" to "heads of great corporations, to engineers, economists, oil
technologists, to coordinated branches of government, in fact to everyone
who seemed competent to contribute to a full and complete survey and
analysis of present petroleum conditions."

THE MID-1920s:
PRESSURE AGAINST GOVERNMENT CONTROL

In response to the FOCB, and to counter the low USGS estimates
(which indicated impending exhaustion and were useful to conservationist
and regulatory positions), the API produced its own "Committee of
Eleven Report" in 1925. This report claimed that "waste in production,
transportation, refining and distribution of petroleum . . . was negligible."
It concluded that there was no imminent danger of the exhaustion of
petroleum reserves in the United States, directly contradicting the implications of the USGS reports.

According to the Committee of Eleven (1925: 3; see also Williamson et
al., 1963: 315-316), oil recoverable by then-existing methods of flowing
and pumping from existing wells—"proved reserves"—consisted of 5.3
billion barrels of crude. Beyond this, the committee estimated that 26
billion barrels remained, recoverable by secondary recovery methods such
as water-flooding, air and gas pressuring and mining, "when price justi-
fies."

Thus, the stage was set for the board's public hearings in the spring of
1926. Chairman Hubert Work's (FOCB, 1976: 1) opening statement was a
model of balanced inquiry:

The Federal Oil Board hopes for views of its guests concerning the
present actual conditions of the industry: whether there is sound
reason for presuming there is or is not an inexhaustible supply of
petroleum in the United States; whether the industry and Government are, through haste and waste, squandering our natural
resources; whether consumption and production are economically
regulated; whether there is or may be practical substitutes at reason-

able prices; whether present statutes should be repealed, liberalized, or made more restrictive insofar as they relate to public lands, pipe lines, common carriers, etc.; whether the oil industry itself foresees the day when it will be possible through legal, cooperative, or other means, to restrict production and reduce consumption with a view to prolong the country's known and potential deposits of petroleum without seriously disturbing national economic conditions.

Actually, sides had been drawn before the investigation began. That the government chose to focus on conservation as the center of the "petroleum problem" indicated an initial preservationist bias. Nonetheless, the hearings began in an atmosphere of accord. The positions of participants, however, basically clashed, since each side expressed differing perspectives. On one side was the production perspective, holding that a barrel of oil is better produced than saved. On the other side was the preservationist principle—a barrel saved is better than a barrel produced.

The first question was, "Is there a shortage or an oversupply of petroleum?" USGS estimates of resources (discussed in the previous chapter) suggested that there might be a shortage. Empirical evidence and fluctuating prices suggested, as of 1926, that there was surplus. Obviously, shortage and surplus pointed to differing policy directions—or did they? The inquiry of the FOCB did not settle that question; large discoveries later on, in the late 1920s and early 1930s, did. For the purposes of preservationists, the answer did not really matter. Preservationist logic was as follows: If there is a shortage of a nonrenewable and vital resource, government action is necessary to protect the people's (or the nation's) interest. Such action should take the form of promoting conservation by regulating production practices, controlling the industry, and encouraging (or enforcing) reduced consumption. The very prospect of future oversupply would encourage wild and wasteful production in a frantic effort to get oil out of the ground. Since temporary abundance means eventual shortage, measures must be taken to regulate wasteful producers.

The key legal issue perceived was not the problematic Rule of Capture, but the disposal of public lands. On the question of the exhaustion of resources, particularly in public lands, the board (FOCB, 1976: 3) said the government was committed to a "policy of protection and practical conservation of raw mineral materials, which, once exhausted, are irreplaceable, and to the protection of the public estate, the guidance of its development and natural resources. The promotion of the best use of these products of the national domain constitutes an obligation both sacred and inescapable."

However, at the same time, the government was also committed to a policy requiring that a considerable portion of publicly held lands be offered for private development, "irrespective of the economic conditions of the oil industry" (FOCB, 1976: 5). If the production practices of private developers were wasteful, then a policy of leasing publicly held lands to private operators would violate the public trust. How could measures be taken for the "conservation and orderly development of the oil resources of the country" (FOCB, 1976: 4), when the "provisions of law force a disregard of the best interests of the general public"? If there were an actual shortage and if production practices were wasteful, then changes in leasing policy and in production practices were necessary. Policy was obscured by uncertainty about actual amounts of petroleum underground in unleased territories.

Increasing demand for petroleum products, and growing civilian and military dependence upon them, also caused government concern. Hubert Work likened the national consumption of oil to an individual's spending his entire income and saving nothing:

> Speaking in round terms, our oil fields in 1925 yielded 758,000,000 barrels of crude petroleum, and the consumption was 750,000,000 barrels. We produced 10,000,000,000 gallons of gasoline and burned up 9,000,000,000 gallons. This is a common ratio. From these figures it would seem that we are proceeding along much the same line as the man who earns $100 a month and spends $100 a month. How long, at this rate, can we, as a nation, maintain our equilibrium in manufacture? [FOCB, 1976: 6].

That argument—assuming a fixed quantity of liquid petroleum irrespective of price or substitutes—prevailed, and persists to this day.

Independents viewed the prospects for legislative change with skepticism and hostility. Basically, independents claimed the federal government had no power to act in these matters and that legislation, if at all allowable, was in the province of the states. According to Amos L. Beatty (President of Texas Oil, an independent producer), no government had the authority to "legislate the uses of a particular product" (FOCB, 1976: 1)—that is, to regulate uses to which private property was put. Moreover, "regulation is less efficient as a guide to conservation than are the inexorable laws of economics. . . . The unwritten but inexorable law of economics affords a perfect remedy and leaves no credit balances for future adjustment" (FOCB, 1976: 16). Consequently, legislation regarding wasteful practices was unnecessary, as was legislation about price or use.

Integrated firms, too, in this case seemed to prefer a free-market definition of conservation. W. C. Teagle (FOCB, 1976: 20), President of Standard Oil of New Jersey, defined true conservation as the economical

use of a resource, not artificial restraints on that use. Scientific development and economics, not government regulation, would lead to conservation:

> The average man fails to realize that true conservation of material is
> its economical use. Government action may bring about the eco-
> nomical use of a raw material but generally conservation is more
> certain of attainment by science and economics. Science, through
> research, improves methods of production and manufacture. Eco-
> nomics, through price, creates the market. Price expands or con-
> stricts production and consumption and is generally the incentive to
> scientific research. Price is the controlling factor in conservation and,
> therefore, the influence of price is paramount in any consideration
> of the subject.

If the situation were to change, however, and if the market were to be
flooded (that is, if considerable new discoveries were to be made), then the
simple rules of science and market would no longer be sufficient to ensure
economic use (conservation in the free-market sense). Regulation would
then be welcome. This statement prefigured accommodation to regulation
in the 1930s. Although the chief integrated-firm position at the moment
was antiregulatory, it was not an inflexible stand.

The sharpest exchange over the issues before the FOCB was between
Charles Evans Hughes and Henry L. Doherty. This debate illustrates not
only the fundamental conflicts between physical and economic interpreta-
tions of conservation, but also their different implications for estimation.
Hughes represented the American Petroleum Institute before the board.
Doherty was a petroleum engineer.

The adversaries were irreconcilably opposed on the major issues of
concern to the board:

(1) the nature of the reserve base;
(2) the constitutionality of federal conservation regulation;
(3) the definition of conservation; and
(4) the importance and credibility of estimation data.

Hughes's objective was to convince the FOCB of both the illegality and
the uselessness of federal regulation. His arguments were based on an
economic definition of conservation, optimistic estimates of reserves presented in the API Committee of Eleven report, and a conventional reading
of the Constitution. Doherty presented the case for strong federal regulation, based on an assumption of shortage and the belief that industry

practices were leading to an inevitable exhaustion of resources. Doherty accused the oil industry of acting against the national interest in refusing to adopt governmental regulation of production practices. Essentially, Doherty's program consisted of limiting production and exploration, as well as limiting efforts toward secondary recovery of depleted fields.

Hughes (FOCB, 1976: 2) argued there was no case for federal regulation to encourage conservation:

> Curtailment of production within the states in a general public interest for the purpose of conserving oil in the ground was not the power to tax and to purchase for governmental uses, but a power to control production upon private property within the States, and subject to the sovereignty of the States, respectively.

Federal conservation legislation aimed at correcting wasteful production practices, Hughes claimed, would violate state sovereignty. Voluntary agreements among producers to achieve the same ends would be in violation of antitrust statutes. Outside the states, then, there was no legal countermeasure; even within the states, legislation aimed at preventing economic waste was invalid. In any event, regulation of the use of resources was best achieved through price, not by statutory conservation.

Was there a real need for conservation? Not in the physical sense suggested by proposed legislation, Hughes continued (FOCB, 1976: 2), for the reserve base was abundant; USGS estimates had been inaccurate: "In connection with all the official estimates . . . the necessary caution has been given that they were conjectural, and the actual results have abundantly justified the warning that they might prove to be wide of the mark."

Reserves, in fact, were more than adequate for the long term. Beyond that, any specific amount of petroleum held underground did not matter greatly, since supply was determined by price. Hughes held that the same pricing mechanism also would assure a smooth transition to substitute energy sources at that distant time when substitution might be necessary. To follow a policy based on a physical notion of conservation and control production would be a foolish rejection of the best regulatory mechanism price: "It is evident that any estimate of future supply and demand that did not embrace the price factor would be futile. Price finds the oil and produces it. Price controls and limits its use" (FOCB, 1976: 3).

What then, was the proper role of government? Hughes characterized as "political" any remedies that involved regulation. Political action, however, since it operated contrary to the more efficient price mechanism, was unlikely to achieve "conservation." The government should, then, make this wisdom more apparent to the public, and ought to stimulate scientific research:

> The great service that this Board can render is to bring about an intelligent conception on the part of the public of facts relating to the industry, of its problems both economic and legal, and to foster the scientific investigations upon which ultimately the conservation of our vastly important oil resources must depend [FOCB, 1976: 21].

Whether participants wanted no action outside of markets or government control of industry, they were sure to advocate more research and better data.

Henry Doherty (FOCB, 1976: 41), in a written reply, accused the oil industry of silencing "men of vision in the industry, who actually know that conservation measures should be adopted." Hughes, he suggested, was simply the industry's errand boy, lending prestige to industry's position, though he himself was ignorant. Doherty maintained that a shortage of crude oil was imminent, that the USGS estimates were correct, and that the Committee of Eleven report (which Hughes had sponsored) was self-interested, fanciful, and exaggerated. Fearful of justified government intervention, the industry had constructed a misleading and inaccurate argument solely to prevent such intervention.

The industry definition of conservation as "economical use," Doherty continued, was "one-sided and false." The economical use of petroleum, once produced, could not compensate for waste incurred at the time of inefficient recovery. Moreover, any "use" of an exhaustible resource meant its eventual depletion. "Economic use" represented maximum use and therefore was antithetical to conservation. As Doherty put it,

> hundreds of millions of barrels of oil are already being produced in excess of our real needs for petroleum purposes, and if we were, under our present system, able to double the efficiency of every automotive engine, it would have but little or no effect on conserving our oil but would simply increase the amount of oil being burned to displace coal [FOCB, 1976: 47].

To achieve true conservation, it was the duty of the FOCB to gather accurate information and lay it before the public. Accurate estimates were crucial in the formation of policy. To rely on the self-serving data offered by the API would be dangerous, Doherty continued:

The decision of what should be done must depend upon how much our remaining reserves of oil amount to. There is no use talking about a "billion acres of land" unless it is used as evidence to enable us to estimate the amount of oil which remains. And if the oil men are unwilling to make an estimate of our remaining reserves, or if this estimate when made is not large enough to insure a future supply, then it is up to us to do something to insure a supply and to act without delay [FOCB, 1976: 52].

Why then, was the industry so anxious to prove a superabundance of petroleum reserves? Because, in Doherty's opinion, if supplies seemed adequate there would be no need to regulate, and because oil men were aware of the shaky nature of their legal case against regulation and wished to sidestep the issue entirely. The formation of the board itself indicated the government's interest in conservation and therefore in regulation; it was in the industry's interest to pretend cooperation while heading off the enemy at the pass. Doherty felt sure that there was no legal barrier to regulation on the part of the states and that if the oil situation were to be viewed as one of national emergency, the federal government "could do whatever seemed desirable to do, based on the powers given to it to provide for national defense" [FOCB, 1976: 59].

Doherty considered that his case rested on the reality of petroleum shortage. If the abundance that his opponents claimed really existed, then he was willing to withdraw his proposals. "It is for your commission to say whether my opponents by their various activities have proved the existence of such an abundance of petroleum that there is no danger of a shortage that might limit our efficiency in the prosecution of war" [FOCB, 1976: 62].

The FOCB straddled the issues. In its first report, it stressed that the best way to achieve conservation was through voluntary cooperation between federal and state governments and the oil industry, and that FOCB activities would

convince Congress that it can do nothing toward the conservation of oil other than legislate in respect of lands owned by the United States; convince the oil industry that it can and should regulate itself; convince the states that they can enact leglislation that will cause the orderly development of the oil resources within their borders; convince the ultra-conservationists that they should give the weight of their influence to the doing of things that can be done without undertaking anything that will start a controversy as to fundamental questions of state and federal power [FOCB, 1976: Report I].

By the time its fourth report was published (1929), the FOCB was convinced that the primary "petroleum problem" was surplus, and by then the it strongly favored control of that oversupply.

THE 1930s:
FROM PRESERVATION TO PRICE STABILITY

By the early 1930s the federal government and the major firms supported a view of conservation that centered on establishing, with the aid of central planning, a balance between production of crude oil and market demand. Government had shifted away from seeing conservation as the preservation of physical resources and prevention of physical waste; major firms had redefined efficiency in terms of price stability. To understand how this shift came about, we will examine some of the events of the late 1920s and early 1930s that changed perceptions of supply, self-interest, and attitudes toward regulation.

The FOCB's original mandate had been to develop a national conservation policy for the oil industry based on the voluntary cooperation of the industry with the government. When the FOCB began its work in 1924, it tended to accept a perception of shortage: Its concerns were with wasteful production and manufacturing practices, and the preservation of the reserve base. The constitutionality of a federally devised and enforced program of conservation seemed doubtful. Therefore, the board's first report (1926) stressed the role of states in developing and enforcing conservation statutes; cooperation among oil-producing states; and the technical and advisory role of the federal government. FOCB recommended a voluntary cooperation model for government and industry.

The problem of "overproduction" emerged in the late 1920s; so did calls for some means to limit production. In 1928, a Committee of Nine—including representatives of the federal government, the Mineral Law section of the American Bar Association, and the oil industry—was appointed by the FOCB. This committee recommended voluntary integration among oil producers and voluntary curtailment of output. The following year, the American Petroleum Institute submitted a proposal to the FOCB calling for voluntary agreements among firms which were consistent with worldwide production limitations. Independent producers were suspicious, and the Attorney General ruled the proposal in violation of antitrust legislation. With voluntary "self-regulation" of the industry ruled out, the FOCB recommended development of parallel state conservation legislation and voluntary cooperation among state regulatory agencies. The board recommended an arrangement called "prorationing," an administrative effort to limit production so as to maintain a minimum price.

The legal and organizational framework for prorationing on a national scale was not worked out until well into the 1930s. The settlement (if it can be called that) was difficult, cumbersome, and served to confirm mistrust already well established.

The development of prorationing followed three stages. The first stage (1929-1933) was an attempt to control production through voluntary industrial cooperation, state enforcement, and interstate cooperation. All of these mechanisms failed. Industrial cooperation was unobtainable because the real interests of independent firms and integrated majors were in conflict. Cooperation was understood by the independents to spell their own destruction. States either chose to limit production within their own borders or, acting together in only an advisory capacity, to control the flow of oil between states.

The second stage (1933-1935) was part of and parallel to the experiment in industrial planning under the National Recovery Act (NRA), which involved suspending antitrust action and redefining "conspiracy in restraint of trade" to mean "industrial cooperation." The NRA has been viewed alternatively as the structure of planning necessary to save American democracy during the social and economic dislocations of the depression, and as the blueprint of American corporatism. Antimonopolists, such as Harold Ickes, heirs to a Progressive tradition, found themselves defending "industrial cooperation" in the name of national planning.

The petroleum industry specifically was dealt with in Section 9C of the NRA, which prohibited interstate shipment of oil in excess of the amounts which states had permitted to be produced within each state. The NRA, however, was invalidated by the Supreme Court on the grounds that its provisions represented an unconstitutional delegation of congressional authority to the executive.

The third stage (1935-1940) of mechanisms for limiting production of crude oil and establishing price stability in the form of prorationing was finally implemented. The framework included a federally endorsed interstate body (the Interstate Oil and Gas Compact Commission) to control and allot production of crude oil; federal regulation of the interstate flow of oil (the Connally Act); and a federally developed indicator to measure market demand (Bureau of Mines forecasts of market demand).

THE FIRST STEPS TOWARD PRORATIONING:
OKLAHOMA AND TEXAS

In 1929 there was still a certain degree of optimism about the prospects for voluntary, self-regulated limitations of petroleum production, but events were to prove this optimism misplaced. Exceedingly rich discoveries (first in Oklahoma and later in East Texas), combined with the general economic depression, were to prove disastrous. Patterns of production in Texas and Oklahoma threatened to drive prices down throughout the industry. Independent operators battled against major firms and state agencies. In essence, the majors could wait for their money, the independents could not.

Attempts to promote voluntary limitation and state enforcement failed. Various conservation statutes had been in effect in the oil-producing states for many years. These statutes usually required conservation technology—well-capping, well-spacing, and some form of prorationing—to prevent physical waste. However, the effectiveness of state conservation statutes often was limited by the resistance of independent producers who were influential in state legislatures.

The Oklahoma Conservation Statute, adopted in 1915, empowered state authorities to restrict output in the interest of conservation. This act prohibited the production of crude oil in conditions which constituted waste, defining waste to include both economic waste and improper production practices. A large find at Seminole in 1926 appeared to threaten the price structure of the industry; petroleum was extracted frantically. The Oklahoma Corporation Commission attempted to enforce the provisions of the statute (in cooperation with the larger companies and the pipeline companies), but its attempts proved futile since independent operators would not shut down or limit production, and the commission had no power to suppress shipment of oil across state lines. Discovery of the even richer Oklahoma City field in 1928 made the restriction of output impossible. By August of 1929, the Oklahoma Corporation Commission ordered a shutdown of the fields, and the governor imposed martial law for thirty days. But not even martial law worked. Actual output for the state continued to increase.

Without the cooperation of the operators, Oklahoma authorities could not enforce their orders. There were many independent producers, and it would always pay at least one operator to continue production, even at marginal prices. If one producer continued operations, others had to do so as well, to defend themselves from the effects of drainage and offset well-drilling. It was a stark manifestation of enslavement to the Rule of Capture.

The enormous East Texas oil finds in 1930 completely and finally dispelled hopes for voluntary cooperation. All efforts to limit the production of crude oil necessarily revolved around Texas, which produced more than 40 percent of all crude. The state legislature often had shown hostility to prorationing and to economic definitions of conservation. On several occasions statutes had been enacted to restrict the Texas Railroad

Commission from applying economic definitions of conservation. Indeed, when the Conservation Act of 1919 was amended in 1921, a specific proviso was inserted to the effect that "prohibitable waste shall not be construed to mean economic waste."

Although the regulatory authority of the Texas Railroad Commission was confirmed in 1931 (and a new statute, the Market Demand Act, was enacted to permit prorationing), conflicting interests, combined with vague regulatory machinery, defeated attempts to stop the flow of oil from East Texas. In 1931, martial law was declared and, as in Oklahoma, the national guard was called up to close the oil field. When production was resumed in 1932, the Texas Railroad Commission was unable to control the flow of "hot oil" (oil produced and sold in excess of the commission's allowable amounts).

The flood of oil from Texas (one million barrels a day, roughly a third of national requirements) was so great that it posed a threat to all attempts at regulation throughout the country. Furthermore, the giant East Texas field was largely in the hands of independent operators. These operators considered the Texas Railroad Commission an agent of the major firms. Independents' views on the activities of the major firms were expressed in an editorial in the *Austin Dispatch,* reacting to a bill before the Texas legislature, which would create a new commission more favorable to prorationing:

> There is only one reason for such a measure, to oust the regulators who fail to do the major companies' bidding and to put in others who will. East Texas is one of the few oil fields where the land-owner, wildcatter and true independent got a handhold and the Octopus means to break that hold by whatever means necessary.

Independents saw prorationing (a statute explicitly citing production in excess of market demand as prohibitable waste) as price-fixing by the majors, intended to destroy or discipline independents by legal means. Naturally, opposition continued. State Senator Joe Hill expressed the opposition to defining prorationing as conservation:

> It is the rankest hypocrisy . . . to say that the purpose of proration-ing is anything other than price-fixing. . . . I sit here in utter amaze-ment and see men . . . talk about market demand as an abstract proposition and contending that it has got no relation to price-fixing [Temporary National Economic Committee, 1978].

PRORATIONING FINALLY "ACHIEVED"

As we have seen, prorationing was not accepted without dispute. The industry was divided. Major firms favored prorationing and by the early 1930s began to look for help from the federal government. At an industry meeting in Chicago in 1932, the president of the API expressed support for federal regulation designed to end the industry's characteristic cycles of shortage and glut "by balancing crude oil products with consumer demand." A vice-president of Standard Oil of California followed up: "If you do not give us price regulation, you can make codes from now to doomsday and you will get nowhere" (Engler, 1961: 138). Independents, however, were not of the same mind; they were suspicious of controls in the hands of the federal government or the major firms.

Originally, prorationing had been part of the preservationists' arsenal. The idea was that prorationing would ensure maximum eventual recovery with minimum physical waste. Preservationists and the majors seemed united. However, when state agencies were empowered to set monthly production allowables based on market demand, prorationing came to be seen as a mechanism which would ensure a "predictable flow" of products to known markets with a minimum of "economic waste" and "price fluctuation." Proponents of prorationing continued to argue that to support prices encouraged exploration, thus assuring a continued and dependable supply while at the same time providing an incentive toward physical conservation. This assurance of a stable supply was an element preservationists found hard to support.

The official justification for prorationing continued to be "conservation," in the service of which state commissions were empowered to restrict rates of output. Individual well production was limited on the basis of "maximum efficient rate" (MER). Wells with the greatest potential were cut back to the lowest percentage of MER, so that smaller wells could produce at MER. Further, spacing requirements for wells were most restrictive on the large properties. In essence, such restrictions prevented rapid exploitation of reserves by the largest producers, so that conservation was achieved by reducing the flow from proved reserves. Ironically, the independents who had fought prorationing benefited from it perhaps more than the major producers.

The importance of prorationing for the future was that, through the actions of state commissions, total state production was limited. Consequently, prices above those which would have occurred without regulatory controls were established and maintained for years.

In 1930 the FOCB had recommended a plan for interstate cooperation which had as its major objective coordination among oil-producing states to "protect the resources of cooperatively operated pools against the destructive competition of sources outside the jurisdiction." The Oil States Advisory Commission was organized to implement the plan, but it was relatively ineffective in dealing with problems of overproduction. The commission, for example, could not stem the torrent of "hot oil" flowing from Texas. After the Supreme Court ended the NRA, and in order to dampen rising interest in federal regulation, the industry again looked for interstate cooperation. The API and Governor Ernest W. Marland of Oklahoma took steps to form an interstate oil compact. In 1935 Congress authorized the Interstate Compact, an agreement among the major oil-producing states.

Under the compact, major oil companies submitted estimates of anticipated imports to the Oil States Advisory Commission. Each state received a monthly statement of existing petroleum stocks and a forecast of demand for that state's oil, prepared by the Bureau of Mines (based on industry-supplied data). Using these statements and forecasts, the states fixed "allowables" for each field, which served as industry production guides. Any production in excess of allowable violated state law and was subject to confiscation, and any shipment of oil in excess of allowables violated the Connally Act. Thus, while state law had been powerless to control interstate oil traffic, the federal government through the Connally Act assumed that power.

PRORATIONING:
PATCHWORK WITHOUT AGREEMENT

There are at least two contrasting views on the origins and significance of prorationing. One view is held by antimonopolists, who see prorationing as a link in a carefully constructed chain of control, one of several mechanisms whereby major integrated firms have strengthened control over the industry and the government. This view postulates that either the government is in collusion with the industry or the government is industry's captive. Analysts such as John Blair or Robert Engler, for example, emphasize the international aspects of firms' behavior. Blair and Engler interpret prorationing in the 1930s as the mechanism whereby American petroleum production was brought within the limits set by the international oil cartel as part of a worldwide price-fixing arrangement. This sort of analysis describes an elegant, elaborate, and effective structure of control.

Another view, more favorable to the oil industry, is that the program set up in the 1930s—mutually cooperative and intelligently planned and executed—culminated in a flexible and rational petroleum policy. In this view, prorationing served both conservationist and industrial purposes. A legal framework was developed to encourage the physical preservation of resources while at the same time preventing excessive fluctuations in the supply of oil.

A third view, to which we would subscribe, is that actually prorationing was disorganized price-fixing, which led the nation to pay more for oil than was necessary, thus depressing the standard of living. As one analyst, Northcutt Ely (1938: 1237), wrote:

> The attempt to maintain a price that will reward this over-investment requires stabilization of an artificial price level. . . . [A]s the ratio of drilled-up reserves to proven reserves becomes more and more top-heavy, the aggregate return, in barrels of total production per dollar invested, becomes less and less attractive.

If the major integrated firms were so powerful, it is hard to explain why they spent so long doing such a slipshod job. Indeed, without the help (however inadvertent) of preservationists, the majors might not have managed to fix prices. Worst of all, prorationing masked, but did not resolve, the basic differences over oil.

What is striking about prorationing, however, is not its elegance but its patchwork nature. That solution did have advantages; general economic conditions were chaotic and supply did appear overabundant. But if those conditions changed, the creaky nature of the arrangement would become apparent. Ely (1938: 1240-1241) concluded, prophetically, that prorationing did

> steer [the industry] away from the Scylla of immediate overproduction. But there is a Charybdis, more distant yet perhaps more ominous. The efficiency of the state control system has yet to be tested by a down-cycle of supply, when the problem may be how to meet the demand at reasonable prices during a period of diminishing flush flow. That day is certain to come. It is an open question whether the conservation laws will be applied to limit production for conservation's sake alone, when stabilization of overproduction is no longer a factor. . . . It is even more questionable whether . . . the consuming public will be content to pay the higher prices which curtailment would occasion. The complex system now governing petroleum production is essentially producers' legislation. . . . [T]he conservation laws have been enacted upon the insistence of the industry, and the indifference of the consuming public.

Ely, then, saw the industry in 1938 as faced with a profound contradiction in objectives: the producers' desire for protection against short-run overproduction, and the national consumers' latent interest in cheap and abundant energy. Prorationing cushioned against the first worry, and appeased conservationists to boot: "The second, thus far (1938) has been distant enough to require none" (1938: 1243).

Prorationing, an arrangement developed to ensure market stability, also ensured the persistence of mistrust. The settlement arrived at in the 1930s did not satisfy the material interests of independent producers, one important group, and subverted the aims of another, preservationists. The settlement laid the groundwork for consumerists who would rise as a powerful force protesting the hidden effects of prorationing. In sum, whether overtly or latently, prorationing confirmed already well established positions.

REFERENCES

Committee of Eleven, American Petroleum Institute (1925) American Petroleum Supply and Demand: A Report to the Board of Directors of the American Petroleum Institute by a Committee of Eleven Members of the Board. New York: McGraw-Hill.

ELY, N. (1938) "The conservation of oil." Harvard Law Review 51.

ENGLER, R. (1961) The Politics of Oil. New York: Macmillan.

Federal Oil Conservation Board (1976) Complete Record of Public Hearings, February 10-11, 1926. Washington, DC: Government Printing Office.

MILLIMAN, J. W. (1962) "Can people be trusted with natural resources?" Land Economics (August).

POGUE (1921) Economics of Petroleum.

Temporary National Economic Committee (1978) "Hearings on the petroleum industry, pt. 14, p. 7603," p. 171 in J. M. Blair, The Control of Oil. New York: Vintage.

WILLIAMSON, H. F., R. P. ANDREANO, A. R. DAUM, and G. C. CLOSE (1963) The American Petroleum Industry. Evanston, IL: Northwestern University Press.

4 WHEN ALL SIDES AGREE
World War I and
World War II

WHERE THERE IS A WILL to disagree, there is a way. Differences over estimates of oil and gas reserves and resources are grounded in a combination of technical and economic uncertainties; these are, after all, estimates and not measurements. There are differences, also, over policy perspectives; when their opposing world views are reinforced by appropriate figures, preservationist perspectives lead to estimates of shortage, and those of major producers to estimates of surplus. Even when overwhelming evidence proves that reserves are substantial, differing perspectives lead to different policy conclusions. While a surplus might be considered an actual surplus to some people, others—preservationists, for instance—see it as an invitation to excess which will lead inexorably to future shortages. And whereas in the 1920s a surplus did not imply the need for government regulation, surplus in the 1930s justified significant intervention to limit production and thus force up prices. Unfortunately, these are necessarily retrospective explanations based on sequences of actual events, not on other concatenations of circumstances that might have occurred but did not. Much as we might like to do so, we cannot rerun history to try out various hypotheses based on different sets of data.

SETTING THE SCENES:
PERSPECTIVES

Fortunately for us, however, events did take place which let us make retrodictive (if not predictive) tests of our hypotheses. We can answer the question of what would happen to estimates and to policies if suddenly there were agreement on perspectives under a specific set of conditions. For during both world wars, with victory as an objective, the structure of the oil industry, its prices, and political and economic practices were not to be questioned or brought to account. The preservationist position had to be modified (World War I) or abandoned (World War II). In return for permission to set prices, the oil industry accepted a large role in national energy policy. Progressive politicians could not, in good conscience, worry about competition when cooperation (even if defined as collusion) was the way to win. Since the idea was to maximize production, independents and majors forged ahead without too much sparring.

What about estimates? Data on holdings above ground were the basis for central planning. After an initial flurry of arguing about whether estimates were too small or too large, those who held various opposing positions adjusted to getting everything possible out of the ground and into refineries. Supply was enhanced by price incentives and cost-plus contracts. Demand was contracted by rationing and rising prices. Apart from some anxiety at the beginning, not much was heard about estimates by the middle of the war. Only toward the end, when postwar problems came to the fore, did estimates, pessimistic as usual, begin to matter again.

WORLD WAR II

We start with World War II because it represents a sharper break with the past. World War I is brought in for comparison, to show how different it was, except in the one, most important respect: that cooperation replaced conflict and that estimates were either agreed on or ignored. In any event, it was not estimates that produced policies but perspectives, which gave meaning to both.

Late in 1941, all factions were still engaged in ancient battles. Independents, convinced that economic recovery had been purchased at their expense, regarded the activities of government and major firms with deep suspicion. Major firms were in an uneasy alliance with the government, having traded some autonomy for price stability yet remaining on the alert for regulatory encroachment. As for the government, antitrust litigation against some of the largest firms was pending. Within a few months, the government-industry quarrels appeared to have been suspended; all participants were organizing, with conscious cooperation, to fight a new, common enemy.

Yet, the old quarrels had not magically vanished. Conflicts were to surface repeatedly during the course of the war, but each time they would be expressed in manageable terms. That is to say, old quarrels were subsumed under new perspectives. For a short while, the miasma of mistrust had dissipated.

The most important question that was settled—almost in passing and nearly without debate—was the relationship of government to industry, at a time when the universally recognized national emergency took precedence over internal conflicts. At such a time, the power of the federal government to determine policy—even if that power included controlling the structure of the oil industry—was not seriously questioned. In fact, during the course of the war the government was to set prices, control production, allocate resources, and supervise the refining, transportation, distribution, and marketing of petroleum. All of this was done with the cooperation of industry.

There was, after all, a single, overriding objective to which most other considerations were subordinated. An agreed-upon objective is not policy, but it can be the foundation upon which the agreement necessary for policy is built. The exigencies of war required a command economy; ideological and material disputes over this fundamental question were suspended for the duration. A self-evident goal, winning the war, and an acceptance of the overall structure for achieving that goal (the command economy) created the climate that made the policy formation possible. The inevitable disagreements and debates would take place in an arena where settlement, compromise, or concession were possible.

Under wartime conditions, government could make concessions to industry which would have been unacceptable in other circumstances. The Petroleum Administration for War (PAW), the central coordinating agency for petroleum matters, was staffed (in important decision-making areas) by high-level industry personnel on leave to the government for the duration. In most instances, their firms continued to pay them (often making up the difference between their original salaries and the much lower salaries). It was understood, also, that these officials would resume their industry positions after the war. The conflict of interest inherent in this situation was discussed during a series of congressional hearings, but eventually was dropped. Harold Ickes, chief of the PAW, justified this personnel policy on the grounds that the oil industry itself was the best source of knowledgeable individuals able to establish an effective agency.

Disputes over estimates did not disappear. The same question, "Is there (or will there be) a shortage?" was asked. The enormous requirements of the war effort served to refocus attention on the nature of the reserve base. Was it declining? If yes, why? Was an administered price a better means to stimulate new discovery? Estimates of reserves were looked to for answers to the first questions, and demand forecasts and production estimates for the second. The paramount difference was that this time there was a mutually acceptable answer.

THE PETROLEUM ADMINISTRATION FOR WAR:
A UNION OF GOVERNMENT AND INDUSTRY

From the outset, it was clear that pursuit of a global war would demand enormous quantities of fuel, lubricants, and other petroleum products. Besides meeting the demand of its domestic economy and war effort, the United States would also have to serve as the "arsenal of democracy" for its allies; the production and transportation required would be on a gigantic scale. Coordination of this effort could be left neither to the choice of individual oil companies nor to the government whose authority was diffused among myriad federal and state agencies.

President Roosevelt appointed Secretary of the Interior Harold Ickes Petroleum Coordinator for National Defense several months before the United States formally entered the war. Ickes was empowered to gather information, make recommendations, and coordinate policy. The agency's name was changed, at first to Petroleum Coordinator for War and, shortly after that, to the Petroleum Administration for War (PAW), under which title it functioned until the agency was disbanded in 1946. The agency began as an information-gathering and -coordinating office, set up only to make recommendations to industry and government agencies. Within a year, as the Petroleum Administration for War, it became an important wartime agency, responsible for formulating basic petroleum policy and reporting directly to the White House. PAW would have to coordinate its activities with the more than thirty governmental agencies concerned with some aspect of oil. PAW also would have to supervise and coordinate the activities of the oil industry, in the face of considerable apprehension (at least initially) that the agency was simply part of another federal effort to control the industry. The OPC, established by presidential letter rather than by executive order or statutory authorization, differed fundamentally from most other wartime agencies in that it had no compulsory power or authority. Nonetheless, as PAW it functioned effectively and, for a government agency, efficiently, even managing to self-destruct when the war ended.

The organizational structure of PAW contributed greatly to its effectiveness. The agency was organized along functional lines paralleling the principal functions of the petroleum industry and was staffed by individuals with practical industry experience. An industry committee was also created (the Petroleum Industry War Council, PIWC), with the express purpose of maximizing voluntary cooperation and minimizing permanent bureaucracy. The PIWC was at the apex of a system of subcommittees set up to correspond with the geographic districts of PAW. This was a cluster of functional committees for each district (production, supply, transportation, distributing, and marketing). The PIWC was staffed by high-level industry personnel with corporate authority to carry out governmental policy decisions. PIWC also had a Foreign Operations Committee, which advised PAW in formulating and administering foreign oil programs.

The necessity for centralized planning was recognized almost from the beginning of the war. Even industrial leaders accepted the notion that "unlimited and undirected competitive activity" could not be relied on to coordinate and produce the petroleum necessary for the war effort. According to Frey and Ide (1946: 16), in *A History of the PAW* (a government-sponsored, industry-written account),

> it was understood that in the dislocation shortages and frozen prices of the emergency situation, undirected competition would give rise to unbalanced production and flow of supplies, failing to meet war requirements, inequities between competing units, and special hardship to smaller companies.

Despite agreement on the necessity for a wartime command economy and the basis of compromise on which that agreement rested, conflicts between industry and government did surface. The most serious conflict was over a sudden dip in reserve estimates and a slackening in exploration that took everyone by surprise. Why the falling-off? How much oil did we really have? But the customary combat over these familiar questions bowed to the more insistent call to combat, the war.

HOW MISTRUST OVER ESTIMATES FADED

On the eve of war, U.S. reserves and production were considered more than adequate—many refineries were actually standing idle. On the average, refineries were still operating at only 87 percent of capacity by 1941. Before Pearl Harbor there had been no realistic forecasts of the volume of petroleum that would be needed for the war, only a general assumption that all the oil required would be obtainable merely by "turning on the valves." Although since the 1920s the industry had possessed excess capacity to produce, refine, and distribute petroleum, that assumption soon proved incorrect.

Harold Ickes's earlier warnings of impending shortages were rejected both by the oil industry, which was seeking to avoid controls, and by the Congress, which essentially viewed Ickes's warnings as a ploy to increase his agency's power. But by 1942 both the atmosphere and the actual situation had changed. The enormous military requirements were by then apparent, and the necessity for controls was well accepted. By 1942 the industry was worried about a slackening-off of drilling, declining rates of discovery, and puzzlingly rapid depletion of proved reserves. These problems were presented to the Congress in testimony before the Interstate and Foreign Commerce Subcommittee in 1943 during a series of hearings on the price of crude oil.

Robert Fell, speaking for the oil industry, attributed the decline to prices that were too low. The current crude ceilings, set in 1937, now seemed inadequate to stimulate sufficient new discoveries (Subcommittee on Interstate and Foreign Commerce, 1943: 35). Figures submitted suggested that exploratory drilling activities for the four years before 1943 had not discovered the expected quantities of new oil. In fact, Fell contended, new oil was becoming more difficult and expensive to find. Therefore, given the emergency situation, it was imperative that the industry greatly increase its exploratory effort. To encourage this, the industry would need higher prices. Furthermore, if the industry did not "obtain for the oil now sold an amount sufficient to replace in quantity the oil produced and sold, the industry [would] impair its capacity to meet further requirements" (Subcommittee on Interstate and Foreign Commerce, 1943: 36). In order to do so, the industry recommended an increase of $.25 a barrel.

What was unusual in these recommendations was not so much that the industry looked to higher prices to stimulate discovery and drilling, but that the industry did not call for a return to market forces to correct the pricing defect.

Requests for price increases had to go through a separate agency, the Office of Price Administration (OPA). The OPA was responsible for general pricing controls during the war. Industry requests for price increases supported by the PAW initially were denied by the OPA: Such increases were both unnecessary and inflationary, said the OPA. Significantly, conflict between the OPA and the PAW took the form of quarrels over who had jurisdiction over oil price increases, over how best to stimulate oil production. These were fairly tame sorts of quarrels. Eventually compromise was achieved.

Harold Ickes, in an action out of character with his antibusiness past, supported the industry claim for higher prices. The OPA, however, wanted to substitute an intricate program of subsidies to stimulate discovery and production. The OPA saw price increases as unnecessary; moreover, they would fuel inflation and destabilize national pricing policy in general.

As to the causes of the low rate of discovery, Prentiss Brown (n.d.) quoted E. E. DeGolyer: "Thus our low rate of discovery seems not to be a result of slackening of effort so much as due to the low quality of prospects, which indicates an exhaustion of prospects discoverable by the present methods of utilizing known techniques." As with every other such prophecy since the turn of the century, events would eventually out-distance and discredit it, but belief in it led to developments that remain with us today.

The problem, then, was believed to lie in the nature of the resource itself—the absolute quantity of petroleum available. Petroleum was said to be nearing the point of exhaustion (shades of past debates). Administrative action, not pricing policy, was the way to go, since higher prices had not increased the number of wildcat wells drilled in California. OPA certainly was unconvinced that the oil companies needed higher prices; oil profits already appeared more than adequate. The effect of a price increase on already nearly exhausted resources was debatable. The real answer lay in the development and increased use of foreign resources, as Prentiss Brown (n.d.) wrote to Harold Ickes:

> In your two letters you have dwelt at length on the necessity for increased domestic crude production, yet I believe your most recent approach to the supply problem, namely, through increased use of foreign crudes, constitutes the real answer. Since it is true that the reserves of this country, both known and undiscovered, are not inexhaustible, it seems only logical that our military and civilian requirements should be satisfied to the greatest extent possible through supplies available in other countries. If "oil is ammunition," according to the popular slogan of the oil industry, let's conserve our ammunition to the greatest possible degree.
>
> My position on the entire matter can be summarized in a very few words. The present price of oil is a fair price, and producers as a whole are showing profitable operations. Exploratory drilling has always depended largely upon financial aid given by large integrated companies, and they are in as good a position today to extend such aid as they have ever been. Shortages of manpower, materials, and transportation are holding up the full utilization of proven areas from a development standpoint, increased drilling from an explora-tory standpoint, and maximum efficient production from present producing wells. Foreign crude and residual oils are available and should be used to the maximum extent of their availability during the war emergency in order to conserve our domestic resources for future years.

All the old debates are encapsulated in Brown's statement: How much oil does this country have? Is there really a shortage? What is the nature of the shortage? Is the reserve base in danger of exhaustion? Is price the controlling factor? Would higher prices lead to discovery and recovery of more oil? Ickes answered by debating the credibility of Brown's data, by reiterating the relationship between price and discovery, and by insisting that a higher price be granted.

It is true that an old issue resurfaced in a new context, but the difference between the peacetime and wartime contexts was significant. Under the unifying force of World War II, the issues were resolved, at least temporarily. Soon after these hearings were held, a compromise between PAW and OPA was reached. Some price increases were allowed, and certain OPA programs were enacted. The compromises, however, remained on a gentlemanly administrative level. Industry had made its requests and had supplied supportive data. At no time did the oil industry threaten to withdraw support from the war effort or refuse to abide by administrative decisions.

BUT MISTRUST DID NOT DIE

When hints of peace began to appear on the horizon, the faint stirrings of the old combatants over estimates could again be heard. The specific impetus to conflict over estimates at the close of the war was the realization that the United States for the first time would be a net importer of oil.

During the war it had been necessary to increase the production of foreign crude oil, mainly from Venezuelan, Colombian, and Middle Eastern sources, and also to protect access to these sources. At the same time, it became evident that petroleum would be even more important after World War II than after World War I, for both civilian and military purposes. Declines in domestic drilling and new discoveries, combined with anticipated future demand, suggested considerable future dependence on foreign oil sources. The United States would become an oil-importing nation. In this scenario, major firms would need government support and protection in the exploitation of foreign concessions. Members of the oil community, however, feared that the wartime experience of government control, combined with the recognition of future dependency, might lead to an indefinite extension of unwanted government involvement in the oil business.

In 1943, spokespersons for American oil interests in the Middle East expressed concern to Ickes about the security of oil concessions in that area. A round of discussions among representatives of the Departments of State, War, Navy, and the Interior followed. What resulted was an instruction from the President to form a Petroleum Reserves Corporation (PRC), empowered to act in many oil situations. The PIWC (and the industry) interpreted this corporation to be a government body with a bald mandate to intervene in the oil business. The PIWC rushed in with a study, "A National Oil Policy for the United States," stressing the importance of private development of oil. The Independent Petroleum Association of America took a similar stand in a resolution that petitioned the government to establish a "consistent" oil policy that would

(1) give support to nationals engaged in foreign oil business;
(2) foster private enterprise for nations; and
(3) establish as a "cardinal principle" that the government of the U.S. will not engage itself directly in the petroleum business (PIWC, 1946: 399).

In February 1944 the PRC announced that it had agreed "in principle" to build and operate a government-owned pipeline from Saudi Arabia to the Mediterranean. The line was to be built in conjunction with two major oil companies, but the U.S. government was to retain ownership and to set aside for its own use a billion barrels of oil reserves in Saudi Arabia. Ickes insisted that this pipeline project would not constitute government entry into the oil business. The government would not compete with private industry. There was no reason to fear future importation of foreign oil; the pipeline's only purpose was to ensure future military petroleum needs. Needless to say, the oil industry did not believe Ickes. They declared the pipeline project to be a "unilateral foreign commitment in a British sphere of influence" (PIWC, 1946: 278) likely to involve the United States in rivalry with Britain. The proposed pipeline was "the beginning of a fatally mistaken policy as grave as the fatally mistaken policy of scrapping much of our fleet at the end of the war ... because it is the scrapping of the internal strength of America itself" (PIWC, 1946: 279). The government was "venturing forth into the post-war world with an imperialistic program in derogation of our Good Neighbor Policy" (PIWC, 1946: 279). The pipeline proposal was set aside and eventually abandoned, but the controversy surrounding it shows that the mistrust temporarily suspended during the war was alive and ready to kick.

SETTLEMENT IN THE TWO WARS DIFFERED IN NATURE

Despite the jostling for future positions on the question of foreign oil policy, a real (if temporary) political settlement did exist during World War II, as it did in the first world war. The nature of those agreements was quite different. Let us compare some of the salient issues in both world wars.

Until 1917 the European war was not regarded as a serious threat to the United States. The importance of petroleum as a fuel was not as clear at the outset of that war as it would become later on. The agreement in World War I essentially was that the oil industry would continue to govern itself. (One might say that the government accepted industry terms in exchange for voluntary cooperation.) Within these limits, industry was prepared (albeit sometimes under threat) to make necessary concessions with a reasonable dash of public spiritedness and patriotism thrown in as well. The terms of agreement were less clear than they would be in World War II, when national danger was evident earlier, the magnitude of the problems involved was greater, and U.S. participation as a belligerent lasted longer. In World War I it was possible for the oil industry to regulate itself and, to a larger extent, continue with business as usual (except for cessation of business with the Central Powers). From 1941 to 1945 this was not possible.

During World War I cooperation between industry and government existed, but a command economy did not. The necessity for a command economy was not clear, and to establish one would have been in violation of an understood social contract. Voluntary cooperation was sufficient, with an implied threat of active governmental regulation, should voluntary controls break down or be insufficient to prosecute the war. By contrast, conditions during World War II were such that the necessity of centrally administered policy was unarguable.

Similar approaches to formal organization of the petroleum industry existed in both wartime periods—a governmental coordinating agency with a parallel industry structure. In both periods the parallel industry structure carried considerable responsibility. In 1917-1918, the government worked through the Petroleum Committee, which conducted petroleum affairs with considerable autonomy. But there was a distinct difference in 1944-1945; although the PIWC performed many functions, there was never any doubt about its relationship with either the PAW or the government as a whole. The PIWC did not set quotas, control prices, or allocate resources; nor did it deal independently with foreign allies. The PAW controlled production, transportation, distribution, and marketing of oil. It instituted rationing and production quotas, and administered prices.

No such official controls on consumer consumption were enacted during World War I. There was no rationing, and distribution of petroleum products and marketing was left entirely to the industry.

The year 1942, like 1917, was a year of fuel-oil shortage. However, in 1942 the government did not allow the free play of the market to correct this, acting instead to alleviate shortages by building pipelines to relieve distributional pressures, by offering subsidies to encourage exploration and drilling and, on two occasions, by allowing price increases. The oil industry was not allowed to govern itself, and acceded, for the duration, to central-government direction.

During the period of the first world war, the United States was a net exporter of oil. Despite the gloomy USGS estimates, the 1920s and 1930s seemed to be swimming in oil. The experience of World War I led to the expectation that greater foreign demand would accompany the second world war and that European oil in storage would soon need supplements from American sources. Moreover, there was a general perception of oversupply in the United States, so that eventual drains on U.S. reserves and stocks were discounted. The expectations of the industry were not fulfilled. European belligerents were trying to meet military requirements by curtailing civilian consumption. By 1942 shortages and problems in transportation and refining capacity were evident, along with a decline in discovery.

This unexpected falling-off of discoveries and reserves during the second world war pointed to America's eventual dependence on foreign petroleum resources. Industry came out of World War II with two new concerns: extreme competition for foreign sources of oil, and direct government intervention in the oil business during peacetime.

CONCLUSION

Despite their differences, what do the war periods tell us about the nature of the political settlements reached? To some extent, what we already know: Political settlements are based on accommodation to a shared perspective or objective. Political settlements, nevertheless, must be grounded in economic and political realities; participants in a settlement must have at least some of their interests satisfied, and the general outlines of the settlement must be consistent with what is publicly acceptable.

It must be noted that these settlements were temporary and that not all areas of conflict were resolved. The question of perspective, however, was. In both wars, the intention of participants—to win—was not seriously questioned. Given that suspension of mistrust, it was possible to address specific differences. Either participants could be reasonably satisfied by compromise, or a losing participant might accept an unfavorable decision. Once the perspective of a command economy was established, for example, the quarrel between the PAW and the OPA over increases in petroleum prices was settled, although the underlying question remained unresolved and proponents of each view remained unconvinced of the opponents' correctness. Temporarily, at least, it was decided that overall inflationary considerations outweighed the question of whether price was a proper stimulus to new discovery.

Such agreement on perspective made it possible also for estimation data to be used, though there was not absolute agreement on numbers. The important question, "What do we want this information to do?" was answerable. That is, specific data needs became clearer, and the reconciliation of differences became possible.

The final lesson to be learned from this comparison is that agreement need not be permanent or all-inclusive. Within the bounds of an agreed-upon perspective or an overwhelmingly important objective, partial and temporary agreements on policy may suffice. In fact, as long as participants can suspend total mistrust, temporary or partial solutions may be preferable, allowing flexibility for unanticipated future developments.

REFERENCES

BROWN, P. (n.d.) Personal communication to the Office of Price Administration.
——— (n.d.) Personal communication to Harold Ickes, Petroleum Administration for War.
FREY, J. W. and H. C. IDE (1946) A History of the Petroleum Administration for War, 1941-1945. Washington, DC: Government Printing Office.
Petroleum Industry War Council [PIWC] (1946) "A National Oil Policy for the United States," in J. W. Frey and H. C. Ide, History of the Petroleum Administration for War, 1941-1945. Washington, DC: Government Printing Office.
Subcommittee on Interstate and Foreign Commerce (1943) Crude Oil Prices and Extension of Cole Pipeline Act. Washington, DC: Government Printing Office.

PART **II** AN ERA OF SHORTAGE

LOOKING OVER THE HISTORY of reserve estimation from 1908 to 1945, the reader may recognize repeated patterns—an endless cycle of accusation and counter-accusation about apparently identical issues. Statements made about estimates in 1908, 1921, 1932 and 1943 are almost interchangeable. Even more remarkably, statements made by participants today could easily be interjected in any past document and appear entirely consistent. In short, the perspectives of participants have endured over time, even if the specific issues under debate have changed occasionally. People holding similar perspectives say the same thing.

We have reviewed public debates surrounding the estimation of oil reserves since 1908 and have found persistent perspectives and unresolved policies, polarization and conflict. From the beginning, as these debates testify, the field has been mined with mistrust.

The seeds for this mistrust were sown with the beginnings of the industry and were brought to flower in the events surrounding the dissolution of the Standard Oil Trust. While public passions flared, all major participants came away dissatisfied, and the fundamental issues remained unresolved. The structure that emerged was neither fish nor fowl: an industry neither permitted to operate on a market basis nor completely integrated into a planned economy. The basis for partial and often-contradictory arrangements between industry and government was formed, but without the overriding perspective of either quantity or price as a determinant mechanism. In such a framework, fundamental philosophical and policy agreement was impossible. The path was marked for unceasing conflict.

Prorationing was one of the most notorious developments to mark this path of conflict. A cumbersome and equivocal arrangement of production quotas through which participants either accommodated each other or quarreled, prorationing denied the logic of either a free or a planned economy. It papered over real differences and fed already established conflicts.

Estimates of resources and reserves began to figure through these early years as counters between spokespersons for antithetical perspectives. The differences over estimates faded, however, under the force of external events during wartime.

What participants deemed to be major issues in the early history of oil policy are still debated today:

(1) What is the extent of the oil and natural gas resource base? How much do we have left? Is it adequate? Is there a shortage?

(2) What does conservation mean, and in whose view?
(3) What is the proper role of the federal government in oil and natural gas policy? Has the industry's own conduct been contaminated by collusion?

Positions on these issues have been determined significantly by the quantity-theory or price-theory perspectives held by participants. Estimates have been plucked up for use in policy debates surrounding these issues. The estimates chosen and how they were used were predictable, once one knew the perspectives of their users, whether supplies were plentiful or short and whether it was wartime or peacetime.

The next section opens with some of the developments of the 1950s and 1960s that led to the unprecedented shortages of 1973-1977. We then examine selected episodes of those years, episodes in which reserve and resource data were at the center of controversy. This examination begins with the "energy crisis" that appeared in the wake of the Arab oil embargo. Suddenly, in 1973, detailed data on oil and gas reserves and resources were demanded from a federal government that had not previously seen any reason to collect such data. Why were data on reserves and resources now so desperately wanted? Who wanted them, and for what purposes? What would a given number tell participants, and what policies would it influence? By 1977, more was indeed understood about oil and gas reserves and resources than ever before. Yet mistrust still overwhelmed knowledge. People knew more but believed less.

 GAPS AND SHORTFALLS

SINCE THE EARLY 1970s the idea of a "shortage" of energy as the central problem has dominated policy and thinking. In addition to hearing after hearing in Congress, numerous studies have repeated the refrain of shortage or gap.[1] Some day, the studies have predicted, growing demand will overtake limited supply. On that day, there will develop a gap between needs and oil production, and consumers will be drawn into a scramble for inadequate supplies. Most studies between the early and mid-1970s assumed an unchanging price for oil and then predicted future demand. Corresponding estimates were made of the likely supply of oil, based on estimates of reserves and resources. Predicted supplies were subtracted from predicted demand to yield a net demand, which then was compared with estimates of available productive capacity. There may be assumed, for example, considerable excess capacity in OPEC, but given the growth in demand and unchanging prices, excesses will dry up and one day a gap will appear.

Even if one adds the assumption of inevitable price rises, the notion of shortage extends beyond perceptions of the market clearing. Constant warnings of catastrophe and massive energy crises bespeak something more than simply a prospect of higher prices for energy: Such predictions envision an actual physical exhaustion under which no energy can be had at any price. Were this quantity theory correct, preserving the precious fluids would be the nation's foremost priority lest life in this industrial society grind to a halt.

Many such gloomy predictions, a price theorist would say, have been made because of confusion among the concepts of physical scarcity, economic scarcity, and shortage. Physical scarcity means that at a given point in time there is not as much of something as we would want at any price. Some goods that are physically scarce can be made available at very high prices; economic scarcity refers to such a situation. Shortage means that, at prevailing prices, the amount people want is greater than the amount available; consumers want more than producers are willing to sell at that low price. In a market economy such a thing as a gap or shortage cannot exist; price itself eventually brings supply and demand into equilibrium. A shortage can occur temporarily due to lag time. But more significant for policy, shortages occur when prices are held below the market-clearing level by government control.

The "energy crisis" was touched off by the Arab oil embargo. But it was a history of price controls that caused continuing energy shortages. Long lines at gas stations and fuel shortages in buildings were the result of a crazy-quilt history of regulation and the incentives and disincentives it generated among suppliers and consumers. The shortages were not caused by OPEC price increases. In fact, in the absence of price controls the embargo and subsequent increases in prices of crude oil would most likely have restricted the amount demanded and rationed the available supply to those who valued it the highest and, it must be added, could pay for it.

In a fully functioning market, there is no such thing as a gap. But under that system of partial and conflicting controls which has characterized the U.S. energy market since the early 1900s, gaps have been possible and indeed actual. Because prices were believed to be more just under even a partially administered system than under a competitive market system, congressional concern naturally focused on the shortage. How large was the gap? To answer this required enormous amounts of data on supply and demand, prices and costs. If legislators could obtain all the data, it would seem possible to move supply and demand into equilibrium through planning—through nothing less than a comprehensive national energy plan.

This chapter looks at oil policies of the mid-1970s to illustrate what happens when officials talk in terms of gaps and the desire to close them, yet are not prepared to act as this reasoning would imply: to take over the energy industry.

THE EMBARGO PROVOKED THE
URGENCY FOR DATA

Before the late 1940s, the United States was self-sufficient in crude oil—not only self-sufficient, but enjoying crude oil inexpensively and in abundance. Actually, this state of affairs resulted in part from certain federal and state policies of the 1920s, which encouraged more supplies at lower prices than would have been the case under a market system.

Over sixty years ago Congress introduced percentage-depletion-allowance[2] tax treatment for oil and gas production, and on its heels allowed intangible drilling-and-development-expense writeoffs (see Mead, 1979: 352). The initial effect of these two federal policies was to increase the after-tax rate of return on investments in oil and gas exploration and production. More capital flowed into exploration, new reserves were found, and production was stimulated (see Table 5.1). Thus, more gas and oil were produced than the economy otherwise would have elicited.

At the state level, production of oil and gas was centered in Texas, Oklahoma, and Louisiana. Under the Rule of Capture, the one company among many in a field that brought the product to the surface seized ownership rights to the field.[3] In M. A. Adelman's (1964: 101) words, "a well on one property would drain every adjoining lot; hence, you must drain your neighbor before he drains you." This way of establishing property rights made for overdrilling, which led to a further physical waste of petroleum, through its inefficient dissipation of the pressure needed to drive oil from its natural reservoirs (Mancke, 1974: 73). Thus, the days of cheap and abundant oil and gas came in part out of federal tax interventions and state conceptions of property rights.

State conservation commissions, trying to counteract the overdrilling and overproduction wrought by these policies, reacted with a new policy: restrict outputs. Under the rubric of conservation, they adopted a policy known as market-demand prorationing (Mancke, 1974: 74-76),[4] which was designed to give each state control over its internal oil supply: Prorationing was a method of dividing among the states the total national output desired during a given period. Each state, then, divided its share of the total output among the fields in the state. In so doing, a state would divide (or "prorate") a field's allowable output into "allowables" for each well according to the the well's "potential" or according to the surface area covered. The intent of prorationing was to keep prices up at a given level; but it had the effect of promoting conservation, too, by reducing output.

While overproduction was in fact alleviated, the cure evidently turned out worse than the illness, as we suggested in Chapter 3. And according to Richard Mancke,

> first, prorationing did not eliminate the costly incentives for over-drilling. In fact, since oil fields with deeper and more closely spaced wells were rewarded with higher basic allowables and since inefficient stripper wells (i.e., wells producing less than 10 barrels per day) were exempted from all prorationing regulations, the incentives for overdrilling may actually have been strengthened. Secondly, by using

prorationing, the large oil-producing states were able to restrict severely their total output, and thereby succeeded in keeping prices for U.S. crude oil far above its competitive level throughout the late 1940s and early 1950s [Mancke, 1974: 75].

We can see that federal and state policies were in conflict. State regulatory policies limited domestic production capacity, while federal tax policy encouraged exploration and production, putting downward pressure on prices and increasing demand. The eventual effect was to put the country in the position of excessively expanding its imports. As we shall see, the end result was an inability to respond flexibly to the 1973 embargo.

Rapidly expanding exports from lower-cost Persian Gulf sources were beginning to be sold in the United States by 1950. Under prorationing, U.S. price and supply stability had prevailed even in the face of rapidly growing demand. Imports from the Middle East thus could penetrate U.S. markets without creating more than a ripple in the domestic price (McAvoy, 1974: 4, n.). Table 5.1 shows how dramatically the United States came to depend on imports.

Eventually, this influx of cheap imported oil undermined oil states' efforts to maintain their own high prices. Under the rubric of national security, therefore, owners and producers of oil and legislators in the oil states tried to persuade the federal government to restrict imports. After several years of study and debate, President Eisenhower established a voluntary import-control program in 1957.[5] But with imported oil so much cheaper than domestic, the voluntary quotas naturally were violated. In 1959 Eisenhower came to the rescue at last to protect domestic markets by imposing mandatory oil import quotas.[6] The official rationale, however, was national security. Thus, proponents of security of supply and proponents of higher prices found themselves allied in the desire to control oil imports.

The effects of import quotas were to restrict the supply of cheaper imported oil, to increase demand for the more expensive domestic oil, to increase domestic prices further relative to world market prices, and artificially to stimulate additional domestic production. (Figure 5.1 shows the growth in domestic demand and in domestic production.) Under the import-quota program, the higher demand for domestic crude oil could be satisfied only by increasing domestic output. But to sustain increased output over a long term would have required yet higher prices to keep up exploration activity and bring on more proved reserves. By 1969 the domestic wellhead price was over $3.00 per barrel, as opposed to about $1.20 for Persian Gulf oil. Still it was not enough to increase exploration

TABLE 5.1   Petroleum[a], 1920-1975; U.S. Reserves,
Production, Net Imports, and Demand

Year	Proved Reserves (billions of barrels)	Domestic Production (millions of barrels)	Net Imports[b] (millions of barrels)	Domestic Demand[c] (millions of barrels)
1920	–	453.9	29.2	483.1
1921	–	484.2	57.0	541.2
1922	–	571.3	61.4	632.7
1923	–	754.2	-2.6	751.6
1924	–	738.4	-22.9	715.5
1925	–	792.4	-36.0	756.4
1926	–	805.4	-51.0	754.4
1927	–	942.8	-70.3	872.5
1928	–	947.5	-63.7	883.8
1929	–	1063.6	-54.8	1008.8
1930	–	953.3	-51.3	902.0
1931	–	896.5	-38.6	857.9
1932	–	822.5	-29.0	793.5
1933	–	940.8	-61.6	879.2
1934	–	946.3	-64.3	882.0
1935	–	1037.8	-76.8	961.0
1936	–	1145.0	-75.3	1069.7
1937	–	1331.1	-116.1	1215.0
1938	–	1267.5	-139.8	1127.7
1939	–	1319.1	-130.4	1188.7
1940	–	1412.1	-46.7	1365.4
1941	–	1486.5	-11.7	1474.8
1942	–	1472.4	-80.9	1391.5
1943	–	1595.7	-86.6	1509.1
1944	–	1780.4	-115.3	1665.1
1945	–	1828.5	-69.4	1759.1
1946	20.9	1851.7	-15.4	1836.3
1947	21.5	1989.8	-5.1	1984.7
1948	23.2	2167.3	53.4	2220.7
1949	24.6	1999.2	116.2	2115.4
1950	25.3	2155.7	199.0	2354.7
1951	27.5	2452.7	154.2	2606.9
1952	28.0	2513.7	190.3	2704.0
1953	28.9	2596.2	230.9	2827.1
1954	29.6	2567.6	254.3	2821.9
1955	30.0	2766.3	321.4	2087.7
1956	30.4	2910.5	368.2	3278.7
1957	30.3	2912.1	367.4	3279.5
1958	30.5	2744.2	520.0	3264.2
1959	31.7	2895.7	572.5	3468.2
1960	31.6	2915.4	590.2	3505.6
1961	31.7	2983.6	636.1	3619.7
1962	31.4	3049.0	698.4	3747.4
1963	31.0	3153.7	698.8	3852.5
1964	31.0	3209.3	752.8	3962.1
1965	31.4	3290.1	832.5	4122.6
1966	31.5	3496.4	866.8	4363.2
1967	31.4	3730.3	813.9	4544.2
1968	30.7	3868.6	954.9	4823.5
1969	29.6	3953.0	1070.7	5023.7

(Table 5.1 continued on next page)

TABLE 5.1   (continued)

Year	Proved Reserves (billions of barrels)	Domestic Production (millions of barrels)	Net Imports[b] (millions of barrels)	Domestic Demand[c] (millions of barrels)
1970	39.0	4123.4	1153.6	5277.0
1971	38.1	4071.7	1351.2	5422.9
1972	36.3	4082.5	1653.8	5736.3
1973	35.3	3995.3	2199.1	6194.4
1974	34.2	3818.6	2150.4	5969.0
1975	32.7	3652.6	2133.9	5786.5
1976	30.9	3563.0		
1977	29.5	3599.0		

SOURCES: For proved reserves: American Petroleum Institute, Reserves of Crude oil, Natural Gas Liquids, and Natural Gas in the United States and Canada, 1978 edition. Also in American Petroleum Institute, *Petroleum Facts and Figures,* 1971 edition, p. 116. For remainder: 1920-1967: American Petroleum Institute, *Petroleum Facts and Figures,* 1971 ed., pp. 283-288. 1968-1975: American Petroleum Institute, *Basic Petroleum Data Book,* Section VII, Table 3; Section IX, Table 2; Section X, Table 1. For domestic production after 1975: Energy information Administration, *Annual report to Congress,* 1978, Vol. 2, p. 5.

at home sufficiently to keep up with production and demand. Figure 5.1 shows how exploratory drilling fell off after 1957.

The import quota, combined with prorationing, created an incentive to invest heavily in low-risk, low-production fields instead of high-risk, potentially high-yield prospects. According to Bohi and Russell (1978: 292),

> producers were more encouraged to develop known reserves intensively rather than to find new reserves. Consequently, known reserves depleted faster, and replacement reserves were coming onstream more slowly than they would have had the price been the same but without market demand prorationing. Given the long lead time in bringing new reserves to production, the responsiveness of domestic output to a change in price was reduced.

What did the oil import-quota program cost U.S. consumers? Bohi and Russell (1978: 285) calculated the cost to consumers as composed of two factors: (1) the additional payment for actual consumption above the world market price; (2) an estimate of how much more oil would have been purchased if the only price had been the lower world price. Both Bohi and Russell, and President Nixon's Oil Import Task Force (see U.S. Cabinet, 1970: 259-263) estimate that this departure from economic market efficiency cost the nation $5-$7 billion a year (in reference to 1968-1970).

Among the political consequences—especially in the populous nonproducing regions of the country—was the emergence of a strong coalition of

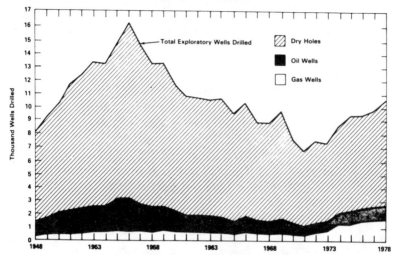

SOURCE: Energy Information Administration, *Annual Report to Congress*, 1978, Vol. 2, p. 26.

Figure 5.1: **Exploratory Wells Drilled for Oil and Gas**

congressmen from New England. They led attacks against oil import quotas and against oil producers and oil-producing states for taking advantage of the situation. Continuous pressure by these congressmen resulted in the controls becoming more relaxed; eventually domestic prices slid downward.

Hence, the quotas did not protect domestic producers' prices. Neither was the other rationale for quotas satisfied, as McAvoy (1974: 11) points out:

> The way in which the program was operated did not provide incentives for holding inventories against embargoes (quotas were extended to companies on the basis of historical production capacity, not on the basis of inventories or of security of the source of supply). . . . The quota controls placed on imports throughout the 1960s had none of the results justifying their existence for either group of supporters.

The apparently abundant capacity was an illusion. And what looked like enhanced national security—increased domestic oil production—was only the initial effect of quotas on top of prorationing; these higher levels of output from already existing, low-risk sources could not be sustained. Despite import controls, moreover, the continuing presence and pressure of cheaper Persian Gulf oil could not be ignored. Under these conditions, domestic producers were not eager to go look for new domestic oil. Furthermore, in 1954 consumerist desires to keep prices low led to price ceilings on field sales of natural gas going into the interstate pipelines. Oil and natural gas are often found together. Thus, the price freeze on natural gas contributed to a winding down of both gas and oil exploration, resulting in substantial reductions in new reserves over the last half of the 1960s. (See Figure 7.1 for natural gas trends.) Whether the physical amounts of U.S. oil and gas actually were on the decline, sellers were concerned about foreign competition, or price controls dampened incentives to bring on new reserves, drilling rates and recovery rates did fall off. By the beginning of the 1970s, U.S. production and reserves seemed to be on a precipitous decline. Then, to further exacerbate the energy supply situation, the administration in August 1971 instituted price controls on oil.

Meanwhile, domestic demand and consumption had been increasing steadily since the later years of the Great Depression. By 1970, with demand up and reserves down, the full comparative advantage of Middle Eastern oil hit home. The United States was drawn into a vulnerable situation, vulnerable not to excessive imports per se, but to embargo, especially since import controls led to far greater use of American oil than market considerations would have justified.

Consumption went on, unabated, with the public still under the impression that energy would long continue to be cheap and plentiful. Yet, because of the circumstances recounted above, domestic refinery capacity was lagging. Quotas might have protected domestic oil production, but they did not help domestic refinery capacity. On the contrary, as Mancke (1974: 160) tells it, "because of the government's oil import controls, refiners were uncertain about where they would be able to secure additional crude oil supplies. As a result of this uncertainty, prudence dictated that they delay making commitments to build new refinery capacity."

Consumption expanded until the effort to refine enough oil to meet the demand for home heating oil in the winter of 1971-1972 led to a gasoline shortage during the summer of 1972, with long lines and gas station closings. There followed another winter shortage of home heating oil. Under these pressures, import quotas were relaxed and finally abolished by a presidential executive order on April 18, 1973.

Before that decision, no major refinery expansions had been undertaken in the United States for several years. Within six months after oil quotas were abolished, plans for more than twenty large refinery expansions were announced (Mancke, 1974: 160). But given lead times of several years, this late start could not alleviate the refined-oil product shortages of 1973.

In October 1973 the Arab-Israeli war erupted. The fighting was accompanied by an embargo of Arab oil sales aimed at achieving pro-Arab changes in the foreign policies of the major oil-consuming nations. To the United States that embargo raised a specter of crisis far worse than the shortages in gasoline and home heating oil.

The 1950s and 1960s had furnished the United States with a set of markets unable to respond flexibly to abrupt changes in foreign supply conditions in 1973 and 1974. Foreign supply had become the market-clearing source. By 1970-1971 significant shortages had developed as production reached technical limits from reduced reserves, and as demand still increased. The effects of prorationing, federal price controls, and import quotas were responsible for shortages; shortages, in turn, increased pressures to import. The web of conflicting federal and state policies made reaction to the embargo virtually impossible.

The embargo took the U.S. energy economy completely by surprise. If one had looked into the past, one would have seen that the U.S. supply situation in 1973 had grown out of the many years of conflicting regulations and in reaction to the consequences of previous regulation. Ignorant of this and alarmed by the sudden appearance of shortages, people cried out, "What is causing the shortage?" As the next section will show, public mistrust quickly transformed that question into "Who is to blame for the shortage?"

WE NEED BETTER DATA, BUT FOR WHAT PURPOSE?

With the 1973-1974 winter approaching and heating oil supplies short once again, the Arab embargo riveted public attention on the oil supply situation. As it became clear that the United States faced an unprecedented crisis, pressure mounted on President Nixon and Congress to do something. But the congressional investigations into what was causing the oil and gasoline shortages turned up precious little useful information.

Senator Henry Jackson (D-Wash.), Chairman of the Senate Committee on Interior and Insular Affairs, in the spring of 1973 had requested the General Accounting Office (GAO) to do a study of "the feasibility of establishing . . . a data bank [for information], independently developed or verified, on the energy supply and demand picture.' It seemed to Jackson (1973) that "the Federal government is making energy decisions on the basis of information which is less than adequate." In partial response, the GAO produced a report, "Actions Needed to Improve Federal Efforts in Collecting, Analyzing, & Reporting Energy Data." The report stated that as of 1973, bits and pieces of energy data had been collected by many government agencies. Philip Hughes, Assistant Comptroller General, told Jackson's committee:

> We have identified 45 bureaus, offices, divisions or administrations of 17 different agencies which are significant collectors or users of energy data. The principal collection agencies are the Bureau of Mines and the Geological Survey in the Department of the Interior, the Federal Power Commission, the Atomic Energy Commission, and the Department of Commerce. The Office of Oil and Gas of the Department of the Interior, the Bureau of Labor Statistics, the Cost of Living Council, and the Interstate Commerce Commission also collect energy-related data.
>
> To further indicate the magnitude and scope of energy data collection, as of March 1973, 15 major Federal agencies were circulating 145 energy-related questionnaires to the State and private sectors, requiring 11 million responses and an annual response effort of about 3.6 million man hours.
>
> Thus, a large volume of data is being collected by a wide range of agencies. Until recently, however, the data [were] collected to meet needs of specific, long established programs or agencies rather than as part of a systematic assembling of energy data [Senate Committee on Interior and Insular Affairs, 1974: 2-3].

Just having data lying around like laundry lists does not necessarily help anyone. As always, the prior question is, "For what purpose was the data collected?" Much of the energy data collected by government agencies was used for specific regulatory purposes. In the Bureau of Mines—the largest energy-data collection agency as of 1973—there was a "broad and long-standing legislative mandate to encourage the development of the mining industry. It therefore collects data relative to some 90 different minerals among which happen to be fossil fuels" (General Accounting Office, 1974: 7). The (former) Federal Power Commission (FPC) had a number of reporting systems to monitor specific regulations. Its annual Form 15, for example, was initiated in 1963 to enable the FPC to keep surveillance over each interstate pipeline's natural gas supply. The Nuclear Regulatory Commission (NRC) was collecting data to judge the reliability, safety, and environmental effects of nuclear-energy production plants.

However useful these arrays of data might be for particular purposes, it was hard to see how they might serve broader policy purposes. Let us specify three types of uses that would convert data, considered as any bit, into information, data arrayed so they make a difference in what is concluded or decided: (1) Data may serve to direct attention to a difficulty by presenting an anomalous or unusual or arresting set of numbers

(Millions of children are malnourished; there are diminishing returns to drilling for oil or gas in the United States.) (2) Data may purport to measure the size of an alleged difficulty. (There are so many million children from x region and y groups going hungry.) (3) Data may tell us how we are doing. (This year is 50 percent better than last year.) But unless they are relevant to policy thinking, data are not information. By "relevant", we mean that the data are tied to a potential policy embodying a theory relating instruments of policy to consequences. When different dispositions of data do matter in determining what a decision maker does, the data are policy-relevant. If size or severity of hunger or type of children involved sets off a sequence of actions or decisions—from food stamps to medical care, for instance—those data have been converted into information. Or, if a medical test suggests stopping or starting a certain treatment, those data then are information.

Whether energy data will become information thus depends on proposed policies. It is not merely those blobs of data, but rather the purpose (the policy-relevance) they are to serve that is crucial. Then we must ask, "For what policy purposes were energy data wanted: Were data sought for insight into particular policy alternatives? Or were data wanted only because they would be nice to have around, maybe handy on some rainy day?" As a historian of the energy issue might suspect, however, policy-relevance was ignored; instead, personal credibility became the criterion of judgment.

The GAO report suggested that the many specifically oriented, scattered data systems were inadequate because of their lack of uniformity, comprehensiveness, and centralized standards of quality; also that "much of the data being collected is reported voluntarily by industry with little verification by Federal agencies. The data collected on individual companies [are] considered proprietary and held confidential by collecting agencies and, with limited exceptions, only aggregate data [are] reported. In addition, there are substantial time lags in the reporting of data and there is a lack of uniformity in reporting" (General Accounting Office, 1974).

Worse, the data were not taken as credible. Again, according to GAO (1974: 14; emphasis added),

> as long as much of the reporting of data by industry is voluntary and unverified, questions will be raised as to the credibility of the data, even though the data may be entirely valid.
>
> Generally, the feeling among Federal officials that we talked to was that they had no reason to doubt the validity of data supplied. However, *much of the public believes the present energy shortages*

have been contrived by industry for the purpose of raising prices and increasing profits. The Federal Government has been unable to demonstrate convincingly the nature and extent of the energy shortage, in large measure, because of the lack of independently developed or independently verified data.

The credibility problem was seen widely, especially among consumer-oriented liberals. Senator Muskie (D-Maine) blamed the entire energy industry for failing to respond to demands for energy which it has encouraged. "The energy companies have failed to plan and provide for the energy needs of this country, to develop alternatives that would make us secure, and to invest their profit in means to satisfy a growing demand" (Senate Committee on Public Works, 1976: Vol. II, 2463-2464). Martin Lobel, a consultant, blamed the majors:

> But why doesn't the Government have accurate oil information? Oil is vital to our national security, to our own economy and, indeed, to the entire world's. Yet the only accurate data base is closely held in the hands of a few international, integrated oil companies—the so-called major oil companies—not by the Government. Why?

> The answer goes a long way toward explaining how these major oil companies are able to manipulate Government policy for their own benefit, to the detriment of the Nation as a whole and, most immediately, to destroy what little competition remains in the oil industry. We must not forget that the small, independent producers, refiners, and marketers have been the first to feel the shortage.

> The majors have set up their own secret, extralegal, and indeed illegal, process through the API to approve information gathering by the Interior Department to keep control over information. And, finally, when pressed for accurate data, the companies refuse to provide it.

Lobel further blamed the National Petroleum Council and the FPC:

> After all, why should government collect data when the API, the National Petroleum Council, oil's official adviser to the Secretary of the Interior whose membership reads like a Who's Who of the oil industry, and others were so expert and willing at gathering and analyzing the needed data. Apparently no one, outside of a few individuals, considered that the industry might be manipulating data.

> These companies' incentive to underreport, knowing that their figures were unlikely to be checked and that they might thus be able to double or triple the price they were getting, is obvious. Yet the

Federal Power Commission has refused to independently gather data on which decisions costing the consumers literally billions of dollars are being made [House Permanent Select Committee on Small Business, 1974: 9-11].

Ralph Nader blamed the Interior Department:

What information is obtained by the Interior Department comes directly from the individual oil companies with leasing rights on Federal lands, onshore and offshore! This is nothing less than a national scandal, Mr. Chairman. The U.S. Geological Survey exists in order not to know. It has repeatedly refused to demand a capability from the Congress to obtain independently the extent of oil and gas reserves from the people's lands. That is, the Federal lands in the United States [House Permanent Select Committee on Small Business, 1974: 241].

If neither industry nor the executive branch of the government could be trusted, who could be? As one obvious solution to the credibility problem, the GAO proposed to create a federal energy-data office entirely independent from the energy industry, and not only independent from industry, but also completely independent of the federal energy agencies.

The GAO report ultimately did not say what sorts of data should be collected for which purposes, perhaps because that would have appeared to preempt the policy prerogatives of Congress. And when Senator Jackson requested the report, he did not give GAO this particular task—understandable then, but also unfortunate. Without a policy there is no purpose in collecting data for a comprehensive energy-data bank; without a purpose for data there is no relevance and, hence, no real information.

COLLECT DATA TO MEASURE THE SHORTAGE

As the majority in Congress saw it, data were wanted first to answer the question, "How large is the shortage?" Having neglected to look into past decades to understand the chain of developments that had produced shortages, Congress saw the gap between supply and demand for energy as the central problem.

At the start of the December 1973 hearings of the Senate Committee on Government Operations, on the Federal Energy Administration Act, Senator Abraham Ribicoff (D-Conn.) had stated that the nation had a right to know the size of the energy shortage:

> We begin these hearings at a time when our Nation is in the grip of a major energy shortage without a national energy strategy. Americans are alarmed by the barrage of halfway emergency measures and speculation of worse to come. And they are frustrated by a lack of reliable information.
>
> The Nation simply has the right to know what the dimensions of the crisis are. I understand that the administration is predicting shortages between 18 and 32 percent of demand for essential fuels this coming quarter.
>
> If we are expected to pull together and make sacrifice after sacrifice, then we must be told just how bad the energy crisis actually is. Americans are not afraid of the truth—as dismal as it may be. But ignorance breeds fear—and fear breeds chaos [Senate Committee on Government Operations, 1973a: 2].

That there might be no straightforward answer to such a question, because it was impossible to sift out of years of conflicting regulation imposed on a historically market economy, was unclear to many participants.

Senator Jackson also stressed shortage. He was introducing a bill to develop contingency plans for reducing demand and assuring supply in the event of an "emergency," to be declared when demand exceeded supply by 5 percent or more. Jackson noted that the embargo

> comes at a time when we already face serious shortages of home heating oil, propane, jet fuel, diesel, residual oil, and gasoline. Domestic production of crude oil has peaked; refineries are operating at the limits of capacity; stocks of crude oil and refined products stand at the lowest levels of the past three years; and our energy distribution system is seriously malfunctioning. . . .
>
> Emergency legislation is needed because of the imminence of serious shortages as a result of [the embargo]. . . .
>
> Although we have faced shortages . . . for two years, the administration has consistently failed to deal with these shortages, or to prevent their occurrence in the future [Senate Committee on Public Works, 1976: 2481].

The administration was accused of not executing mandatory allocation schemes for gasoline or home heating oil (Senate Committee on Public Works, 1976). The bill's measures to close the gap between supply and demand—reducing speed limits, ending all advertising to induce more energy consumption, requiring car pools, urging regular tune-ups—reflected the shortfall logic that supply and demand must be pressed into equilibrium by the hand of administration—in this instance by forcing down demand.

By October 1973 everyone was churning out his own estimate of the size of the shortage in producive capacity. Representative William L. Hargate (D-Mo.) found this enormously frustrating:

> For years witness after witness has come forward to tell us that there was no problem. Last May Mr. Simon appeared before this committee and was asked if the administration needed additional legislation and his response was "No."
>
> On October 12th Mr. DiBona, then the White House energy expert, estimated that the shortage would be 1.2 million barrels per day.
>
> On October 20th, Mr. DiBona estimated the shortage would be 1.6 million barrels per day.
>
> On October 30th, the Department of the Interior estimated that the shortage would be about 2.5 million barrels per day [House Permanent Select Committee on Small Business, 1974: 5-6; see also Senate Committee on Government Operations, 1973b: 7].

Henry Kissinger, in a letter to the House Foreign Affairs Committee, estimated the shortage at 3 million barrels a day (House Permanent Select Committee on Small Business, 1974: Vol. 1, 526).

Different estimates could be subject to at least the following interpretations: (1) No one knew, so all had to guess. (2) Everyone knew, but instead each supported his own policy preferences. (3) Essential data were lacking. (4) Theory or policy to give meaning to the data was missing. (5) The diversity of estimates was desirable to allow comparison of different views. (6) Diversity, by confusing everyone, was a disaster. (7) All of the above. (8) None of the above.

Finding diversity intolerable, however interpreted, the Senate Government Operations Committee and the Senate Committee on Interior and Insular Affairs assigned the new Federal Energy Office (FEO) the task of producing one believable estimate of the shortfall. The weekly *Petroleum Situation Reports,* Which the FEO began issuing in December 1973, thus tried to estimate the size of the near-term gap between energy supply and demand, but only by projecting (assuming the past was a straight-line path to the future) the government's already existing spotty data. John Sawhill, FEO deputy administrator, told a subcommittee of the Government Operations Committee:

> Our best estimates of the average shortage in the first quarter of 1974 is 3.27 million barrels per day or 16.4 percent of uncon-

strained demand.... [T]hese estimates are subject to forecasting errors for which variances of 200,000 barrels per day in the total deficit would not be surprising and variances of 100,000 barrels per day in each major product are believed reasonable [Senate Committee on Government Operations, 1973b: 5].

But federal energy-data-collection efforts, intended for specific uses as they came up, were not meant to be used in the enormous systemwide accounting needed to measure the size of the energy gap, if, indeed—without aditional assumptions as to price and technology and recoverability—the energy gap could be measured at all. In this context, then, what could shortage mean? Was there a natural right to a given supply at a fixed price?

What is the size of the shortage? The question is neither simple nor straightforward. Conceptually, the question neglects the dynamics of price, cost, and technological developments. If cost were not a consideration, then one might consider calculating a shortfall as between demand (at zero cost) and supply. But if demand was dependent on price, and price on technologies and their costs, then the target was not standing still but moving. It would make no sense to answer a static question implied in terms like "gap," "shortage," or "shortfall" with a necessarily dynamic answer about present and future prices. Also, it would be a formidable task to try to measure static supply and demand at one point in time. However, a gap could not be measured at all without necessary assumptions concerning price, cost, technology, and recoverability of resources.

In any case, there is no evidence that President Nixon even had gap measurement in mind. In fact, FEO Administrator William E. Simon actively lobbied against Representative John Dingell's (D-Mich.) amendment to the Energy Emergency Act, which would have required reports on the size and causes of the energy gap. The Nixon Administration apparently took a different approach to energy data.

To Simon the situation was clear: The days of cheap and abundant energy were over; the time had come to be more energy-efficient. Conservation, not better data, was needed; but failing to achieve conservation by exhortation, Nixon sought to induce it by stimulating market mechanisms. Amid congressional protest, he began to raise the price of oil (Senate Committee on Government Operations, 1974: 605).

The opposing position, which dominated Congress, was that Americans should continue to be assured low-priced and plentiful energy supplies. The paramount desire of those dissenting was to prevent a massive redistribution of income from 200 million energy consumers to a handful of producers. Since private industry could not be trusted to uphold this principle, the corollary position was that the federal government would have to step in to manage the nation's energy supply systems. Planning would require complete data—on supply and demand, prices, and costs—at each phase in the production process for every type of fuel. Planning to keep supply-demand gaps closed, moreover, would call for forecasts of future supply and demand.

Was Congress prepared to take over the energy industry? So long as the argument appeared to be about data alone, that question needed neither to be asked nor answered.

After the embargo ended in spring 1974, the majority in Congress passed legislation endorsing a policy framework requiring detailed data to assess the current and future size of the gap. Included was the Federal Energy Administration (FEA) Act of 1974, which established the first agency to be responsible for regulation, "truly independent" data-collecting, and planning intended to keep the energy gap closed. Congress had responded to the cries to do something about the crisis by creating that new bureaucracy—the Federal Energy Administration—to collect data for eventually determining the size and causes of the shortfall. In adopting this "gap mentality," market interaction and price were rejected as moderators of energy supply and demand.

Historically, energy provision had been rooted in the market system. As the MIT Energy Laboratory Policy Study Group expressed it,

> in the past, energy provision has been left to the workings of private markets—some regulated and some not. Energy prices and the relation of those prices to the costs of domestic supply and conservation measures have been the principal determinants of the magnitude and composition of the energy sector, and of energy imports. The driving force has been profits, with the government as one of the determinants of what was profitable. . . . The hypothesis adopted here is that for the foreseeable future we are *not* likely to institute fundamental changes in the structure of the energy sector, or move in a determined, decisive way to a more centrally-controlled energy economy. For better or worse, the market system will predominate in the U.S. [Policy Study Group, Energy Laboratory, MIT, 1976: 27-28].

A legislative focus on demanding data served the function of avoiding choice between market and administered prices. After all, who could object to more, better, unbiased, complete data? Failure to act may be excused by lack of information, as if data determined choice. Once one realizes that the usefulness of data depends on policy purpose, the continuous call for data takes on a larger significance.

DATA WANTED FOR "POLICY AND PLANNING"

The hearings in Congress of January and February 1974, "Energy Data Requirements of the Federal Government," are studded with complaints of how frustrating it was "trying to make policy determinations and make policy recommendations without comprehensive and adequate and accurate data" (House Permanent Select Committee on Small Business, 1974: 29). Experience proved that the vague concept of "data needed for the formulation of energy policy" was empty also. Certainly the general notion that policy may require data could not be gainsaid. But constant repetition of that phrase masked the relevant questions: First, for what purposes were the data wanted? How would having one or another set of data—or a high as opposed to a low estimate—influence a given decision or line of thinking? Second, exactly what kind of data would be wanted?

FOR WHAT POLICY PURPOSES
DID CONGRESS WANT DATA?

Legislators who championed low-priced and abundant energy for consumers—mostly liberals from populous northern and eastern regions and some other non-oil-producing states who dominated on energy matters in Congress—suspected that the crisis and the shortages were contrived by the oil companies. Said John Dingell (D-Mich.) in January 1974 at the opening of his subcommittee's hearings on "Energy Data Requirements of the Federal Government,"

[in calling for these hearings] I cited the growing public skepticism of the American people over whether the energy crisis is real or contrived. I queried whether the oil shortage was fact or fiction. To the latter question I have no answer. I believe that the documented shortcomings of our Federal energy data collection system preclude a reasoned answer to that question [House Permanent Select Committee on Small Business, 1974: 2].

The Federal Government has enacted regulations to deal with the apparent shortages. Yet, without the fundamental data, the Government cannot assure itself, let alone the consuming public, that the crisis is real [House Permanent Select Committee on Small Business, 1974: 5].

In Congressman Silvio Conte's (R-Mass.) words, "Is there a credibility gap between data designed for Government information and the total picture known only inside the fortress of solitude that is the oil industry?" It was possible that the industry knew and would not tell. It was possible also that industry did not know and could not tell. Indeed, if the oil industry relied on markets while government held out for regulation, the kind and quality of data each needed might be markedly different.

In expressing their mistrust of the oil industry, Congress members brought back from their December 1973 trips home the refrains of their constituents. Constituents' cries of outrage were aired in no fewer than four separate sets of hearings in January 1974 (House Permanent Select Committee on Small Business, 1974: Part 1, 2). The public wanted information that would determine whether the crisis or shortages were contrived by the oil producers to push up fuel prices. As Conte put it,

> Let me say that the energy crisis is tragically real in Massachusetts. I brought back enough cases with me to fill the Library of Congress' new annex.

> The real question is not whether there is an energy crisis, ask any consumer, but whether this crisis has resulted despite the oil industries' best efforts or because of them.

> I am still . . . to be totally convinced, as is the public, that a shortage of the fuels we all depend upon exists. Never minding a lot of sophisticated double-talk, most people cannot comprehend an energy crisis characterized by the reported presence of "tankers" waiting in New England harbors to be unloaded, storage tanks along the east coast filled to the brim, and soaring corporate profits [House Permanent Select Committee on Small Business, 1974: 5].

In Massachusetts the emergency was real enough, but reasons for the crisis were not evident. Not knowing who to trust and unwilling to say constituents would have to pay higher prices, members of Congress took the path of least resistance: "[We will get] better information than we have been getting. The testimony of the witnesses called will . . . serve to emphasize this point and help us to organize strategies for gathering the reliable data we need for future planning" [House Permanent Select Committee on Small Business, 1974).

The search for data to answer the question, "Is the crisis fact or fiction?" was grounded in the belief that the oil companies were creating and/or using the threat of shortage to push up prices and increase their own profits. On the House side, Congressman John Dingell, chairman of the Oversight and Investigations Subcommittee of the Commerce Committee, was saying:

> [H]omes are cold, workers unemployed, children go to school by candlelight or flashlight in the predawn darkness, and, a host of products are in short supply at even higher prices. The Federal Government has enacted regulations to deal with the apparent shortages. Yet, without the fundamental data, the Government cannot assure itself, let alone the consuming public, that the crisis is real. The Government cannot delineate the scope of the shortage or pinpoint its cause. We lack the factual basis for solving the crisis if a crisis exists. How, then, can regulations solve problems or correct situations the characteristics of which we are not certain? [House Permanent Select Committee on Small Business, 1974: 2].

And on the Senate side, Senator William Proxmire (D-Wisc.) put the question to the FEO administrator:

> Mr. Simon, there is a great skepticism in the country. A shockingly large proportion of people, perhaps most of our people, doubt the existence of the energy crisis. They believe it is a Government-oil-industry-sponsored put-on to raise prices and increase profits at the expense of consumers. Others say the oil shortage is real but it is being manipulated by the oil industry and Government to increase oil industry profits and the shifts and changes from day to day in statements from the Government add to the turmoil.

> The first objective of these hearings, therefore, is to establish the facts and to get from those who make public policy the basis for their facts, the question of who provides them, how reliable they are, and what means the Government and the public have of verifying their accuracy [Joint Economic Commission, 1974: 89].

The primary data—shortage experienced by citizens—caught wide attention, to be sure, but did not extend to proving causation. Who or what was responsible? If the shortage was contrived, oil companies might be compelled to disgorge their hoard. But if only so much was available at the going price, the prospect of price increases had to be faced. Obviously this was undesirable, since the actual policy was to keep down costs to consumers by subsidizing imports. Thus, it is not clear whether just any answer to what caused shortages would do. Indeed, when possible answers were proferred, the presence of data satisfied critics no more than their absence.

WHAT DATA WERE WANTED?

While it would be convenient for the historian of oil and gas reserve estimation if Congress had been interested only, or even primarily, in reserve estimates, the development of the mandate for a National Energy Information System was not so accommodating. When the oil crisis broke (Fall 1973), Congress initially defined the situation as a problem of oil supply—a formulation then expanded to include gas and coal supplies and, finally, all energy supplies. The question of the extent of oil and gas reserves was introduced as a side issue to the problem of supply.

Throughout the 1973-1977 period, the extent of oil and gas reserves remained a secondary concern. Indeed, the whole problem of energy data was but one of the energy issues with which Congress struggled during this period; price regulation and allocation of available oil and gas were of much greater concern. Within this universe of problems, let us isolate the issues Congress addressed bearing on oil and gas reserve estimates, and the place of these estimates in the envisioned National Energy Information System.

The terms "reserves," "resources," and "holdings" were used so frequently in Congress that it is well-nigh impossible to say what Congressmembers meant by them. As used during 1973 and 1974, "reserves" meant whatever oil or gas was in the ground. The distinction between reserves and resources had not entered the province of congressional discourse. Further, most officials assumed (incorrectly) that reserves could be accurately measured. With the exception of one brief exchange—in which someone tried to convince Dingell that the term "reserves" itself carried several different meanings—debates over the 1973 oil crisis ignored the technical complexities of reserve estimation. "Holdings" was a blanket term in Congress for oil or gas from the time it emerged from the ground to the time it was sold to end-users. Thus, holdings included all oil produced but not yet consumed, such as oil in pipelines, in storage, and in transport. Often in debate over what data would be needed, "reserves" and "holdings" either were lumped together or used interchangeably.

It would be easy to suggest that the Congressmembers seeking industry data on "reserves and holdings" did not know what they were talking about or what they wanted; but such a suggestion would be misleading. What these legislators wanted to know was whatever the oil companies knew about the nation's supply of oil and gas. The phrase "data on reserves and holdings" served as an emblem of whatever was known, whatever that was. No one thought to ask whether anyone, oil companies

included, knew (or could know) what data were necessary to make policy
without first knowing what kind of policy anyone wanted to make.

FEO DATA CONCLUDED
"THERE IS A SHORTAGE"

FEO Administrator William E. Simon spoke to the fact-or-fiction issue
many times during the winter of 1973-1974:

> Many people still do not believe there is a shortage, but let me assure
> you that the shortage is not contrived. Certainly it is not contrived
> that the demand for energy in the United States has been growing at
> a rate of 4 to 5 percent a year for the past 20 years. It is not
> contrived that if the present trend continues, our energy needs by
> 1990 will be twice as great as they were in 1973. It is not contrived
> that domestic exploration peaked in 1956. It is not contrived that
> domestic production began to decrease in 1970. All these things are
> real, and have led to our current energy crisis. The very fact that
> even with the embargo, we are importing about 5 million barrels a
> day and post embargo that we will import about 7 million barrels a
> day shows the imbalance between domestic supply and demand
> [Senate Committee on Government Operations, 1974: 605].

But his words did not achieve their intended effect; mistrust in Congress
and in the public persisted. The consumerists' new line of attack was that
FEO data ignored oil company behavior with respect to costs, prices, and
profits. Thus, more data were wanted to prove that the oil companies were
using the crisis to increase prices. The issue was not whether prices should
respond to the shortfall between supply and demand, but, rather, when
one could say that normal price increases had become "price-gouging,"
and profits "excessive." Senator Abraham Ribicoff (D-Conn.) put it
bluntly: "The oil companies are exploiting the American people. Their
profits are going through the roof and the American people just will not
take an increase in prices at the same time of unconscionable profits"
(Senate Committee on Government Operations, 1973a: 2).

In the hearings he chaired, Senator Proxmire (D-Wisc.) called for data
which would let Congress determine whether profits were excessive:

> We want the facts on production, reserves, inventories, and con-
> sumption. We want the facts for both the immediate short-run
> problems and about the long-run issues. And we want the facts not
> only about supply and production but we want them about costs
> and prices. The full audit that you have pledged of refineries may

give us some of the answers, I suspect not all the answers, and perhaps only a small part of it. Furthermore, at the present time, there seems to be little or no concern on the part of the Government itself as to whether or not the huge, unprecedented, and inflationary rise in fuel prices are related in any direct way to costs [Joint Economic Committee, 1974: 90].

Since oil companies were treated as a monopoly that could raise prices at will, virtually all price increases seemed unjustified.

PRICE WAS CONSIDERED THE PROBLEM

What the advocates of cheap and abundant energy (our low-pricer consumerists) wanted was any data that might be used for the following policy purposes:

- to measure the size of the shortfall between supply and demand;
- to determine to what extent oil companies were contributing to the shortage and,
- once blame for the shortage was apportioned, to design policies to control energy prices, close the shortfall, and keep it closed.

If price was not to relate supply and demand, administrative means would be necessary to acquire and allocate oil. Since oil is not free, some people would be paying for other people. So data were also desired on costs and needs.

Given this perspective, the desire for data was immense. As Dingell pressed Eric Zausner of the FEO:

If you do not know the amount of reserves, if you do not have audited, viable information regarding reserves, if you do not have information to know what the maximum efficient rate of production is, how are you going to know whether or not there is a conspiracy afoot by the oil companies and the oil suppliers of this country to skin the consumers? We've had an absolutely astronomical increase in price despite your controls [House Permanent Select Committee on Small Business, 1974: 521-522].

Price was considered not part of the solution but the problem itself. In market terms, price relates supply to demand. Price is therefore a dynamic variable. Suppose, however, that price is presumed to be constant, either because the energy industry sets its own prices or because people should not have to pay more than a certain price. Then price becomes the problem. Distrust of an unregulated energy market—suspicion that its prices would be unnecessarily and unfairly high—suggested that the federal government would have to take energy into its own hands. To become the decision maker on energy, government would need data on every aspect of supply and demand.

Accordingly, in the seemingly endless deliberations of 1974 through 1977, only those price increases which elicited "substantial" new supplies were to be allowed. This raised impossible problems of evaluation: attributing x new supplies (discoveries? proved reserves?) to a y percent increase in price; the question of what size price increase is not worth approving, or barely worth it in terms of producing new supplies; balancing the principle that prices should reflect cost with the principle that price should match one's ability to pay; and so forth.

Prices reflect a process of discovery; they are products not of prediction but of markets. Yet the main problem perceived throughout the hearings, debates, and reports was that those very market forces were being denied.

The question of whether oil prices were related in any way to oil company costs became the hub of the lengthy debates in the Senate and House on taxation of windfall profits. These debates dragged on through the winter and spring of 1974. Congress finally reached a temporary compromise, what was incorporated in the Energy Emergency Act. In March, however, Nixon vetoed this act, partly in objection to its provisions against windfall profits. Eventually, the legislation Nixon signed did allow the FEA to monitor retail prices for heating oil, gasoline, and propane. But that legislation contained no provisions to obtain data that would have permitted a detailed scrutiny of oil company records.

In the House, an attempt by Dingell to include data on internal energy industry costs and petroleum product prices among the data to be gathered by the proposed FEA was quashed. The amendment, reintroduced on the floor of the House, was stripped of its financial data requirements.

Thus, countless hours had been spent vainly trying to figure out, as Dingell put it, "whether we are going to allow the producers to steal a little, to steal some, or simply to raid the public" (House Permanent Select Committee on Small Business, 1974: 521).

Not only were efforts to get data that yielded profit information repeatedly dashed; efforts to obtain data on reserves also came under question. During the oil embargo, Congress seemed to be dealing with a supply problem that could be understood, in principle, by improving certain existing data series and gathering additional data. The properties Congress looked for in the data were partly a function of the embargo problem as Congress members saw it, and partly responsive to the barriers Congress had discovered that kept industry data beyond government scrutiny. The point is that, initially, the problem to be solved was relatively clear: to get data to help explain the near-term crisis as it related to imports. The data wanted were about the process whereby imported oil arrived at the points of consumption.

Unless data could interpret themselves, of course, no set of figures would answer questions about imported oil. Such answers required a framework of understanding to interpret the numbers. Viewed either way, however, domestic oil and gas reserves were not relevant to planning the routes of imports.

WANTED: DATA TO SUPPORT ANY FUTURE POLICY PRESERVING CHEAP AND ABUNDANT ENERGY

By spring 1974 the import crisis had abated. But a pile of legislation to deal with shortages was still churning its way through Congress. A certain momentum had built. In January 1974 many members of Congress had committed themselves publicly to finishing the work they had started to resolve the oil crisis. Even though the embargo ended in February, legislators could hardly go back to their districts and admit nothing had been done to solve the problem.

Besides, as those taking the lead on the oil crisis saw it, there was indeed a clear policy framework. The object was to ensure that consumers could buy all the fuel they wanted at prices as close as possible to the rates to which they were accustomed. This object would be achieved by tracing the flow of oil and gas through the entire system from reserves to end-consumption. Once the stages in this system had been identified, the data collected for each stage would lead to defining policy alternatives relevant at that stage; such alternatives then would be resolved by policy decisions. The outcome of these decisions on the oil supply system would be to assure a cheap and abundant oil supply, and a guarantee against massive redistribution of income from consumers to producers.

But what use would data on the oil supply process be if the policy framework changed? Suppose the object of the policy became to lower the balance-of-payments deficit, for example, or to impose the same price restraints on American oil consumers that consumers in other countries had to bear. Policies with these objectives probably would not engender issues that could be well served by detailed data on the oil supply system.

What would happen if the data base were expanded? Suppose Congress were to receive the report it had mandated on oil and gas reserves. Would the imprecision of reserves estimates, and the conclusion that reserves are a function of price, have an impact on the original policy objective of ensuring cheap and abundant oil supplies? If reserves increase with price—

if price is not an acceptable variable because the object is to keep price low—and if the reserves estimated to exist at a given price cannot be estimated with precision, of what use could a report on reserves be to policy makers?

Such an attempt to drive policy with data will inevitably produce large quantities of numbers which cannot be information because they do not measure concepts that fit into a policy framework. It is one thing to ask for comprehensive data to determine whether the oil supply system is producing abundant, cheap petroleum products. It is quite another thing to ask for a comprehensive, accurate data system which will contain data relevant to any future oil policy issue. Unless policy frameworks are first defined, the endless variety of measurements which could be made (on each of a host of potentially relevant phenomena) would lead to a monumentally expensive bank or series of figures, none of which might turn out to be information.

In extending its mandate from gathering import data to gathering data that could inform decisions on how to maintain a cheap, abundant supply of oil—and, finally, to the everything-for-everyone task of collecting data that could be used to deal with any future energy shortfall or problem—Congress succeeded only in creating abundant conceptual confusion.

THE IMPLICIT POLICY FRAMEWORK

To ask whether policy should drive data or data should drive policy may be deceptive. The statement "policy drives data" could be misinterpreted to mean that we start with a solution to a problem (a policy) and proceed to justify the policy by collecting certain data. Epistemology and experience teach that some framework or theory must exist to convert sensation to data and data to information; therefore, the idea that data could "drive policy" is absurd. The question then becomes whether the policy framework is explicit or implicit. When it appears that data are driving policy, the policy framework is implicit.

The record of legislative discussion leading to the FEA Act and the Energy Supply and Environmental Coordination Act shows that these laws resulted from many compromises among these groups.

But the energy-data mandate was the product solely of consumerists and preservationists. They were thinking in terms of fixed quantities rather than price relationships, so they needed data for decisions rather than data to define arenas for finding each other.

In addition to advocating price and allocation controls over oil and gas,[7] these groups oriented toward quantity theory wanted to order supplies produced at their "maximum efficient rate of production" and, under certain circumstances, in excess of this maximum (Senate Committee on Government Operations and Committee on Interior and Insular Affairs, 1974: Sec. 107). Refineries were to follow suit "to produce refined products in proportion commensurate with national needs" (Senate Committee on Government Operations and Committee on Interior and Insular Affairs, 1974: 195). These explicit policy preferences had formidable and (perhaps necessarily) unspoken implicit implications: taking over the entire management of the oil and gas industries without quite saying so. Central management of resource quantities would supersede decentralized markets. The unspoken desire for this fundamental shift constituted the implicit policy framework.

The implicit policy framework was grounded in quantity theory. It assumed, in a sweeping departure from historical practice, that energy should be provided by a centrally planned economy. If this assumption seems to assume too much, we need only say that supply was to be severed from price by allocating quantities of resources through administrative means. Central management would supersede decentralized markets.

It was unlikely that Congress would follow through with this and actually legislate conversion of the energy industry from a private to a centrally managed economy, even in the most acute energy crisis. But Congress was also unwilling to allow private markets to operate fully. Busy assessing data "requirements," Congress did not have to face the real choice.

CONCLUSION:
TOO MUCH AND NOT ENOUGH

Between 1973 and 1977, Congress passed a series of mandates imbued with a majority conviction that there was a need to know the precise extent of all U.S. oil and gas reserves and holdings. The key motivating factor was a mistrust of the oil companies manifested in shortages, rising prices, and apparent stockpiling. The investigation of why oil and gas were no longer cheap and plentiful could have focused on either prices or supply. But the oil embargo riveted attention on supply. Given this focus, and given the sense of urgency and congressional responsibility, the questions were about shortfall: Was there a shortfall? How great was it? Were the oil companies causing, or taking advantage of, the shortfall to increase prices?

The focus on shortfall led to an increasingly detailed demand for complete and accurate data on the nation's energy supplies. This mandate could be met by nothing less than tracing oil and gas from below the ground through production, transportation, refining, and final distribution. Also the mandate called for short-term and long-term forecasts of oil and gas supplies. Accompanying this focus on supply were laws which artificially kept oil and gas prices low. Thus, in order to assure a cheap and abundant supply of oil and gas, supply must be disassociated from price; supply and price must be regulated separately; and by substituting observations of consumption severed from cost, demand would be ignored.

Today the all-inclusive models which the energy-data mandate envisioned still have not been produced. Why? The legislation failed to specify a clearly defined, clearly limited framework within which policies regulating oil supply would be formulated. Nor, within that framework, were there any examples of the issues that might be addressed. By enacting an approach to the National Energy Information System in which data would drive policy, Congress blocked thoughtful efforts to construct that energy information system. Instead, Congress's continuing demand for oil and gas data was met by the undiscriminating collection of countless figures and projections.

So it happened that the groups in Congress that wanted to know enough about oil and gas supplies to be able to identify and address problems through regulation did not get the data they wanted. Congress had elevated the energy-data function to make it an independent office within the Department of Energy. But the conceptual (not to mention the measurement) problems underlying the energy-data mandate possibly were not recognized and certainly were not addressed. The resulting data turned out to be at once too many and not enough—that is, not enough relevant information. Put differently, there were far too few data for government to control oil and gas, and far too much for what markets would have needed.

Nonetheless, if one believes there is a gap between supply and demand that must be closed, the size of the shortfall is essential information. Estimating the extent of the gap thereby became the most important of the federal government's data-collection and analysis activities. Once the size and scope of the shortage was known, the task was to allocate scarce quantities to those designated as needy. The next chapter describes the FEO's desperate attempts to collect the data necessary for these tasks.

NOTES

1. See Central Intelligence Agency, 1977; Congressional Research Service, 1977; Workshop on Alternative Energy Strategies, 1977; and Ford Foundation Energy Policy Project, 1974.

2. For the percentage depletion, see IRS Code sec. 114(b) [3]. For the expensing of intangible drilling costs, see IRS Code, Regulations 111, sec. 29.23(m)-16. A description of their workings is found in Mancke (1974: Ch. 6).

3. All producing states now restrict capture-related practices.

4. For a more detailed explanation, see Bohi and Russell, 1978.

5. Eisenhower was responding to the recommendations of the Report to the President of the Special Cabinet Committee to Investigate Crude Oil Imports. For a thorough history of oil import control policy, see Bohi and Russell, 1978.

6. Presidential Proclamation 3275, March 10, 1959.

7. As detailed in the Emergency Energy Allocation Act. See also Chapter 7, in which these groups are shown to have wanted price ceilings maintained for natural gas at the wellhead.

REFERENCES

ADELMAN, M. A. (1964) "The efficiency of resource use in crude petroleum." Southern Economics Journal (October).

BOHI, D. R. and M. RUSSELL (1978) Limiting Oil Imports. Baltimore: Johns Hopkins University Press.

Central Intelligence Agency (1977) The International Energy Situation: Outlook to 1985. Washington, DC: Government Printing Office.

Congressional Research Service (1977) "Project Independence," in Hearings before the Committee on Energy and Natural Resources. Washington, DC: Government Printing Office. (U.S. Senate Publication 95-31)

Ford Foundation Energy Policy Project (1974) A Time to Choose America's Energy Future. Cambridge, MA: Ballinger.

General Accounting Office (1974) "Actions needed to improve federal efforts in collecting, analyzing, and reporting energy data," in Energy Information Needs: Study by the General Accounting Office. Washington, DC: Government Printing Office.

House Permanent Select Committee on Small Business (1974) "Energy data requirements of the federal government," in Hearings before the Subcommittee on Activities of Regulatory Agencies. Washington, DC: Government Printing Office.

JACKSON, H. M. (1973) Personal communication to Elmer Staats, Comptroller General of the United States, April 6.

Joint Economic Committee (1974) "Energy statistics," p. 89 in Hearings before the Subcommittee on Priorities and Economy in Government. Washington, DC: Government Printing Office.

MANCKE, R. B. (1974) The Failure of U.S. Energy Policy. New York: Columbia University Press.

MEAD, W. J. (1979) "The performance of government in energy regulations." American Economic Review (May).

McAVOY, P. W. (1974) "The separate control of quantity and price in the energy industries." Massachusetts Institute of Technology. (unpublished)

Policy Study Group, Energy Laboratory, MIT (1976) "Government support for the commercialization of new energy technologies." Prepared for the U.S. Energy Research and Development Administration, November.

Senate Committee on Government Operations (1974) "Current energy shortages oversight series: the Federal Energy Office," in Hearings before the Permanent Subcommittee on Investigations. Washington, DC: Government Printing Office.

——— (1973a) "To provide for the effective and efficient management of the nation's energy policies and programs," in Hearings on S. 2776. Washington, DC: Government Printing Office.

——— (1973b) "Current energy shortages oversight series: conflicting information on fuel shortages," in Hearings before the Permanent Subcommittee on Investigations. Washington, DC: Government Printing Office.

——— and Committee on Interior and Insular Affairs (1974) "Standby Energy Emergency Authorities Act," in Joint Hearings on S. 3267. Washington, DC: Government Printing Office.

Senate Committee on Interior and Insular Affairs (1974) "Actions needed to improve federal efforts in collecting, analyzing, and reporting energy data," in Energy Information Needs: Study by the General Accounting Office. Washington, DC: Government Printing Office.

Senate Committee on Public Works (1976) "A legislative history of the Energy Supply Environmental Coordination Act of 1974." Congressional Research Service Series 94-7.

U.S. Cabinet (1970) Oil Import. Washington, DC: Government Printing Office.

Workshop on Alternative Energy Strategies (1977) Energy: Global Prospects, 1985-2000. New York: McGraw-Hill.

POOR POLICY OR INADEQUATE IMPLEMENTATION?
Federal Energy Office Regulations

IT IS DECEMBER 4, 1973. You, the Federal Energy Office, have just been created by President Nixon through executive order. Parts of you are scattered about in nine different office buildings.

You are to operate within the legislative framework of the Emergency Petroleum Allocation Act of 1973, which only became law on November 27. The purpose of this law is to protect the people and the economy from the harmful effects of any petroleum shortfalls.

Congress has given you two immediate tasks: to measure the size of the oil shortage in all its manifestations, and to design and implement supply and price regulations for allocating these now-scarce quantities equitably across the country. It is your job also to collect the data necessary to accomplish the tasks. Finally, you are to gather data to use in planning against future shortfalls.

By April you are spent. For all your effort, your implementation of Congress's mandate could be judged a failure. Some shortages seem to have abated apart from anything you have done. On other fronts you are constantly fighting (and never putting out) fires—supply problems no one had expected. Were the failures due to errors in implementation: working with the wrong people, collecting inappropriate data, or misinterpreting data? Or did the failures stem from congressional inability to envision how the mandates were to be carried out? After all, those who pass policy must foresee its practical execution and, indeed, weave implementation and the policy objective together into an integrated formulation. If policy makers do not think ahead to the details of implementation, the goal may never see the light of day. Thus, while implementation depends on foresight in policy design, the ultimate fate of the goal depends on that implementa-

tion. Another possible source of failure might be poor policy conceptualization from the very beginning.

Policy ideas and their implementation, alike, evolve over time. Both
questions—whether the ideas are worth carrying out in the light of new
events and whether their implementation has been faulty—remain open to
discussion.

This is a case study of an implementation effort, one that depended on
the collection of voluminous data—in this case, data pertaining mainly to
supplies *above* ground and presumably less laden with physical uncertainties than reserves and resources below ground. We shall examine the
Federal Energy Office's information apparatus to ask whether the FEO
might have been a more effective implementing agency, or whether even
the most talented staff would have failed because of poorly conceived
policy expectations or lack of foresight on the part of policy makers.

CONTRADICTORY POLICY GOALS

One implicit policy framework was the inclination to take over management of the oil industry without quite saying so. Central management of
resource quantities, as in a planned economy, would supersede tradition-
ally decentralized markets. Congress would not follow through and actually convert the oil industry from a private to a central operation; neither
could Congress tolerate full operation of a private market. This ambivalence between desire for central control and unwillingness to go all the
way was reflected in the policy goals set forth in the Emergency Petroleum
Allocation Act. Witness the list of objectives in the Act:

(1) Insuring adequate petroleum supplies for specific high-priority
    uses, viz., national defense, safety and welfare, public health
    (including residential heating), public transportation, agricultural
    production, and energy production (e.g., thermal electric power).
(2) Preservation of a sound and competitive petroleum industry, with
    emphasis on protecting the market share and competitive viability
    of the independent sector of the industry.
(3) Equitable distribution of petroleum supplies at equitable prices
    among regions and areas of the country.
(4) Avoidance of unnecessary interference with market mechanisms.

Government ambivalence toward the business of central management is
reflected in the inherent conflicts over objectives. Objectives 3 and 4 are in
basic conflict. There is no guarantee that a free market will allocate goods
and services equitably. Leaving aside the problem of defining "equitable,"

to assure equitable distribution usually involves interference with market mechanisms. There is a similar conflict between objectives 1 and 4, ensuring supplies versus avoiding interference. Notice also the conflict between 2 and 3, preserving industry and maintaining equitable prices, moderated only by weasel words such as "unnecessary interference" (4) and "equitable distribution" (3). These contradictory objectives formed the legislative framework within which the FEO was supposed to operate.[1] Resolution of these conflicts was passed along to the bureaucracy, which had to choose which objectives to emphasize and the implementing actions.

POLICY MAKERS WERE NOT IMPLEMENTORS

The Arab embargo of oil exports to the United States meant a loss of about 17 percent of this country's oil supplies. To meet impending shortages and to respond to Congress's policy goals, President Nixon issued Executive Order 11748 on December 4, 1973, which established the Federal Energy Office. The FEO was given the monumental tasks of measuring and monitoring the shortfall and of alleviating ill effects of the shortages.

Who was in the FEO? To say "a mixed bag" would be putting it mildly. The office was headed by William Simon, Deputy Secretary of the Treasury Department. There, George Schultz, then Secretary of the Treasury, had already made Simon head of the Oil Policy Committee. In taking over the FEO, Simon brought along a staff of about a dozen analysts, who were to grapple with most of the day-to-day implementation problems.

In addition, the FEO brought together people from at least two other federal organizations that had recently dealt with energy matters: the Department of the Interior and the Cost of Living Council. Within the Interior Department was the Petroleum Allocation Office, in which staff people were trying to set up a monitoring system of ten regional offices (plus an office in each state) to keep track of where oil and petroleum products were going. Also in Interior was the Office of Energy Data and Analysis, which had been compiling data from other parts of the government, especially the Bureau of Mines. A third bureau of the Interior Department to join the new organization was Energy Conservation. Across town, the Cost of Living Council was trying to regulate gasoline prices. Thus, one entity (Interior) was trying to control quantities while the other (Cost of Living Council) was trying to control prices. The broad policy aims (keep down prices, restrict quantities) of Congress not only were in conflict, but also were being carried out by two separate bureaucracies.

There were leftovers, too, from the old White House Energy Policy Office. From the Domestic Council came James H. Falk, whose job was liaison with state and local governments. A tight group of top White House staff people also participated: Alexander Haig, Bryce Harlow, Melvin R. Laird, and Roy Ash. This group had a hand in such things as selecting John C. Sawhill to be Simon's deputy. Also there was the cabinet committee chaired by President Nixon, the Emergency Energy Action Group; it was supposed to be the chief decision-making body for energy policy. Then there was the Energy Emergency Planning Group, an interagency task force with OMB leadership, on hand to feed policy options to the cabinet committee. Remnants of all these entities came to inhabit the Federal Energy Office.

The individuals who made up the FEO had virtually no day-to-day relationship with Congress. Legislators were not thinking about day-to-day implementation. In addition, most FEO staff members lacked industry experience and so did not understand the workings of the industry they were assigned to regulate. FEO now was being asked to do what government historically had refrained from doing, and in an atmosphere charged with mistrust. An internal study done for the Energy Information Administration describes the degree of suspicion that the shortage was not "real," setting the scene for many of the FEO's informational problems:

> First, there was widespread disbelief among members of the general public that the U.S. would even be affected by an embargo. A poll taken at the time showed that a large proportion of the public did not even know that the United States imported oil. When shortages did become manifest, the popular belief was that they must somehow have been contrived by the oil industry. Second, the average person had very little knowledge of the vastness and complexity of the oil industry. He was obviously aware of the major companies, but only dimly aware of the multitude of independent producers, jobbers, and retailers that together account for an extremely large proportion of the industry. Third, there was no precedent for emergency governmental regulation of the oil industry. The government had brought oil executives to Washington to run the industry in wartime, but that had been a matter of ensuring that the nation's war effort went smoothly. National survival was at stake and industry-government cooperation was a matter of patriotic duty. None of this was the case in the embargo. The United States was not at war and its survival was not at stake. Oil company profiteering, a possibility in wartime as well, was to be decried, but was not equated with treason. Fourth, because the United States was facing a novel problem, the government did not have trained cadres of individuals

possessing the kind of detailed knowledge necessary to control the industry's activities.

For the above reasons, the executive branch of our federal government found itself with a mandate to do something that it has historically been extremely reluctant to do, vis., centrally manage an industry without nationalizing it and without a trained, "industry-wise" staff [Yurow and Levy-Pascal, 1979: 4].

IMPLEMENTATION PROBLEMS WERE INEVITABLE

Data to Assess Shortages

Given such tasks—measuring shortages, regulating the quantities of oil that flowed across the country, and controlling prices—estimates became extremely important. In many situations, supply outcomes were quite sensitive to differences in estimates. National Journal Reports remarked:

> Federal energy policies often are based on upswings or downturns in statistics that are so small they can barely be seen with the naked eye.
>
> Even when they can be seen, they cannot always be believed.
>
> For example, the Administration has been trying to guess the extent of heating oil shortages this winter. In making their estimates, officials have figured that the nation's oil refineries will produce distillate fuels at the rate of 23.4 percent per barrel of crude oil. A change of a point either way in the calculation might spell the difference between shortage and surplus [National Journal Reports, 1973a: 1513].

Everyone clamored for estimates that could be trusted. Yet, as we know, just about all the data that FEO used at the beginning were suspect, including data on stocks above ground. As things stood early in 1974, according to Ralph Nader, the government could "produce a shortage just by announcing one" (National Journal Reports, 1974a).[2]

What data were available to help assess shortages when the FEO first came into being? The Bureau of Mines canvassed all 140 refineries in the United States every month for certain supply data. Refinery personnel completed Bureau of Mines forms voluntarily, and over time a high response rate had been achieved. The data were published in the monthly *Mineral Industry Survey* for petroleum with a two-month lag. Though the American Petroleum Institute (API) solicited fewer refineries (60 percent of them), it covered about 85 percent of total refining volumes. API data were gathered weekly, by mail, telephone, telegraph, and teletype. The reports, again volunteered, were published in the API *Weekly Statistical Bulletin.* The kinds of data covered by both forms included crude oil production, quantities coming into the refinery from domestic and foreign sources, quantities in storage, and quantities of various refined products leaving the refinery.

Critics argued that Bureau of Mines data were unaudited, not timely, and not mandatory. They objected also to API data for not being mandatory or all-inclusive, as well as for being unaudited. These qualities had never bothered the API. As John E. Hodges, publisher of the API's *Weekly Statistical Bulletin,* said, "The weekly statistics were never intended to be a definitive record of everything going on in the petroleum industry" (National Journal Reports, 1974c). Hodges expressed the impossibility of going in and auditing refineries' estimates of quantities that are always in motion: "The refineries are reporting unaudited data to us right off the worksheets" (National Journal Reports, 1974c). Moreover, the semi-cooperative, semicompetitive structure of the industry militated against questioning the validity of each and every submission of data. Informal discussion among API staff weeded out the worst estimates. For the rest, time would smooth out deviations so that estimates were good enough—that is, better than nothing in general, but not revealing in particular.

As for checking to see whether companies cheated on the numbers they supplied, Hodges indicated it was not worth the effort: "[P]eople feel it goes up to the chairman of the board who says we have got to juggle these numbers. The numbers are not reported that way. These companies are too large and too complex to do that, and we get raw data from too many sources within a company to have it juggled" (National Journal Reports, 1974c).

Bart Holaday (director of the Office of Energy Data and Analysis when it was part of the Interior Department) vouched for the trustworthiness of API data: "I have no reason to think the Institute is not reliable" (National Journal Reports, 1974c). Holaday had checked certain of the Institute's weekly data with the Bureau of Mines' monthly data and had found little variation. Holaday had plenty of company within the administration. Said the New York *Times* (1974b): "Publicly and privately, the energy planners have said that they have found the Institute's weekly report substantially accurate. But outside the administration, Holaday's opinion was not shared by all. What critics demanded was nothing less than mandatory, timely, and auditable data. So the FEO, with some reluctance, proceeded to build its own refinery information system—a five-part Weekly Petroleum Reporting System (WPRS), which was almost an exact duplicate of the API system.

FEO forms basically used the same questions, data elements, definitions, and procedures as the API system. The difference was that the FEO forms were all-inclusive and mandatory, with persistent follow-ups of slow respondents. In addition, each FEO form had to be "certified" by a company officer. For the refineries, this meant filling in the same numbers on two sets of forms—one for the API and one for the FEO—with the added nuisance of getting an officer to sign each FEO form. Responses telephoned in to the FEO had to be confirmed separately by letter, again "certified" by a company official.

The FEO had its period of start-up problems. When Wednesdays rolled around, said Paul Chapman (1979b), who worked extensively on the WPRS, "I'd come in around 11 a.m. and leave about 8 a.m. the next day. . . . Oh, sometimes I'd go home for dinner, say around 6 to 10 p.m., and come back."

Not surprisingly, the FEO and API results usually came within about one-half a percentage point of each other. It was a classic situation of "you're damned if you do and damned if you don't": The FEO, formerly criticized for relying on API data, now was damned for spending taxpayers' money only to replicate the API system. The closeness of results, the "certification" of FEO forms, the fact that the forms were universal and mandatory, did not assuage mistrust. Finally, after one year, the WPRS was abandoned. As Al Linden (1979), formerly with the FEO, put it, "we couldn't justify sustaining 15-20 man-years of effort, and three-quarters of a million dollars, if we were coming out so identically with the API. So we went back to using the API."

Data to Allocate Quantities

More critical than the general state-of-the-shortfall assessments dependent on the WPRS and the API weekly bulletin, was obtaining data to help the FEO allocate scarce oil and gasoline throughout the country. The first albatross was the problem of who should have how much oil, how much gasoline. Charles Owens (1979), involved with price regulation in the FEO, described the hopelessness of the task: "The overall policy was 'jobs first,' to keep the economy going. . . . What happened, of course, was that in implementing that policy nobody had any idea of what fuel of what type was necessary to achieve this optimum. . . . [U]nder the circumstances, anybody that needed fuel was going to take all they could." And the FEO people were no experts. His impression, Paul Chapman (1979a) said, "was that everyone was so new to the game that no one really had a handle on what it was that we were trying to cope with."

The attempt to distribute gasoline equitably throughout the country was by far the most ambitious part of FEO's all-inclusive allocation program. After listening to countless demands from individuals and interest groups, the FEO decided to guarantee for six groups of "high-priority" gasoline consumers all the gasoline they needed. These groups included agricultural producers, emergency services, energy producers, sanitation, telecommunication, and public transportation. Other business activities were to get an amount related to that which had been consumed during the same month in 1972, the designated "base-period" year. One can imagine the information problems involved in enforcement: Are airplanes that spray crops "priority" agricultural users? What about florists? What about taxicabs? How could one determine what everyone had used in a given month of 1972?

Our story gets more tangled. The rules required that after meeting specified high-priority needs, oil companies had to allocate their remaining gasoline "equally" among all their dealers. For example, if Exxon's remaining gasoline was 77 percent of what Exxon had had in February 1972, Exxon was to give all its retail dealers 77 percent of each dealer's February 1972 supplies. Finally, in each state each oil company had to set aside 3 percent of its supplies. The governors had discretion to use these set-asides for emergencies.

Impossible as it is to list all the data problems, we can give a few illustrations. The FEO decided to try to measure for each state the gap between supply and demand for gasoline. The first big problem was to figure out where the nation's gasoline was, that is, how much supply each state had. Oil companies were to furnish these data. The companies were supposed to fill out FEO "Form 1000s," including data on how much gasoline and other products the companies were sending to each state in February 1974, the first month of the mandatory allocation program.

John A. Hill, FEO assistant administrator for Policy, Planning and Regulation, said the FEO did not receive Form 1000s from some of the oil companies until the middle of February. By then, some of the data were clearly out of date. For example, some companies deducted the 3 percent state set-asides from the supplies to each state as entered on the form; others did not. FEO officials also made halting attempts to estimate gasoline demand for each state in February. They estimated 1973 use, as reported in tax records, and multiplied it by the increase during 1973 in motor-vehicle registrations. With these very rough manipulations, the FEO came up with a shortfall figure for each state. Great variatio s showed up. Virginia and New Hampshire apparently were getting only 63 percent of their demand, while Wyoming was getting 22 percent more. These examples only hint at the supply side of problems the FEO had in trying to measure each state's gasoline gap.

Even when the policy is realistic in its expectations, it is hard enough to specify and collect the data needed to apply it. When it is impossible to implement a policy, such as a program to distribute all gasoline equitably throughout the country, enormous data problems are bound to arise. FEO officials said privately that many oil companies simply could not gear up in a hurry to distribute gasoline "equitably" (National Journal Reports, 1979d). John Sawhill told the Senate Interior and Insular Affairs Committee and the House Commerce Committee during a joint hearing on February 27, 1974, that even if every oil company could equalize supplies, those states having many gasoline stations of a particular oil company with low supplies would suffer in comparison to other states (National Journal Reports, 1979d). Other behavior also could not be assessed: Motorists who topped off their tanks, for instance; or northerners who usually went south during the winter, staying home a particular winter and causing more gasoline consumption than expected in the north, but less in the south. Thus, the difficulties with data—like the problems with enforcement, which we will describe—were symptoms of conceptual weakness and lack of foresight in the policy-making itself.

DATA AND ENFORCEMENT PROBLEMS ACCUMULATED

There were problems of data definition. Because of the congressional objective to preserve competition, for instance, which meant small refiners and independents, one had to define "small refiner." Robert Copaken (1979), who had been involved with allocation policy in the FEO, explained: "Your definition of a 'small refiner' is a subject of some variability. Some said the limit should be 50,000 [barrels], some said 100,000, some said 150,000, some said 175,000. There had to be some cutoff. In some respects this was an arbitrary number." The stronger the desire to help small refiners, the higher was the ceiling number fought for.

Then there were problems in finding out what had happened in 1972. Commonly, state and local governments were unable to come up with 1972 data on which allocations of petroleum and propane supposedly would be based. As Edmond F. Rovner of the National Governors' Conference said, "the states don't have the numbers. Petroleum allocation districts don't conform to state lines, so it's hard to tell how much oil was coming into a state a year ago or several months ago" (National Journal Reports, 1973b: 1977). David E. Piper, executive director of Oregon's

Office of Energy Conservation and Allocation, added: "We didn't have any figures for November of last year. The suppliers told us they didn't have the figures. . . . We're just allocating. We don't know if we're meeting the proper limits or not" (National Journal Reports, 1973b: 1978).

The FEO found itself having to assign some firms artificial base periods. For example, according to Copaken (1979), "if you had a gas station or a propane dealer, or whatever, who was not in business when the base period was established, but only came into business a year later, he didn't have a base period. So you had to assign him one."

The FEO was trying to measure quantities that were constantly on the move, that refused to be fixed in the way planners wanted. This difficulty affected many aspects of the petroleum industry. What was the amount of "primary" inventory (in the hands of refiners)? or "secondary" inventory? As for consumers, as Charles Owens (1979) put it, "how could you estimate what was on hand in terms of supplies, small storage amounts, even down to the amounts that might be moving around in vehicles or home heating tanks?"

Historical data and trends covering many processes were missing, because no one had needed them before the emergency. Furthermore, much of the data that did exist before the emergency was no longer relevant to the emerging situation. On the question of how much gasoline was available in various regions of the country, and how to get more to where it was needed, Lawrence Luhrs (1979a), a former FEO analyst, observed: "the problem was that the data which was needed didn't really exist, because it required very fundamental, detailed information, which no one had ever been collecting. Then you had the case of the Florida vacationers who decided to stay home . . . so the figures, the trends you normally used were suddenly not relevant."

What about the desire for accuracy? Accuracy took last priority within the FEO. Copaken (1979) explained: "We were in a crisis. We wanted something that was not clearly wrong, not clearly arbitrary." As for validation: "Validation was something that came very much after the fact, if at all." Timeliness? Normally, when collecting data, one considers tradeoffs between the importance of accuracy and timeliness. For the FEO, desparate for any data at all, both qualities took a back seat. Said Copaken, "I don't think timeliness was our main criterion. I think availability of data was our main criterion." With all the data problems generated in trying to fulfill the mandatory allocation program, Al Linden's (1979) remark may have been true: "The noise in the data may be greater than the damn shortfall itself."[3]

In the face of the enormous difficulties in gathering data to enforce the allocation regulations, the FEO staff tried to cope by seeking information through informal contacts they had developed. Lawrence Luhrs (1979a) described coping:

> We needed extremely detailed information which wasn't available. So we had to rely to a large extent on judgment and what we could get. Because there were only eight of us [moreover,] not everybody was knowledgeable in this area either, because covering the whole industry involves so many sectors that to swing somebody who doesn't know marketing, or transportation, or refining, and to operate efficiently or effectively without any learning period was just a deadly, deadly problem.

Luhrs was talking of two distinct, crippling limitations: the FEO staff's ignorance concerning the oil and gas industry, and the impossibility of obtaining data about that industry. To try to overcome both limitations, an FEO staff person would get to know someone from a company or from one of the trade associations or from a particular state government office. These acquaintances would send reports to that individual—figures, explanations, or opinions—over the phone. In this way an FEO staff person developed his or her own bailiwick of knowledge and data. Another information-gathering method used by the FEO as an organization was to hold hearings on a proposed regulation. The FEO would learn from listening to reactions to the proposal. A third, widely used strategy for coping was the option to grant "exceptions." Allowance for exceptions would be written into a regulation, and those who wanted to be excepted would apply to have their cases judged individually. Specific data would be collected for each case.

This method of using a core of already existing data providing a general picture (such as the API weekly bulletin) plus detailed data on a case-by-case basis evolved not out of inclination but out of necessity. The administrators of gasoline allocation did not seek the best system; they sought survival.

"Behavior" Problems

The implementation consequences of policies regulating quantities of oil were not limited to difficulties with specific data. FEO people were confronted constantly with unexpected disincentives and other behavioral problems. In monitoring gasoline-pricing regulations, for example, the FEO not only had to worry about designing data forms to check on implementation, but faced all manner of unexpected behavior. Retail sellers of gasoline would not obey the rules. Retailers were required to

post on each pump the current ceiling price. This posting was intended to
be easily auditable by the army of 2,000 of Internal Revenue Service field
agents, who were to monitor price regulations. The pump sticker was to be
direct and visible, creating a "compliance consciousness" among retailers.
But retailers found ways to wriggle out from under the controls. Charles
Owens's (1974) account shows how easy this was:

> Some applied the stickers to their pumps but in areas that were
> totally invisible to their motorist customers. Others would place the
> stickers on their pumps but would not write in the ceiling price, and
> still others would write in the price in a manner that could be easily
> altered. Many methods of circumventing the regulations came into
> being. The prices of car washes went up, trading stamps and self-
> service pumps were discontinued, and the prices of tires, batteries
> and accessories reflected increased *gasoline* costs. Some retailers
> were less subtle and simply ignored the ceiling price rule, charging
> whatever price the market would bear.

With 250,000 retail outlets and but 2,000 IRS agents to enforce not only
gasoline but all price controls under Phase IV of the Economic Stabilization Act, enforcement was a lost cause. Any hope for data forms to help
implement controls was nothing but dreaming, given the number of outlets
to watch over and the varieties of creative disobedience such rules naturally invited.

In addition, the FEO was forever juggling competing demands of
interest groups trying to get the most for themselves under the allocation
policy. Robert Copaken (1979) grew weary just listing them: "[T]here
were independent refiners. There was a New England caucus and other
groups of states. You had the petrochemical groups. You had the agricultural interests. Propane, for example, was used for crop-dusting. It's also
used for home heating, so you had that constituency." Then there were
individuals. Lawrence Luhrs (1979a) recalled: "We were getting thousands
of letters from people—a woman, or a man who suddenly didn't have any
gasoline to sell, and they're out of business. Could Mr. Simon do something? We had to answer these letters." The FEO received up to 4,000
letters a day.

There were lawsuits and threats of lawsuits. The Gulf Oil Corporation
went to court over the crude oil allocation program. Pan American World
Airways threatened to sue over jet fuel allocations. The State of Maryland
filed suit to try to get more gasoline, and New Jersey threatened to do the
same.

There were the states to worry about. The states were supposed to
recommend distribution schemes to wholesale purchasers, keeping in mind

the "needs" of particular end-users. What state wanted to face the politically sensitive decision of who should get how much? Edmond F. Rovner complained, "States are faced with allocating the shortfall. And the guy you say 'no' to is going to be mad" (National Journal Reports, 1973b).

How some emergency quantities of gasoline were allocated can illustrate the plight of the states in implementing federal policy. It fell to state energy officials (many of whom had been hastily designated within their state governments to cope with the energy crisis) to decide how to distribute emergency allotments of gasoline given to states by the FEO. This meant setting up an information system to receive requests from gasoline stations and local governments, and to plug in some formula for distributing the gasoline.

One day in February 1974, New York's governor, Malcolm Wilson, was promised eight million gallons above New York's expected gasoline allotment for February. As a result, New York's information system had to deal with inputs from the FEO that changed unpredictably. To add perspective, we are talking about an average of roughly one gallon per registered vehicle, allocated throughout New York. The FEO communicated by telegram what would be the quantities of gasoline. The "eight-million-gallon telegram" reached John S. Edwards, who had the thankless responsibility for allocating New York's gasoline. Edwards and his staff were in the middle of "trying to cope with 3-hour line-ups, frazzled motorists and angry retail dealers" when the telegram arrived (New York Times, 1974d).

The volume of work required to decide who deserved how much of this extra state gasoline slowed the allotment program to a snail's pace. New York had nine thousand gas stations. Government people in Albany and the several dozen "county coordinators" alike were bombarded with demands from service stations. Edwards assembled a three-man task force to sit down and decide—by debate, discussion, and a few data—which were the neediest areas, and just how needy those areas were. The task force then fed into a computer these decisions concerning who, proportionately, should get how much. The computer produced several thousand individual printouts, showing the name of each service station and the quantity to be allocated to it. This process took longer than anyone had imagined. Once the printouts were ready, the staff had to mail copies (by special delivery) to to oil company suppliers and to the service stations.

Since the letters went out not all at once but in bundles over a period of a few days, at the same moment that a staff person was complaining of delays, Martin Igel, the owner of a Manhattan service station, got his special delivery printout.

"This is my lucky day!" said Igel, whose pumps were dry.

"Present this letter to your distributor to receive your allocation," the letter told him. Mr. Igel tried; he journeyed to his Exxon distributor in Pelham, just over the New York City border in Westchester County. But the manager declined the request, saying that he had not received any notification from the state.

As if there were not enough problems in implementation, the FEO also had to explain its data results and decisions to the public. As Paul Chapman (1979a) put it, the FEO was "constantly dealing with even trying to explain to people how a barrel of oil is split up into gasoline and its component products—very basic kinds of things that ought to be known but weren't. "And naturally they didn't want to see changing numbers," said Al Linden (1979). "They wanted a firm number. We always run into that. They never want the number to change."

An incident involving one number off the Weekly Petroleum Reporting System—gasoline inventories for the week—illustrates the inflamed sensitivity that pervaded the interpretation of data. Recall the announcement in February 1974 of a small extra quantity of gasoline that would suddenly be made available to certain states; that quantity amounted to only about one gallon per automobile. It so happened that on the day of the announcement, Simon cited on the *Today* show "substantial inventories of gasoline"—a total of 219 million barrels. (There are 42 gallons in a barrel.) The emergency quantity to be allocated had amounted to less than 1 percent of total inventory. The cry arose: If there was so much inventory, why was there so little emergency relief? One FEO official tried to be helpful: "You can mislead with statistics. That new gasoline is going to be put under the control of the Governors to help solve spot shortages. And if they use it where the situation is worst it will help a helluva lot" (New York Times, 1974c).

Even the more substantive explanations for the large inventory figure gave no solace to skeptics who thought that the shortage was spurious: Much of the gasoline included in the inventory figure was unusable; it was in pipelines, in transit, in refineries, in storage, or in service station tanks "below extraction valves," whatever that tells the layperson. Besides, winter is the time when oil companies build up gasoline inventories against summer demand.

Thus, all the elusive characteristics of every quantity begged to be explained whenever a single number was printed or announced. How could people understand that "219 million barrels" was not a fixed quantity, available instantly? Add distrust, and you had a no-win situation in the attempt to communicate quantities to Congress or to the public.

The FEO's own organizational problems made implementation even more difficult. The agency was scattered all over town. At any moment some staff members were found, or lost, moving from one building to another. Much duplicative work resulted. According to the *National Journal* (1974a), "Simon . . . had several divisions of the FEO working on the same project at the same time, sometimes at cross-purposes. For a time, four FEO offices were writing petroleum allocation regulations, and not all of them always knew what the others were doing." This did nothing for employee satisfaction: "Personnel turnover has been a problem at all levels. At the beginning, the FEO had to rely on other federal agencies to detach some of their employees to work for the energy office. Some agencies hesitated to give up their good people, and some of the detailed employees quickly decided they did not like the FEO and returned to their home agencies."

What was the relationship between policy makers and data collectors inside the FEO? It goes almost without saying that the relationship had no pattern. The question did not even come up during the life span of FEO. Despite the signs on office doors, there was no clear separation of policy units from data units. Divisions names such as Office of Policy, Planning and Regulation, Office of Data Analysis and Conservation, and Office of Operations and Compliance betrayed a certain amorphous definition of function within the agency. While there were some "policy" people, and while others were involved only in data collection, many FEO officials wore both hats. As Paul Chapman (1979a) remembered, "things were happening so quickly that the people with the data were sometimes directly involved in policy. The distinction there was difficult to tell."

There was little sharing of data or information. For one thing, people were dispersed physically. Second, because often a staff person needed some data—any data—quickly, he or she would develop informal contacts from within the industry. An ambitious analyst with a "good bailiwick" had a certain advantage over colleagues, and guarded information sources.

During the existence of FEO, its organization grew more complicated and confused. Describing the atmosphere in which the FEO tried to operate, one high-level congressional aide told the *National Journal* (1974b),

> Major federal reorganizations normally have taken strong, persistent Presidential pressure combined with the backing of influential congressional leaders. But the situation that has developed in this case is almost unprecedented.
>
> Watergate has resulted in an increasingly immobilized President, and recently the Administration has spoken with many voices about what it wants on energy policy. . . . To this, you add the usual clash of strong personalities . . . the usual jealousies regarding committee

jurisdictions, and the fears of constituent groups that their comfortable arrangements will be jeopardized.

THE STRUGGLE FOR DATA TO REGULATE PRICE

The goal of price controls was to assure that no price was "excessive." What was desired was a system to track all pricing changes from crude oil producers through the refiner, the wholesaler, and on down to the retail level. Unwilling to attempt such far-reaching control, the FEO decided to concentrate on refiners, of which there were only 140 in the United States.

The strategy was to make certain that all refinery price increases reflected only justifiable cost increases. In the months preceding the FEO, the Cost of Living Council had held this responsibility. When the FEO was created, the energy unit of the Cost of Living Council moved over to the new agency. The regulations allowed a refiner to raise prices once a month to reflect increased costs of crude oil or of refined products purchased for resale. Refiners were to produce calculations to justify price increases. In addition, refineries were forbidden to hold "excessive" quantities in product inventories. The regulations thus limited both prices and quantities stored.

As one step toward implementing the complicated regulations, the Cost of Living Council issued worksheets to all U.S. refiners. These worksheets were to be the basis of the price increase requests the refiners sent to the Cost of Living Council. The thirty "major" refineries also had to submit the actual worksheets, along with their final figures. Staff people at the Cost of Living Council then went over these worksheets. By the time the FEO came into existence, a new reporting form emerged which required "certified" information on a monthly basis. This form, FEO-96, would be the core of a reporting system for refiners to monitor their price increases and to check for "excessive" increases in certain prices or costs.

To validate the data, the Internal Revenue Service was enlisted and sixty-four IRS auditors went into training. The auditors actually would "live" in the offices of major refiners for weeks at a time, examining records and observing day-to-day practices. Smaller refiners would undergo "desk audits" in Washington, to be expanded into field audits when necessary. Thus began the Refiner Audit and Review Program (RARP), which Simon unveiled on January 10, 1974. The program had great aspirations: It would monitor all price, profit, and supply records of every refinery, to assure nothing less than "fair" prices on everything sold. Simon expressed optimism that the reporting system would "verify the accuracy of refiner reports ... and is a major step toward establishing an independent reporting and information system ... at FEO" (New York Times, 1974a).

It helped that these particular regulations were photogenic, so to speak. The questions, "Are your prices just? or do they only fatten your profits?" appealed to Congress and to the public. The information system would produce such results as: "As of the end of May 1974, major refiners were retaining approximately $3.2 billion of increased crude and product costs which would have been passed on to consumers in the form of increased prices." It would not have mattered if the system had caused retention of only $1 billion, or even half that, for Congress was drawn to the image: FEO planners had designed a limited, apparently visible information system which produced numbers that made it look as though real progress was being made.

Indeed, perhaps the system's main virtue was that it served ceremonially to show critics of industry data that the FEO really was doing something about restoring credibility. This show itself overshadowed any other substantive attributes of the system—of necessity. No amount of government auditing, after all, could realistically expect to uncover "excessive prices" or "excessive profits" of integrated oil companies.

There were several reasons. Refineries are complex and variegated operations. The refinery is the place where the raw material, crude oil, is transformed into a multitude of petroleum products. They include gasoline, alcohols, propane, home heating oil, petroleum jelly, jet fuels, kerosene, asphalt, and numerous other products. A refinery might make many of a few of them. Because there are different types of "crude" oil, refineries vary in their processing methods and their mix of products.

The simplest type of refinery, called a skimming plant, boils products out of the crude oil and disposes of the remainder as heavy fuel oil. Complex refineries take the carbon and hydrogen atoms in crude oil and rearrange them into the molecules of products desired, adding other atoms to increase the yield, to improve the quality, or to produce new products. The site of the refinery and the processes it uses depend on many things, including the quantity and type of crude oil available to the refinery, the kinds of products desired to supply its particular market, and competitors' prices. Integrated refiners also control a significant portion of the downstream distribution of their refined products. Distribution and marketing companies have their own separate profit centers, costs, and facilities. The complex structure of an integrated oil company challenges efforts at regulation. To assign meaningful refinery costs, to determine an "excessive" profit or price to a given customer, or even to verify stocks on hand, is virtually impossible.

Overcharging was hard to prove, even when data on the FEO-96 form looked questionable. It took a great deal of time and effort for a validator to pursue a suspicious-looking report. During March and April of 1974, FEO and IRS agents thought they had possible evidence (from the FEO-96 and field audits) that some companies had paid excessive "transfer" prices for crude oil to their foreign corporate affiliates, and then raised prices to customers to cover the higher "costs." To check on this, auditors had to trace through long strings of transactions involving corporate affiliates. Were the affiliates middlemen? Were there third-party brokers between two affiliates? On the small chance that the FEO could pin down a violation, how would the government force the company to make price rollbacks, once it determined the amount to be rolled back or refunded, and to whom? The FEO would issue an initial notice of probable violation. The company had ten days to reply. If the company's answer seemed unsatisfactory, the FEO would "press" the company to agree to an order specifying the amount to be rolled back. If the company contested this order, the FEO would have to go to court to seek an injunction. If there was evidence of willful overcharging, the matter could go to the Justice Department for possible presentation to a grand jury for criminal indictment. The FEO could also seek civil penalties for each violation. Would each day of sales at excessive prices count as a separate violation? The point of this exhausting tale is to show how, even if the data were useful in pointing to violations, data results were not the end but rather the beginning of a convoluted path toward restitution. In fact, according to the acting director of the Division of Audit Program Operations in the Department of Energy's Office of Special Counsel (in the Economic Regulatory Administration), people are still bent over old FEO-96 forms and audit reports trying to unravel alleged violations (Dorcheus, 1980).

The refinery audit program pinned down little cheating, which took excruciatingly long to substantiate, if it could be substantiated at all. Mistrust prevailed. It assuaged no one's suspicion when Simon stated periodically that he found no evidence of conspiracy or of data manipulation by refineries.

Early in 1974, congressional investigations began. Simon tried to give the impression that he fully understood the mistrust, yet believed also that industry was not entirely responsible for it: "[L]et's face it, we've got a terrible credibility problem in this country today. We've got a mood in this country where people really don't believe the institution of government, it seems. That's why I look forward to these dialogues that are going to be held in Congress, to get the facts and figures on the table" (New York Times, 1974a). This optimism, if it existed, was misplaced.

CONGRESS'S CONFLICTING EXPECTATIONS OF THE FEO

The FEO's relations with Congress were distressing. In the first place, Congress had given the FEO a mandate of conflicting policy objectives. Now Congress was giving the FEO conflicting signals on implementation tasks. There were two sets of conflicting expectations:

(1) The majority in Congress wanted the FEO to collect detailed data on everything, but many members of Congress were unwilling to pay for it; nor did Congress understand the difficulties such collection would entail.

(2) Congress wanted the FEO's data collection to be completely clean, independent of industry; Congress did not want FEO people to have prior industry experience, but where would officials get the insight into the energy industry unless they had worked for it?

Let us look at how the FEO perceived each set of contradictory expectations.

(1) Despite all the refinery data—the WPRS, Form FEO-96, and so forth—for many in Congress, there was not nearly enough. One constant demand (and there was no way for the FEO to satisfy it) was for data on companies that were withholding oil and natural gas from production. Congressman John Dingell (D-Mich.) confronted Sawhill during a hearing in January 1974:

> I note in your statement, and I find this most troublesome, that . . .
> you indicate that under your present capabilities . . . you are really
> only able to achieve information on the marketing end, on refinery
> runs, what goes in and what comes out of the refinery. You are
> really not able to get factual, audited information as to (a) reserves,
> (b) what would be the basis of those given reserves and (c) informa-
> tion as to whether or not the maximum efficient rate of production
> is being achieved. . . . We hear continuously that reserves are being
> over- or under-estimated [House Permanent Select Committee on
> Small Business, 1974: 507].

Sawhill responded, speaking about the uncertainties surrounding reserve estimation. But Dingell persisted. Were there capped wells? Were the producers underreporting their reserves? Were producers withholding oil and gas from production? Sawhill could put an end to this dialogue only by postponement: "Let me ask Mr. Zausner, who is our Assistant Adminis-trator for Information. . . ."

Then there were questions of "policy-relevance." During a House Census subcommittee hearing, Eric Zausner had just finished enumerating

all the data the FEO had to collect to satisfy the congressional policy
mandates. Congressman Andrew Hinshaw (R-Calif.), his patience worn
thin, put the question to Zausner: "To what extent has your office
compiled details of the descriptive terms with descriptive types of information you would like to get, and fit that into a definitive statement as to
precisely how you would use each piece of information?" Zausner
answered by referring to a new "interagency task force" and a new
"advisory group" that were to "look at data needs" (House Committee on
Post Office and Civil Service, 1974: 61-62). Given the uniqueness of
energy policy, and given Congress's sweeping mandate to collect everything, a satisfactory answer to the policy-relevance question, as Hinshaw
raised it, could not be expected.

Bruce Pasternack, Zausner's aide at the FEO, spoke of their relations
with Congress:

> It was a terrible environment to work in. Congress was always
> breathing down our necks.
>
> On the one hand, it was Congress who mandated that FEO find out
> the size of the shortage, and collect data on every aspect of the
> industry. . . . On the other hand, when we'd go up for budget
> hearings, they would always ask, "Why do you need so much staff?"
> And there was no pattern: Sometimes it was the same congressmen
> asking both things, sometimes different congressmen.
>
> And they wouldn't leave us alone. We were spending all this time on
> the Hill, testifying about the same things to every little subcom-
> mittee, answering the same questions, defending ourselves. We
> couldn't do our work because there was always another meeting to
> go to [Pasternack, 1979].

(2) The other great source of frustration in Congress was members'
suspicions of anyone with industry experience. Bruce Pasternack (1979)
told us, "Here they were calling for all this data in great detail. But they
didn't want anyone at FEO to have any ties to industry."

Congressman Benjamin S. Rosenthal (D-N.Y.) requested a list of all
former oil industry personnel hired by the FEO, criticizing the "incestuous
game of musical chairs that is played so frequently by industry and
government. . . . [This game] is particularly inappropriate in the government's principal energy office at a time when government credibility is at
an all-time low and when consumers are being asked by that very office to
permit higher fuel prices" (National Journal Reports, 1974d). The FEO
disclosed that 58 of its professional employees formerly held management,
consulting, or technical positions with petroleum industry corporations or

trade associations. However, "it is not surprising," FEO wrote in reply, "to find among the 2,030 employees working for the Federal Energy Office throughout the nation 58 who have had past employment experience in the oil industry" (from the text of the FEO's reply letters; National Journal Reports, 1974d). Indeed, what was more disturbing was that so few were familiar with the industry.

AN AMBIVALENT CONGRESS, A RELUCTANT FEO[4]

For all its show of effort to procure data, the Federal Energy Office did not satisfy Congress's demand for complete, objective, validated, and accurate data. Whose fault was it? Does it make sense to apportion x amount of blame to FEO administrators and y amount to congressional policy makers? Implementing policy is a tandem process, not a unitary operation of setting a goal and then enforcing the plan that embodies it. At each point in the process, implementors must cope with new circumstances that allow (or cause) them to adjust and reformulate whatever policy ideas they are implementing. When we implement a policy, we change it. When we vary the amount or mix of resource inputs, we alter outputs also. Through implementation, the policy idea is transformed to produce different results. As we learn from the experience of implementation what objectives are feasible or preferable, we correct errors and adjust to circumstances. To the degree that these changes make a difference at all, they alter our policy ideas as well as the policy outcomes, because the idea is embodied in the action. Since both policy ideas and their implementation evolve together over time, it is inappropriate to apportion blame between implementors and policy makers.

It might seem reasonable to ask, simply, "Did difficulties stem from Congress's own failure to envision realistically how its policies were to be implemented?" After all, those who make policy must think ahead to its practical execution. But this view ignores the important point that many, perhaps most, constraints are hidden in the policy-making stage and surface only in the implementation process. Moreover, conditions of feasibility keep changing over time: Old constraints disappear or are overcome (e.g., through learning) while new ones emerge. Because of cognitive limitations and the force of external events, there is no way for policy makers to foresee all the exigencies of implementation. These demands can be discovered and dealt with only as the implementation process unfolds. As long as policy makers cannot predetermine what is feasible, implementors cannot carry out a policy unequivocally.

Does this let Congress off the hook? Or were there some things Congress should have been able to envision? If Congress could generate a well-defined policy, shouldn't Congress also have been expected to foresee execution of that policy, at least to some extent? Again, it is not so simple. The essential constituents of any policy are objectives and resources. In most policies of interest, including energy, objectives are multiple (because we want many things), conflicting (because we want different things), and vague (because that is how we can agree to proceed without having to agree on exactly what to do). We want abundance but we also want low prices, and these objectives conflict. But there is such a thing as policy that is too multiple, too conflicting, or too ambiguous. The mandate of Congress to the FEO was an apt example, with its concurrent objectives to assure oil supplies, preserve competition, achieve equitable distribution, and avoid interference with private-market mechanisms.

Policy content shapes implementation by defining the arena in which the process is to take place, the identity and role of the principal actors, the range of permissible tools for action, and by supplying resources. The theory underlying the policy provides not only the data, information, and hypotheses on which subsequent debate and action will rely, but also (and most important) a conceptualization of the policy problem.

The congressional energy policy mandate in 1974 was not blessed with a "theory" or "conceptualization" of the policy problem. There were only extremely conflicting objectives set forth by a deeply divided Congress. The contradictory expectations the FEO faced with respect to its informational duties were reflections of the basic ambivalence that divided Congress: an inclination to manage the industry as in a planned economy against an unwillingness to carry it out.

The administration and the FEO, in turn, were reluctant to go through with the implications of central management. "We're developing a planning system that could very easily develop into a full-blown managed economy," said Robert T. McWhinney, Jr., of the FEO Resource Development division. "It's frightening. Sometimes I have to sit down and ask myself if we really want to do this" (National Journal Reports, 1974a: 158).

Establishing the mandatory allocation program was a perfect example of that tension between what the universal mandate of Congress implied and the administration's reluctance to carry it through. A. Baron Holmes, executive secretary of South Carolina's Energy Management Policy Council, expressed the heart of that tension: "Formally, the Administration told us they didn't have the authority to tell the major oil companies what to produce. But privately some of those people told us they couldn't take the heat politically" (National Journal Reports, 1973b: 1979).

Former FEO officials did not place primary responsibility for failures in implementation on initial shortcomings in concept or foresight. Charles Owens expressed a commonly held view, not questioning the conceptual sense of Congress's original mandate but instead blaming failures on the difficulties in coming up with data needed for program implementation. Owens (1979) believed that if only the FEO had been able to determine the needs of all energy consumers, if only it had been possible to gauge the flexibility of the oil industry to move quantities across regions of the country, if only the FEO could have known the quantities in secondary stocks, then "that kind of information would have made my job a lot easier at the time in helping me do what I was supposed to do."

Neither did Lawrence Luhrs (1979b) hold faulty conceptualization or lack of foresight responsible: The primary failure in FEO as far as information was concerned was the lack of a core of expertise. Luhrs believed most of the blame lay with the Federal Energy Office as an implementing body. When reminded that Congress did not want FEO people who had past experience with industry, Luhrs still did not regard that as ironic.

Most former officials tended not to think in terms of who was responsible. During their days at FEO there was no time to think and, later, when they assumed other jobs, they were not inclined to look back and ruminate on the old FEO days. Some officials philosophically attributed implementation failures to "the nature of emergency itself." No one reflected on the origins of this emergency. No one reflected that the FEO faced impossible tasks given by an ambivalent Congress.

Given such contradictory policy to carry out, couldn't the FEO have seen in this an opportunity to reshape policy? Might there have been room for FEO officials to be creators as well as implementors? "This particular set of tasks may not be achievable," they could have told Congress, "but how about substituting a set of tasks that can be executed?" Those who made up the FEO were not of this disposition. They were government employees who saw their jobs as the faithful translation of congressional mandate into practice. Presumably, they are still waiting.

Chapters 5 and 6 told what happened when a history layered with contradictory policy culminated in an oil shortage of "emergency" proportions in 1973. In the atmosphere of mistrust the shortage inflamed, and given a monumentally ambivalent policy-making body to serve, data collectors faced impossible tasks.

In this case, the data referred to oil supplies above ground. Yet, the data turned out to be as elusive as if they were undiscovered resources. Skeptics who maintained that the oil companies contrived the shortage distrusted any data, above or below ground, that did not confirm their belief. All data submitted by refiners or producers were suspect. Only a comprehensive, permanent government activity—a National Energy Information System—could get the unbiased truth. The National Energy Information System, as more and more people envisioned it, would replace all industry data-collection systems.

We go underground again to understand the effort required to accomplish this replacement. Chapter 7 describes the industry's own reserve estimation system, the system that became the prime target for takeover by the government.

NOTES

1. The ambivalence was well recognized in an internal study by Jerry Yurow and Ehud Levy-Pascal of the DOE's Energy Emergency Management Information section of the Energy Information Administration. Results of the study are found in Yurow and Levy-Pascal, 1979 (see p. 5).

2. Nader was testifying before the Joint Economic Committee on January 14, 1974.

3. Linden was talking about the Iranian crisis and production cutbacks of early 1979, but the comment could pertain equally to the post-Arab-embargo period.

4. The comments on implementation in this section are based on Giandomenico Majone and Aaron Wildavsky, 1979.

REFERENCES

CHAPMAN, P. (1979a) Personal communication with Jerry Yurow, June.
——— (1979b) Personal communication with Ellen Tenenbaum, August 17.
COPAKEN, R. (1979) Personal communication with Jerry Yurow, June.
DORCHEUS, W. E. (1980) Personal communication with Ellen Tenenbaum, March 27.
House Committee on Post Office and Civil Service (1974) "Future requirements for energy data and alternatives for meeting such requirements," in Hearings before a Subcommittee on Census and Statistics. Washington, DC: Government Printing Office.
House Permanent Select Committee on Small Business (1974) "Energy data requirements of the federal government," in Hearings before a Subcommittee on Census and Statistics. Washington, DC: Government Printing Office.
LINDEN, A. (1979) Personal communication with Jerry Yurow, June.
LUHRS, L. (1979a) Personal communication with Jerry Yurow, June.
——— (1979b) Personal communication with Ellen Tenenbaum, August 15.
MAJONE, G. and A. WILDAVASKY (1979) "Implementation as evolution," in J. L. Pressman and A. Wildavsky (eds.) Implementation. Berkeley: University of California Press.
National Journal Reports (1974a) February 2.
——— (1974b) February 16.
——— (1974c) February 23.
——— (1974d) March 9.

——— (1973a) October 13.
——— (1973b) December 1.
New York Times (1974a) January 11.
——— (1974b) January 26.
——— (1974c) February 21.
——— (1974d) February 24.
OWENS, C. (1979) Personal communication with Jerry Yurow, June.
——— (1974) "History of petroleum price controls," in Department of the Treasury, Historical Working Papers on the Economic Stabilization Program, August 15, 1971, to April 30, 1974, Part II. Washington, DC: Government Printing Office.
PASTERNACK, B. (1979) Personal communication with Ellen Tenenbaum, August 29.
YUROW, J. and E. LEVY-PASCAL (1979) "Study of information use during four energy crises." Prepared for the Energy Information Administration, July 16.

7 THE API-AGA RESERVE REPORTING SYSTEM

MORE THAN JUST NUMBERS, data are artifacts which arise out of a social context to serve human purposes. In order to interpret data, we need to understand not only their technical standing but also the cultural context out of which they come—the values and beliefs of those who compile and (mis)use them, the social structure they are meant to sustain.

What is said about data is even more appropriate for estimates, which are data deliberately arrayed to serve one or more specific sets of purposes. Human volition is stamped all over estimates. Divorced from their social surroundings, estimates make no sense, as we shall see. The pleasure or pain they give is not inherent, but belongs to social processes. In the context of this report, the processes involve institutional actors in oil and gas policy whose first fifty years we have just discussed.

The mistrust of oil and gas reserve and resource estimates that pervaded the history of energy policy can be interpreted if one knows the social context of the positions of participants, the institutions in which they work, and the purposes they hope to serve. Therefore, to comprehend the part played by estimates of oil and gas reserves and resources in stimulating or stultifying energy policy requires understanding how and why estimates were made, who made them, and how the relationships among the senders and receivers of this data guaranteed disagreement.

We begin by describing the origins of the American Petroleum Institute's (API) estimates of oil reserves as well as the structure of that estimation process. Having done this, we can satisfy ourselves with a truncated discussion of how the American Gas Association (AGA) estimates gas reserves. Next we will see how these estimates were drawn into the vortex of governmental policy, making oil and gas prices dependent on the direction of the estimates. We will end with brief illustrations of the type of disputes that break out about the validity of estimates. Though it may appear that the reader is learning more than anyone needs to know about origins and evaluation of these estimates and the institutions that prepare them, everything that follows depends on knowing enough about the social structure of estimation to be a good anthropological observer of these strange tribes and their peculiar customs.

ORIGIN AND STRUCTURE OF
THE AMERICAN PETROLEUM INSTITUTE

Estimation of oil and natural gas liquids is a chancy business at best, because of the hidden and fluid characteristics of the resource. Estimation as a process is embedded in the historical conflicts between the oil industry and the government, as well as in conflicts between various interests within this sector of the economy. Estimation had several uses: for planning in the industry; as a means to stem internal conflict and deflect criticism from the government and preservationists; as a means to smooth out the vagaries of supply; as a means to stabilize the price structure of oil and natural gas; as evidence supporting the securing of loans for exploration and drilling.

How did the estimation process develop? Who estimates, and how? How can the estimation process accomplish these goals? We will deal with these and other questions by reviewing the history of the API and its Committee on Proved Reserves and Productive Capacity.

Estimation of oil and natural gas liquids is affected by the structure of the API, as well as by internal and external constraints on the oil industry as a whole. These constraints are technical, financial, legal, and political. Before we elaborate on the constraints we will look at how the structure of the API affected estimation.

The American Petroleum Institute was created as a means to continue privately what the government had done officially during and preceding the U.S. entry into World War I. The API's predecessors, the National Petroleum War Service Committee, and before that the Petroleum Advisory Committee, were created by the Wilson administration. These bodies were deemed necessary in light of the international emergency; Europe was embroiled in a world war and petroleum was a vital commodity to Allied survival (Davis, 1974: 46).

The Wilson government came under criticism by antimonopolists who cried that the administration's National Petroleum War Services Committee (NPWSC) was letting the oil industry accomplish through the "mantle of Patriotism what was impossible through greed." They charged that the oil industry was using the NPWSC to stifle competition and set up an industrywide trust that was greater than the old Standard Oil Company (Davis, 1974: 47-48).

To meet these criticisms, but not to defeat the purpose of the committee, Wilson created the United States Fuel Administration. The new American Petroleum Institute was created in 1919 as a means for the oil industry to continue privately what it had done publicly for the Wilson administration.

Once the war emergency faded and the future relations between government and industry became more uncertain, the American Petroleum Institute was created to defend the interests of the industry. The central figures in the new private Institute had also served on the public National Petroleum War Services Committee. With the war's end, mistrust loomed again as the enforcement of antitrust legislation was reintroduced. So the API had to tread rather lightly. The API developed a system of committees that would discuss industrywide problems and adopt rules of professional conduct to solve such difficulties without restraint of trade. Larger committees would appoint smaller, regional subcommittees with technical expertise. Individuals appointed to these subcommittees were employees released from activities at their parent firm for a year or more at a time. Salaries would continue, but without supervision by employers. Subcommittee members—free of company control but knowledgeable about practical problems in their localities—were supposed to give advice and judge the merits of proposals aimed at solving technical problems within the industry. A subcommittee member was never to discuss the antitrust laws or details about his parent firm's competitive position.

Through its structure, the API dealt with external relations with the government, particularly legal relations. The subcommittee form of organization kept the API on the safe side of antitrust law. The API also started sponsoring research and collecting data pertinent to the industry (not only on estimates of oil resources, but also on production capacity and refining facilities). In this way the API became an intermediary institution, supplying information, acting as a public relations firm for the industry, and lobbying.

Furthermore, the API was a mechanism to vent intraindustry conflicts. Oil is a hidden fluid—simple enough, yet so troublesome. How can a firm request investment capital if it must rely on future production of an unknown nature? Since oil is a fluid, moreover, it can flow across property lines. To get sufficient investment capital from banks and stock markets you need proof that oil exists, yet you must keep discoveries as secret as possible to avoid losing the oil to a competitor who could drill just outside your property. Samuel Pettengill (1936: 19) put it neatly: "Given two thirsty—if not greedy—boys, two straws, and one glass of lemonade, and you have the cosmos in microcosm. It becomes a sucking contest in which the one who sucks the *least* is the bigger sucker."

The factor of pressure, arising from the fluid nature of oil, is a consideration that early producers ignored. The oil field would be vented of natural gas (no economic value of any consequence existed for the gas because there was no technically feasible way to ship it) and as much oil as possible would be pumped out. Loss of the natural gas made for loss of pressure, and with the crude oil being pumped out so fast, reduced pressure caused a large percentage of crude to be left underground. This crude oil could not be pumped out by the unsophisticated methods in existence at the time. Yet, competitive tensions forced people to try to get as much oil out as they could. The resulting waste spurred attacks by preservationists and geologists. Eventually, the larger oil companies came to see their long-term interest as better served by conserving pressure and pumping out the gas and crude oil in a slower, steadier fashion.

Still, certain interests were best served by the quick draining of oil fields. Small producers and wildcatters specifically—who had little back-up collateral and were heavily in debt—would act on short-term interests. The individual wildcatter, able to gamble because of no heavy investments, acted differently from an oil company, small or large, with responsibilities to a bank or to stockholders. In addition, it mattered whether one had the means of marketing or refining the crude after it was discovered. A large refiner holding many contracts with large crude producers could afford to turn away some crude and could last out a time of slow discovery and slow production. On the other hand, the small refiner with a strategy of handling the crude that big refiners would not handle, would find that even a small shortage could erase his surplus margin. A large independent firm owning oil wells, large refineries, and pipelines—all domestic—would behave in one way with respect to price controls on imported oil. A major oil firm with very little domestic production but with much foreign oil production mostly marketed in the United States, would behave differently. The position a faction in the oil industry would take on a host of issues depended on the location and scope of ownership of the oil production process.

The differences among interests within the oil industry thus have been much more complicated than merely "majors" versus "independents." The

API, formed with the majors and largest independents as the main movers of the association, managed to ease certain conflicts chiefly between these two largest groups. Some of these biggest firms were crude-poor with excess refinery capacity; some were crude-rich and short of refinery capacity. The API managed to patch up these differences so that the most efficient use of capacities by each firm could be made.

The divisive nature of the industry, the breadth of technical problems over drilling rights, prorationing, and estimation all necessitated some type of conflict-resolution mechanism acceptable to those concerned. The only way for the API to obtain legitimacy was to make participation as broad as possible. The interactive nature of the API thus evolved to manage conflict.

The API's semisecretive way of making decisions resulted from the proprietary nature of information, on the one hand, and the concerns of the government over antitrust laws on the other hand. This meant duplication of representation at multiple levels: geographic, functional, horizontal, and vertical. If information could be shared freely by phone or interviews with subcommittee members not within your own firm, then your company would not need a member on each subcommittee to secure information. So to some extent it was economical to share information.

Interaction was somewhat slow and redundant, but it helped to stabilize a very divided industry in a relatively cheap way. No interest lost completely. Small producers did not lose because they were important in helping to find new fields or to explore fields anticipated to be too small for a large firm to concern itself with. This conservative system moved slowly and cautiously, and had to achieve a majority of majorities before real changes could be made.

The organization of the API has affected the system of estimation it has developed. To understand the history and structure of the API's Committee on Proved Reserves—the group concerned with estimating oil and natural gas liquids—is to know a good deal about how estimates are made and, therefore, why estimates turn out as they do.

THE HISTORY AND STRUCTURE OF
THE ESTIMATING COMMITTEES

The Committee of Eleven

Estimation of oil and natural gas liquids by the API has been going on since the first report of the ad hoc Committee of Eleven in 1926. That report made the first distinction between "proved reserves" and "resources" (Pew, 1945: 20). Proved reserves were defined as oil and natural gas liquids shown to exist by sinking a drilled well, and technologically feasible to recover at existing prices. Resources were defined as all oil and natural gas liquids presumed to exist: proved and unproved, economic and noneconomic.

The importance of the distinction between proved reserves and resources underscores one of the major reasons for creating the Committee of Eleven. The oil industry had been attacked by preservationists, USGS geologists, and academics, all of whom claimed that this country's oil was quickly disappearing. In addition, the industry was accused of wasting oil by using irresponsible recovery techniques and for having little regard for fluid pressure maintenance. The preservationists and geologists made no distinction between proved reserves and resources.

Such attacks gave rise to a new government agency created to deal with these perceived problems in the oil industry. The Federal Oil Conservation Board (FOCB) was created in 1924; in 1925, as a response to that government board, the API created the Committee of Eleven.

At first the Committee of Eleven was seen as a one-shot, ad hoc body that had put together figures on the industry's own view of resources. With the Committee's new distinction between long-term resources and short-term proved reserves, a brighter picture of the oil supply situation was painted. Thus, the Committee of Eleven's report achieved several goals at once—a public-relations function, a display of scientific expertise to elevate the debate over reserves and resources, and a new perspective for viewing the issues of scarcity and waste.

Such estimation, a costly and difficult enterprise, had not been deemed necessary before this period. Until then the danger to the oil industry had been chiefly Progressives who wanted reform through antitrust legislation and divestiture of large sections of oil companies; their interests focused on the *structure* rather than the *processes* of the industry.

The Institutionalization of an Estimating Committee

The oil industry suffered in the late 1920s and early 1930s from that other problem of supply—too much. Discoveries in Oklahoma and Texas, including the giant field in East Texas, glutted the market, and the price for domestic crude oil dropped to $.10 a barrel. In 1936 the API responded to this roller coaster of shortage and glut by setting up an elaborate system of estimation, with a committee on reserves and with geographic subcommittees all over the country. The aim was to achieve stability—in estimates over time, in price, and in planning for bringing in future supplies. Procedures to add new proved reserves to previous estimates were established. As API Chairman Edgar Pew (1945) stated,

> illustrative of the manner in which "extensions" add to the "proved reserves" of a field are the facts in regard to the East Texas Field. Discovered on October 3, 1930 in Rusk County, Texas, at 3,592 feet, this field constitutes the greatest oil find in United States History [up to that time]. Had there been an API Reserve Committee in that year, following the procedures which this group has observed, I have no doubt that the figure reported as of 1930 for the "proved reserves" of this field would have constituted but a very small fraction of the amount which we now know existed.

The new Committee on Proved Reserves institutionalized the oil industry's definition of conservation: Whereas to a preservationist conservation meant making oil last longer, to industry it meant keeping the price up to mete out oil in a stable fashion to conserve the industry.

At that time the industry's association had little interest in short-term maximization of profits (by stripping wells and rushing to add new reserves to existing stocks) because the API represented the largest corporations in the oil industry. Those large producer members, who were losing money at the wellhead, preferred to ensure a long-term, consistent income that would maintain the stability of a firm well into the future. Short-term goals were of benefit primarily to small producers, wildcatters, and other minor oil companies.

Small refiners, less concerned with maintaining prices at the wellhead, were much more eager to cash in on lower wellhead prices and to maximize quantities at the end of the refining process. Small refiners had no reason to look twenty or thirty years down the line; they were in business to sell as much refined product as possible.

The API did not conspire deliberately to under- or overestimate oil reserves; it merely reacted within the context perceived at the time. The API had certain needs for planning and public relations, as well as for institutionalizing industry's definition of conservation. Its members wanted to ensure that repeated instances of mistaken cries of shortages and scarcity gained no further credence either in spurring government intervention or in unnecessary increases in exploration (resulting in gluts of new oil). Nor did the API want to depress the market with vast new amounts. Its members wanted to show that a lot of oil was in reserve, but not enormous amounts at any one time. In short, the API wanted to assure people that there were enough *reserves* without suggesting that there might eventually be a problem with *resources.*

The API required the use of measurements and methods that provided concrete evidence of the existence of recoverable oil and gas. Specifically, estimation included such techniques as core and electric log samples, and production flow tests. Both require test drillings and therefore a degree of start-up capital and commitment by some firm or group of individuals willing to take the risk. Enough information on the risk has to exist before money will be put down to verify an actual oil find. When an oil find is made and the necessary drill-dependent tests can be carried out, only then are these figures added to API estimates.

An additional factor manages to delay full estimation of how much oil is in a discovered field or reservoir. The very system of estimation, as in other API committee systems, has two built-in institutional constraints: proprietary information must be safeguarded, and government antitrust laws have to be obeyed. The API subcommittees follow an interactive method, with selective sharing of information in compliance with these constraints. Delays result also because all firms with new finds are unable to have representatives on all committees at once, or on all subcommittees of the Committee on Proved Reserves. Thus, if a firm with a new find is not represented, the find can be estimated only on the basis of public information or information held on that field by other firms, if any—and sometimes there is none. Therefore, a new field could be neglected or partially reported for a number of years until data were made public or until a release-time employee of that firm was put on that committee.

The physical nature of estimation technology makes for further restraint. One really cannot know how much is in a well until it is all pumped out. As one gets more information about a well over time—as production continues and new wells are drilled in a field or old wells of a new field run dry—more exact estimates can be made. The system of estimation continuously updates information on discovered wells, reevaluating past estimates, downgrading some, and upping others. The process is cumulative and historical; as time goes on, information about how much there *was* becomes more accurate. The very basis of the definition of proved reserves is such that revisions and extensions are normal components of the concept of proved reserves.

Estimation of oil reserves is a tricky business; the only way to begin is to drill holes. If the demand for oil is not there or if the price is too low, there is no incentive to incur the risks of looking for oil. During the war years reserves were quite low, not because exploration was not going on—it was—but because demand outstripped the ability of the industry to meet it. Resources for exploration were tied up in the war. As E. W. Zimmerman (1962: 365) said,

> if a heavy demand for motor fuel was to emerge—as it quickly did—the industry faced the further problem of readjusting its crude supply position. The reproduction rate [difference between marginal additions to proved crude reserves and gross annual consumption] of crude supply during the war years had slipped under the pressure of shortages of steel and labor and the near peak producing capacity of existing oil fields. Between 1935 and 1939, for example, new discoveries averaged about 2.4 billion barrels annually and so much exceeded current production that there was a net increase in proved reserves averaging 1.3 billion barrels of crude per year. During the six-year period, 1940-1945, however, new discoveries averaged 1.9 billion barrels, but the inflated consumption demands of war resulted in a net average annual increase in known reserves of only 0.4 billion barrels. . . .
>
> The total of new oil through discoveries estimated as proved in each year is comparatively small, because development is usually not extensive during the first year. The total of new oil through extensions, on the other hand, is comparatively large. As knowledge of factors affecting production and reservoir performance becomes available, and as these factors are studied, reserves in older fields can be estimated with greater precision and revised accordingly. Therefore, the total quantity of the new proved reserves for the year includes the oil from discoveries and extensions, modified by revision of previous estimates where new data have made better information available.

The API system of estimation was institutionalized in 1936 for yet one more reason—finances. Banks had little experience and less familiarity with the oil business and with that industry's methods for estimating how much was in a proved well. Once the industry convinced the financial community that geologists and engineers could estimate with some accuracy how much oil is in the ground, after it has been discovered, banks were willing to make oil and gas loans. These loans did not become widely available until the late 1930s, after the API created its Permanent Committee on Proved Reserves, which began issuing estimates in its annual Blue Book (Zimmerman, 1962).

The next basic change took place thirty years later, in response, as usual, to conditions that suggested the desirability of a different portrayal of estimates.

What's in a Name? Committee Structure Changed When Production Declined.

In 1966 the API expanded its statistical programs to provide additional information pertaining to reserves and productive capacity of crude oil and natural gas liquids in the United States. Why? That same year, the API changed the name of its committee to include "productive capacity" as well as petroleum reserves. Why? To answer these questions, we have to go back to 1962, when the Petroleum Study Committee of the Federal Trade Commission reported to the President of the United States:

> Satisfactory information concerning petroleum reserves, productive capacity, and deliverability, and their expansibility under normal and emergency conditions is seriously lacking. . . . A great deal of fragmentary and sometimes contradictory data [are] available. . . . There is, in addition, a related inadequacy in analytic studies.[1]

The U.S. Budget Bureau responded to this criticism by organizing a Petroleum Statistics Study Group, its membership drawn from various federal agencies. In 1965 this interagency group issued a report with specific recommendations for improving petroleum data. Examples of new data the government wanted to see included:

- statistics on original oil-in-place and ultimate recovery categorized by:
  - (a) geologic age and reservoir rock
  - (b) reservoir lithology
  - (c) type of entrapment
- allocations back to year of discovery of:
  - (a) current estimates of ultimate recovery
  - (b) current estimates of original oil-in-place
- reserves and production data by subdivisions for the states of California, Louisiana, New Mexico, and Texas
- crude oil potentially available from cased-off reservoirs and from the future installations of fluid injection projects in known fields—reported as "indicated additional reserves" [General Accounting Office, 1973].

The Department of the Interior was designated the main agency to carry out the Petroleum Statistics Study Group's recommendations. That department went about its task with the aid of the industry and managed to identify areas for which the government lacked adequate statistics on petroleum. The oil industry was more than happy to participate; it had become apparent, back in the 1950s, that exploring for oil within the United States was becoming more expensive (and less productive). The problem for the industry was to get that message across. As they were, the API/AGA estimates on additions to reserves did not have the desired effect on critics (certain antimonopolist legislators, consumer advocates, and environmentalists) of the oil industry. Those critics were unwilling to accept the interpretation that it was becoming more expensive to find oil in the United States. The new statistics and presentation were an attempt by the industry to "package" the record of declining returns on oil exploration.

Several agencies voiced the suspicion that more oil did exist—in old wells, in cased-off reservoirs, and from fluid injections into known fields. The credibility of the overall estimates was challenged, also, because of suspicion that estimates over time were being "manipulated." Thus, comparisons were requested to show allocations for current estimates of ultimate recovery back to the year of discovery.

ESTIMATION AS A PRODUCT OF CONSTRAINT: API'S ESTIMATES OF PROVED RESERVES

The history of API estimation of oil and natural gas liquids suggests three conclusions: (1) Estimation serves many purposes, only one of which is to know how much oil and natural gas liquids exist. (2) The organization of the process of estimation results from the way the API and its Committee on Proved Reserves and Productive Capacity are organized. (3) Estimation is affected by technical, financial, legal, and political factors. The purposes that estimation serves include: planning; institutionalizing and operationalizing the oil industry's definition of conservation; smoothing out the vagaries of supply to protect the price structure of oil; deflecting criticisms that come from government and conservationists; providing evidence to secure loans.

How does the oil industry deal with these manifold constraints and purposes? It develops a system of information-sharing to meet the multiple objectives, and it patterns the system so as to avoid, or deflect, external criticism. The oil industry does what groups always do in a pluralistic situation; it finds a way to band together against a common foe. Here, an industry association is formed to represent its overall long-term interests to outsiders—specifically the government—and to help manage internal conflict.

Problems of mistrust exist both inside and outside the industry. We have described the many factions and interests involved in the oil industry, but we have not shown how the government's own policies have exacerbated internal conflicts in the industry.

External Constraints

External constraints on estimation result from two governmental policies: (1) Antitrust legislation has made it hard, even impossible, for oil companies to cooperate on prices and sharing data about crude oil reserves. (2) Price controls that depend on estimates of crude oil reserves, which originate with the industry, make industry-produced figures suspicious. If either set of imperatives—antitrust or price regulation—were not in effect, the figures produced by the industry would have looked more credible (and less interesting).

(1) Antitrust legislation has constricted the sharing of proprietary information on grounds that such behavior is anticompetitive. This inability to share proprietary information makes it impossible to replicate or independently evaluate different firms' methods of estimation. Antitrust laws make it illegal for the industry to speculate publicly on prices in the future, or to affect future prices by publicly discussing proprietary information. The secretive manner in which such proprietary information is handled further increases the public's suspicions of the validity of this information.

(2) Price-control legislation posed a different difficulty; fear of the market power of the largest oil companies to drive up prices is what brought controls about. However, because the government needed statistics on reserves, it had to go to industry for figures to use as a basis for setting prices. The lower the reserves were, the stronger was the case for government allowing a higher price. In the early years of price ceilings, the 1960s, reserve estimates began falling. This made it seem as if the industry were manipulating those figures to get the highest prices possible. If price controls were taken off, the industry would be more subject to the market and the prices would move accordingly. Whether or not firms had sufficient market power to affect the price of oil, at least it would no longer appear as if they were manipulating estimates to affect prices.

Double controls (price controls as well as antitrust laws) inhibit the free exchange of information. There is little exchange of information on oil reserves within the industry, between the industry and government, or, between the consuming community on one side and the government and industry on the other. (Here the consuming community includes pipeline companies and service station operators as well as the public at large.) This inhibition of information exchange exacerbates mutual mistrust; for example, the consuming community believes that government has been co-opted by the majors.

The organization of API/AGA reserve estimation is calculated to accomplish two other important tasks, entirely apart from the task of preparing estimates as good as possible given the inherent constraints: (1) to avoid charges by the government of collusive activities in restraint of trade, and (2) to protect each firm from competitors within the industry. How? By protecting the confidentiality of proprietary information; by having decentralized subcommittees of estimators spread over ten geographic areas; by giving each fairly independent firm responsibility for a number of fields within its assigned area; by assuring that subcommittee members come not only from companies but from state government agencies and universities as well. Accordingly, an individual who comes from a private company might be assigned to fields not owned by his or her company. If so, that individual may check first with his or her own company for any information on these or adjacent fields, and also looks for publicly recorded information to use in making an estimate. Most states now require some data on new discoveries, drilling, and reserve estimates. If there is no such information available, or if confidentiality rules require that the information not be released for a time, no estimate is entered. Because fields are constantly being reassigned, over a period of many years, eventually an estimator who comes from a company will have that company's field to report on, and the reserve estimate will be updated.

These proved reserve estimates are more useful for understanding long-term trends than for assessing the current equation. The method of estimation is so carefully set up to prevent sharing proprietary information that independent verification becomes nearly impossible; but, of course, the charge of collusion by various firms is thus avoided. The problem then becomes that these methods of estimation tend to increase suspicion that the figures are manipulated.

Internal Constraints

The mechanism for venting and dealing with intraindustry conflict is the API's complex committee system. Fifteen members sit on the API Committee on Proved Reserves and Productive Capacity. Each member (except the secretary) appoints one or more subcommittees for the purpose of preparing reserve estimates for his or her area of responsibility. As of December 31, 1977, there were twenty-three subcommittees with a combined total of 150 members (subcommittee chairs included). No one on the API Committee on Proved Reserves and Productive Capacity sits on any subcommittee. This committee includes representatives from the largest oil companies (Phillips, ARCO, Mobil, SUN, Shell, Texaco, AMOCO, Exxon, Cities Service Co., Marathon, Union, Chevron, and Continental), as well as one member from the Indiana Geological Survey and a staff member from the API who serves as secretary.

The API's Committee on Proved Reserves and Productive Capacity produces its estimates by having each of its members appoint teams (subcommittees) of geologists, engineers, and industry specialists for specific regions and areas of responsibility. Who actually collected data for the estimates eventually prepared by the committee? These subcommittee members (none of whom were on the API's Committee on Proved Reserves and Productive Capacity) had communications with "field men" in their respective firms. Information sought was on certain existing geological and petrological conditions, as well as on production flow tests and core samples (Allaud and Martin, 1975). In the earlier years, subcommittee members sometimes made actual site visits to fields for estimation purposes. Today telephone calls will often do. Such interviews and other research into public information are the basis for the subcommittee members' judgments about what proved reserves existed in a field. These judgments are discussed, sometimes in detail, but are never formally audited by the whole subcommittee, the overall committee, or any other body. A discussion might take place within the subcommittee over what the "ballpark" figure for a group of fields would be if a member had no access to the production flow tests or core samples (the most accurate means of testing for oil) for those fields.

The subcommittees are expected to make multiple assignments of selected fields to their members when doing so will contribute "beneficially" to the quality of reserve estimates and will promote the exchange of expert views. However, there are no published criteria concerning when such conditions exist, or which fields are selected, on what those selections are based, or what "objective" means. How, then, are these assignments made? Do they result from rules and procedures, or from bargaining between firms?

Experts appointed by the subcommittees are "release-time" employees, nominated by their respective organizations for a period of several years. The time each serves varies; some have served for only two years, others as long as ten (Allaud and Martin, 1975). During each year the members devote about two months to estimation. Sometimes they are released from their regular jobs; sometimes they perform this service simultaneously with their regular duties. The experts have experience estimating reserves and an intimate knowledge of the areas assigned to them (specifically, of the important fields in their areas). It is common for these experts to represent various segments of the producing industry which have prominent owner-ship holdings in the subcommittee's assigned area (Allaud and Martin, 1975). However, nowhere is "prominent" defined. Is it defined on the basis of land owned or leased, investment in facilities, or actual output of oil? Is it 10 percent, 5 percent, or some larger percentage of the assigned area that qualifies a firm as "prominent"? Is there a set standard based on some formula? or is there some form of bargaining and logrolling between firms, across subcommittees? Where are these decisions made? In the full committee?

Members of the API Committee on Proved Reserves and Productive Capacity, subcommittee chairs, and subcommittee members operate under the API policy on petroleum statistics:

> Statistical information is published under Institute sponsorship in the maximum degree of detail consistent with the safeguarding of proprietary information of individual companies, while mindful of the cost and utility of data involved. Data gathered by the institute are confined to current and historical data. The Institute does not participate in the publication of forecasts of future demand for crude oil, natural gas, petroleum products, or estimates of crude oil, natural gas, or natural gas liquids, recoveries that are speculative in nature or based upon conjecture regarding future physical or eco-nomic conditions [API/AGA, 1979].

The API maintains that members of the Committee on Proved Reserves and Productive Capacity, along with the subcommittees under it, adhere to the policy of keeping strictly confidential the basic data and reserve estimates used in preparing state totals. No committee or subcommittee member is authorized to release to anyone (including his or her employer) reserve information beyond that which is published in API reports on reserves or specifically approved by the API Management Committee.

How can such a policy be enforced sufficiently for the member firms to trust their proprietary information to those individuals? Obviously it is impossible; firms really do not try, because they themselves give only outdated proprietary information to their own release-time employees. (If these employees want to maintain a good reputation in the industry and if they want to return to a job, they will not leak information.) Others firms' employees cannot be trusted; therefore, assignments to them that are not among their parent firms' holdings are assumed to be hard to estimate accurately. This assumption of inaccuracy can be considered an agreement to disagree over the accuracy of some estimates.

Thus, the mechanism for venting and dealing with intraindustry conflict channels the conflict by breaking it into discrete parts. Issues are divided along geographic and functional levels, with much repetition in assigning parts of problems. (Several subcommittees will receive the same problem but deal with it differently, according to which firm's interests are most affected in particular geographic areas.) Firm A will win in the geographic region where A's investments and facili_ies dominate, for example, while firm B, with a minority of interests in the same geographic region, will lose. Howeve , in the geographic region where B predominates, A will lose. It balances out as a sort of logrolling that differs according to region rather than issue.

The same type of conflict resolution figures in the estimation process. The Committee on Proved Reserves and Productive Capacity divides its problems (i.e., How much oil and natural gas liquids are in the nation?) down to a regional level, which is then further subdivided into specific fields. If a firm has something at stake in an area that it does not wish to subject to the process, it will merely inform its representative on the subcommittee that such information is proprietary.

In one respect, this process is an agreement to disagree in the short run, with the understanding that in the long run either both firms will agree or agreement will not matter. As time goes on, estimates do become more accurate; initial estimates are almost always different from late¯ ones, as they are adjusted for additions and subtractions in the particular field. If such an agreement to disagree (and, therefore, to let inaccurate estimates stand for the time being), were not in effect, competition among the larger firms would become destructive. Each time a firm were to take a risk in a potential field, all other firms would have to assume the risks to be low and therefore worth taking. Extrapolation to the entire universe of exploratory operations would obligate each firm to duplicate every other firm's exploratory drill size. There would be no division of labor and no rationalization of risk.

THE AGA RESERVE ESTIMATION SYSTEM

It should be recognized that the American Gas Association (AGA) does not primarily represent producers. While the AGA is open for limited purposes to all in the trade, its voting membership is composed mainly of distribution and pipeline companies in the United States and Canada. Some firms do have producing affilitates, but for AGA purposes they are considered distribution or pipeline companies. The API and the Independent Producers Association represent natural gas producers more directly. Thus, as Edwin F. Hardy, Manager of Gas Supply of the AGA, testified,

> AGA's member companies are distributors and transmitters of natural gas. There is no benefit to them to create or perpetuate a notion of a gas shortage. Quite the contrary, the fact of the gas shortage is being used against these companies by competitors in selling energy—whose supply difficulties, although as great or greater in some cases, are not as well advertised. It also affects their ability to achieve the financing necessary to seek and provide increased supplies which is severely impaired, they cannot serve customers they have sought for years, and indeed are forced into the unfortunate position of curtailing deliveries and allocating sales among existing customers [House Committee on Interstate and Foreign Commerce, 1975: 438].

Among many things concerning the AGA, the Committee on Natural Gas Reserves interests us most.[2] The chair of this reserves committee is appointed by the AGA president, acting for the AGA's board of directors. A member of the Bureau of Mines (Department of Energy) is a member of the committee, and its staff executive comes from the AGA Directorate of Gas Supply and Statistics. The chair appoints all other committee members and assigns each to one of ten geographic areas of responsibility. Though a significant minority come from pipeline companies, most members are employees of gas producers. Each main committee member becomes the chair of a subcommittee for his or her geographic area. With the approval of the main committee chair, the subcommittee chair for each area selects subcommittee members from among organizations active in the area: companies, universities, consulting firms, or state commissions. Typically, these members are experienced engineers and geologists who may serve on the subcommittee for many years, covering the same fields. Their longevity is the reserve committee's claim to consistency in methodology.

Subcommittee members, though usually professionals from various segments of the natural gas industry, have access to several sources of information: internal records of the companies; conversations with operators in the field; data on discoveries, drilling, and reserves that state regulatory commissions may require; private commercial data sources, such as the Petroleum Information Corporation. These sources form the main basis for estimates. Individuals are expected to make independent judgments based on personal experience. Those who come from private companies are expected not to act as representatives of their companies.

The AGA system is based on trying to provide accurate data of interest to a variety of organizations without trespassing on domains of private data. Data are based on what can be agreed upon among more or less competitive companies rather than on what would necessarily be optimal if one set out to estimate total reserves. The AGA justification is that only a relatively small part of the total is lost, and that its absence is essential to let the operation continue.

Occasionally, moreover, even a company with a representative on an area subcommittee will deny information to its own employee. It could be that the company is involved in contract disputes, that competitive relations are involved, or that there are internal disagreements. If this were to happen too often (it is apparently rare, but the extent is unknown), the utility of AGA estimates would be at an end.

The main function of the subcommittees is to update reserve data annually, adding to or subtracting from the prior year's submission. A list of new fields is compiled from numerous sources, including weekly publications of commericial scouting reports, made in consultation with a member's company scouts. Then responsibility for covering these new fields is divided among subcommittee members, primarily on the basis of which company is active in the field. Should several companies hold a field, the most knowledgeable firm will be chosen, and then (if there is no one on the committee whose company has an interest) another firm, possibly one with holdings adjacent to the field, will be chosen. If there is no committee member from a firm that meets that criterion, anyone who seems able to handle the job gets the assignment.

After their research and field contacts, subcommittee members enter on worksheets data for particular fields. During the first year in which a field is reported, the member estimates proved reserves. This is known as the "ultimate recoverable proved gas reserves." If there has been production from the field, the amount taken out is subtracted from the amount estimated to be ultimately recoverable. Should there be new reservoirs discovered in the same field, additions can be made; such changes are called "extensions." Reserve additions may be made also when new drilling (or other new information) persuades a member to revise estimates or possibly when a new member does the estimating. Reserve subtractions occur not only when production takes place but also when evidence appears that the original estimates were too high. Thus, reserve estimation is a continuous series of additions and subtractions.

Once each member has completed his or her worksheets, the sub-committee meets to go over the results. Estimates are discussed, judged, questioned, sometimes double-checked, and finally accepted for submission to the central committee.

The critical criteria in the AGA definition of proved reserves of natural gas lie in phrases such as "reasonable certainty," "recoverable in the future," and "under existing economic and operating conditions." All these phrases make for ambiguity; reasonable individuals may differ on what is reasonable, what is certain to be recoverable, and what are existing economic and operating conditions. The AGA definition of proved reserves of natural gas follows:

> The Committee's definition of proved reserves defined the current estimated quantity of natural gas and natural gas liquids which analysis of geologic and engineering data demonstrate with reasonable certainty to be recoverable in the future from known oil and gas reservoirs under existing economic and operating conditions. Reservoirs are considered proved that have demonstrated the ability to produce by either actual production or conclusive formation test.
>
> The area of a reservoir considered proved is that portion delineated by drilling and refined by gas-oil, gas-water contacts or limited by structural deformation or lenticularity of the reservoir. In the absence of fluid contacts, the lowest known structural occurrence of hydrocarbons controls the proved limits of the reservoir. The proved area of a reservoir may also include the adjoining portions not delineated by drilling but which can be evaluated as economically productive on the basis of geological and engineering data available at the time the estimate is made. Therefore, the reserves reported by the Committee include total proved reserves which may be in either the drilled or the undrilled portions of the field or reservoir [API/AGA, 1979].

Though there might exist what some would call reserves in a physical sense, the absence of a producing platform and associated facilities might lead an estimator to omit a particular portion. Controversy has raged over whether the AGA definition of proved reserves must include a flow test. The answer appears to be "probably," for the AGA definition refers either to actual production or to some kind of geological test believed to be conclusive. When a member of an AGA subcommittee was asked what he did when his fields were controlled by other companies, he said he would often ask his own company's exploration department for information it might have on externally controlled fields. Usually, he said, they had very little information on these sections. This member went on to say that he realized the proved reserve estimates he submitted on these fields were not what he "would actually call proved reserves under AGA standards, but it sometimes is the only way you can come up with any kind of reserves" (API/AGA, 1979: 60). Evidently, more than a little judgment is involved in these matters. Knowing that additional drilling will take place and that estimation of reserves is a sequential process which may improve with additional data over time, estimators may be inclined to report only what is certain and exclude the "almost certain." But how far they should go in this direction is not (and cannot possibly be) covered by rules.

From this account it is clear that the AGA series cannot claim to be consistent in definition or results, though the same people are following much the same methodology over the years. The definition is not entirely operational and the scope is incomplete. If one says, "Compared to what?" however, there is no answer, because there is no alternative. Furthermore, the important thing in reserves reporting, from the standpoint of the AGA, is not a point estimate but trends over time. Equally, it would be very hard to justify a charge of collusive underreporting. Indeed, it is the absence of the necessity for collusion that highlights this process of estimation. Because the national estimates are made by aggregating regional estimates without subjecting them to formal auditing, a national figure appears on which gas companies can agree, even though no one is individually responsible for the figure. What the AGA series accomplishes is a total estimate on which there is general industry agreement without the need for excessive industry collaboration. If the credibility of this figure is challenged by significant users of the data, however, its value is necessarily called into question. Why would credibility be questioned? Distrust of the industry has been discussed. To this, however, we must add changes in governmental policy that make certain kinds of estimates appear more profitable to companies than other estimates.

RESERVE DATA WERE NOT ALWAYS IMPORTANT

Before the mid-1960s, reserve data were not central to national policy. In 1954 a Supreme Court decision opened a door for new regulatory policies that would eventually call for such data. The Supreme Court in Phillips Petroleum Company v. Wisconsin (1954) held that the Natural Gas Act of 1938 required the FPC to regulate field prices for natural gas sold to interstate pipelines. The Supreme Court's opinion was formal, focusing on the language of the Natural Gas Act. The only hint of a rationale for regulation came when the court said that "protection of consumers against exploitation at the hands of natural gas companies was the primary aim of the Natural Gas Act."

As long as wellhead prices were low, there was no opposition to the FPC's rationale for not regulating wellhead prices. However, opposition rose quickly when rapid expansion of interstate pipeline capacity encouraged great increases in natural gas demand and, concomitantly, higher prices. Consumer interest groups asked the FPC to reverse its practice and start controlling wellhead prices.

It took the FPC six years to issue its own decision on how it would regulate wellhead prices. During the period just after that Supreme Court case, the FPC (under the Eisenhower administration) continued to advise Congress to exempt producers (Ross, 1972: 92). Oil companies also lobbied hard to get Congress to overturn Phillips.

In 1956 the industry almost achieved its goal when Congress passed a deregulation bill that President Eisenhower favored. But the president vetoed it after charges surfaced that an oil industry lobbyist had offered a thinly disguised "campaign contribution" to Republican Senator Francis Case of South Dakota, allegedly in return for a promise of support.

During this interim period, the FPC tried to carry out Phillips by individually regulating thousands of natural gas producers. The commission became swamped with paperwork. Moreover, because the FPC did not review the initial price on a new contract, requesting only *increases* in price, *new* contract prices on gas went essentially unregulated (Mancke, 1974; 111).

In 1959 the Supreme Court ruled (Atlantic Refining Company v. Public Service Commission of New York, that the FPC wellhead price regulation procedures were inadequate. This and the enormous backlog of individual cases forced the FPC finally to respond with a decision to adopt areawide wellhead price regulation in September 1960.

A two-tiered (1965) and then a three-tiered (1968) price ceiling system evolved.[3] Under the two-tiered system, according to Ralph Spritzer,

> one ceiling was established for "old" . . . gas (defined to include gas-well gas sold under pre-1961 contracts and all oil-well gas); a second, higher ceiling was fixed for "new" gas (that is, gas-well gas sold under a contract executed after January 1, 1961). The industry . . . had developed . . . capability to engage successfully in directional drilling, that is, to search for gas reservoirs separately from oil reservoirs. Thus, it was feasible to employ a price mechanism that would provide incentives to engage in the independent search for gas without according the same "premium" price to gas

already found or to gas that might be found as a by-product of the
search for oil [Spritzer, 1972: 118].

Under the three-tiered system,

so-called "first vintage prices" fixed ceilings on both associated gas
and "old" gas sold under pre-1961 contracts; "second vintage
prices" fixed a one cent per Mcf higher ceiling on all sales of
nonassociated gas consummated between January 1, 1961 and Oc-
tobber, 1968; "third vintage prices" raised the ceiling an additional
one-half cent per Mcf on all subsequent sales of nonassociated gas
[Mancke, 1974: 112].

These policies were designed to elicit new supplies, but Mancke concluded:

Because these, and subsequent liberalized price ceilings, have been
far below the level necessary either to elicit large increases in natural
gas supply or to significantly reduce the ever-growing level of
demand, the natural gas shortage . . . worsened [Mancke, 1974:
112].

ESTIMATES WERE CRITICAL AFTER 1968

In 1968 additions to domestic reserves of natural gas started dropping
dramatically, as shown on the chart entitled "U.S. Natural Gas Reserves"
(produced by the AGA Committee on Natural Gas Reserves). Four explanations could be given for this decline. The first, a consumerist's viewpoint
to which many subscribed, stemmed from the Permian-Basin decision of
the Supreme Court (1968) which accepted the FPC's general method for
determining gas prices at the wellhead. In a general way, the price allowed
by the FPC depended on *additions to proved reserves,* divided by the *cost*
of obtaining them, together with an allowable *rate of return.* The most
significant factor in calculating cost was a *productivity* factor, calculated
for any one year as

$$\frac{\text{annual nonassociated gas reserve additions}}{\text{total successful feet drilled for natural gas wells}}$$

Thus, federal regulatory policy put the gas-producing industry in the
position of having gas prices depend to some degree on reserve estimates
supplied by that very industry. An incentive was perceived to report low
additions to reserves, which would drive down the productivity factor.

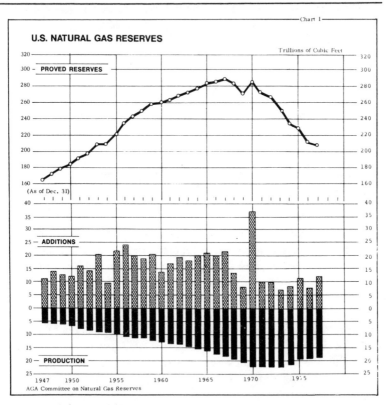

SOURCE: API/AGA (1978).

Figure 7.1: U.S. Natural Gas Reserves

Low productivity, inversely related to cost, meant higher costs, and since the price allowed the directly reflected cost, a higher cost pointed toward a higher price allowed. In short, price went up as reserve additions went down.

A second explanation for the downturn in reserve additions was the expectation of higher regulated prices in the future: It might be more profitable in the long run not to produce so much now. This was the variable marketer's explanation. As the late Senator Philip Hart (D-Mich.) put it, "it would indeed be an imprudent businessman who signed a contract today to deliver natural gas for the next 20 years at 51 cents per thousand cubic feet when there is every possibility that by waiting he may get $1, $1.50 or even more" (National Observer, 1975). Numerous charges were made between 1973 to 1977 that natural gas producers were withholding new gas supplies in anticipation of future price increases.[4]

Haskell Wald, Chief of the Federal Power Commission's Office of Economics, put substantial blame on "regulatory uncertainty":

> Regulatory uncertainty has a pernicious effect on gas supply. *Especially when the uncertainty fosters expectations of higher future prices,* as seems to be the case at present, it encourages producers to defer making new capital commitments even though a pay-out calculation may show a good profit at today's ceiling prices. A profit-maximizing producer or royalty owner will ask whether the cost of forgoing an early sale is likely to be more than offset by further appreciation of the value of his asset [Wald, 1973: 6; emphasis added].

These two explanations were interrelated. The underreporting inference suggested short-term incentives to report current reserve additions conservatively; the waiting-for-a-higher-price explanation suggested long-term incentives to do so. To provide evidence for the two explanations, many investigations would dig into a third: reserve reporting practices of producers.

This third explanation—a reflection of the constant marketer view—was that at some point withholding is a natural producer reaction to prices kept below the level at which a market would clear. At some point, it is not worth the investment to go on drilling for new gas; investing in something else may have become more profitable. To people who inferred this from opportunity costs, the AGA estimates did not look unreasonable. A number of economists and producing-industry interests held the FPC's regulation at below-market-clearing prices responsible for failure to elicit substantial new supplies—despite the FPC's intent, through the several-tiered price system, to encourage new supplies.

A final explanation for the drop in reserves was a physical one: Natural gas and oil are physically depleting resources in their last phases of availability. When a resource is being exhausted, there will naturally be fewer and fewer discoveries and reserves.

It was the first two explanations that most worried the major actors during the late 1960s and early 1970s, for consumerists and the majors dominated the stage. The extent to which an *individual* producer (let alone producers acting in collusion) had an incentive to report low (or to "underreport," as an FTC investigation we will look at in Chapter 8 charged) was unclear. For one thing, the FPC area (later, nationwide) price was based on averaging the data of thousands of producers. For another, the FPC decided that those data on additions to reserves covering only a few years were insufficiently reliable. Instead, the commission used reserve additions for the ten-year period from 1963 through 1972 to get a more balanced figure. In rendering this Solomon-like judgment, the FPC balanced out earlier reports of higher reserves with more recent reports of lower reserves and, in addition, adopted a formula for the range of costs associated with AGA reserve additions to reflect uncertainty, so that base costs were adjusted downward. Some benefits that gas producers perceived from low estimates thus were attenuated by the FPC's rate-making process.

Nevertheless, the inference was widely held (among liberal legislators and consumer groups, as detailed in Chapter 8) that producers were underreporting their reserve additions on their AGA forms to influence the FPC to raise the price allowed for new gas. Many saw the "coincidence" in the timing of Permian and the sudden reporting drop in reserve additions as signs that data manipulation was going on.

After Permian confirmed the basis for FPC calculation of wellhead gas prices, the FPC began an attempt to collect its own reserve data from producers. In the South Louisiana Area Rate Case, the FPC announced it would require producers in that area to fill out a detailed questionnaire, submitting reserve estimates on a lease-by-lease basis.[5] The companies vigorously objected to this, saying they would pursue the matter through the courts for five years if necessary. After all, the companies argued, the FPC had relied on AGA data in its original formulation, and this source was also available in Southern Louisiana.[6] As the staff of the Bureau of Competition of the FTC, who recommended that charges be brought against the AGA and a number of producers, stated in their 1975 report,

> this action by the producers and an unprecedented decline in AGA proved non-associated reserve additions in 1968 and 1969 caused serious concern among many participants in the proceeding because of the suspicions that reserve estimates were manipulated for the purposes of obtaining a higher maximum well-head rate [House Committee on Interstate and Foreign Commerce, 1975: 42].

Suppose, however, that government had made the estimates itself. Would that have established their validity? Based on our readings, which included a vignette we share below, we doubt it.

WHAT IF THE GOVERNMENT HAD COLLECTED RESERVES DATA?

It was June 1977, and the issue was natural gas price deregulation. The Senate Energy and Natural Resources Committee was holding hearings on the natural gas pricing proposals in President Carter's energy program. One policy question was to what extent an increase from $1.42 (the FPC's most recent ceiling) to $1.75 would elicit new supplies of gas. (The FPC's pricing decisions were still influenced by the additions-to-reserves component of the formula.)

As we shall see in the next chapter, Senator Howard Metzenbaum (D-Ohio) was asking FEA administrators the same question legislators had been asking for several years:

> I hope the administration will explain to us what they used as their documentation for the question of the entire matter of determining what the reserves are. Are they basing their calculations only on the figures as supplied by the oil and gas industry, or do they have some separate information which has not yet been made available to the American people so we might share those figures with them? We have heard time and again, the only information available comes from the industry, although it is my understanding both the FPC and the FEA do have the authority to make their own independent conclusions [Senate Energy and Natural Resources Committee, 1977: 43-44].

Senator Henry Jackson (D-Wash.) persisted:

> This thing has been discussed continually since since 1954. . . . How can I do my job here in a conscientious way, a judicial way, asking for the facts and trying to make a decision when we don't have any data? [Senate Energy and Natural Resources Committee, 1977: 56].

John O'Leary, FEA administrator, could reply only:

> [W]e are chipping away at the edge of this problem. We are . . . in the course of a very serious discussion . . . concerning the replacement of the current industry system of collecting both oil and gas data in [their] entirety with a Government system. . . . This is a costly business, and it is going to cost a lot of money. Unfortunately, although this has been recognized for the last 5 or 6 years as one of the linch-pin problems associated with the whole business now before the Congress in developing a national energy plan, the fact is we have not done the fundamental work that permits us to definitely answer Senator Metzenbaum's questions [Senate Energy and Natural Resources Committee, 1977: 55].

Presumably "fundamental work" meant governmental, rather than private, estimation. Suppose the government had been collecting and thoroughly validating oil and gas reserves data all those years; and suppose the government's estimates still showed the same pattern of decline in additions to gas reserves that the AGA data showed. How could the downturn be explained?

Advocates of low prices ("consumerists") would still suspect producers of underreporting. At the level of the single firm, underreporting reserves is a charge extremely hard to verify. To substantiate the existence of sizable hidden reserves would require examination of much geological data, and considerable expertise to evaluate the data. And it would be virtually impossible for even the best data-collection system to substantiate a charge of *collusive* underreporting on the part of many firms. The most sophisticated government data-collection system would not reduce low-pricers' suspicions, especially when, under the FPC pricing formula, incentives for a company to report conservatively were apparent. The related explanation for the decline in reserve additions—that producers were holding out for anticipated higher future prices—would be equally hard to prove. Suspicions would not be alleviated under even the most thorough government system, because always there might be hidden supplies, especially if supplies were presumed to be unknown.

What about the third explanation, advanced by high pricers and a number of economists, that at some point, given a too-low price, output was bound to fall off? To support this explanation would have required a great deal of additional data—and in a more detailed form than the FPC was using in its formula to answer the questions, "Was the price really below a market-clearing price? What would a market-clearing price have been? Was it reasonable to have expected the percentage drop in reserve additions that was reported?" To answer the questions that are central to the supply-price type of analysis, voluminous input-cost data would have been needed.

The one conclusive method would have been to increase the price and see what happened—exactly what low-pricers were bent on preventing. If the government had been in charge of reserves data collection, and if the results had shown declines similar to the AGA's results, low-pricers would have showed that the government system was inadequate because such economic data as cost of exploration, drilling, development, and extraction were not included.

Knowing additions to proved reserves would not have been enough. Consumerists might have accepted such figures as credible, but still would have rejected the pricing policy implications on grounds that the data collection failed to capture cost factors. In search of a more perfect regulation, they would have begun to create a tar baby—reserve data are not enough; cost data are now needed. If the new data still seemed to support a higher price, they would have asked, "Were those cost figures reasonable?" New layers of data validation and a need for more expertise would mushroom; regulators would crumble under the weight of their own requirements.

Now suppose that the government had collected the reserve data and the numbers did *not* decline. Low-pricers probably would not have protested. Of course, if the existing AGA system had produced higher reserve estimates, they probably would not have protested either.

Had the government collected the reserves data, then, what would have been improved? There would be no guarantee that the major congressional users would have given more credence to the results. On the contrary, Congress might have called for yet more data collection and validation, at great expense. As to the use of government reserves data to inform supply-price analyses, reserves data alone would not have been enough. Volumes of additional, detailed cost data would have been demanded, with no possibility of testing the crucial hypotheses of the responsiveness of supply to cost. The weight of collecting and validating enough data to achieve a more perfect regulation might have crushed respondents and regulators alike, in addition to overwhelming consumerists themselves.

This is all supposition. How well is it grounded? The reader will have an opportunity to judge based on reports of actual experience. However horrendous disputes over data may have been before the great oil price increases of 1975, they were much worse afterward.

NOTES

1. The types of estimates the government wanted had to meet three criteria originally: (1) satisfactory information concerning petroleum reserves, productive capacity, deliverability, and the reserves' expansibility under normal and emergency conditions; (2) comprehensive and consistent data; and (3) adequate presentation to facilitate analytic studies. Instead, the government received additional data on productive capacity, defined as showing decreasing rate of return in exploration. (See General Accounting Office, 1973: 18.)

2. The following description is based largely on the FTC Bureau of Competition investigation (see House Committee on Interstate and Foreign Commerce, 1975: 29-33) and on the API/AGA (1979) Blue Book.

3. The two-tiered system was solidified upon the FPC's Permian Basis decision of 1965: Area Rate Proceedings, AR 61-1, 34 FPC 159 (1965). The three-tiered system developed out of the Southern Louisiana Area Rate Proceedings of 1968: AR 61-2, Op. no. 546, 40 FPC 530 (1968).

4. The second explanation, expectation of higher prices, was advanced to explain two occurrences: (1) The conservative reporting of new reserves. Legislation was frequently introduced that would allow a higher price for newly discovered gas and a

lower price for "old" gas. In anticipation that one day such legislation might pass, a company could plausibly withhold knowledge of "new" gas until the legislation passed. (2) The slackening-off of production. There was much suspicion that companies were not producing as much as they could have—that they were holding gas "behind the pipe." The charge was that the producers were holding back until they could get a higher price. Indeed, this was the subject of a hearing whose investigation was still continuing as of 1980 (see House Committee on Interstate and Foreign Commerce, 1977).

    5. 34 Fed. Reg. at 5760.

    6. Related in the FTC Bureau of Competition's investigation recommending that complaint be issued against the AGA and several natural gas companies (March 25, 1975). The FTC report is reproduced in House Committee on Interstate and Foreign Commerce (1975: 15-120).

REFERENCES

ALLAUD, L. and M. MARTIN (1975) Schlumberger, The History of a Technique. New York: John Wiley.

American Petroleum Institute/American Gas Association [API/AGA] (1979) of Crude Oil, Natural Gas Liquids, and Natural Gas in the United States and Canada as of December 31, 1978. Volume 33. Washington, DC: Author. (commonly referred to as the Blue Book)

——— (1978) Reserves of Crude Oil, Natural Gas Liquids, and Natural Gas in the United States and Canada as of December 31, 1977. Washington, DC: Author.

ATLANTIC REFINING COMPANY v. PUBLIC SERVICE COMMISSION OF NEW YORK (1959) 360 U.S. 378

DAVIS, D. H. (1974) Energy Politics. New York: St. Martin's.

FRANKEL, P. H. (1969) Essentials of Petroleum. New York: Augustus M. Keeley.

General Accounting Office (1973)

House Committee on Interstate and Foreign Commerce, Subcommittee on Oversight and Investigations (1977) Behind-the-Pipe Natural Gas Reserves. Washington, DC: Government Printing Office.

——— (1975) Natural Gas Supplies, Volume 1, Part 1. Washington, DC: Government Printing Office.

MANCKE, R. (1974) The Failure of U.S. Energy Policy. New York: Columbia University Press.

National Observer (1975) March 29.

PETTENGILL, S. B. (1936) Hot Oil: The Problem of Petroleum. New York:

PEW, J. E. (1945) Testimony in Hearings of the Senate Special Committee to Investigate Petroleum Resources. Washington, DC: Government Printing Office.

PHILLIPS PETROLEUM COMPANY v. WISCONSIN (1954) 347 U.S. 672

ROSS, C. R. (1972) "A commissioner's viewpoint," in K. C. Brown (ed.) Regulation of the Natural Gas Producing Industry. Washington, DC: Resources for the Future.

Senate Energy and Natural Resources Committee (1977) Natural Gas Pricing Proposals of President Carter's Energy Program: Part D of S. 1469. Washington, DC: Government Printing Office.

SPRITZER, R S. (1972) "Changing elements in the natural gas picture," in K. C. Brown (ed.) Regulation of the Natural Gas Producing Industry. Washington, DC: Resources for the Future.

WALD, H. (1973) Summary remarks presented at the AMR Seminar on Oil and the Gas Shortage, New York, January 31.

ZIMMERMANN, E. W. (1962) History of Petroleum.

THE CREDIBILITY OF NATURAL GAS RESERVE ESTIMATES
Is It What You Say or How You Say It?

POLICIES ON ENERGY, objects of derision abroad, are also subjects of satire at home. Whatever else may be said about energy policies, all admit that no participant trusts another. Not only do the opposing sides disagree on solutions, they cannot come together even on the configurations of the problem. Pose any question—How much oil and gas is underground? How much can be recovered? How long will it last? How much does it (and should it) cost? How much is in reserve, available for production?—and the participants will differ over the answer. Unable to agree on what they are talking about, it is no wonder they cannot agree on what to do. Much insight into this mutual incomprehension may be achieved by a bottoms-up view of disagreements over data.

In the mid-1970s all-out controversy over oil and gas reserve data broke out. Federal agencies, Congress, producing companies, trade associations, and consumer groups hurled charges of conspiracies to "cook" data, to use it inappropriately, or to misuse it deliberately. Several separate investigations were conducted to check the validity of some of the charges or to get credible estimates. Yet, all went away as they had come: dissatisfied.

In what ways did the collection, preparation, or presentation of oil and gas estimates make a difference in how that material was received by people who would use the data? Did attitudes toward data depend more on how reports were prepared or on the results themselves?

Can anyone, in government or out, certify that estimates of gas reserves are accurate or acceptable? That depends on what is at issue: the data, or the decisions data are used to justify. Is the difficulty with the message or the messenger? Does the fact that the industry prepares the estimates make them impure? As always, the messenger may be blamed for the bad news. Suppose, then, that government replaces industry in making estimates. It may easily be imagined—in fact, it has happened—that others arise to say that government officials (because they also have policy preferences that may be supported by higher or lower estimates) cannot be trusted and, therefore, are also suspect. The question of who will guard the guardians is as relevant to oil or gas estimates as it is to anything else. Conflict or impropriety exists not only in the world but also in the eye of the beholder. If anyone, no matter how knowledgeable, with a conceivable interest in the matter is excluded from making estimates of reserves, then no one who may be deemed trustworthy remains.

We are left with rival hypotheses, the first of which takes these declarations at face value and says that as soon as there is an intellectually respectable and evidently unbiased preparation of estimates, hosannas will fill the sky and debate will move on to matters other than who is manipulating the figures. This hypothesis assumes that the difficulty lies in some combination of inadequate method and various biases. The alternative hypothesis is that disagreement over estimates is not the cause but the consequence of disagreement and mistrust among participants making policy on oil and gas. The assumption here is that no opposing estimates, set against arguments used to bolster one or another set of policy preferences, would be accepted. Just as Clausewitz spoke of diplomacy as the conduct of war by other means, so may arguments over estimates be a convenient cover for differences over policy.

We shall try to test these hypotheses by looking at the historical record to see whether alternative arguments or methods have made a difference; whether participants inconvenienced by certain results of estimates nevertheless express admiration for the methods and, with reluctance, acquiesce in the policy results; or whether such individuals damn the entire enterprise. Are there other modes of presentation, yet to be tried, that might put both hypotheses to a stronger test? Does the reserve estimation *process* have to be legitimized (made credible to its clients) so that whatever outcomes are produced, however inconvenient, will be accepted? or must there be agreement on *outcomes*, so that the processes that produce them are considered credible?

Our rival hypotheses are:

(1) A user's perception of reserves data depends primarily on the technical and process aspects—how the data are estimated, collected, and validated.
(2) A user's perception depends primarily on the results themselves and which policy position the users of the data support.

THE CONTEXT OF PERCEPTION

A user of data may perceive any number of biases as undermining the credence he or she gives the estimates. Whether these biases actually exist is one matter; whether the user merely assumes (that is, claims to perceive) them is another. If the user has a strong policy preference, for example—*and* if the policy outcome depends on a low or high estimate, *and* if the user thinks that the estimate is too low or too high given the particular interest or preference—that user may claim biases that are nonexistent, or may exaggerate the degree of a particular bias. Therefore, it is important to identify and separate the actual difficulties in a survey of those users believe to exist. Our focus is on users' perceptions.

The techniques and processes behind a set of results are open to a multitude of perceptual criticisms. The user of data could consider troublesome the *criterion* of what is to be estimated. Is a single criterion indicated, or does the respondent have some discretion in interpreting the data? The user of the data probably wants to know that a single criterion was followed. But that is not enough. In the example of proved reserves, even within the standard API/AGA definition, there was much room for a user to make a broad or narrow individual interpretation. Since at one time industry stood to gain by low estimates, criticis of the AGA system held that the producer probably gave the definition a narrow interpretation and, thus, a downward bias to the result.

A user could perceive the *method of estimation* to be problematic. On the one hand, if all estimators used a single method, consistency would be achieved, but with the possible danger of built-in, systematic bias. For example, if everyone used a single approach, a user of data could charge not only that this method resulted in a downward bias but also that there was no way to validate such bias in the absence of estimates. If the survey did not call for using a single method of estimation—and no survey we have looked at did require this—one would have to live with inconsistencies, some tending toward bias in one direction, some in another. The net effect would be hard to find. However, a user might claim the inconsistency to be a discrepancy and therefore give the results less credence.

The user could question many characteristics of the *sampling plan.* Is the list of potential respondents in the universe really complete? If the universe used actually lacks some parties, or is thought to, noncoverage bias might be charged. Moreover, selection bias (the sample picked did not truly represent the population) is a common criticism.

The user might find the level of *aggregation* in the data collection of little use. Many who want to keep a closer eye on the producers think field-by-field data are not detailed enough. Here, irrelevance is perceived to be bias, that is, reporting data in a form that fails to fit the user's purpose.

One may believe the *collection process* introduces or perpetuates biases. The AGA system, for example, featured industry employees collecting data from their own companies. Any incentive a respondent had to report low would be reinforced by this collection method, and the user could suspect the results because of this seemingly self-serving characteristic of the collection process.

The user might perceive a number of *validation* problems: problems in auditing or double-checking results and the processes that contributed to those results. One criticism of the AGA reporting system was that there appeared to be hardly any validation. Worse, the collection and validation processes seemed difficult to decipher. While this quality did not produce systematic bias, critics of AGA data did believe it allowed already existing biases to remain.

Whether data are submitted *under oath* is another defect the user might bring up. Supposedly, there is stronger presumption of accuracy if a respondent supplies data under oath. That AGA material did not have to be so submitted came to be seen as a defect. It could also be argued, of course, that data submitted under duress are equally deficient.

Users might perceive problems in the way the data are *presented*. If they are displayed in a more summary form than suggested by the detail required on the survey instrument, users might suspect something is being hidden or, alternatively, find aggregated results not very useful to them.

Whether *point* or *spread estimates* are presented, someone is sure to be dissatisfied. If the results are presented as a single figure (point estimate), the user might suspect overconfidence and say the presenters were covering up for weaknesses. After all, how could the presenters claim to arrive at such a specific number when we users know there must be a degree of judgment error involved? If the results are presented as probabilities or as ranges or with other qualifications (spread estimate), some usefulness may be lost. Some users are always bound to think either that results are too pinpointed or too laden with qualifications.

Our first hypothesis suggests that if technical and process-related biases are corrected or accounted for, users will accept the results, whatever their policy implications.

The alternative hypothesis says that a user who does not want to believe the results—who does not trust the source of the numbers—can find many legitimate opportunities for suspicion. Such a user can point to biases and shortcomings in sampling, in validation, or in any of the other technical aspects of a data-collection effort. Thus, to test our two hypotheses involves some fine-combing through statements users made when they discredited one effort or another.

Even if the data are technically flawless—sampled without bias, with clear and thorough collection and validation processes, perfectly balanced in presentation, and so on—the user still may reject the results because of characteristics perceived in the data *suppliers*. A user of such data could discredit the results solely because the respondents are producers who may have an interest in reporting proved reserves conservatively. It is not what you say but who you are that matters.

Finally, even if the user can find no fault with the technical aspects (the process, the presentation, or the source of the data), it is possible that a user with a strong policy preference will reject the result outright, especially if the policy outcome depended on whether the results were high or low and whether they were damaging to that user's policy stand.

In testing hypotheses about what influences perception of reserve estimates, the issue's context is important. Users' perceptions of gas reserves data were tied to their policy preferences on the issue of price. Federal regulation had put the gas-producing industry in the position of having its ceiling price depend, to some degree, on reserve estimates supplied by the gas industry itself. After 1968, reserve estimates became entangled with the policy issues of wellhead price: Should the price be higher or lower? Should it be regulated or deregulated?

Division over deregulation was clearly drawn between liberal Democrats (on the side of controls) and conservative Republicans and oil-state Democrats (on the side of deregulation). The price issue was basically dichotomized between proponents of low-pricers and high-pricers. Low-pricers, equivalent to the "consumerists" of our earlier discussion, included legislators as well as the FTC Bureau of Competition, staff for the majority on the Oversight and Investigations Subcommittee, and consumer groups. High-pricers included other legislators from gas-producing states; minority counsel to the Oversight and Investigations Subcommittee; the AGA and the API; oil and gas producers; and a number of outside economists. The FPC, for the most part, was of this persuasion. Some FPC commissioners were appointees of a Republican administration sympathetic to industry preferences. The issue of price regulation, then, was polarized; legislators' policy preferences were generally well established and well known.

Furthermore, it was clear how reserves data influence the FPC's price ceilings. It seemed clear enough to participants in this issue, at least, that the lower were the estimated additions to reserves, the higher was the price implied. Given this context, participants on both sides knew what the data results would mean to them. Low-pricers would find support in seeing high reserves estimates. Alerted by the fall in these estimates, low-pricers turned to suspecting the producers of deliberate underreporting and of withholding production. If this could be shown, low-pricers would have a strong case for maintaining regulation of the prices producers could charge. High-pricers did not see their own interests endangered by low reserves estimates, which signaled that insufficient exploration had resulted from a low regulated price. Low estimates argued, instead, for raising the price to induce more exploration and more supply.

Our question, then, is: Did it matter to participants how the results had been reached? or were participants interested only in the results themselves? Is it how you say it that matters? or is it what you say?

As in *War and Peace,* to keep things straight we present the actors and their surveys. A glance at the scorecard (Table 8.1) shows the House Commerce Committee Democrats and the Federal Trade Commission's Bureau of Competition already pitted against the Federal Power Commission and the AGA.

THE FTC INVESTIGATION: ARGUMENTS OVER ESTIMATES WERE A COVER FOR POLICY PREFERENCES

It was June 1975. If mistrust was the message, the medium was the running dispute over whether those who took part in the AGA reserve estimation system were deliberately underestimating the extent of reserves of natural gas after 1968 in order to get a higher price from the Federal Power Commission. The forum was a series of hearings before the Subcommittee on Oversight and Investigations of the House Committee on Interstate and Foreign Commerce, conducted by John E. Moss (D-Calif.). The emotional loading was one of suspicion and anger.

Congressman Moss's opening remarks reveal how critical he thought reserve figures were to policy:

> The Nation faces a number of difficult questions relating to natural gas policy. Should the wellhead price of natural gas be allowed to rise to increase incentives to produce greater quantities of gas? Should gas prices be deregulated altogether or should the Federal Power Commission act to insure adequate production?
>
> Without exception, those questions can be intelligently answered only if we know how much domestic natural gas is available for

TABLE 8.1   You Can't Tell the Players Without a Scorecard

1. *The American Gas Association*—Committee on Proved Reserves.
    Survey: Annual survey of U.S. natural gas reserves is performed by the
                    Committee on Proved Reserves. AGA reserve data were questioned
                    for possible underreporting.
2. *Federal Trade Commission*—Bureau of Competition
    Investigated underreporting of reserves by natural gas producers to the AGA
    reporting system. Concluded there were strong incentives to underreport.
3. *Federal Trade Commission*—Bureau of Economics
    Refuted the conclusions of its colleagues in the FTC Bureau of Competition.
4. *House Committee on Interstate and Foreign Commerce*
    Held hearings on the FTC Bureau of Competition investigation. Majority
    numbers concurred with belief that underreporting was occurring. Accused
    FPC of passively accepting AGA data.
5. *Federal Power Commission*—Bureau of Natural Gas
    Survey: *National Gas Reserve Study*, a one-time survey conducted by the
                    Bureau of Natural Gas, to check AGA data. Found no evidence
                    of underreporting.
    Survey: *FPC Form 15*, an annual survey of pipelines conducted by the
                    Bureau of Natural Gas. One item asks for information about
                    reserves owned by pipelines. This item was hauled into the fray,
                    even though repondents were not producers but pipelines.
6. *Energy Research, Inc.*
    Consulting firm that evaluated the FPC's National Gas Reserve Survey and
    concluded it was a reputable effort.
7. *Federal Power Commission*—The Commission
    Issued Opinion 770 in 1976, raising significantly the ceiling price for natural
    gas at the wellhead. One element in the pricing formula is "additions to
    proved reserves." The lower this is, the higher the price. Reserve data used in
    the formula were AGA data.
    Survey: *FPC Form 40 and FPC Form 64*, a proposed pair of FPC forms
                    to collect annual reserve data from producers. These forms were
                    used on a pilot basis in 1975 and 1976. When these numbers were
                    plugged into the formula, they pointed to a higher price.
8. *American Public Gas Association*
    Protested FPC's Opinion 770 for its significant price increase. Objected to use
    of AGA data in its formula.

present and future consumption. Current regulatory policy, moreover, directly relates to assumptions as to the magnitude of U.S.
natural gas reserves. The price, for example, of new natural gas, as
set by the Federal Power Commission, is determined by a formula
based on current reserves estimates. The smaller new gas reserves,
meanwhile, have been cited by deregulation advocates who cite the
industry's declining reserve estimates as proof of the failure of
Federal natural gas price regulation [House Committee on Interstate
and Foreign Commerce, 1975b: 1].

Low numbers militated against Moss's policy preferences. Low-pricers thus had a strong predisposition to discredit any numbers that looked low—and especially so if the source was the producers themselves. Moss continued:

> Do the American people realize that the information on natural gas reserves relied upon by the Federal Power Commission and other Government agencies is furnished primarily by industry? Do the American people appreciate that reserve information relied upon by those who would deregulate the price of natural gas has been provided not by Government, or some other impartial source, but by those who would benefit from the resulting threefold increase in natural gas prices? Very serious questions would be raised if this Congress deregulated natural gas on the basis of the industry's own self-serving data regarding diminishing gas reserves [House Committee on Interstate and Foreign Commerce, 1975b: 2].

The major, unarticulated premise was that it was possible to have such accurate knowledge of the extent of estimates that it would make a significant difference to national energy policy. What seemed so obvious to everyone that it was never discussed, however, is not necessarily self-evident in retrospect. What is clear now is that, instead of coping with the threat of interruption of supply and the manifold increase in oil prices, the United States engaged in bitter internecine warfare over who was responsible for (or had tried to profit from) circumstances so unfortunate for the welfare and prosperity of the United States. Among the major weapons were several divergent estimates of oil and gas reserves.

The immediate subject of the hearing was a report by the FTC's Bureau of Competition charging that the AGA's reserve reporting system bred deliberate underreporting of reserves (House Committee on Interstate and Foreign Commerce, 1975a). The Bureau of Competition had concluded its report by recommending to the Federal Trade Commission that a complaint be issued charging that gas companies violated Section 5 of the FTC Act "by concertedly maintaining a deficient natural gas reserve reporting program which influences the price at which producers sell natural gas to interstate pipeline companies (House Committee on Interstate and Foreign Commerce, 1975a). The evidence was alleged underreporting of proved reserves in the offshore Louisiana region (and underestimates compared to other studies) leading to "the creation of a false picture of reserves . . . and an increase in the pressure exerted upon the FPC to raise wellhead prices to stimulate additional exploration in the area" (House Committee on Interstate and Foreign Commerce, 1975a: 57).[1]

Now there is a considerable difference between a technically deficient system, which may or may not be better than any known alternative, and a concerted effort among producers to underreport to raise their profits. The Bureau of Competition tried but found it hard to choose conclusively; it did claim that susceptibility to manipulation is additional evidence of deficiency in data estimation. As the Bureau of Competition said,

> certain evidence illustrates both the effect of a deficient system and the effect of conscious manipulation. All of the evidence presented does, however, show the effects of a deficient system. Because the evidence of possible manipulation is circumstantial and inconclusive, an agonizing debate was had over whether evidence tending to show manipulation should be presented at all. It was included primarily because some of the evidence tending to show manipulation is also evidence of a tendency to show a deficient system. . . . One of the reasons the AGA system is deficient is that it could so easily be manipulated for the gain of producers. Whether or not the evidence we have gathered so far is indicative of conscious manipulation is a close question. The inescapable fact, however, is that the system is seriously inadequate and should not be allowed to continue [House Committee on Interstate and Foreign Commerce, 1975a: 70].

According to Kenneth C. Anderson, assistant director of the Bureau of Competition, "we cannot and do not say that these 11 companies sat down and deliberately set about to manipulate the AGA reporting system so as to produce a contrived shortage of natural gas" (House Committee on Interstate and Foreign Commerce, 1975a: 370). But in data that they were able to procure from four of the eleven companies, Bureau of Competition staff believed that the estimates were deficient and could have been manipulated.

"Deficient" for what purpose? Estimates were claimed to be deficient for technical reasons; they could not be validated, for one thing. For the FTC Bureau of Competition, however, the main concern was with the source of data. The collection effort was deficient because it was controlled by the producing companies that had an incentive to underreport in order to influence FPC regulatory practices. The source formed an improper basis for the legitimate FPC rate-making. As Congressman Moss put it,

> if these companies submitted inaccurate and misleading reserve data to the Federal Power Commission . . . this would amount to a flagrant abuse of the regulatory process to achieve an end adverse to

consumer interest [House Committee on Interstate and Foreign Commerce, 1975a: 2].

The AGA system was now considered deficient because the interests of those supplying the data undermined legitimate regulatory intent. Thus, the Federal Power Commission was pulled in. Congressman Andrew Maguire (D-N.J.) charged FPC Chairman John N. Nassikas with "simply taking the information that the industry gives you and then, in effect . . . acting as a tool for the industry." Maguire's indignation was directed to Nassikas's support for gas deregulation, for one of the arguments made on behalf of deregulation was that it would increase supplies allegedly reduced by regulation. Let us put it another way: Short of looking over an estimator's shoulder, knowing a person's position on regulation enabled one to determine what sort of estimates that person would accept.

The question of estimation had become entangled with the quest for energy policy. Many in Congress thought that low estimates were used by industry as a bid for deregulation (i.e., that industry claimed artificially low prices had prevented additional exploration). Today, low estimates are used to argue that the higher prices expected to result from deregulation are not likely to elicit significant new supplies because there is very little gas to be found.

Throughout the story of the FTC investigation runs an ironic undertone: The government itself had made the AGA estimates important. As the FTC Bureau of Competition put it in its proposed complaint, "at the outset it is important to recognize that until wellhead price regulation began in earnest, the accuracy of AGA reserve data was not a matter of critical importance (House Committee on Interstate and Foreign Commerce, 1975a: 42).

The AGA reporting system had not been set up in 1946 to serve government policy implementation; rather, it was initiated "to get an idea of the supply outlook for . . . end-use customers—utilities, homeowners, etc."[2] Later the FPC, under pressure from consumer interests and their congressional representatives, reluctantly began to regulate wellhead prices. Under evolving formulas, the FPC came to depend on the AGA system in government pricing decisions. Now the FPC was being pressed by consumer interests and their congressional backers to abandon the AGA system and establish a more believable one—a system that did not feed the interests of the producers. Having made gas association data important, Congress proceeded to challenge the accuracy of that material for purposes that no one had in mind when the AGA system first was initiated. At the same time, industry was using the same data to show a shortage in discovery of new natural gas that was attributed to regulation.

Willy-nilly, therefore, we must probe the differences over estimates to understand whether the nature of the estimates caused the disagreements, as our first hypothesis suggests.

Perhaps it would be best to let Chairman Moss set the record straight: "Let the Chair say that we don't start from the premise that we are faced with possible impropriety. We are looking for the accuracy, the inherent credibility of the treatment that is employed as a result of the AGA compilation by our regulatory bodies in this country." What is the inherent credibility of AGA estimates of gas reserves, and how might this be ascertained?

Since one could not see into the AGA reporting system to do a technical validation, all one could do was compare AGA reserve estimates with other people's reserve estimates. Thus, the FTC Bureau of Competition looked at the reserve numbers reported on Form 15, the survey conducted annually by the FPC. Form 15 reserves came in higher than AGA reserves, and the Bureau of Competition embraced Form 15 reserves as "better." But what was Form 15 about? Was it better? Were Form 15 reserves and AGA reserves appropriate to compare?

Form 15 collected data from interstate pipeline buyers for the purpose of pipeline regulation. Since 1963, Form 15 has been filed annually by interstate pipeline companies which own or control 50 billion cubic feet or more of natural gas reserves. Respondents report the amount of gas reserves under contract to them for subsequent resale in interstate commerce. In order to fill out the form, a pipeline company employee contacts the producer's office, where reserve data are kept. The two meet in the producer's office, where the pipeline representative works up a reserve estimate for the amounts dedicated to that pipeline (House Committee on Interstate and Foreign Commerce, 1975a).

From time to time FPC staff audit the supporting information underlying a company's Form 15 estimates. To validate Form 15 filings of natural gas reserves, "teams of geologists and engineers are sent to the offices of the pipeline respondents to review the basic production and well data on which the estimates are based, to review the methodology of the estimates, and when necessary, to recommend changes . . . to insure greater accuracy."[3]

In regard to the FPC's Form 15, the results—what was said—had the dominant impact on the way that system was perceived by the FTC Bureau of Competition and congressional opponents of the AGA method. Technical differences between the AGA and Form 15 systems were not considered important. The Form 15 definition was more inclusive than the AGA definition, but this did not bother the Bureau of Competition, nor did its lack of systematic validation. Even the undeniable fact that the ultimate source of data was still the producers did not make the Bureau of Competition wary. It was what was said that mattered. Form 15 reserves were higher than AGA reserves when the Bureau of Competition compared the two, and this supported the BOC charge of AGA underreporting.

Tables 8.2 and 8.3 illustrate how unimportant scientific quality was to people in the Bureau of Competition. For example, they protested against the lack of auditing in the AGA system, but were not bothered by the sporadic nature of Form 15 auditing.

Enter the forces against the Bureau of Competition! First came its own brethren in the FTC, the Bureau of Economics. Economics Bureau staff complained that the Bureau of Competition had not sought the economists' "analytical assistance or interpretation." The Bureau of Economics objected strongly to the results and recommended that the Bureau of Competition not file its complaint. The Bureau of Economics felt that the Bureau of Competition's charges were wholly unsubstantiated. The Bureau of Competition data lent themselves to quite other interpretations, said the Bureau of Economics, claiming there were "plausible alternative explanations ... for virtually all of the perceived suspicious behavior" (House Committee on Interstate and Foreign Commerce, 1975a: 612).[4] Moreover, Economics Bureau people continued, it was inappropriate for the Bureau of Competition to compare AGA data with other data: The gas association's definition of "proved reserves" was different from the definition implied in other reporting forms. In any event, and given the state of the art of reserve estimation, it would be hard to say which definition (or even which number) was "correct." The Bureau of Economics' memorandum flatly dismissed the Bureau of Competition's charge of concerted misreporting by the gas association: "There are, of course, no hot documents to support this claim. There are no hotel meetings. There are no suspicious telephone calls. There are no damaging memorandums. Thus, the conspiracy alleged is an inferential one. We believe that inferences of conspiracy in this matter are impossible to draw" (House Committee on Interstate and Foreign Commerce, 1975a: 613).

Then the Bureau of Economics added a new dimension to those arguments. The main concern of the Bureau of Economics in defending the AGA was that "supporters of continued regulation would be able to point to the complaint as proof that the natural gas shortage was a contrivance of the producers." That is, the Bureau of Economics was interested in promoting deregulation of the gas-producing industry. The Bureau of Competition wanted to maintain controls over the industry. A legal complaint against the industry data system would further the Bureau of Competition's interest and would hurt the Bureau of Economics' aims.

TABLE 8.2 FTC Bureau of Competition Perception of AGA Reserve Reporting System

Major features	How it was	How FTC Bureau of Competition perceived it	Did it raise or reduce credibility?
Results	Additions to proved reserves were low, with decline starting in 1968	Suspiciously low; indicated too high a price would be allowed the gas producers	AGA results were rejected by the Bureau of Competition
Technical/ Process Aspects			
Definition of proved reserves	Allowed variously narrow/broader interpretations	Allowed too narrow an interpretation, resulting in lower reserve estimates	Reduced the credibility of the system in the eyes of the Bureau of Competition
Data collection	By Reserves Subcommittee members who were company employees; collected mainly from own companies	Totally controlled by companies; invisible	Reduced
Data validation	Not apparent	No validation	Reduced
Under oath?	No	Not a problem in the FTC investigation (only later in the 40/64 study was it introduced as a problem)	N/A
Voluntary or mandatory?	Voluntary	To its discredit	Reduced the credibility of the system in the eyes of the Bureau of Competition
Suppliers of the data	Producers	Producers controlled entire system	Rejected

TABLE 8.3 FTC Bureau of Competition Perception of Form 15 Reserve Estimates

Major features	How it was	How FTC Bureau of Competition perceived it	Did it raise or reduce credibility?
Results	Additions to proved reserves committed to interstate commerce—higher than AGA for year compared; but sharper downtrend than AGA	Form 15 data estimated higher reserves than AGA	Reduced *AGA* system's credibility in the eyes of the Bureau of Competition
Technical/ Process features			
Definition	Modeled on AGA but broader	Equivalent to AGA (even though Form 15 people have criticized the AGA definition)	Did not matter that the two definitions were not comparable; credibility depended on thinking the two definitions equivalent.
Data collection	From pipelines, who conferred with producers	Did not mention	N/A
Data validation	Validated irregularly by FPC	Noted that FPC validated (did not mention frequency or nature of validation as possible problem)	Raised Form 15's credibility and usefulness for comparison in eyes of Bureau of Competition

TABLE 8.3 (continued)

Major features	How it was	How FTC Bureau of Competition perceived it	Did it raise or reduce credibility?
Under oath?	Yes	Did not mention this as a plus (only later in the 40/64 study did it emerge as an important quality)	N/A
Voluntary or mandatory	Mandatory	Did not mention this as a plus (though they *did* criticize the AGA system for not being mandatory)	N/A
Suppliers of the data	Pipelines (interstate)	Assumed comparable with producers for the AGA/15 comparison. Did not attack source of Form 15 data as they had attacked source of AGA data (though producers are part of the source of Form 15 data)	N/A

Trying to put it less bluntly, the Bureau of Economics feared that "rational debate on the issue of deregulation would be much diminished. ... The result might be continued FPC regulation into the distant future. At a time when the FTC ... is engaging in a thoughtful review of the efficacy of various regulatory institutions, the FTC might be taking steps which would entrench one of those institutions" (House Committee on Interstate and Foreign Commerce, 1975a: 615). Knowing the rules now, we know also that it was unwise for the Bureau of Economics to enter the fray openly in favor of deregulation at this point, because such arguments immediately were dismissed out of hand. The brief statement above got economists Joseph Mulholland and Joanne Salop into hot water as they testified before an unsympathetic subcommittee majority. After Mulholland and Salop were grilled on deregulation, the original Bureau of Economics critique of the Bureau of Competition report lost credence.

The Federal Power Commission also attacked the Bureau of Competition's report by calling forth technical and process-related aspects of reserve estimation. To take one example, the FPC emphasized the noncomparability of definitions: The Form 15 definition did not require that a reservoir be demonstrated able to produce (through actual production or conclusive formation test) in order for the reserves to be considered proved.[5] Thus, the pipelines could include some "probable" as well as proved reserves in their Form 15 submissions. The FPC dug out old letters, forms, and memoranda to discredit the FTC Bureau of Competition's presumption that the definitions were equal. Arguments over this bogged down the hearings. Finally the disputants were reduced to squabbling about whether conversations the FTC Bureau of Competition staff had with staff in the FPC were accurately reported.

Wayne M. Thompson of the FPC Bureau of Natural Gas told the Subcommittee on Oversight and Investigations that the raw data used by the FPC staff when preparing the estimates were obtained from pipelines and producers pursuant to pipeline certification applications, and that the staff adhered to the AGA definition of proved reserves when calculating the estimates. He said:

> I do not believe that in either of the contacts that I asserted that the staff adhered to the AGA definition of proved reserves when calculating the estimates because I did not believe it then and I do not believe it as a factual statement now for reserve estimates made in past years. On the contrary, in the second meeting I specifically stated that the reserves estimates on the FPC Forms 1149 and 1150 may not always be proved reserves by AGA definition [House Committee on Interstate and Foreign Commerce, 1975a: 675].

To this the FTC Bureau of Competition replied that Thompson's testimony was "contradicted not only by our interview reports but also by every other pertinent piece of evidence we have seen" (House Committee on Interstate and Foreign Commerce, 1975a: 682).

On another technical front, FPC Chairman Nassikas told the Moss subcommittee:

> Proved reserves figures, regardless of the definition used, are only estimates. . . . The *accuracy* of an estimate . . . cannot be fully determined until the reservoir has been depleted to the abandonment stage, a point usually reached years after the initial reserves estimate is made. The *reliability* [of the estimate] is therefore dependent upon the ability of the estimator as well as on the quality of information available about the gas reservoir. . . . [I]nitial and intermediate estimates should be continually revised. . . . Changes in economic and operating factors also affect the reserves estimate . . . adding a set of non-physical variables to the problem of estimation.[6]

Aware that a sudden decline in reserve estimates would exert upward pressure on price, the Federal Power Commission averaged reserve additions over ten years and made modifications so that the range of base costs was adjusted downward. Thus, in its rate-making, the FPC was not simply taking producers' data at face value.

Indeed, it is not clear that the natural gas industry could be spoken of as a single entity. The reader should beware of the assumptions that there is only a single type of gas company and that there is a single interest within each company. If companies are coalitions, as one group of scholars suggests (Cyert and March, 1963), and if there are different types of companies doing different things within the industry, then the notion of a single-industry interest may be called into question.

Belief in a single-industry interest in low estimates of gas reserves was fortified by the FTC Bureau of Competition's charge that companies kept separate ledgers of proved reserves that were consistently higher than data submitted to the AGA.[7] If, indeed, the proved reserve ledgers were calculated on the same basis as gas association estimates, yet did show up as consistently higher than the data submitted to AGA—which was what the Bureau of Competition claimed—something was wrong. Every one of these premises was contradicted by the FTC Bureau of Economics. Basically, the Bureau of Economics claimed that there is no comparability between AGA and proved-reserve-ledger reserve estimates, because "in general the proved reserve ledgers appear to be influenced by many nongeological factors such as tax laws, stockholder relations and executive egos" (House Committee on Interstate and Foreign Commerce, 1975a:

653). Moreover, not all these uses would lead to low estimates; since the proved reserve estimates are used to obtain loans and to appeal to stockholders in annual reports, estimates might as easily be biased upward as downward. Furthermore, the Bureau of Competition's own data show that proved reserve ledgers exceeded AGA reserve estimates more than half the time.

None of this made any majority member of Congress think twice. In the hearings, the same fate befell the FPC as befell the FTC Bureau of Economics: Amid claims that the FPC was for deregulation, and at industry's beck and call anyway, every claim supporting a higher price was attacked. With every figure contested and every inference disputed amidst arcane language and technical terms, one wonders what any legislator could make of these arguments. If you doubt my credibility and I doubt yours and we all doubt each other's, we might ask whether the dispute is about energy estimates or whether estimates have become merely a convenient mode of continuing hostilities over policy.

THE FPC RETALIATES WITH
THE NATIONAL GAS RESERVE SURVEY

We saw that the Bureau of Competition's attempt to compare the low AGA figures with the higher FPC Form 15 figures and the companies' own ledgers did not seem to work. Another comparison, the FPC's one-shot National Gas Reserve Survey (NGRS), would deflate the low-pricers even further. This study had been initiated under pressure from Congress to get some independently collected and independently validated gas reserve data. Credibility was the call, and the FPC tried to give the impression they were making a good-faith effort.

The organization of the study revolved around a show of scientific quality and independence from industry influence:

(1) The University of Oklahoma compiled the list of all gas fields in the United States.
(2) Independent teams of government professionals went into the field to do their own estimates.
(3) An independent accounting firm selected the sample and wrote up the findings.
(4) A statistical validation team prescribed the sampling procedures.

Near-fanatical attention was given to making the NGRS as scientifically valid as possible. In this way the FPC hoped to regain credibility. Certain techniques for collecting natural gas data for this study had been tested earlier by the FPC's Bureau of Natural Gas in its "Uncommitted Gas Reserves Study." In particular, it appeared that "a government field team working in a company office with the required basic data could prepare an independent field reserves estimate and conduct its work in a manner which did not jeopardize the confidentiality of the company data (House Committee on Interstate and Foreign Commerce, 1975a: 8). Companies in the field furnished working space and provided raw data for the reserve analysis people. The teams generally did prepare their estimates from company-supplied data, but "in some cases reserve estimates were developed using data purchased commercially or obtained from public sources" (House Committee on Interstate and Foreign Commerce, 1975a: 4). Usually, these raw data consisted of various types of well logs, core analyses, other types of well test data, temperature measurements, gas analyses, maps, pressure history, and production history, from which teams made their own estimates of reserves. Rather than rely solely on the various factors developed by the company, teams worked up their own factors for porosity, water saturation, temperature, pressure, and so forth. The estimate for an individual field was developed on a reservoir-by-reservoir basis, then summed for a field total. Worksheets generated by the independent reserve teams were to be saved and sent to the Bureau of Natural Gas office in Washington. The technical director of the National Gas Survey was to keep these worksheets.

Results from the independent reserve teams were transmitted "on a confidential basis" to the team supervisor, who compared those estimates with AGA reserve estimates and could call for a recheck of the team's work. A final reserve estimate for each field then was submitted to Arthur Young and Co., which consolidated all the findings and produced a report on the study for the National Gas Survey. The AGA definition of proved reserves was used; however, certain additions to that definition's vague assumption of "existing economic and operating conditions" were made for the NGRS:

> These reserves estimates ... include gas ... reserves of all types regardless of size, availability of market, ultimate disposition or use.
>
> A ready market will exist for all volumes of gas produced.
>
> The estimator will not limit his consideration to the "prevailing practice" in the field ... but should consider the possibility of adding compressors or other equipment and base his estimate on the recovery efficiency which would result from installation of such equipment.[8]

Careful enough? If anything could serve as a basis for our first hypothesis, that process matters to users of data, it was the National Gas Reserves Study. However, the study concluded that the results "put the total proved gas reserves for the U.S. for 1970 at 258.6 Tcf, about 10 percent lower than the AGA estimate for the same year. Given the margin of error involved in any estimate . . . the practical effect . . . was generally to confirm the AGA national gas reserve estimates for that year" (Federal Power Commission, 1976a). As if this were not enough, the NGRS suggested that "the American Gas Association's Natural Gas Reserves Committee continuously update the proven gas reserves estimates so that the most current reservoir . . . data are incorporated into their annual report on proven gas reserves" (Federal Power Commission, 1975: 26).

Incredulous, the FTC Bureau of Competition obtained NGRS estimates for 24 offshore fields on the Gulf Coast, made a comparison, and determined that AGA estimates were 2 percent higher. Thus, if the NGRS estimates were accepted as a reasonable approximation, it would appear that AGA estimates, if anything, came out on the high, rather than on the low, side. The counterattack was on.

In Congress, both the Moss Subcommittee on Oversight and Investigations and the Senate Interior Committee (chaired by Henry Jackson) objected to the NGRS numbers. Jackson asked the Congressional Research Service (CRS) to do a critique of the results of the NGRS effort. CRS engaged Energy Research, Inc., to do the job. The critique concluded that the NGRS was a good-faith effort and a good study.

Members of the Senate committee—who thought that Energy Research's report was not critical enough of the NGRS—was not impressed. Neither was the FTC Bureau of Competition. Both expressed dissatisfaction with various aspects of the NGRS estimates. Looking into the process, the Bureau of Competition perceived certain sampling biases, objecting in particular to the NGRS emphasis on large fields with established production histories: Since large fields are likely to be reported most accurately, this introduced a selection bias. "It is in the reporting of relatively underdeveloped fields that we have found the AGA to be deficient," that is, in reporting of fields that "contain relatively nominal amounts of natural gas" (House Committee on Interstate and Foreign Commerce, 1975a: 117). Besides, by contacting only a single producing office for each field, the NGRS was unlikely to get all the data, because producers do not usually lease or own an entire field.

Even if the Bureau of Competition had perceived no selection biases, it probably would have rejected the NGRS data results on the ground that the source of the data still remained the private, natural gas producing industry. Theodore Lytle of the Bureau of Competition doubted whether the teams really had been able to see all the company data (House Committee on Interstate and Foreign Commerce, 1975a: 373). Further, the touted advisory committees to the study had been "dominated by the very same corporations that we are recommending that complaints be issued against. The directors of all the three advisory committees were from Exxon" (p. 373). In addition, "the Gas Survey was not aided by compulsory process. As a result, the producers supplied such raw data on particular fields voluntarily, the completeness of which is doubtful and not attested to under oath" (p. 764).

If the root of the evil is that private companies prepare the data, then the only way around it would be either to nationalize the companies or to give the government the right to conduct its own detailed studies on a large proportion of this heretofore private property. Up to this time, all data had originated with private producers because the industry was private. At another level, concerned with interpretation of data, the evil could be mitigated by removing private-industry personnel from the structure of advice. The trouble here is not only that might industry be unwilling to cooperate on this basis, but also that most of the expertise does belong to those professionals who are employed with companies. As far as the FTC Bureau of Competition and those legislators who agreed were concerned, the NGRS only compounded rather than cleared up the biases of the AGA.

THE FPC'S NEW PRICE INCREASE

We leave the stormy hearings to look at a final episode that will put the hypotheses once more to the test. It was summer 1976, time for the FPC to make the biennial review of its ceiling price for natural gas at the wellhead. We recall that in the FPC formula for determining the price, the lower the reserves, the higher the price. In turn, the higher this price was, the more consumers perceived they would have to pay. In setting the price, the power commission shouldered the delicate and difficult task of balancing two priorities: to establish rates that would be (1) high enough to stimulate additional gas supplies, but (2) not so high as to burden consumers with prices in excess of those needed to elicit such supplies. The FPC did consider its main mission to be "to assure an adequate supply of natural gas for the nation."[9]

By 1976 the issue, overwhelmingly, was price, dichotomized between (a) those who wanted continued regulation to ensure lower prices, and (b) those who wanted higher prices on the ground that prices had long been too low to elicit new supplies. This second group included proponents of deregulation as well as those who favored some form of continued regulation, but at higher prices. The episode of the FPC price increase reveals the role of gas reserves data in the issue of price and profit. It shows also how changeable were the criteria for credibility: It depended on whose ox was gored.

On July 27, 1976, the FPC, in its biennial rate review, increased the ceiling price for new gas from $.52/Mcf (Mcf = 1000 cubic feet) to $1.42/Mcf, about a threefold increase (Federal Power Commission, 1976b: Docket R-389-B).

What the differences show is that where there's a will to disbelieve, there's a way. Table 8.4 highlights the Bureau of Competition's view of the NGRS. Again, we note inconsistent opinions about technical and process-related aspects of these reporting efforts. Clearly, the second hypothesis is borne out: It's what you say that matters.

The source of the reserve figure in the formula had been, as always, the AGA. This year, though, it was not entirely by choice. A new FPC survey, using Form 40, was just beginning to collect "independent" reserve data from producers; many in Congress had hoped that Form 40 data would be ready to use in the 1976 rate-making formula.

Form 40 (and its companion, Form 64) held out high hopes for low-pricers, who were calling for credibility. It had all the technical qualities that could possibly enhance "credibility": For example, it was to collect detailed data, reservoir by reservoir. The figures would be transparent to government validators and to the public. Moreover, to keep the source truthful, Form 40 was to be mandatory and taken under oath.

When FPC's $1.42 price was released, Congressman Moss (1976), in strong objection, instructed his staff to do a study of the productivity factor of the formula the FPC had used, "the key element in setting the price of new natural gas." For this study, Moss asked the staff to review FPC Form 40 and FPC Form 64 filings to see what productivity factors could be derived from them, as opposed to the AGA data which the FPC had used.

How was the productivity factor computed? The formula for wellhead price was composed of the cost of nonassociated natural gas (gas not associated with oil) plus a specified rate of return. A principal component of the cost was the successful well cost, which the FPC computed by first estimating a productivity figure. Productivity for any given year was calculated as the ratio of nonassociated reserve additions to successful gas and well footage drilled, and was usually expressed as x units per successful foot drilled. Thus, if 200 feet of gas wells were drilled in a year and

TABLE 8.4 FTC Bureau of Competition Perception of FPC's National Gas Reserves Study

Major features	How it was	How FTC Bureau of Competition perceived it	Did it raise or reduce credibility?
Results	Proved reserve estimates lower than AGA estimates by approximately 10%	AGA should have turned up lower than NGRS	NGRS results were rejected; credence unchanged for AGA system
Technical/ process features			
Definition	Modeled on AGA but broader due to assumptions written in	Did not mention	N/A
Sampling	Small sample of mostly large fields	Poor plan, as it omitted newer fields where underreporting was most likely	Reduced for NGRS in eyes of the Bureau of Competition
Data collection	By government teams in producers' offices with producer-supplied raw data	Companies could control process (yet companies could control Form 15 process, but this was not been to be a problem in Form 15)	N/A
Data validation	By team supervisors	Did not mention (yet validation was more thorough than for Form 15)	N/A
Voluntary or mandatory?	Voluntary	Not aided by compulsory process; may have gotten incomplete data	Reduced for NGRS in eyes of the Bureau of Competition
Suppliers of the data	Producers ultimately, though government teams made the calculations and furnished reserve estimates	Controlled by producers ultimately (yet ultimate control of Form 15 lay with producers, but this was not brought up as a problem in the Form 15 case)	N/A

400 Mcf of reserves were added, productivity would equal 400 Mcf/200 feet, or 2 Mcf per successful foot drilled. In the overall formula, the higher the productivity is, the lower is the cost and the price.

The staff's resulting productivity factor was much higher than the FPC's AGA-based productivity factor: 411 Mcf compared to 300. The higher the productivity factor was, the lower was the resulting price. The Form 40 and Form 64 data suggested to the subcommittee staff a price for new gas of $1.00 (as opposed to $1.42).

The subcommittee staff report was endorsed immediately, not only by Congressman Moss but also by Senators John Durkin and William Proxmire, and by Congressmen Berkley Bedell, William Hughes, Andrew Maguire, Toby Moffett, James Oberstar, Richard Ottinger, John Seiberling, and Gerry Studds—all Democrats (Federal Power Commission, 1976b: 36). These congressmen submitted the subcommittee report, as a group, in formal reaction to Opinion 770. Their comment, in accordance with procedure, was sent in via the prominent public-interest law firm of Spiegel and McDiarmid.

What about this Form 40/64 data embraced by congressmen? As for Form 40, by August 1976 the FPC had not even sifted through the 225 returns. The subcommittee staff, in performing this task, found only 94 usable forms ("judged complete and free of obvious error"). The power commission *had* been able to sift through the 360 Form 64s and judged only 113 to be usable. These 113, plus the 94 Form 40s, were used by the subcommittee staff in its comparative study. Use of Form 40 data for the year 1975 was precluded, however. Since none of the 25 largest producers had volunteered a usable Form 40, the staff could not compute a productivity factor for 1975 using Form 40s. In short, the staff was primarily using scraps.

The few volunteered 40s and 64s in no way resembled a statistically sophisticated sample. Yet, the FPC Bureau of Competition staff report embraced these data as preferable to the AGA data. In fact, it concluded that

> the Commission has before it a sufficient number of usable Form 64's and 40's to derive a statistically valid productivity series for the ten-year period 1965 to 1974. And certainly the data from the Forms is more trustworthy than that supplied in industry publications [Federal Power Commission, 1976b: 9-10].

Why did the Bureau of Competition give credence to the Form 40 and Form 64 data? "[T]he report acknowledges that the Form 40 and 64 data had not been audited or verified. But *whatever the infirmities of unaudited data, the presumption of correctness is higher for submissions under oath* than the American Gas Association reserve data employed by the Commission in Opinion 770" (Moss, 1976; emphasis added).

Submission under oath was the major criterion for acceptability in this study. This criterion had not been a factor in the FTC investigation of underreporting reserves, and that Form 15 was submitted under oath was not even mentioned.

What about the fact that the 40 and 64 data had been voluntary? This did not occur to the subcommittee staff or the congressmen. Yet, some of the same individuals had criticized the AGA reporting system and the FPC for relying on data voluntarily supplied by the producers.

Further, the 40 and 64 data had not been audited, yet were accepted. A main criticism of the AGA system had been that it was not audited. Moreover, the Form 15 data had been acceptable to the FTC Bureau of Competition and to a number of subcommittee members because the FPC audited them, even though the FPC's audits were only sporadic.

The final chart recapitulates how low-pricers perceived the results (and the processes underlying them) of the four data-collection efforts. Observe how the process-related criteria fluctuated; for one set of data a certain criterion mattered a great deal, while in another it did not matter. Consistency of standards in the way estimates were reached was not at the forefront of low-pricers' concerns; a consistent policy position was. The apparent inconsistencies in these consumerist views of how the surveys were conducted had a certain logic, given their policy preference, and given the data's consistent relationship to the price into which that policy was translated.

IT'S WHAT YOU SAY

Proponents of lower price and continued regulation viewed the sudden drop in estimates of reserve additions in 1968 with suspicion that the producing industry was underreporting to push up the price. If the AGA system had been visible and auditable, would consumerists have accepted the low numbers? Not likely. Other limitations in the process could have been brought up, and the ultimate source of the data might still have come under fire. For many with an already well-established policy preference, the low results were a sign to continue with price regulation.

It was hoped that the Federal Power Commission's study of gas reserves (the NGRS) would lead to evidence of purposeful underreporting by the producers. The results failed to do so. Proponents of continued regulation, therefore, looked for process-related weaknesses in the survey that would

TABLE 8.5   Oversight and Investigations Staff Perception of Forms 40 and 64 Reserve Estimates

Major features	How it was	How Oversight and Investigations staff perceived it	Did it raise or reduce credibility?
Results	The productivity factor derived by staff with 40/64 reserve data was higher than with AGA data	Results justified calling for lower price. Staff accepted 40/64 data results	Reduced for AGA in eyes of sub-committee staff and members of Congress who applied to FPC for rehearing
Technical/ process features			
Definition	Similar to NGRS; broader than AGA	Did not mention problems (though there may have been comparability questions between AGA and 40/64 definitions)	N/A
Sample	Not a true sample	Not perceived as serious obstacle (though NGRS sampling plan had been scrutinized and reduced credibility of NGRS results)	N/A
Data collection	By mail from producers	Not mentioned	N/A
Validation	Not validated	Still acceptable (yet there had been strong objections to AGA lack of validation)	N/A
Under oath?	Yes	Stressed as a plus (though not even considered a criterion in the other surveys)	Raised for 40/64, and reduced for AGA—in eyes of subcommittee and members of Congress
Voluntary or mandatory?	Voluntary	Not seen as serious obstacle (though NGRS and AGA were criticized for being voluntary)	N/A
Suppliers of the data	Producers	Did not question them (though they were same source as AGA and NGRS source, ultimately)	N/A

TABLE 8.6 Summary: Perceptions of Low Pricers

Major features	AGA	Form 15	NGRS	40/64
Results	*Too low, discredited*: The AGA system and the credibility of gas producers	*Higher* than AGA; *acceptable*; hoped would help show deliberate under-reporting	*Lower* than AGA; *discredited*	Higher than AGA; *acceptable*: argued for lower price
Technical/process features				
Definition	Allowed too narrow an interpretation	Comparable to AGA (but acceptable)	Did not mention	Did not mention difficulties
Sampling	–	–	Faulty: undersampled less-developed fields	Not a good sample but acceptable anyway
Data Collection	Invisible; controlled by companies	Did not mention	Companies could control	Did not mention problems
Data validation	No validation at all	Satisfied that the FPC validated them (though the FPC did so irregularly)	Did not mention	Lack of validation not a serious problem
Under oath?	Not mentioned as a criterion (until the 40/64 study; then criticized for not being under oath)	Not mentioned as a criterion	Not mentioned as a criterion	Praised for being under oath; all its credibility hung on this legal compulsion
Voluntary or Mandatory?	Deficient because voluntary	Was mandatory, but was not mentioned as a plus	Deficient because not mandatory	Voluntary, but not seen as problems
Suppliers of the data	Producers controlled entire system	No problem accepting the source of these data	Producers had ultimate control	No problem accepting the source of these data

suggest the NGRS results should have been higher than AGA. But they were again unsuccessful.

For policy purposes, it was the message of the results that mattered. In the Oversight and Investigation Subcommittee's comparison of the 40/60 data with AGA data in deriving a productivity factor, the 40/64 data produced a result favorable to the subcommittee's policy stand. The 40/64 results were embraced, although they were not a valid sample, were not audited, and were not mandatory.

Those who wanted continued regulation attacked the ultimate source of the AGA and NGRS estimates. They did not criticize Form 15, or Forms 40 and 64, on grounds of the ultimate source. Proregulationists merely urged the federal government to take charge of reserves data collection. It is unclear whether, in urging this, they fully realized that the government would still have to rely on the same original source for the data. The expectation that a new collection system would be mandatory—collected "independently" of industry and validated by government—seemed to hold out promise for enhanced credibility.

In conclusion, the second hypothesis—it's what, not how, one estimates that is important—seems to explain events better. Given (1) the fluid, judgmental nature of the "science" of reserve estimation and the many estimates possible; (2) a clearly drawn issue of price as the problem, which elicited strong policy preferences among elected representatives account-able to their constituents; and (3) that the outcome, due to regulatory practice, was dependent on these reserves estimates, it did not really matter whether the processes of gathering the data were perceived to be perfect or problematic. What ultimately mattered was whether the result strengthened one's policy preferences.

NOTES

1. The Federal Trade Commission, after reviewing the Bureau of Competition report and a conflicting report by the Commission's Bureau of Economics, did not want a complaint issued. The Commission did not permit public release of the Bureau of Competition report. But the Moss subcommittee subpoenaed the report and also required the FTC to appear before the subcommittee in hearings. Therefore, the documents were printed in the hearings and thus were available to the public.

2. Telephone conversation with Richard D. Lambert, Manager for Radio and TV, American Gas Association, on January 1, 1979.

3. John Nassikas made this statement before the Subcommittee on Oversight and Investigations on July 14, 1975 (see House Committee on Interstate and Foreign Commerce, 1975a: p. 50 of statement).

4. From a memorandum dated April 16, 1975 from the Bureau of Economics to the Federal Trade Commission (see House Committee on Interstate and Foreign Commerce, 1975a: 612).

5. From the FTC Bureau of Economics report, attachment B (see House Committee on Interstate and Foreign Commerce, 1975a: 667).

6. Statement of John Nassikas before the Subcommittee on Oversight and Investigations (see House Committee on Interstate and Foreign Commerce, 1975a: p. 4 of Appendix A of statement).

7. Theodore Lytle of the Bureau of Competition explained what he thought was meant by a proved reserve ledger:

"When we got documents from ... three of the four companies, we found that they had a compilation of reserves that they sometimes called an annual report or else they called it a proved reserve ledger. Usually, it was a computer printout. What is showed was the lease designation and estimated quantities of proved reserves there and amount of production in a given year. It was the company's books" (House Committee on Interstate and Foreign Commerce, 1975a: 10).

8. The AGA definition of proved reserves with additions to the definition of "existing economic and operating conditions" was made for the NGRS.

9. S. William Yost, Chief, FPC Bureau of Natural Gas, in a form letter response to letters protesting the FPC's Opinion 770 of July 1976, which raised the ceiling price on new gas to $1.42.

REFERENCES

CYERT, R. M. and J. G. MARCH (1963) A Behavioral Theory of the Firm. Englewood Cliffs, NJ: Prentice-Hall.

Federal Power Commission (1976a) National Gas Survey, Volume 1. Washington, DC: Government Printing Office.

––– (1976b) Opinion 770. Washington, DC: Government Printing Office.

––– (1975) National Gas Reserves Study. Washington, DC: Government Printing Office.

House Committee on Interstate and Foreign Commerce, Subcommittee on Oversight and Investigations (1975a) Natural Gas Supplies, Volume 1, Part 1. Washington, DC: Government Printing Office.

––– (1975b) Natural Gas Supplies, Volume 3, Part 1. Washington, DC: Government Printing Office.

MOSS, J. E. (1976) Personal communication to all subcommittee members, October 27.

9 OIL AND GAS RESOURCE ESTIMATES
How Relevant to Policy?

IN CHAPTER 8 WE SAW that the chief disagreements were about estimates of additions to proved reserves: How much has been added each year that is producible under current conditions? Note that the time horizon is a single year, that fields have been discovered, holes drilled, and, for the most part, gas has been demonstrated to flow.

Suppose, however, that the time horizon were almost infinite, that fields had not been discovered nor holes drilled nor flow demonstrated. Suppose also that instead of assuming current technology and prices, these had to be predicted or postulated into the future. What would be the chances of gaining agreement on the results of such an enterprise? "Nil" might not be too negative an answer. Yet this is precisely what we have asked ourselves to do when attempting to estimate recoverable resources. Resources refer to the total amount of oil and gas, including reserves, estimated to be under the ground, whether discovered or yet undiscovered. Any recoverable resources are those that estimators think can be brought to the surface and produced (Schanz, 1978).[1] We are now asking ourselves: Having already produced X amount of oil and gas, how much is left underground that is technologically feasible and economically worthwhile to pump out in the future?

Whether this is a hopeless or a heroic task, that conjunction of joint probabilities—estimates of resources in place times estimates of recoverability—also multiplies the prospects of poor performance. The concept of recovery itself includes estimates of the ratio between drilling and finding, and finding and extracting. Diogenes might well find his honest man before the estimates of recoverable resources are either accurate or agreed upon. With every increase in complexity—number of variables, types of variables, serial dependence of one upon another, time horizon, method of estimation—confidence in estimates may be expected to decrease.

What to do? As usual, there are two ways to go: increase the accuracy of each stage of the estimation process, or decrease the demand for accurate data. Since resource estimates are bound to differ and policy preferences are powerful, different estimates may be taken as pointing to preferred policies. Decreasing the demand for data calls for dominant solutions that are entirely independent of estimates or that are tied to an extreme estimate. To have an estimate of virtually unlimited or terribly small amounts of oil and gas resources would suggest that no policy is necessary because resources are either superabundant or nonexistent. However one proceeds, whether by improving data or lessening the need for it, the path is strewn with obstacles.

Substantial differences in estimates of recoverable oil and gas resources have been the rule rather than the exception since early in the century. Based on the historical record, one would be more surprised if estimates came close than if they were within several magnitudes of each other. What has changed, at least since the fourfold price increases brought on by the Organization of Petroleum Exporting Countries (OPEC) cartel, is not that estimates have gotten worse but that we care more about them. But why do we care? Alas, the answer to this question is considered so self-evident that it is seldom raised. Estimates would almost never dominate policies in the sense that a difference would rule out one alternative or rule in another. Obviously, if there were an extreme abundance of oil and gas recoverable at present or contemplated future prices, this would matter. Conversely, it would make a difference if existing resources, recoverable or not, were so small that effort could substantially increase the amount produced and available for use. Soon, however, one learns that the difference between the highest and lowest estimates would not be enough, by far, to dominate the policy debate.

So how does one assess the situation? Public officials want the hard facts, partly because their constituents, upset by widely varying estimates, need reassurance that somebody up there knows what is going on. In order to maintain legitimacy, for themselves as well as for the political system to which they belong, public officials must appear to be in control. It is especially important that such officials not be victims of false or foolish presentations, to recognize at least the dimensions of the problem if not the shape of the solution. The appearance of ignorance is intolerable.

Keeping up appearances, however, is insufficient to explain the heat of passion generated by energy resource estimates. Somebody out there must think these estimates make a difference. To understand what this difference might be, we must know something about the cognitive maps (how people relate estimates to policies) of users of energy data.

We describe two events useful for this purpose. The first is a hearing held by the late Senator Hubert Humphrey in February 1975, on the adequacy of U.S. oil and gas reserves. The dispute was over ten different estimates of undiscovered, recoverable resources; the question was, "How much do we really have left?" The second event describes three conflicting projections of future gas supply, all of which emerged in 1977 from the Market-Oriented Program Planning Study (MOPPS), sponsored by the Energy Research and Development Administration (ERDA). Both events show that where the political arena is polarized, small differences among estimates are magnified if participants feel they have a stake in the estimates.

ONE QUESTION WITH TEN ANSWERS

The Humphrey hearing was held in February 1975 under the auspices of the Joint Economic Committee. The subject was the adequacy of U.S. oil and gas "reserves"; the question was, "What is the size of America's remaining oil and gas *resources* and the resulting projections of attainable future production rates?" Officials and experts from the United States Geological Survey (USGS) and the National Academy of Sciences (NAS) as well as private research organizations attempted to explain why the NAS estimated recoverable oil and gas resources at lower levels than most estimates generated by the USGS. The NAS had reviewed the data and estimation procedures used by nine parties with divergent estimates of recoverable resources. Based on those, the academy then proceeded to give its own estimates. Table 9.1 shows the range of estimates produced by the ten parties. The NAS estimates of resources were markedly lower than estimates of the USGS. Great frustration ensued on the part of many in Congress and the public: Why were these scientists unable to agree?

NEEDED: A PLURALIST VIEW OF RESOURCES

The problem lies partly in the character of these estimates of recoverable oil and gas reserves. They do not measure what is known or tangible

TABLE 9.1   Estimates of Undiscovered Recoverable Resources
             of the U.S.

	Oil and Natural Gas Liquids (billions of barrels)	Natural Gas (trillions of cubic feet)
Oil Companies		
1. Company A (Weeks, 1960)	168	
2. Hubbert, 1967	24-64*	180-500*
3. Company C (1973)	55	
4. Company D (1974)	89	450
5. Company E	90	
USGS		
6. Hendricks (1965)	346	1300
7. Theobald et al. (1972)	458	1980
8. McKelvey (1974)	200-400	990-2000
9. Hubbert (1974)	72	540
10. National Academy of Sciences	113	530

SOURCE: Chapter 5 of report prepared by the Committee on Mineral Resources and the Environment (COMRATE), Commission on Natural Resources, National Research Council, National Academy of Sciences. Reproduced in hearings, page 21. The designation of companies A, C, D and E was made by COMRATE. The names of the companies could not be matched to those designations from a reading of the hearing.
*exclusive of Alaska

or can be seen. After all, if there were knowledge, conclusions rather than estimates could be produced. Everyone involved agreed with John D. Moody, a member of the NAS Panel on Estimation of Mineral Reserves and Resources, when he said, "We have no real way of seeing under the ground, and all of these estimates are subjective at least to some extent, and there is no way of getting away from that" (Joint Economic Committee, 1975: 27). Everyone also agreed with him that "it is conceivable that the lowest estimate is too high and that the highest estimate is too low. Policy decisions are going to have to be made with these unresolved uncertainties" (Joint Economic Committee, 1975). This was after a study in which the people involved had worked for two and a half years. Here, however, we leave that small area of agreement by asking how the inevitable uncertainties are to be overcome or accounted for.

If the sources of uncertainty are thought to be centered in the judgments of estimators themselves, it might be wise to seek independent estimates. Presumably, this was the idea of asking the National Academy of sciences to appoint a panel to review various prior estimates. Since there are only a relatively small number of people who do this sort of thing, however, and since they came either from industry or from government, by definition those with the expertise cannot be new to the field. In fact, four of the nine estimates under review were prepared by members of the Geological Survey, and these estimates (as Table 9.1 shows) ranged from rather low to rather high. Furthermore, the chairman of the NAS panel was formerly with the Geological Survey, and its cochairman was employed there at the time.

One way of looking at the problem is to ask whether there is a single best approach or whether, given the state of the art, more than one will be equally valid. If a pluralist approach is taken, the aura of science may be tarnished, but disagreement also serves a positive function. The tradition called on here is one in which science proceeds by proposing and refuting hypotheses so that disagreement marks a healthy state of science. The alternative view—that there is a single best way to estimate, resulting in a single set of conclusions—suggests a stronger Science (with a capital S). There are better and worse methods of estimation; the better ones, used by unbiased investigators, will be correct. The tradition here is one in which science is seen as Scientific Method, of which there is only one kind and from which there is no appeal. This is not the science we know from the last twenty years of philosophy of science, but it may be the science that is more readily understood by public officials.

The pluralist approach suggests a startlingly simple method. First, one eliminates the estimates which are most extreme; then one takes the best-supported estimates at the high and low range in order to come out someplace in between. The National Academy of Science Panel combined the pluralist method with the pronouncement of universalism and arrived at a single figure. A pluralist disagreed, expressing the view that "we should not place great reliance on any single estimate of the magnitude of undiscovered resources—the unknown in a very real sense—but there is value and meaning in all of the estimates available if one understands what each of them is trying to assess and how each one has been made" (Joint Economic Committee, 1975: 9-10).

The legislators listening to this debate, not surprisingly, wanted an estimate they could hang their hats on. Senator Humphrey's evocative phrases captured the frustration:

Now, we have had all kinds of estimates made. They always make the headlines, and immediately people are writing letters that flood the mail. The mail is incredible. You cannot imagine, gentlemen, what hits us when these stories come out.

First of all they want to know, what are you doing about it, like somehow or another a Member of Congress can immediately go out and drill 10 oil wells and assure us of an extra million barrels a day. Incredible.

I was on a radio show yesterday up in Philadelphia. I took some questions, and when I got through I asked myself whether this was really necessary, because the questions were not the kind of questions that sought thoughtful analysis. It was—why aren't you doing this: why aren't you getting us some more oil. Senator: why haven't you started the coal gasification: why haven't you done this: and, didn't you read that report.

One said to me, didn't you read that report that came out from that group of scientists: aren't you frightened: what are you going to do about it.

Now, help me. Where do you come down in this wide range of estimates? Do you feel it is the upper or the lower end or where is it? [Joint Economic Committee, 1975: 53].

Would it be helpful for the senator to tell his constituents that there is a wide range of estimates that depend on assumptions about prices and technology? To go further, would it help if the senator said that these estimates were subject to great uncertainty, depending, as they did, on the time period involved, the methods used, the models employed, and so on? If there were only three variables subject to such uncertainty (such as drilling and extraction ratios) and if five values were assigned to each, at least seventy-five estimates would emerge. That is quite a point spread. To answer our rhetorical questions: No, it would not help, because for the purpose of communicating with constituents a point estimate was what legislators were seeking; that is exactly what the disagreement was about in the hearing.

No one wanted to hear why each of several oil and gas resource estimates might be plausible in some aspect and why these estimates call for a pluralist view. First, of course, is the sheer physical uncertainty of trying to estimate the undiscovered, let alone the inability to measure what *has* been discovered. Moreover, methods of estimation differ widely. In fact, the existence of several methods derives partly from the physical unknowns. The volumetric approach uses successful past exploration as a yardstick to predict the success of future exploration in unexplored areas.

A second approach, like the first, also involves extrapolation, but of a different character: Past yearly production trends and past discovery trends are analyzed. Then, noting the dependence of production trends on discovery trends, these trends are projected into the future. If the past is like the future, then the future may be well served by these two types of estimates. Since it is possible, however, that the richest areas have already been found and taken, the future may be worse than the past. A third, "geologic," approach is a probabilistic appraisal of undiscovered, recoverable oil and gas. To the volumetric information this appraisal adds some statistical integration of estimators' subjective judgments about areas that contain oil and gas. Resulting estimates could indicate, for example, a 95 percent chance of a certain amount of recoverable resources but also a 5 percent chance of there being quite a bit more.

The volumetric approach used alone tends to yield higher estimates than do approaches based on production-discovery patterns. According to "Mineral Resources and the Environment," the NAS committee report, the amount that could be recovered (under current prices and technology) was around 113 billion barrels of oil and 530 trillion cubic feet of gas—totals "considerably smaller" than the 1000-2000 trillion cubic feet of natural gas and the 200-400 billion barrels of oil estimated only the year before by the USGS, which had taken a volumetric approach. The two estimates differed by a factor of two. The academy's main conclusion was that its lower estimates of the likely additions to proved reserves made a substantial increase in the production of oil and gas "very unlikely." Knowing the policy debate, we may conclude it would be argued that no price increase could generate nonexistent oil.

The "News and Comment" section of the journal *Science* reported that M. King Hubbert (formerly an exploration geophysicist for Shell Oil), using a discovery-production approach, predicted that production in the United States would decline in the late 1960s. Generally, Hubbert held there was much less oil and gas than claimed by industry or government. For two decades his predictions were at odds with the much higher estimates associated with Vincent McKelvey, the geologist who in 1971 became head of the Geological Survey. It was after the OPEC price increase (and acceptance by the Project Independence Report of 1974 of the National Petroleum Council's claim that higher prices would result in a doubling of production) that NAS, according to *Science,* agreed to arbitrate among the various estimates [Science, 1975a: 723-725].

Even if all estimates used the same approach, assumptions might differ on physical and technological matters. For example, what do you assume to be the rate of discovery in totally unexplored areas? NAS, in trying to reconcile the differences between the high estimate attributed to McKelvey and the lower ones attributed to Hubbert and several oil companies, noted:

> It became evident that certain factors used in Estimate 8 [McKelvey's] could have been more rigorously derived. [See Table 9.1.] Particularly critical is the discovery ratio assumed for unexplored parts of basins in making Estimate 8. . . . The low figures for undiscovered resources were calculated on the basis of a discovery ratio of 0.5, the high figures on the basis of a ratio 1.0. Both ratios appear to be too high to be used in calculating undiscovered resources of the coterminous 48 states in which exploration has been carried out for more than 100 years.

The NAS report goes on to praise Hubbert's conclusion that the discovery ratio ("with a high degree of certainty") is nearer to 0.1. Applying this ratio to McKelvey's estimate brings it down to about 123 billion barrels (Joint Economic Committee, 1975: 21).

Is the method criticized intolerable and untenable? That depends on how you look at it. Speaking in his own defense, though he disclaimed sole authorship of the 1974 estimates, McKelvey believed "that it is useful to know that the undiscovered presently recoverable oil and gas resources in this country" might be as large as he said it was "under favorable circumstances." The volumetric method he used, he continued,

> is likely to give higher estimates than those obtained by the other methods because it allows for presence of oil and gas in rocks in which no specific targets have been identified. While this is obviously a disadvantage if it is misinterpreted as an assurance of what will in fact be found, properly understood it is also an advantage, for it tends to indicate the maximum that can be expected in a given area if unexplored rocks are nearly as prolific as those already explored [Joint Economic Committee, 1975: 8].

A different conclusion, taken from those same data in the NAS committee report, however, was reached by Professor S. Fred Singer of the Department of Environmental Sciences at the University of Virginia. The crucial figure is Hubbert's claim to have derived (rather than guessed) a 0.1 conversion from drilling to the discovery of oil. Whereas from 1860 to World War II the ratio was around 200 barrels per foot drilled, after 1950 the ratio leveled off to 35 barrels per foot drilled. Singer believed that changes in geological techniques are responsible for the difference, since early oil was found rather than drilled, and only lately has extensive drilling been required. "There is no guarantee," Singer concluded, "that the curve will decrease exponentially in the future, as Hubbert assumes, and thus there is no reliable way of estimating" (Science, 1975b: 401). Should the cost of drilling go up, for example—either because of price changes or because drilling is not treated so favorably in the tax laws—less speculative drilling will occur and the amount recovered per effort is likely to go up. Besides, there is some general agreement that most of the new oil is likely to be found offshore and in Alaska, where there has been no extensive drilling.

How did the NAS Committee on Mineral Resources and the Environment make its estimates? One of its members, K. O. Emery of the Woods Hole Oceanographic Institution, insisted that the NAS committee was not organized in order to review the work of Project Independence—whose conclusions were announced after the committee began working—but rather to provide a balanced, long-term view of problems concerning mineral resources in the environment.[2] Emery believed that "estimates of future supplies of oil and gas are so dependent upon unknown scientific factors and unknown environmental and political factors as to be almost unknowable, and they are by no means susceptible to simplistic solutions." Yet nothing could be simpler than to end up someplace between the highest and lowest estimates. As a committee member testified, "from our point of view, we thought it advisable . . . to accept more conservative estimates, thinking that most of the Geological Survey estimates are relatively high, and most of the oil company estimates are relatively conservative" (Joint Economic Committee, 1975: 14). This is Science?

Acknowledging that the dates of the events Hubbert predicted had been amazingly accurate, McKelvey expressed a point of view that still deserves to be heard:

> Because Mr. Hubbert's estimates are in essence based on the product of human activities, which in turn are influenced by economics, technological development and public policies, I believe that they are most useful in indicating what is likely to happen if things continue to go the way they have in the past. This also is useful to know. . . . Projections of this type, however, assume that the course of future petroleum exploration and production is an inexorable one, regardless of major modifications in economic conditions, technological advances or public policies [Joint Economic Committee, 1975: 9].

It should now be evident that no resource estimate has a monopoly on plausibility. A number of them can contain elements of equal validity. Resource estimates are products of uncertainty; they vary depending on the method of estimation, and on the assumptions of estimators. Equally important, estimates vary depending on how one interprets the question one thinks one is trying to answer, and on the context behind the request for the estimate. A private producer in the business of exploring may see the question as, "How much evidence is there that a company, with today's technology and today's prices, will consider it worthwhile to produce over the next five years?" A government estimator may interpret the same question to be, "How much can the United States reasonably expect to have available to use over the next 25 years, so the government can plan the shift to alternative energy sources?" Finally, to some degree, resource estimates or predictions depend on what industry and government do or do not do to make them happen or to keep them from happening. One who sees little likelihood of finding oil may not search for it. If a natural gas explorer does not think the government's price will cover costs and leave an acceptable profit, it may seem unprofitable to explore. The question, "How much oil and gas does the United States have?" reminds us of the old Buddhist proverb: If twelve wise men give different answers to a single question, then it must be the wrong question.

HOW WOULD RESOURCE ESTIMATES INFLUENCE POLICY?

To what degree are predictions of potential resources a species of self-fulfilling or self-defeating prophecy? If we believe there is less oil and gas to be found and we therefore drill less or encourage less drilling, then less is bound to be discovered, even if there is more oil and gas found per foot drilled. The more worthwhile we make it to search harder, the more oil and gas may be discovered. Only if there were stringent known, natural limits—meaning that the oil and gas are not there—could these predictions be invalidated.

"In a way," K. O. Emery writes, "debates about the environmental and political controls on oil and gas production are akin to the medieval debates about how many angels can dance upon the head of a pin" (Science, 1975c: 973). Consider the nature of the question: How much oil and gas *might* there be underground that *might* be technologically feasible and economically worth producing at different future times? Do two "mights" make a maybe?

A pluralistic estimate cast in uncertainty is a breeding ground for mistrust. The inherent uncertainties in estimating resources underground are compounded by the uncertainties of what technology is or will be capable of doing and how much is worth spending. Technological doubt, multiplied by human judgment, can easily produce mutual mistrust. There is mistrust of knowledge and mistrust of will, as if estimation had become a mirror reflecting only what partisans of policy wish to see rather than what is there.

Every estimate that has come to our attention so far, moreover, includes more variables than are apparent in whatever main estimation method is being employed. There appears always to be some judgment about the consequences of technology or price levels or of secondary or tertiary recovery of tar sands and oil shale. Facts are alleged to be fictions so that whatever anybody says, not only about estimates but about how they were made, is challenged by somebody else.

After the hearings were over, McKelvey was asked to explain in writing why the major differences between himself and the other experts were not on the outer continental shelf and Alaska, which had been little explored, but on the lower forty-eight states, which had been explored substantially more. In response, McKelvey pointed out that this disagreement was not with the NAS committee, which made no calculations of its own, but with the Mobil and Sun oil companies whose estimates the committee had used.[3]

In totally unexplored areas, McKelvey believed, everyone was at a similar disadvantage. "The agreement of experts on the oil potential of undrilled areas is more apparent than real—it denotes a common level of ignorance of what geological conditions are rather than a high degree of accuracy on what they are" (Joint Economic Committee, 1975: 60). In regard to well-explored areas, companies that do the exploring are interested in what they can find and extract themselves, rather than in what might be available. Again, McKelvey stated:

> An oil company will tend to estimate the amount of oil which it knows how to find, and if the estimates are to be made public, it would further consider whether all the extent of its knowledge should be revealed. This is a legitimate bias in a competitive business such as oil exploration, but it should be kept in mind. On the other hand, a public agency such as the Geological Survey tends to estimate what could be found given the proper policies and steps to

be adopted by government; such estimates are targets for exploration and technologic advance rather than predictions of what will be
found and produced [Joint Economic Committee, 1975: 59-60].

Aside from the potentially valuable information about the direction of
bias among various estimators, McKelvey's comments indicate a volitional
element in estimation: Among the purposes of estimation are not only to
predict what might be there, but also to encourage exploration and drilling
to test the hypothesis. Alternatively, these estimates might be said to
contain ingredients of conditional prediction: If government enacts certain
incentives and if private companies adopt the required policies, the predictions may be made good. Thus, the borderline between estimation and
incentive becomes blurred.

MOPPS

The controversy over the Market-Oriented Program Planning Study was
not about differences over how much natural gas would be produced at
any given cost, but about larger political issues of energy policy. The furor
over MOPPS shows that it is not what numbers are produced but who
produces them and on what side of the controversy such data are perceived to be that influences their interpretation. If differences between the
various estimates were policy-relevant, the relationships between cost and
supply produced by each of the three MOPPS groups would have been
different. As it was, all three estimates agreed on the fundamental relationship between cost and supply, but disagreed about what to include in
calculating the cost of producing additional undiscovered reserves. If the
relationship were more "pessimistic" (no matter what the cost, little gas
will be discovered), the ratio of cost to supply (the slope, as it is called)
would have to approach a value greater than one.[4] If the relationship were
more "optimistic," the slope approaching zero would indicate that the
slightest increase in cost would produce large increases in supply. Estimates of potential natural gas production supplied by the three working
groups produced remarkably similar relationships. Even where the most
substantial difference occurred, the fundamental relationship was basically
the same. Yet, the groups were treated as if they were in blatant opposition.

The Market-Oriented Program Planning Study was undertaken by the
Energy Research and Development Administration to help policy makers

understand the relationship between costs and supplies of natural gas. However, MOPPS did more to confuse and confound than to clarify the policy area. It generated heated conflicts that went beyond its function as a simple set of studies to determine cost/supply curves. MOPPS became controversial not because its various estimates were so different from each other, and not because the relationships on which each estimate was based were qualitatively different from each other; rather, the interests involved were sharply divided, and each had a stake in the MOPPS results. The alternative predictions of natural gas supply—no matter how little difference there was between estimates—took on a magnified importance for each interest.

Although, on the face of it, the blow-up was about why the Energy Research and Development Administration (ERDA) squelched an optimistic estimate in favor of a more conservative one, the underlying issues are tied to the larger historical questions on energy policy in the United States. The importance of MOPPS for policy makers should have been to understand the shape of the relationship between costs and supplies. The actual size of that relation is of little consequence for policy makers because all of the studies within MOPPS indicate the positive position of cost to supply: As the amount spent goes up, the supply of natural gas increases until some point near the end of the curve where, no matter how much money is expended, a decreasing amount of natural gas will be produced.

The differences between various estimates are not important in answering the overall policy question concerning what to do to produce greater supplies of natural gas. You go either to $1.50 per thousand cubic feet to produce 635 trillion cubic feet of natural gas (Estimate 1) or $3.50 (Estimate 2) or to $5.00 (Estimate 3). Whatever you choose to believe, natural gas costs are going to get more expensive. (See Figure 9.1 and Senate Committee on Energy and Natural Resources, 1977: 95). To put this in some perspective, as of 1975 there were 237 trillion cubic feet of natural gas proved reserves. Even taking the lowest estimate, we could double our supplies at $3.00 per thousand cubic feet. These differences are not of the type that would change policy when the cost of alternative fuels keeps climbing, especially when we consider that most of the difference is due to assumptions about what to include in determining the curves. Estimates 1 and 2 (the optimistic and less optimistic estimates, respectively) *both* include proved reserves in calculating marginal costs to increase the next unit of natural gas. The third estimate (the truly pessimistic one) does not include proved reserves in its calculations but instead starts from the point of how much it will cost to find new, yet undiscovered supplies. Here, incidentally, is the greatest discrepancy between Estimates 1 and 3. Thus, again, if it made little difference to policy, why was there such controversy over MOPPS?

People Had a Stake in MOPPS

The Market-Oriented Program Planning Study was requested in January 1977 by Robert W. Fri, acting administrator of ERDA, as an instrument to help in ranking research and development policies. One part of the study involved projecting quantities of supplies that could be expected at various future costs for oil, gas, coal, and electricity. This part of MOPPS was headed by Christian W. Knudsen. Knudsen was in the planning section of the assistant administrator for Fossil Energy within ERDA when he went, "on loan," to the MOPPS project. Knudsen's group, using USGS estimates of undiscovered recoverable resources, arrived at a "high" estimate: Substantial quantities of natural gas could be made available at relatively low production costs.

On April 7, preliminary MOPPS results were presented at a meeting of ERDA senior officials. Knudsen's projections, indicating that low-cost gas was still to be found in abundance, shocked most ERDA officials in attendance: It would mean a significant setback in ERDA's plans for all kinds of research and development projects for substitute technologies. As Knudsen later testified before the Senate Energy Committee, his low cost estimates "put many of the technologies that ERDA is developing in some question about their urgency and priority" (Senate Committee on Energy and Natural Resources, 1977: 12).

Knudsen's results were the only ones officially described to the assembled administrators on April 7. But the results of an entirely separate, conflicting, ad hoc study were handed out at the end of the meeting. What was this second study? It turned out that during March, Knudsen's team had begun to get hints that their projections were going to be unexpectedly high. During that same month, elsewhere in ERDA's Fossil Energy Office, Martin Adams (unbeknownst to Knudsen until April 1) was conducting a separate study of oil and gas cost/supply projections. The Adams study had been requested by Philip C. White, assistant administrator for Fossil Energy. White told the Senate Energy Committee that he had wanted a balancing alternative to the Knudsen results:

Because of the critical importance of these conventional oil and gas estimates, the study directed the second ad hoc group to parallel the

Intermediate Supply Group of Dr. Knudsen in developing independent estimates of the future outlook for oil and gas [Senate Committee on Energy and Natural Resources, 1977: 65].

Adams, following a methodology different from Knudsen's—using a model developed and supported by Gulf at the Stanford Research Institute—reached much more "pessimistic" conclusions: There was less gas to be found than Knudsen suggested, and only at significantly higher costs.

Here, then, were two apparently conflicting sets of results facing the ERDA administrators. Harry Johnson, executive director of MOPPS, was scheduled to meet with Secretary Schlesinger in six days (on April 13) to brief him on the results. On April 20, President Carter would address the nation with a message to the effect that the United States was fast running out of oil and gas; that we must sacrifice by conserving energy; that research and development on substitute technologies would receive high priority; and that prices should be allowed to rise somewhat in the hope of eliciting larger conventional supplies. This agenda and ERDA's own agenda were better supported by Adams's low supply estimates than by Knudsen's vision of plenty.

Johnson had expected that Schlesinger might find MOPPS useful in making recommendations to Carter as backup for the President's speech. But now, in the wake of conflicting estimates, what was ERDA supposed to tell Schlesinger? The Schlesinger briefing was canceled. On April 19, in a meeting charged with moral outrage, ERDA senior officials battled with their MOPPS colleagues. Many favored Adams's results as more advantageous to both ERDA and to the administration's policy preferences—despite the fact that much of the Gulf/Stanford Research Institute model (i.e., documentation, computer procedure) was not open to ERDA examination, while the USGS data were available to all.

ERDA Assistant Administrator White was especially disturbed by Knudsen's high estimates, and feared those estimates would be disseminated as "the White study." Finally, on April 26, White had Knudsen removed from MOPPS and sent back to his old desk in the Fossil Energy Office.

Meanwhile, a third "independent" estimate was sought. Seventy experts from government (ERDA, USGS, Bureau of Mines, and FEA), with supplemental private-sector assistance and three congressional staff committee observers, met in Reston, Virginia, to assemble a carefully documented data base for public review.

The Reston study was to come up with a "stronger" quantitative basis for cost estimates of resources. Government experts invited representatives of the private sector to participate in part of the meeting. Nine subgroups considered individual oil and gas basins in various parts of the country, both onshore and offshore. The subgroups gave their "best considered judgments" about the basin's potential and the cost of realizing that potential. Unlike previous studies, *all* of the basic information used and developed by the Reston group participants between May 24 and 26, 1977, was open for public inspection as part of the public review of the entire Market-Oriented Program Planning Study. The results of the Reston study were "significantly more pessimistic than [those of] the other two MOPPS groups."

On June 23 and 28, the Senate Energy Committee got in on the act by holding hearings on MOPPS. The key figures in these hearings were Democratic Senators Howard Metzenbaum (Ohio) and John A. Durkin (New Hampshire). These senators found the difference between Knudsen's and Adams's results highly significant. After all, this was a period in which estimates of reserves and resources had assumed great importance. The two senators, and many others, objected to much of the administration's proposed National Energy Plan, particularly to the administration's inclination to raise prices and to turn to coal and other environmentally degrading technologies. Many Democrats did not think there was a shortage at all—only that the producing companies were underreporting or underproducing. Therefore it was not surprising that Metzenbaum and Durkin sympathized openly with Knudsen and favored his high estimates of natural gas still to be found at low cost.

During the hearing Metzenbaum and Durkin treated Knudsen as a man of integrity who had been wronged by ERDA bureaucrats seeking only to preserve their own interests. In Durkin's words, "to complete parallel studies and accept the one most in line with administration policy, as seems to be the case here, is at best unprofessional. In this situation, it has cast doubt on the Government's capability regarding the entire energy crisis and energy supply situation. The MOPPS controversy has also demonstrated the continuing need for knowing precisely what our national energy reserves really are." Senator Durkin harbored a profound mistrust of the industry and, increasingly, of the administration: "Is the arbitrarily and politically motivated rejection of the Knudsen findings, and his summary removal, part of a double coverup—a coverup of the true extent of our national gas reserves, and a coverup by the bureaucrats of that coverup?" (Senate Committee on Energy and Natural Resources, 1977: 3-4).

Then Senator Durkin tried to pull Knudsen into agreement about policy:

> So possibly, and there is no hard evidence yet to dispute your findings, it is quite possible that at a time when we are literally swimming in natural gas, that to put in a wellhead tax is building a floor under the OPEC price and making it impossible to force down the OPEC price even if it's true, if it's demonstrated that we are swimming in natural gas?
>
> And added to that, we have the cost of billions and billions of dollars that are going to be spent digging up the coal in the West, and the East, building railroads or building slurries to get it to areas in this country, costs for scrubbers, for precombustion, cleaning of coal, costs of CO_2 in the air, the greenhouse effect, costs of changing electric boiler generation, industry boilers in the South and Southeast from natural gas to a much dirtier fuel—coal, when we well may be swimming in natural gas?
>
> *Dr. Knudsen.* Well, I have tried very hard through this whole study, Senator, to maintain an engineering and professional posture and stay away from drawing individual conclusions, so we—
>
> *Senator Durkin.* But based on your experience and your expertise, I can understand a reluctance to get into the political field—the last time, it cost you your job. But if you could, elaborate for the record?
>
> *Dr. Knudsen.* Well, that scenario you describe is possible, if indeed gas is found in large quantities, if the estimates that we have used are substantiated in future practice, and if indeed the cost figures that we have used prove to be reasonable. We produced them from the best available information that we can lay our hands on; we said they were preliminary. In phase 2 we planned to go and look at some of the points in great detail, and determine the range of uncertainties, particularly in our cost analysis. We were proceeding—beginning—to do this when our efforts were terminated.
>
> So I would be much more satisfied in making that kind of a statement, Senator, if I had been allowed to finish phase 2 of the effort, to get a better idea around the estimate. But I must say I am somewhat handicapped in not having been given the possibilities of that scenario, because I don't have any basis of knowing the uncertainty, the "error band," if you will [Senate Committee on Energy and Natural Resources, 1977: 40].

A few minutes later, Durkin tried again;

> Don't you think this situation—whether you're right or wrong, don't
> you think this situation—and I am not in a position right now to
> determine whether you are right or incorrect; I believe you're a
> dedicated public servant, trying to do a job that you inherited when
> Whitehall moved up—but don't you think this—before the Congress
> acts, before the Senate acts, with the wellhead tax, and for coal
> conversion, and these many other things—don't you think this cries
> out for an immediate and thorough investigation of the amount of
> natural gas in this country, measured, inferred and probably undis-
> covered?

How was Knudsen supposed to answer such a question? "Well, I—yes, sir; I
believe it's a very important thing to make decisions based on the best
available information" [Senate Committee on Energy and Natural
Resources, 1977: 41].

Results Were Not Different Enough
to Influence Policy

The three estimates are far less divergent than the furor over them
suggested. Curves representing the results of all three studies appear in
Figure 9.1.

What is the issue? Is it the size of natural gas proved reserves? No; all
three studies agree on proved and probable reserves. The controversy is
over undiscovered resources—natural gas not yet known even to exist. In
the latter sections of the curves, showing the play of undiscovered
resources—in which discrepancies in estimated absolute quantities occur—
one would expect the curves to be quite dissimilar. But are they? In Figure
9.2, where we have superimposed the curves on each other to show their
slopes and actual differences, notice how similar they are. The slopes (or
rate of change) of all three curves are almost exactly the same. For each
additional $.50 increase in cost of production, one can expect almost the
same amount of new gas to be found. What happens at the margin should
be the focus of attention. It is not the absolute quantities but the
additional quantities at the margin that are potentially important for
policy. Further, all three cost/supply curves suggest that the marginal cost
for adding another trillion cubic feet of natural gas is the same for each
estimate.

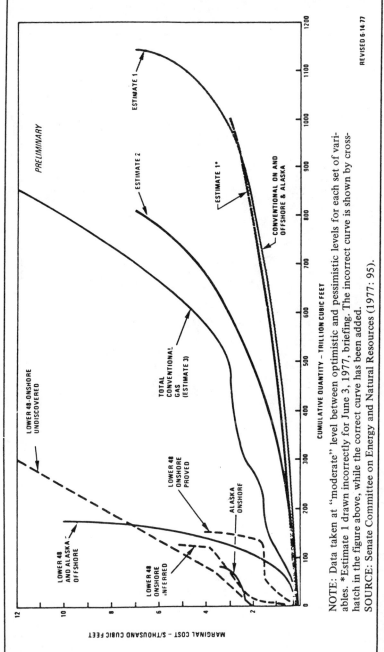

NOTE: Data taken at "moderate" level between optimistic and pessimistic levels for each set of variables. *Estimate 1 drawn incorrectly for June 3, 1977, briefing. The incorrect curve is shown by cross-hatch in the figure above, while the correct curve has been added.

SOURCE: Senate Committee on Energy and Natural Resources (1977: 95).

Figure 9.1: Conventional Domestic Gas (MOPPS)

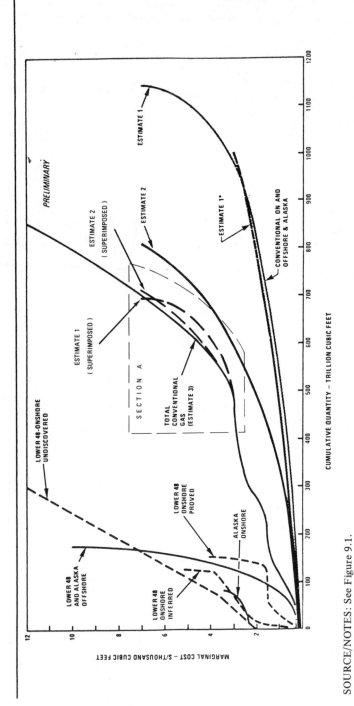

SOURCE/NOTES: See Figure 9.1.

Figure 9.2: Conventional Domestic Gas (modified)

In a letter detailing the different approaches of the three MOPPS groups, Larry Oppenheimer, a Congressional Budget Office analyst, wrote that while

> the fundamental issue about gas reserves which the MOPPS exposes . . . might be very important after 1990 . . . none of the findings [of the three sets of estimates] of the MOPPS study are especially important in a policy sense before 1985. . . . In my view, the three estimates within MOPPS are all credible and valid. . . . Actual estimates of potential resources which can be produced in this century are very conjectural; so it should not be surprising that competing studies would come to somewhat different conclusions. . . . If the difference between estimates I and II or III leads to a different decision on policy, then the policy should be questioned, because there is no basis at this time to conclude that one estimate is more credible than the other.[5]

The MOPPS controversy and the Humphrey hearing are but two illustrations of an important question about the relationship between data and public policy: If the difference between estimates mattered for policy-making—if a decision, or action, or theory is sensitive to a higher or a lower number—then one can understand why there were such bitter arguments estimates. But if we are dealing with great unknowns, as resource estimates are, and if the differences between the estimates are too small to matter for policy-making, why have these estimates generated so much passion and hostility? The answer, we think, is that the disagreements at bottom are not about estimates but about ideologies and institutions. Where values and political aims are polarized and where certain numbers appear to strengthen or weaken one's position, small differences between the estimates are magnified. Even when the technical experts agree, the political process converts their agreement into disagreement.

NOTES

1. Definitions of "resources" and "recoverable resources" are taken from Schanz (1978), whose essay is reproduced in the appendix to this book.

2. Using a similarly informal method, we may imagine that the NAS committee was already in existence when it took on this target of opportunity, a well-publicized difference in estimates.

3. Based on McKelvey's written response to questions. It was not possible to identify, on Table 9.1, which companies (designated by letters) represented Mobil and Sun.

4. The slope indicates the rate of change in supply resulting from a change in cost.

5. Letter from Larry Oppenheimer, Congressional Budget Office, to Elizabeth Moler, Staff Counsel, Senate Committee on Energy and Natural Resources (p. 69-70).

REFERENCES

Joint Economic Committee (1975) Adequacy of U.S. Oil and Gas Reserves. Washington, DC: Government Printing Office.

SCHANZ, J. J., Jr. (1978) "Oil and gas resources: welcome to uncertainty." Resources for the Future 58 (March).

Science (1975a) February 28.

——— (1975b) May 2.

——— (1975c) June 6.

Senate Committee on Energy and Natural Resources (1977) Hearings, Market-Oriented Program Planning Study. Washington, DC: Government Printing Office.

PART  THE CURRENT
DILEMMA

SINCE ESTIMATION OF OIL AND GAS reserves and resources is so riddled with uncertainty and with volitional elements, it seems of questionable value to beat our heads against the wall searching for a "more perfect" estimate. The alternative approach would be to lessen our dependence on such estimates. Decreasing the demand for data requires dominant solutions that are insensitive to a wide range of estimates; or it requires solutions that are tied only to an extreme estimate. To recognize a solution as dominant, in turn, requires a common conception of the problem. There must be some formulated idea, some potential action in mind to guide and limit collection of data. Data are meaningful in terms of a policy hypothesis ("If this is done, then that will happen."), not as random bits.

This shared view has been missing from energy policy in the United States. Congress had no agreed purpose; instead, policy preferences on energy were sharply divided and irreconcilable. Under the system of partial and conflicting controls which has characterized this country's energy policy, shortages were possible and did indeed result. Because even partially administered prices were deemed more just than prices under a market believed to be dominated by a monopolistic industry, the majority in Congress focused its attention on pricing and allocation policies to close the gap and prevent future shortages.

Planning on this scale would have required an enormous amount of data. Standing out in the energy legislation of the mid-1970s was a desire for any data that would enable policy makers to measure the shortage, determine the extent of industry responsibility, and close the gap. Despite all the effort to fulfill this mandate, the data produced left everyone dissatisfied. Responsibility for shortage, underreporting of reserves, excessive profits—none of these charges had been confirmed.

What was the problem? It was not that industry was "innocent." The large producers and refiners plainly were on the defensive, trying to explain why they were doing so well while millions were enduring shortages and paying more. Industrialists in their own way contributed to dissension. They used government intervention variably to maintain profits. In earlier years, for example, producers had urged government regulation to limit oil production—and thereby raise profits. Now they were calling for price deregulation to encourage more production—and increase profitability. Industry, itself divided, nevertheless often came across as a united force ready to unleash a torrent of oil and gas if only the government would lift its price controls. Thus, the majors and large independents provoked mistrust and suspicion. How, then, do we explain the pattern of unsubstantiated allegations over industry data and estimation systems? The Scottish verdict, "unproven" is apropos. All we can say is that the allegations could not be substantiated. The particular charges were virtually impossible to prove. After all, except for offshore areas, only the companies had the original data. Moreover, to belabor the obvious, only the companies could be accused, because they were the entities that did the estimating. That is one major reason behind their current intention to give up making reserve estimates.

The accusations and refutations are best placed in the context of "the politics of mistrust" that produces data that are ipso facto suspect. The political arena was polarized, on one side by a disposition to control the energy industry, and on the other side by a disposition to favor private enterprise. Majority opinion was itself divided between a suspicion of industry and a reluctance to nationalize it with all that implied. This deep ambivalence underlay the political turmoil over energy, the unproven allegations, the obstacles to implementing regulations, and the battles over estimates.

The final section brings us to the present time. Chapter 10 begins with a theoretical approach to the relationship between energy data and energy policy. We then look closely at recent policy alternatives that are assumed to be sensitive to estimates of undiscovered, recoverable oil and gas resources. Exactly how would a high or a low estimate influence a particular policy choice? If either the high or the low estimate were "correct," we conclude, this knowledge would exert little influence on the most important policy variables, world oil price, and the relative prices of other energy sources in a world-market context. But if estimates are not relevant to policy, why are we Americans still beating ourselves over the head about it?

Through the experience of the Department of Energy's own Oil and Gas Information System, we examine the relationship between the credibility of data and the relevance of data to clients' purposes (Chapter 11). Basically, those clients who actually use data already have what they want. And those whose main purpose is to abuse data so as to abuse their enemies will not be satisfied in any event. The conclusion explores several paths toward the kind of settlement prerequisite to making data more closely reflect what clients want.

DO ESTIMATES INFLUENCE POLICY DECISIONS, OR DO POLICIES INFLUENCE ESTIMATES?

TWO PEOPLE ARE RIDING IN A CAR. The driver looks at the gas gauge and exclaims, "I won't get there. The gas tank is half empty." His passenger replies, "We're getting where we're going. Besides, the tank is half full." Expand this illustration to a busload of people with various destinations and differing proclivities to fret about, and a gas gauge that works accurately only post-factum, (i.e., telling you how much you have used but not how much is left). Expand the example to a multitude of people with a laundry list of goals (often vague and at times conflicting) and you have an array of fuel gauges decipherable only by a few, each of whom comes to a different conclusion.

No doubt there would be mistrust and dissension; any appeal to the facts would be the exception rather than the rule, and made only as a last resort. Why, then, do people view irrelevance of data as an aberrational rather than an enduring trait against which, in fact, the brief interludes of "rationality" need to be explained?

We suggest that this topsy-turvy view of what is normal and what is surprising results from a misleading and incomplete view of the relationship between data and politics and how the two are forged to produce policy. As we see it, data, far from preceding policy, are inextricably intertwined with politics; moreover, in formulating energy policy, there is no unalterable need to get the number straight before doing anything else. We conclude that the view that data drive policy stands at odds with recent experience in gas and oil resource estimation. As we have shown in the preceding chapters, that particular history is best characterized as one of continuing mistrust and contention among polarized factions, interrupted only by episodes of wartime political consensus.

If data and politics were not intertwined, one would be led to focus on improving the data without regard to the policy context. On the other hand, and just as futile, one could try to formulate policy guided only by personal preferences, without acknowledging the resource constraints suggested by data.

In policy formulation neither data nor politics has claim to primacy. Both political preferences and resource estimates (the number estimated, as opposed to the physical quantity of oil that is denoted) are in flux. The nexus of estimates and policy, that tangle of fact and value, evolves through time. Data drives politics under certain circumstances, in that data set the outside parameters for policy debate. The data are not sufficiently precise to fine-tune policy. If there is no oil, pretending there is will not get you far. For the most part, data constrain rather than suggest. In other circumstances, political settlements override data disputes and may be prerequisites to agreement on estimates.

As a heuristic guide to untangling the Gordian knots of data and politics, visualize a two-dimensional matrix, which shows agreement on estimates measured on one axis, and the degree of political consensus on the other. The "data" axis is divided into two segments: when the range of supply estimations is deemed narrow, and when the range is judged wide. The "political" axis also is divided into two segments: when there is political consensus, and when there is political polarization.

Periods in the history of gas and oil reserve estimation can be sorted by this fourfold typology. Other observers of the history of resource estimation may wish to include other explanatory variables by adding other dimensions to the matrix; we want to highlight those themes we believe to be most important.

When there is political consensus and the range of supply estimates is deemed narrow, facts support values and vice versa, and policy is easily determined.

When estimates vary widely, when political factions are powerful and the cleavages run deep, then facts and values are at cross-purposes. Mistrust has surrounded peacetime reserve estimates from the outset. The series of estimates produced by the USGS between 1908 and 1922 were consistently pessimistic: The message was that resources were being used up (sometimes wastefully) and government should regulate the oil industry. Industry responded by providing its own more optimistic series of estimates, hoping to head off government regulation. Mistrust grew as subfactions multiplied—preservationists, consumerists, the constant and the variable marketers. What mattered in the end was whether the estimated number supported one's possition. Reserve estimates were drawn into the vortex of clashing fundamental views.

When there is tight political consensus but estimates vary widely, the estimates are likely to be considered irrelevant, and data will have no

TABLE 10.1

	Data *narrow range* *of estimates*	*Data* *wide range* *of estimates*
Consensus	Data and policy will be mutually supporting.	Variations in data will be deemed unimportant.
Polarization	Differences between estimates will be magnified and subject to multiple policy interpretations.	Data will be subject to multiple policy interpretations.

traction on policy. During World War II, victory became the overriding objective, subjugating most other considerations, including the relationship between government and the oil industry. Antitrust activity was temporarily suspended and industry tolerated government control over prices and production. Estimates were accepted by most or ignored or worked out. Although no faction was persuaded that its position was fundamentally incorrect, differences were put aside.

When technical experts agree on the numbers but the political context is highly factionalized, estimates are subject to the "half full or half empty" dispute. Differences are magnified and data provide no guidance for policy. The experience with the Market-Oriented Program Planning Study (MOPPs, see Chapter 9) shows how wide political differences can overshadow fundamental agreement on the data. As a result, remarkably similar estimates become ammunition for policy debate, each side ignoring the similarities and interpreting the numbers for its own advantage.

That prior agreement on data leads to subsequent direction in policy is a notion with widespread currency among public officials. Drawing from positivist and empiricist traditions, this epistemology holds facts to be distinct from and immutable to values. Science and technology stand value-free and apart from value-laden politics. Objectivity reins in political emotions or, at best, science presents the alternatives from which the political process selects. The question of epistemology is: How do we know what we know? Certifying facts translated into the policy realm results in calls for more data (for data provide the foundations for policy), more data validation (for the foundations of policy must be firm), and, yet again, for double-checking the validators (for small tilts in the foundations can topple the entire edifice of policy).

Between 1975 and 1977 Congress passed a series of mandates for "comprehensive, adequate, and accurate" data. Data on oil and gas reserves were part of a larger collection pertaining to all energy supplies which, in turn, belonged to a larger set on regulatory, environmental, and foreign policy questions related to energy. Better to have asked for too much rather than for too little, thought Congress.

In our simple typology (see Table 10.1), it as if history were viewed solely as movement from the lower-lefthand corner to the upper-lefthand corner—when data consensus (i.e., agreement among estimators, their validators, and the validators' auditors) crystallizes a policy consensus from diverse political factions.

This is well and good, so long as the data are hardy enough to contain centrifugal political strains. In the area of oil and gas reserve estimation, the data are rarely that robust. What can happen also is that confusion among estimators and their retinue of validators and auditors can unravel political settlement. When data estimates multiply, so do political factions. In short, we move from the upper-righthand corner of the matrix to the lower-righthand corner. Data still drive policy, but if data are confusing, so, perforce, will be policy.

As the preceding chapters have shown, the history of resource estimation is, more often than not, one in which politics dominates the data rather than the converse.

Themes discussed by philosophers of science may help us understand why data have so little traction on policy, and why policies are so little determined by data, for where policy scientists speak about translating data into information (and subsequently into knowledge), philosophers of science talk about converting sensory perceptions to fact, and about the links between fact and theory.

Recent philosophers of science have meshed the supposed distinction between facts and theory, introducing a more thoroughgoing pragmatism to supplant the empiricist tradition formerly understood to be an advancement over metaphysical speculation as the method for acquiring knowledge.

At one time, it was thought that the truth could be discovered through divine revelation or by metaphysical introspection. If people could escape the corruption of their natural senses and the idiosyncracies of experience, they could apprehend the world as it truly is, rather than as it appears. Truth resided in a metaphysical or theological realm; the physical world was ephemeral. Only by that direct apprehension, made possible by perceptual or spiritual purification, could verification be achieved.

That the natural senses could be trusted, and that experience could provide the foundations for knowledge, was the premise later, for empiricists. The flight into the metaphysical or the theological realm was no longer necessary or desirable. Human beings in their world were sufficient. For empiricists, to see the facts is to know. The foundation for knowledge is the world, parceled into sense data, denoted by neutral observation terms, and strung together logically into a set of facts. As Quine (1961) stated, "modern empiricism has been conditioned in large part ... by the belief that each meaningful statement is equivalent to some logical construct upon terms which refer to immediate experience." Quine called this belief the "dogma of reductionism," and argued that it was ill-founded.

Whereas empiricists contended that statements could be divided into two classes—those that depend on facts for verification and those that do not—Quine proposed that the unit of empirical significance was not the statement, but the whole of science: "Our statements about the external world face the tribunal of sense experience not individually but only as a corporate body." Quine suggested the metaphor of knowledge as a man-made fabric which impinges on experience only along the edges. No particular experience is linked with any particular statement. Thus, recalcitrant experience can be accommodated by any of a variety of shifts in the web of beliefs. Two implications follow: Come what may, any statement can be held true so long as we make sufficiently drastic changes elsewhere in the conceptual web. Conversely, no statement is immune to revision or holds special status as "factually based." In reweaving that conceptual fabric in light of new experience, considerations which lead to changes in one part rather than another are, Quine argued, rational, pragmatic.

Thomas Kuhn's (1962) work in the philosophy of science amplified this holistic view of scientific knowledge. Denying that there are statements of fact anchored in the real world and independent of vacillating theory, Kuhn argued that "observation statements" are embedded in, rather than outside of, theory. Sensory experience is filtered and codified into "meaningful" perceptions, but the filtering and codification are theory-specific. The conversion of sense impressions into data depends on the particular theoretical framework of the viewer. To see is not to know, for what we see depends on what we know.

This theoretical framework, a "paradigm," may be acquired implicitly as part of one's scientific and cultural heritage; conversion of phenomena into a set of linguistic statements does not occur without some implicit paradigm. Fundamental shifts in the paradigm result in and are indistinguishable from a recasting of the "facts." Theories do not change inde-

258 The Politics of Mistrust

pendent of fact; a theory, with its associated statements of fact, supplants another theory, with its associated statements of fact. Viewed as a statement about energy estimates, we might add, this conclusion contains a critical truth: Estimates and policies go together.

During periods of "scientific revolutions," if Kuhn is correct, there is no final appeal to the facts to reconcile conflicting hypotheses, because the "facts" themselves, being theory-specific, are in question. Change occurs not as a matter of persuasion but as a result of conversion, not as piecemeal modification but as wholesale acceptance of a new paradigm.

Crucial experiments (the empiricist's ideal of verification) fail during these revolutions. As Quine points out, the data are not linked directly to one particular hypothesis. Thus, contrary data can be explained away: The process of observation, the integrity of the experiment, and the motives of experimenter are questioned, as is the significance of the measurement or any of the dozen assumptions and premises. And as Kuhn says, the description of a phenomenon itself may be couched in theory-specific language, the language of the same theory that phenomenon purports to refute.

Statements of fact, according to pragmatists, are statements which owe their "factualness" not to some unique connection to the world (theory-determined perception severed that link), but to humanity's preference for those statements rather than others. Almost tautologically, "facts" are fact because we treat them as facts, relative to other statements.

In a community of scientists, facts are statements stipulated to be facts. That judgment often is tacit, resulting from implicit acceptance of the broad conceptual framework or from socialization into a common discourse. At other times, the stipulation as to what counts as fact may be explicit and indirect. Scientists, by explicitly describing a process (so others may replicate an experiment), by using "standardized," "accepted," or "conventional," methods (all forms of stipulation), accord the status of "factual observation" to an experimental finding. Scientists acknowledge the "objectivity" of results by certifying among themselves the integrity of the process, not by direct apprehension of the fact.

Appeal to the facts to resolve disputes is possible only when there is *prior* consensus, both concerning the implicit conceptual framework (the language of discourse) and the rules of resolution. Though no statement is immune to revision, we must agree to hold some statements stable if we seek reconciliation on the basis of facts. If everything were up for grabs all the time, if fundamental questions were raised with every new experience, progress through incremental adjustment would cease.

While recent philosophers have undermined the supposed objective foundations of the scientific enterprise, some policy makers have gone on trying to model their enterprises on science because of its presumed objectivity. Empirical facts, first denigrated by the Platonist, then deified by the empiricist, and recently held to be no more mystical than pragmatic constructions, seem to hold conceptual currency for some policy makers. Natural science is the ideal, which policy science (because policy makers have to live with the messiness of values) can only approximate.

Does this mean that observation and experience should play no role in policy formulation and that we can "imagine" away constraints? Hardly. To have knowledge constrained by experience, even though only at the edges, is not the same as to have no empirical constraint on knowledge.

Though estimates may not generate policy, they may contradict policy. Such clashes with experience may produce proposals for new policies. As Karl Popper might put it, conjectures (read "policy") can never be positively justified. Conjectures, however, can be controlled by criticism, by attempted refutations which include severely critical empirical tests. Through such criticism, we are able to propose more mature and deeper conjectures. Thus, knowledge progresses by "learning from mistakes" and correcting error.

A second check against rampant policy solipsism—total isolation of policy from data—is provided by the social context within which policy analysis is conducted. The product of a community, policy analysis presupposes some common discourse, some shared view of the world, though these views need not be totally shared or even completely articulated. These shared views constitute the "background" knowledge. Although we can legitimately challenge any item in the background knowledge (for no statement could remain unproblematic in all contexts), for practical reasons most knowledge remains unquestioned. That there is a finite quantity of oil, that in the short term (i.e., decades rather than geological eons) oil is a nonrenewable resource, that the price of oil is positively related to the exploration activities (and inversely related to the amount consumers demand) are examples of such background knowledge.

Acceptance of background knowledge, whether tacit or explicit, makes for a conservative bias among people in the relevant policy community. Farfetched theories gain little audience. This community of consent screens out both the madman and the genius.

That most things have to be taken for granted in order to apply analysis to energy policy does not mean that values are removed from the discussion. It may mean that a smaller range of values can be discussed with greater discernment, and that more interesting and answerable questions can be posed. Values can be added to the realm of scrutiny, but only bits at a time; otherwise they overwhelm. As happens during scientific revolutions, conversion would replace persuasion as the mode of change.

ESTIMATES AS DATA

The amount of reserves and the amount of resources are not known through direct apprehension. In some respect, all estimation is inference from past experience—projections of the unknown based on what is known, and whether or not these projections employ geophysical, econometric, or engineering techniques. The estimate (a number) is the end-product of a chain of conditionals: If the technology is this, if the price is that, if geophysicsts interpret their soundings correctly, if the instruments measure accurately, if statistical technique is valid, if past results are any indication of the future, and so on.

Without consent to suspend some of the skepticism inherent in estimates, a set of data cannot be established. Just as "objectivity" is a status accorded a statement by the relevant community rather than from any inherent characteristic, an estimate has the force of "objectivity" more through common consent than from its relationship to the world. It is the relationship of the number to the quantity of oil that is itself in dispute (that is why numbers are called "estimates"), so we cannot appeal to that relationship to tell us whether or not the number is "objective." If the method of inference is deemed legitimate and other things are judged beyond dispute, then the estimate produced is accorded "dataness." Question the inference or open the range of dispute, and few estimates will survive as data.

Estimates produced by the oil industry, for example, are affected by the very process that produced those estimates: Organization as a decentralized network of committees; internal constraints, such as respect for an individual firm's proprietary interests; and external constraints, such as antitrust prohibitions of collusion and the government's price regulations. The numbers produced reflect what companies in quasi-competition can agree upon. These estimates may not be the same as those produced under different rules, and may not be the same as the public's perception of "what's left underground."

Political consensus can reduce the importance of a seemingly wide range of supply estimates, since estimates are a function of political decisions with regard to such factors as the price of oil, tax regulations or other incentives for drilling, and foreign policy regarding national security and balance of trade. Agreement on these broad policies leads to (rather than results from) more acceptable estimates of supply. Political consensus also can make an apparently wide range of estimates smaller or less important: To go back to our simple matrix (Table 10.1), the context changes from the upper-righthand corner, where we agree on policy but disagree on the data, to the upper-lefthand corner, where policy and data support each other.

ESTIMATES AS INFORMATION

Just as facts do not wear meaning on their faces but have significance hidden deep in the context of a broader theory, reserve estimates have no significance in and of themselves. To have any standing as information, estimates must be linked to a policy question. This linkage is not indicated by virtue of an estimate's standing as data. A collection of randomly assembled estimates cannot generate policy direction any more than a telephone directory tells us who to call.

The result of little or no agreement on politics, or on visions of the desired future, is a plethora of estimates, no one of which is more methodologically sound than any other, though each may support a particular policy position. Estimates of vast reserves support the preference for little government regulation, while estimates of limited reserves call for government regulation and price support. But wait. Depending on circumstance, just the opposite argument is maintained: Short supply, says industry, calls for total decontrol so higher prices can stimulate exploration and production. These estimates are sought, obtained, and touted as the truth after policy preferences have crystallized. Here again, politics drive data; values need corroborating facts.

Just as there is no recourse to the facts to settle large-scale theoretical disputes, the facts themselves being part of the dispute, so energy policy cannot resort to the estimates to settle fundamental disagreements. If estimates as information are to have import, the area of disagreement must be limited either by tacit consent to a policy framework or by explicit stipulation.

ESTIMATES AS KNOWLEDGE

Just as knowledge is little determined by experience, energy policy is little determined by reserve estimations. There is no direct link between the estimate and the policy position. In the face of contrary estimations, a policy position may be maintained through a variety of accommodations: It may ignored, impugned, accepted tentatively pending further confirmation, or explained away. Policy positions need not necessarily change, given but one example of "recalcitrant" evidence. Policy is constrained only at the extremes.

If estimates show a nearly infinite supply of oil or, at the other extreme, that the amount of oil is so small that no rise in price would bring forth substantially more, such information would have direct significance for policy. Once these extreme and limiting cases are bracketed, however, both high and low estimates of domestic oil reserves have similar implications for the broad outlines of an energy policy: We should encourage exploration, develop alternative sources, and practice conservation more widely. These policy decisions are relatively insensitive to ranges in the estimates.

Information contributes to knowledge when we learn to ask better questions. Questions of timing—With what urgency should these measures be pursued?—supplant questions of size—How much do we have left? To solve the more finely tuned policy problem of timing, however, means a degree of precision on estimates unattainable with current techniques, and a comprehension of worldwide markets and resources beyond present sophistication. Perhaps, instead, we should be asking about ways to cope with the uncertainty in estimates, ways to make policy less dependent on precise estimates.

THE SENSITIVITY OF ESTIMATES TO POLICY

Whether a variable matters to public policy depends on how sensitive the policy outcome is to a specified difference in that variable. Whether we should worry about these differences in estimation depends on how relevant to policy such differences are. How relevant to strategic choice in public policy about oil and gas are estimates of reserves and resources?

To begin with, the statement that Senator Humphrey used to pen the hearing on the adequacy of U.S. oil and gas reserves (discussed in the Chapter 9) will help to further understanding of the proposed connections between data and policy:

I have called this hearing to clarify one of the most fundamental elements of information needed to formulate an enlightened national energy policy. I refer to information on the size of America's remaining oil and gas resources and the resulting projections of attainable future production rates.

The U.S. Geological Survey has made various recent estimates that place recoverable U.S. resources of crude oil and natural gas liquids in the range of 200 to 400 billion barrels, including those under the Continental Shelf. If we take the midpoint of this range—300 billion barrels—then we have enough oil to continue present output rates for about 80 years and potentially to produce at significantly higher rates for a substantial period. Based on these and other data, the Project Independence blueprint estimates that U.S. oil output could be increased by more than 50 percent by 1985 and could be sustained at such levels for several years. This would enable us to reduce or eliminate import dependence over this period.

A new report by the National Academy of Sciences, however, amasses evidence from various sources that potentially recoverable

U.S. oil resources are much less than indicated by the Geological Survey. It reaches an analogous conclusion for natural gas and concludes that "a large increase in U.S. annual production of petroleum and natural gas is very unlikely." It also warns that world resources of oil and gas will be seriously depleted by the end of the century if present production and consumption trends continue.

If the Geological Survey is correct, then increased oil and gas production may grant the Nation a longer period to reduce dependence on oil and gas while still holding our oil imports to a prudent level. If the National Academy panel is correct, however, then it becomes far more urgent to find acceptable ways to mine and utilize more of the Nation's coal; to get more nuclear capacity into operation; to substitute solar power for fossil fuels wherever feasible; to push energy conservation more rapidly; and to accelerate research and development on revolutionary technologies to relieve our dependence on conventional energy sources [Joint Economic Committee, 1975: 1-2].

Thus, the policy-relevance of these estimates was seen to be *timing*: Should actions to reduce import dependence be relaxed or rushed? Humphrey continued:

So the issue is drawn. Some of the main participants in this debate will testify before the committee this morning. I hope that they can clarify the basis for the diverse estimates of oil and gas reserves and suggest ways to reduce the extent of uncertainty. I hope also that they can guide Congress in taking proper account of the unavoidable uncertainty of such estimates in its effort to formulate policy on energy production and conservation and on energy research and development for the medium- and long-term future [Joint Economic Committee, 1975: 1-2].

Now we know that in this debate-dispute, as in all others affecting oil and gas, Senator Humphrey's hopes were disappointed. Clarification did not take place (at least if clarification includes agreement on what is clear), and there is still no agreement on how uncertainty should be taken into account. But would it be correct to say, as Humphrey suggested, that if the Geological Survey is right one sort of policy is indicated; if the National Academy Committee is correct, another (and different) line of policy is called for?

A first clue, as Sherlock Holmes said in referring to the dog that didn't bark, is not what Senator Humphrey mentions but what he leaves out. There is no reference to price. The senator speaks of the size of oil and gas resources without mentioning price, and goes immediately into "the resulting projections of attainable future production rate," as if the one came automatically from the other. If the ratio of resources recovered to resources drilled is important—and we have already seen that it accounts for most of the difference between the Survey and the Academy—so, also, is the amount of drilling undertaken, which, in part, must be a function of price. If the discussion were only about resources estimated to be physically underground, of course, the price at which they might or might not be extracted would have nothing to do with how much was thought to be there. As Hubert Humphrey put it, "I never could understand what price had to do with what was under the ground" (Joint Economic Committee, 1975: 55). But if we take Jack Carlson's view (he was then Assistant Secretary for Energy and Minerals in the Department of the Interior), that "recoverable resources is the only meaningful figure," then price is primary, because "when you start having incentives to go out and explore for recoverable resources, you are going to find some more that are recoverable, so your total universe may well increase in time, because you have an incentive to be out there more" (Joint Economic Committee, 1975: 55). If the estimates are not only estimates of what is underground but about what it takes to get it out, then estimates may be predicated on the policy rather than the other way around.

The prices that are part of the estimates are also part of the policies. After all, public policy about energy is centrally concerned with price. When we hear about regulation versus deregulation, or whether OPEC should impose its rates within the United States, the discussions essentially are about price. The phrase "resources recoverable under existing conditions" includes in its estimates the current price. But resources estimated to be recoverable in the future depend on the postulation of an anticipated price. It is understandable that public officials could complain that estimates of recoverable resources are biased; the estimates, after all, are based on a price that those very officials will decide through policy deliberations.

Presumably, a way out of this dilemma is to assume a variety of possible prices. Instead of a single estimate, therefore, this approach would produce a variety of estimates, depending on their sensitivity to prices. So far, so good—but not good enough. The variety-of-prices approach is good in that it has sent economists scurrying to develop curves representing the price elasticity of oil and gas. But this pluralist approach is not good enough—partly because existing knowledge is insufficient, and partly because the very question of whether demand is price-elastic (that is, whether demand for oil and gas by classes of consumer will vary substantially according to their price) is precisely what the dispute is about. Knowledge is necessarily limited; after all, there have been import restrictions and regulations since the 1950s and price controls since the early

1970s, so that it is hard to say what the market would do in the presence of counterfactual conditions (i.e., if it were allowed to operate uncontrolled). The argument has to be that if the market were unfettered, one would discover what the market could do. To this, the counterarguments are either that recoverable resources are so limited (according to estimates such as those prepared by M. King Hubbert) that there will not be much more at any price, or that demand will not slacken, so that the only result will be to increase revenues to the oil and gas industry. Everyone is arguing about things unseen or experiences unknown. Can these conceptions be changed by improving estimates, or is it necessary for the parties to agree on desirable policy before they can or will agree about the validity of data?

WHAT DIFFERENCE DOES THE DIFFERENCE MAKE?

Since it does not look as if conflicts over oil and gas resource estimates can be resolved, is it possible, at least, to agree on whether the magnitude of variation in these estimates makes so substantial a difference in formulating public policy that we should be concerned? Turning the question around, if the participants were disposed to agree on policy but estimates showed wide variation, would not the participants move to minimize the importance of those variations? In doing so, participants may be motivated to state that while all estimates are somewhat subjective, each approach is valid and based on legitimate assumptions. In short, if there were agreement on a policy preference, the attitude toward divergent estimates would be pluralistic and magnanimous.

One can begin to think along these lines by proposing that the differences between the highest and lowest estimates are not large enough to dominate debates over energy policy. In McKelvey's view, "What . . . is really important . . . is to recognize that in all of these estimates, even the lowest, they are saying a very large amount of oil remains to be discovered, 70 billion barrels, or 72 billion . . . recoverable at present prices and with present technology. . . . That is a lot of oil." (Joint Economic Committee, 1975: 54). It does not matter here which estimate—70 billion or 500 billion barrels—is right. The implications for energy policy are the same. In McKelvey's words, "the right thing in this case is to be encouraging exploration, looking for other oil and trying to develop alternative sources, and practicing energy conservation more widely" (Joint Economic Committee, 1975: 54).

We can then consider McKelvey's suggested policy for conservation—eliciting new oil and gas and bringing on alternative energy technologies—

The Politics of Mistrust

and ask whether the differences between the highest and lowest estimates of U.S. oil and gas resources are large enough to influence debate or actions.

The view that differences in estimates do not matter greatly is based on a belief that the relevant time horizon is fifteen or twenty years away. In the short term of the next five years, the accuracy of either reserve or resource estimates is not likely to have important price or supply effects. Actions taken now to affect what will happen twenty years from now, therefore, need not be based on short-term problems of supply, thus allowing attention to focus on how good or bad things might be if there were more, or less, oil or gas available at that distant time. Given a long time perspective, certain points of agreement among the various estimates of recoverable resources come into focus. For one thing, the various estimates agreed that there is enough oil and gas out there to be worth exploring, and enough known to be in the ground to make it worthwhile to work on extracting techniques. Second, there is agreement that the best prospects are in Alaska and the Outer Continental Shelf. Third, and most important, if energy consumption were to continue to increase as it has in the past, we can agree that

> energy conservation and vigorous attempts to develop other sources
> of energy must be important objectives, regardless of which of the
> estimates proved to be correct. This is true partly because the period
> separating the time in which production would begin its final decline
> under the lowest and highest estimates is only a couple of decades or
> so, and partly because of the long lead time required to develop a
> new energy supply apparatus [Joint Economic Committee, 1975:
> 10].

Whether all reserves run out a little sooner or a little later, it seems reasonable to agree that the nation still will have to depend on other sources of energy.

Not everyone, to say the least, believes that there is little or no difference between high and low estimates. Harry Perry, a consultant to Resources for the Future, but not a spokesman for that research organization, has a different view: "If the lower resource estimates for oil and gas are believed to be correct," he testified, "there would be little use in letting the price of oil rise or deregulating natural gas prices. . . . It would not be prudent to let the price of oil and gas rise merely to develop small increments of supply" [Joint Economic Committee, 1975: 29].

Thus, we see that low estimates of recoverable resources may be used either to advocate deregulation and higher prices in order to increase supply, or to justify price controls because higher profits could not increase supply. Except for the limiting case—extreme physical limits to recoverable resources—neither high nor low estimates appear to produce different policy implications. Perry, for instance, says that if the NAS committee's low estimates are believed, its recommendation for "a massive conservation effort" must be accepted also. But immediately Perry qualifies this recommendation by observing that too swift a reduction in consumption could cause economic dislocations and that, for national defense purposes, it is desirable to have a stockpile—small encouragement to conservation.

Apparently, timing is the key dependent variable for policy. Perry believes that

> for the longer run—the next 30 to 40 years—the direction of energy policy is likely to be the same no matter whether the higher or lower estimates in oil or gas resources are correct. By that time, the nation will have had to shift away in large measure from these energy sources to other more plentiful ones. This will be so almost no matter how favorable the oil and gas supply function will turn out to be and under almost any reasonable assumption about reduced energy per unit of GNP [Joint Economic Committee, 1975: 30].

Now it appears there is another dominant solution which says that, whether we are wildly optimistic or unduly pessimistic, energy sources other than oil and gas will have to be developed by the first and second decades of the twenty-first century.

What, then, is the policy-relevant question? It appears to be: How much time do we have (and how much effort is required) for adopting policies to induce shifts to other forms of energy? Again, Perry maintains that "no matter which of the resource estimates will someday turn out to have been accurate there is currently very little time in which to switch to alternative fuels that are in ample supply in order for the Nation to achieve a position of reduced vulnerability to another embargo of our oil imports or to other supply interference" (Joint Economic Committee, 1975: 29). To Perry, acceptance of low estimates means a shift to other sources of supply "without delay." With the benefit of hindsight, it is clear that this change, in fact, has not taken place.

Since the short run is over and the middle run is here, the question remains as to whether differences in estimates have any policy potential. At best, if you believe that estimates are likely to be either very high or extremely low, you might differ with others on the speed with which it is necessary to act—that is, not what should be done, but how soon and how

much. Let us therefore ask whether estimates of recoverable resources
matter now (or should have mattered earlier) in determining how far and
how fast to go with subsidizing synthetics or other alternatives to oil.

On January 14, 1979, Secretary of Energy James R. Schlesinger said:

> Above all, we must recognize—as we have failed to recognize before
> the passage of the Natural Gas Policy Act—that we are under no
> immediate pressure. We have the opportunity to develop our policies
> intelligently as uncertainties about domestic supply are reduced and
> as our understanding about prices and availability of alternative
> supplies is in hand [New York Times, 1979].

The ensuing months brought unexpected events—oil production cuts in
Iran, another OPEC price jump in June, and gasoline shortages in the
United States. Suddenly President Carter (1979) was heard proclaiming
the extreme urgency of moving to alternative, domestically provided
energy sources.

> To give us energy security, I am asking for the most massive
> peacetime commitment of funds and resources in our nation's
> history to develop America's own alternative sources of fuel—from
> coal, from oil shale, from plant products for gasohol, from uncon-
> ventional gas, from the sun.

Every important event elicits a change of tune about the importance of
timing.

There is no consensus among Department of Energy officials or in
Congress concerning the best timing of federal support for alternatives to
oil and gas because, among other reasons, officials do not know what the
private market would do on its own. This uncertainty is in large part due
to the fact that prices have been administered for several decades now. No
one knows how long it might take the private market, during the current
transition toward deregulation, to foster alternative technologies.

Given the lack of consensus about policies based on timing, we might
think that a sudden agreement on high estimates of U.S. resources or,
conversely, an agreement that we have very little oil, would make a
difference: A choice would help bring about consensus on timing. If, for
example, we somehow knew that there was little recoverable oil, if there
was consensus that "energy independence" was a prime goal, and if the
private market could not be relied on to make the transition "fast
enough," then the government might invest heavily and immediately in
new technologies. On the other hand, if data told us that we had a great
deal of oil, the timing for new technologies would be less critical. But

these wishful "what if's" would apply only to the extremely high or low ends of the range of estimates. The actual state of resource estimation today is in no position to determine the timing of government policies toward alternatives over the next fifteen years.

If we add the realities of world-market prices to the already numerous factors affecting timing, the chances become still slimmer that American resource estimates can influence timing decisions. The relative importance of these estimates takes its place as part of the following chain of reasoning: Although in the long run a transition away from heavy reliance on depletable sources of oil and gas will take place, over the midterm oil and gas will continue to dominate the energy market. Since newly discovered oil and gas deposits typically are more expensive to work than older ones, the price of conventional oil and gas can be expected to rise steadily. How fast prices will rise depends partly on the rate of discovery of new oil and gas. And whether these prices rise quickly or slowly, smoothly or erratically, the U.S. economy will be greatly affected. Indeed, the impact of world oil prices on the economy is a key motivation behind a national energy policy. The path of price increases, for one thing, will affect the ease with which the United States can make the transition to alternative sources. Thus, when one talks about timing, one is really talking about price. The timing under which alternative sources of energy will be developed depends mainly on the changes in relative prices of different energy sources. The question then becomes: How sensitive are these prices to our estimates of U.S. undiscovered, recoverable oil and gas resources? Taking the current world price of oil as the benchmark, suppose we knew today that the United States had between 150 and 200 billion barrels of undiscovered, recoverable oil left. That is, if instead of the presumed 55- to 458-billion-barrel range confronting the Humphrey hearings of 1977, we reach a consensus, through some effort (including large information costs), on a narrower range (say between 150 and 200 billion barrels), would this new estimate touch off a change in the world oil price? Would such relative price changes, if any, in turn alter the timing under which the United States shifts to alternative energy sources?

This question about the impact of U.S. resource estimates on world prices is a subject, one of many, that "price-path" models have been asking. Uncertainty over the price of oil arises from at least three sources (Blankenship and Gaskins, 1979).

First, it arises with regard to world oil resources, not just those of the United States. The amount and location of recoverable oil can affect the price of oil in two ways: Oil found in the United States and other noncartel suppliers affects OPEC's ability to raise its prices, and larger estimates of OPEC's own oil resources would exert some downward pressure on price. Though we may see estimates of U.S. resources as plagued with uncertainty, they seem models of precision by comparison with estimates of world resources. Estimates vary enormously, from about 1.2 trillion to almost 6 trillion barrels of ultimately recoverable crude oil (Powell, 1979). This world difference dwarfs domestic estimates. For perspective, compare this range to the estimate of what the world has already consumed, about .4 trillion barrels. Or compare the world estimates with the range in U.S. estimates, of .06 trillion to just under half a trillion, with the National Academy of Sciences averaging out at .1 trillion barrels. Under the most extreme differences in estimates, world estimation is ten times more important.

Second, OPEC behavior can affect world oil prices. Price-path models tend to classify OPEC actors as either foresighted wealth maximizers or rather unpredictable actors who make decisions on the basis of political or strategic, as well as economic, considerations.[1] Either assumption can lead to widely varying production and prices.

Third, future demand will be interrelated with future prices. We do not know now how much consumers will have to pay for oil in the future; this will depend on costs of substitutes for oil, the ease of making substitutions, and general trends in economic growth.

Two models (ICF and Fossil2 in Figures 10.1 and 10.2) have estimated what would be the effect on world oil price if (a) OPEC's resource base were to double; (b) the non-OPEC world's resource base were to double; or (c) the entire world's resource base were doubled.[2] If resources were known to be double what we think they are, the effects, models suggest, though not very great, would be worth considering. In the ICF model, doubling the supply would lead to perhaps a $10- to $15-per-barrel reduction in world oil price. In today's "spot market," that means a third to a half of the going price. As world prices rise, the difference would be still less. A doubling of domestic resources would mean ten times less. Under the Fossil2 results, OPEC would turn out to be "kinder" to us. The models did not include the question, "What if only the U.S. resource and not the non-OPEC base were to double?" The reason is that the effect of this change in U.S. resources on world prices would be too miniscule to make the query worthwhile.

Whatever influence oil and gas resource quantities might exert on prices derives from world resource estimates. And these estimates are surrounded by such uncertainty that what we know about them now (and what more we can expect to learn about them over the next ten years?) would not make even a small ripple in world prices over the medium term.

Unless we suddenly knew we had either enormous quantities or almost no U.S. resources left, policies related to the timing of alternative energy

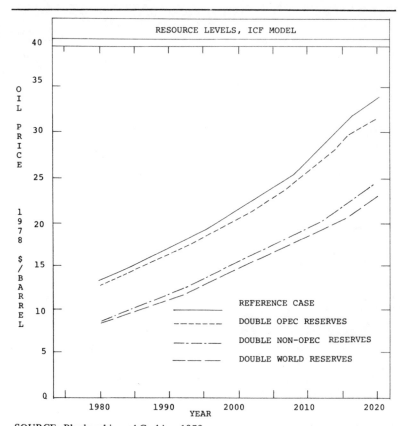

RESOURCE LEVELS, ICF MODEL

REFERENCE CASE

DOUBLE OPEC RESERVES

DOUBLE NON-OPEC RESERVES

DOUBLE WORLD RESERVES

SOURCE: Blankenship and Gaskins, 1979.

Figure 10.1: Resource Levels, ICF Model

sources would not be sensitive to U.S. estimates. As Thomas Schelling (1979: 4) put it, "it is extraordinarily difficult to devise policies in the face of the good news that there is one chance in ten that we shall discover unexpected great wealth within the decade."

Timing is not a policy issue that stands alone, for timing ultimately is a matter of price. Yet, many policy makers persist in giving timing policy a life of its own. The rationale for this thinking can be traced to quantity theory. The importance given to timing parallels the importance given to the goal of self-sufficiency in energy. If energy independence (maintaining a certain quantity) is a primary national goal, then it becomes very important for federal policy to orchestrate the shift to alternative energy sources within the United States. It becomes equally crucial to have better estimates of native oil and gas, coal and shale, and other resources.

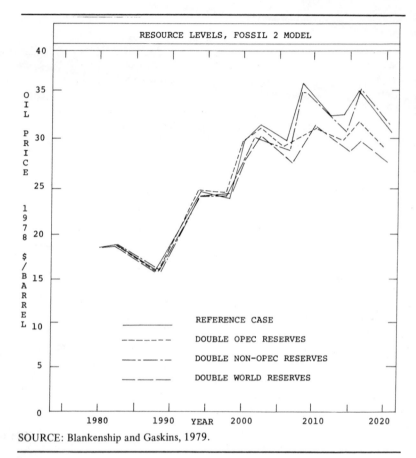

SOURCE: Blankenship and Gaskins, 1979.

Figure 10.2: Resource Levels, Fossil 2 Model

The premise behind the desire for energy independence is that not just any source will do. Increasingly, domestic pride as well as national security call on us to free ourselves from dependence on OPEC supplies. As President Carter (1979) said in his televised address of June 15, 1979,

in little more than two decades, we have gone from a position of energy independence to one in which almost half the oil we use comes from foreign countries—at prices that are going through the roof. Our dependence on OPEC has already taken a tremendous toll on our economy and our people. It is the direct cause of the long lines which have made millions of you spend aggravating hours waiting for gas. It is the cause of the increased inflation and unemployment we now face. This intolerable dependence on foreign oil threatens our economic independence and the very security of our nation.

Price, and the rejection not only of OPEC but of all foreign oil, illustrate a quantity theory in operation. To achieve an insulated U.S. energy supply system calls for a major central planning effort; central timing decisions and enormous amounts of federal research and development funds are required. For this purpose, accomplished by this process of allocating quantities, better estimates of our reserves and resources will be critical.

Returning to our original interest, it seems doubtful that in the near future technical improvements in estimates will aid or influence energy policy. A high or low estimate of U.S. oil resources would have very little impact on the most important policy variables: world oil price and the relative prices of alternative energy sources in a world-market context.

Having said all this, do we want to try for a better estimate? How badly do we need to know the amounts of recoverable oil and gas left to be discovered? Everyone has more or less assumed a cognitive approach to estimation: Through one method or another it will be possible to derive an accurate, or at least an acceptable, estimate. But an interactive approach, in which prices would be regarded as surrogates of scarcity, is possible. Over time, efforts to find oil and gas lead to a better understanding of how much there might be that could be extracted under existing technology and at different price levels. We learn by reacting to the results of our actions. Alternative fuels would be developed if the price rose high enough. Prototype plants are the price the country will pay for increasing its understanding. The difference with interaction is that no one would have to understand the whole thing, that is, how much exists underground that is worth getting out—now. To improve the information base, it would be sufficient for exploration to continue.

The answer we get to the question of recoverable resources will be historical rather than futuristic. The pursuit of an interactive approach has been not so much rejected as never considered, because interaction appears to lead not to an estimate but to a disjointed series of decisions on prices—the very thing, apparently, that one wishes to avoid rather than to encourage. Still, hundreds of thousands of sequential choices eventually will tell us, empirically rather than theoretically, how much has been found underground that is worthwhile to get to the surface. The insistent pursuit of a better estimate here and now, however, will leave legislators, policy makers, and the public frustrated.

What kinds of data, if not quantities of oil and gas, would be relevant to mid-range policies which encouraged exploration and developing other sources? To consider gathering data on costs and on expected relationships between costs and prices, would be very useful. John Schanz (1978: 13, 15; see also this volume's appendix) spoke for many others we interviewed when he recommended including cost data in oil and gas information systems:

> To the economist, it is important to know how much and for what period of time oil and gas production rates might be increased by a change in the economic structure of the industry or in the cost-price ratios. Or how sensitive future oil and gas production rates are to changes in technology. Answers to these kinds of questions are not contained in the usual published estimates of future oil and gas reserves. . . .

> Cost data should be assembled so that it will be possible to analyze better the responses to economic change. Attention must be directed to the effect of technological change on increasing the recovery factor of existing reservoirs and the lead times needed to accomplish this.

As for the quantities of oil and gas this country has left, Schanz (1978: 15) says that "the definitive study of future oil and gas supply and how it may be altered by economic and technological parameters that have not yet emerged still remains to be done. It is of little comfort that the final, reliable appraisal of the oil and gas resources of the United States will prove to be historic rather than predictive."

POLICIES ARE SENSITIVE TO UNCERTAINTY

Whether an estimate of oil or gas resources matters for public policy depends on how sensitive that policy outcome would be to a specified difference in that variable. Our view of the key question, "What difference would different estimates of U.S. resources make?" suggests that these estimates would not matter significantly for energy policy-making. But it is not enough to let the matter go at that. There are circumstances (e.g., under the perspective of a quantity-oriented leadership) in which policy makers and planners do believe that resource estimates make a significant difference. Many officials in the Department of Energy and Congress would agree with Lincoln Moses (1979: 8), head of the Energy Information Administration, who said: "Let us think of the next 10 to 20 years [1985 to 1995] as the medium term. Here, the size of undiscovered resources can be expected to affect supply and price, because the conversion of resources to reserves, and their development to production have time to go forward more slowly or more quickly as resources are perceived to be smaller or larger." While a price-theory perspective would lead one to suspect that energy policy in the midterm is not very sensitive to differences in U.S. resource estimates, there are other perspectives. Lincoln Moses (1979: 9) expresses that view of timing which dominates today's policy thinking: "[I]n the medium term we have good reason for believing that estimates of resources being high or low will exert quite different effects on the domestic supply, and thus would entail policy implications concerning planning for the medium term."

What do you do, then, if you believe that estimates of a certain variable do make a difference, but that no one can come up with the correct estimate (as with oil and gas resources)? And what do you do when the very number of variables and uncertainties makes "How much oil and gas do we have?" a poor question? There are two ways to go: Try harder to increase the accuracy of the estimation process in order to achieve more precise estimates, or make policies that do not depend on the estimate. Given the costs of the first alternative and the ultimately historical nature of the answer, we look at the second path. Decreasing the demand for accurate data requires flexible policies that can ride with a variety of estimates or with the changing conditions that affect estimation; it also requires an understanding of the variables, those sources of uncertainty that go into all estimates. To understand these factors and their relative contributions to the whole picture takes the place of trying to know the unknowable. With this understanding, and the ability to communicate it to policy makers, decisions can be considered that would be sensitive to these uncertainties but not dependent on accurate data.

NOTES

1. Two price-path models, by way of example, were described by Darius Gaskins, Deputy Assistant Secretary for Policy Analysis, Policy Evaluation, DOE, in a conversation of June 26, 1979. See also Blankenship and Gaskins, 1979.

2. The ICF model is a model of imperfect competition in the international energy market, developed for DOE by Stephan Salant and ICF Inc. The Fossil2 model actually refers to a combination of models; these are systems dynamics models of the world oil market (OIL) and the U.S. energy market (Fossil2). These were developed in DOE's Office of Analytic Services under the direction of Roger Naill.

REFERENCES

BLANKENSHIP, J. and D. GASKINS, Jr. (1979) "World oil prices." Prepared for the Office of Policy and Evaluation. Washington, DC: Department of Energy. (preliminary draft, May 31)

CARTER, J. (1979) Televised address of June 15, in New York *Times* (June 16).

Joint Economic Committee (1975) Adequacy of U.S. Oil and Gas Reserves. Washington, DC: Government Printing Office.

KUHN, T. (1962) The Structure of Scientific Revolutions. Chicago: University of Chicago Press.

MOSES, L. (1979) "Importance of assessment of oil and gas potential." Paper, EIA, Department of Energy, Washington, D.C., January.

New York Times (1979) January 14.

POWELL, S. G. (1979) "Impact of world oil and gas reserves on energy prices," Office of the Assistant Secretary for Policy and Evaluation, Department of Energy, April 10.

QUINE, W.V.O. (1961) "Two dogmas of empiricism," in W.V.O. Quine, From a Logical Point of View. Cambridge, MA: Harvard University Press.

SCHANZ, J. J., Jr. (1978) "Oil and gas resources: welcome to uncertainty." Resources for the Future 58 (March).

SCHELLING, T. C. (1979) Thinking Through the Energy Problem. San Francisco: Committee for Economic Development.

11

CREDIBILITY VERSUS RELEVANCE
Estimating Reserves under the Department of Energy

FOR OVER FIFTY YEARS, reserve estimation has been done by industry. But when many in Congress and a sizable portion of public opinion suspected that industry was slanting these estimates for its own profit, the government felt compelled to take the estimating process into its own hands: Enter the Oil and Gas Information System (OGIS), a yearly survey of lease operators begun in 1979, housed in the DOE's Energy Information Administration (EIA). This government move, however, has opened up a Pandora's box of new difficulties.

President and Congress alike wanted EIA's data validators to ensure the accuracy and credibility of oil and natural gas reserve estimates; yet the very nature of estimation makes accuracy unattainable. If there were trust, credibility might substitute for accuracy. But trust is in even shorter supply than accuracy. Thus, in the eye of the beholder, credibility as it were does not always reflect the quality of the estimate. Moreover, high-level policy makers have not specified exactly which of the different reserve and resource categories they want estimated. Such difficulties leave the EIA treading on very thin ice and open to much criticism.

Because there was mistrust, government officials who were suspicious of industry wanted the EIA to certify estimates based on EIA's own firsthand information. This has raised the question of primary versus secondary sources of data. Primary data are obtained by those who make measurements and handle the bits of data. Secondary data are based on bits of data already obtained by a primary source. Primary data present only their own uncertainties and are not burdened with the uncertainties that come from subsequent handling. But primary data, also, are more costly for government to gather. Most reserve estimation, moreover, is carried out on private property, and in privacy that will have to be violated if government wants to certify accuracy. Therefore, government has compromised by accepting, when appropriate, secondary information after validation. But since the number of primary respondents is large—50,000 fields encompassing 517,000 producing oil wells and 157,000 producing natural gas wells—validation has to be carried out by sampling. This opens still another can of worms: How much checking is enough?

The geological entity on which the government was to base its estimates became controversial. Should the data be collected by field? or did one want to examine reserves for each reservoir in a field? Several members of Congress who did not trust oil companies or their lease operators wanted a geological entity based on individual reservoirs. A number of EIA analysts who would be involved with the survey preferred estimating by field and felt that, for large fields containing several reservoirs, data should be collected reservoir by reservoir. The economy-minded General Accounting Office, on the other hand, urged field-level estimates only.

The burden upon industry to prepare estimates, and the cost to the government of collecting and validating them, loomed as issues. A compromise was reached that divided producers into three categories with decreasing reporting loads, the most detailed reports to come from the largest-volume producers.

The usefulness and hence the need for the detailed data collected by EIA have been challenged. Thus far, few policy makers or analysts can be found who need those data enough to warrant the effort. Indeed, it is not easy to find one client in government who uses any substantial part. Why not? Because the data are not collected with any particular policy in mind. The "data" could only be "information" to someone willing and able to regulate or take over functions of the industry. Even there, industry is an amalgam of companies and the data are insufficiently disaggregated to serve any of these firms. Thus, the data seem never to be at the right level for potential users.

Although the original mission of the Oil and Gas Information System (OGIS) was global, including both reserves and total resource estimates, the effort thus far has been limited to answering only two questions: What is the annual U.S. production of oil and natural gas? What are the estimated U.S. proved reserves? The entire reserve estimation effort is focused on the near-term time horizon. This limitation at least reduced the effort required.

At the same time, however, the short-term nature of proved reserves estimates makes them not very relevant to policy-making. The long lead time (about six years) between exploration and production means that very little can be done to expand production in the short run by increasing the quantity of proved reserves, unless the price of petroleum were raised to convert uneconomic proved reserves into economically profitable proved reserves. And if the price were allowed to rise so that market prices prevailed, government would not need its detailed reserve reporting system. The link of proved reserves to policy is through price.

ORGANIZING FOR CREDIBILITY:
THE BEGINNINGS OF OGIS

The GAO (1974) had called lack of credibility the most important defect in energy data. Reserve data were unvalidated, were not proved accurate, were dependent on the API and AGA, were not certified as truthful, were only voluntary, and were devoid of consistency in defining and interpreting terms. These qualities were considered the components of credibility; as long as any of them was missing, credibility was jeopardized.

After the 1974 report, the Federal Energy Administration made a major attempt to restore credibility. The agency conducted an independent appraisal of U.S. oil and gas reserves as of December 1974 and arrived at estimates that happened to concur with API and AGA estimates. Though the FEA survey was mandated and responses were given under oath, its results lent plausibility to the API and AGA system, and the study was heavily criticized. No one who distrusted the industry was about to embrace the FEA results as credible.

In June 1976 the GAO (1976) reassessed the state of credibility in energy data, judging the FEA's survey to be a step in the right direction; but the bureau still gave bad marks for credibility. The GAO report stressed again the components necessary to achieve credibility, considering validation of the estimator's methodology as essential. But unless all data were mandatory and certified as both accurate and truthful, not even the most methodologically valid data would be accepted as credible, warned the report. Moreover, the API and AGA could no longer be relied upon; consequently the data must be collected by government, independent of industry, and housed in a unit set apart from any policy-making responsibilities. Finally, all energy data should be consolidated into that single, independent data-collection bureau.

A year later the National Energy Plan emphasized again those GAO requirements for restoring credibility:

For the Petroleum Production and Reserve Information System, the Federal Government would assume the data collection responsibilities now performed by the American Gas Association and the

American Petroleum Institute. The oil and gas industries would be required to open their reserve estimation processes to Federal officials, who would supervise the collection and preparation of reserve data. Information collected and submitted to the Federal Government through the processes would be verified and randomly audited at the company level. Existing law regarding the protection of confidential proprietary information would not be changed. . . .

The reporting program would restore confidence within the Congress and among the American people that the Government, not the oil industry, is in charge of national energy policy [Executive Office of the President, 1977].

Many conditions had to be specified to ensure that the new Energy Information Administration (EIA) within the proposed Department of Energy would be truly neutral. Section 205 of the Energy Information Administration Act had to declare EIA's independent authority (that is, independent from the Department of Energy as a whole) to require and audit company data, although under certain disclosure constraints. Section 205 was also obligated to state that *someone* would evaluate the EIA. The legislation, therefore, assigned yet another independent body, a Professional Audit Review Team, to watch EIA. The EIA was not to be subject to certain Department of Energy dictates; but neither was the EIA allowed to enter the policy domain of the DOE. As Energy Secretary Schlesinger asserted, "the credibility of EIA as a neutral source of energy data and information will be substantially strengthened by the action which separated it from any responsibility for formulating or advocating national energy policy" (Schlesinger, 1977).

It is unclear whether the main objective actually was to have more credible data or only to assure critics that the data were more credible. A memorandum by Bert Concklin of the Executive Office of the President, Division of Energy Policy and Planning, on primary versus secondary data sources (dated August 12, 1977) states that

the basic concern in this issue is not the actual sources of data and information but rather the credibility of data and information collected from any source. Often the government has been accused of using "bad" data and information for release to the public and in formulating policy. Therefore, to fulfill the mission of the DOE, credible data and information must be obtained irrespective of the source from which they came.

Several attributes for establishing "credible" data and information can be identified. An important factor is *uniform standards*, which would include standard definitions, terms, codes, units, reporting,

> activities, standards for confidentiality, etc. The capability and utility of *verifying* (or *auditing*) will enhance the credibility and utility of data or information. . . . From a credibility standpoint, primary sources of data are more acceptable than secondary sources. However, reliable secondary sources, which are usually more cost effective, are adequate for many purposes and they should be used when appropriate.

The document ends on a familiar note:

> To guarantee uniform standards for energy data and information for the DOE, it is necessary to organize in the EIA the function which is responsible for data and information collection, verification, dissemination, and credibility. Likewise, an EIA audit function responsible for the verification and evaluation of reported energy data and information is essential for obtaining and disseminating credible data and information.

Concklin implicitly defines primary data sources as data produced by those (such as oil well operators) who made the original measurements and estimates. By secondary data sources Concklin means data obtained from organizations, such as the API, who have collected the data from original data producers.

We might then ask why primary data are judged more credible than secondary data. The obvious answer is that data twice handled are doubly prone to error, bias, and distortion. But because it costs more to collect disaggregated primary data, Concklin compromises, stating that secondary data, when verified and appropriate, are adequate for many purposes and should be used. In the same way, according to Concklin, data collected by the government from primary sources also must be validated. Energy Secretary Schlesinger (1977) seemed to be carrying the banner for validation. He wrote that

> to insure an aggressive and positive effort for verifying the accuracy and validity of energy information, the data validation function has been separated and elevated to an Office of Energy Data Validation, headed by an EIA Assistant Administrator. This office is one of three major offices in EIA. . . . A firm commitment has been made to staff the office with the necessary resources.

In order to validate properly, government experts would have to be on the scene to ascertain accuracy when measurements were being made and to inspect all the methods of data-handling, methodology, and estimation processes. This would be a large and expensive operation.

The government solution to this problem was to inspect by statistical sampling. But since validation of oil and gas reserves can be practicably carried out only post-factum, (after measurements have been made, so that government experts can only take them on trust), credibility remains flawed. In order to correct this flaw, one would have to propose that government experts should either be present (to participate in the measuring) or carry out independent measurements later (provided those experts can relate such later measurements to conditions existing when the first measurements were made—not an easy matter).

What is missing from the OGIS's formal approach to validation is the traditional role of collegiality, discussion, and informed judgment. How can government validators become experts without ongoing experience or easy contact with private-sector geologists and engineers who perform estimation? On the other hand, if government validators meet with industry estimators too often, these government estimators will be accused of bias.

The issue of government validators being present in the field whenever a private entity is making a pertinent measurement or carrying out independent measurements on private property, raises a serious problem of property rights and of the boundary between the private and public sectors within the energy industry. Do such activities mean that government is violating the privacy of the private sector and taking over some previously uncontrolled part of free enterprise? Furthermore, if government assumes the responsibility of generating data from the private sector, would government not also become an obvious target for accusations about generating "bad data" by those whom the data may hurt? The result simply might be transfer of blame from private operators to the government, at significant additional cost to the latter.

The government has a composite solution to this problem in the reserves estimation area. Government will collect data from well operators who must certify upon risk of penalty that, according to their knowledge, theirs is the most complete data available. In addition, government intends to conduct random sample audits and independent estimations.

This combination of private penalties and public samples still does not resolve the question of credibility of reserve estimates. Government data verification, no matter how thorough, is carried out using only a relatively small sample. To what extent is the remainder of the unverified data acceptable? What happens when industry and government results are in significant disagreement? Does the question arise as to who validates the validators?

We have described some of the credibility problems surrounding energy data and how it was planned to organize for their correction. The next section will examine the new Office of Energy Information Validation's (OEIV) activities in validating oil and gas reserve estimation. Could OEIV implement the new procedures designed to secure independence from industry and from the executive branch? If so, would that matter for enhancing its credibility and usefulness? The solution adopted to assure credibility raises important questions for students of the relationship between information and policy.

The usual idea is to convert data into information by having in mind its relevance to policy: If information is treated as if it makes a difference to someone, that someone is an integral part of the policy-making. By isolating EIA both from industry and from policy-making in the administration, would the resulting independence of EIA from policy sacrifice relevance to policy? Is there a tradeoff between credibility and usefulness?

THE OIL AND GAS INFORMATION SYSTEM: CREDIBLE OR USEFUL?

The Department of Energy came into being on October 1, 1977. It was equipped with its new, "independent" Energy Information Administration within which several new information systems were forming. One, the Oil and Gas Information System (OGIS), was to be the final answer to the call for credibility in reserve reporting. OGIS (and its reporting form, EIA Form 23) was a renewed attempt to collect data that the Federal Power Commission's Form 40 had failed to get. Form 40, as we learned in Chapter 8, had been developed under congressional pressure in 1976. That survey form had been a response by the FPC to the accumulated charges that producers were underreporting reserves in order to push up the FPC's allowable price for natural gas at the wellhead. Form 40 was delayed in court, however, before it could be distributed; intended respondents had filed protests, and to get the form out seemed an interminable process. At the same time, the new Department of Energy and EIA were coming to occupy a great deal more attention than Form 40. Form 40 never rose out of the quagmire. In the new EIA, a fresh attempt (OGIS) was launched to produce a form. The new survey form, EIA-23, was designed in 1977 and 1978. Since momentum was strong for creating a long-demanded, credible reporting system, and clearance by the Office of Management and Budget

(OMB) was likely, the inclination naturally was to welcome it and not to ask nagging questions about usefulness.

Objectives of the OGIS included the intentions to:

- develop credible reserve and production statistics for crude oil, natural gas, and natural gas liquids (categories of reserves are not specified beyond "proved" reserves);

- furnish information on the operation and ownership of oil and natural gas reserves;

- provide basic data to support estimation of undiscovered resources and analysis of factors affecting availability of such resources;

- support regulatory requirements of DOE, including the FERC; and

- replace annual statistical reports currently published by the API and AGA.

The primary means for attaining the objectives agreed upon included:

- Oil and gas reserves and production data would be obtained on a field basis by surveying operators of oil and gas wells. But for fields containing nonproducing reservoirs, each such reservoir would be reported separately rather than in aggregate. All reservoirs in each new field would be reported separately, and each newly discovered reservoir in oil fields would be reported separately, rather than as field aggregates. Reservoirs that had revisions, extensions, or corrections, as well as all reservoirs in federal lands, were to be specified.

- Completed survey forms would be audited for internal consistency.

- Industry oil and gas production data would be checked against state records to assess the completeness of the survey's coverage.

- Industry records would be audited to verify data supplies on the form.

- Independent reserve evaluations of selected reservoirs would be conducted by government and by independent contractors.

For the first time, government personnel would be scheduled to take part in reserves estimation, instead of just relying on and checking information collected and handled by others. EIA planners hoped that these activities on the part of government validators would be a major step in increasing the credibility of their energy data. The survey covers all "large" producers and samplings of "intermediate" and "small" producers.[1] As summarized above, some respondents must report reservoir by reservoir in certain circumstances; most others report by field only; and the smallest operators report by a more general geographic area, not by field or reservoir.

In order to execute the validation plan thoroughly, government field agents must familiarize themselves with geological, seismographic, pressure, and hydrocarbons flow measurements taken in the particular fields to be covered. These data will have to be used in making independent estimates, to be compared with those of industry. The process is lengthy, annual, expensive, unprecedented. But the objective of OGIS planners is nothing less than to obtain the most credible and useful data possible while, at the same time, minimizing respondent burden, definitional differences, and costs (both government and private).

The political assumption behind the OGIS survey is that a mandatory form submitted under oath, and evidence of more independent validation, will enhance credibility. The administration assumption is that accurate data can be collected at a reasonable cost. The information assumption is that what Allan Newell (1969) called power (relevance to a particular circumstance) and generality (adaptability to a variety of circumstances) will be compatible rather than at odds. This is like maximizing simultaneously in several directions. Something, one can be sure, will have to give.

Can OGIS Achieve "Credibility"?

During the period when OGIS was being designed, Congressmen Dingell and Moss were urging the EIA to require finely disaggregated data from respondents—meaning reservoir by reservoir. C. William Fischer of the EIA replied to the Dingell and Moss request by saying that not only would this be a monumental task both for the companies to report and for the government to process and validate, but also that the congressmen must be aware of

> the high inherent uncertainty in reserve estimates, which error may be much greater than any of the more detailed refinements in the estimation process that they discuss. On top of the problems discussed, the present scientific and technological limits of reserve estimation methods may cast a serious doubt on the meaningfulness and the value of the ultimate use of these estimates. The inherent uncertainty caused by these limits can by itself raise sufficient doubt and diminish the credibility of the estimates despite all the refinements in statistical sampling and the size of the measured fuel resource unit.[2]

Why do all this work for reservoir-by-reservoir data if the results contain inherent limitations?

The central problem for the Office of Energy Information Validation in validating OGIS is how to validate estimates that are characterized by physical uncertainty and the assumptions of individual estimators.

For two major reasons the validation program is built on shaky ground. First, and common to all estimates that cannot be fully verified when made, is that, by nature, estimates are uncertain. The second reason is more serious: In making reserve estimates, no actual measurements are technically possible until all of the product is out of the ground; since different methods of estimation yield different results, each involves subjective or selective judgment.

These two reasons for undermining credence are general. There is a third reason, however, particular to the way EIA approaches the problem. In its plan to validate well operators' reserve estimates, the government intends to check the process only by conducting independent estimates on a few fields. For these fields, OGIS validators will make their own estimates, "using the best available raw data from the respondents." This is an important step forward in government validation of energy information. But if distrust of the private sector's information lies behind the entire OGIS operation, then why accept industry's raw data, even after review? Why not go all the way and get your own raw data by conducting independent measurements over a period of time? Suspicion of industry's estimation processes may be cast similarly on its raw data generation. These industry-generated data may be inaccurate or mishandled or distorted or falsified, or submitted in ways that make such undesirable qualities difficult for a review process to uncover. How can the government know it is "using the best available raw data from the respondents" unless government does participate in measurements on which those estimates are based? How much (if any) reliability and credence can exist under such circumstances?

EIA's *Annual Report to Congress* of 1978 recognized these field validation problems:

> Certain key systems, involving very complex information requests, require ongoing and individualized field validations of respondents' submissions, because they are especially liable to suffer from bias due to misinterpretation of questions or effects of unknown differences in the methods different respondents used to prepare their submissions. These complex information requests may be directed to respondents who could have considerable incentive to make their response less than a clear and accurate representation. Two promi-

nent cases are the OGIS and the Financial Reporting System (FRS). . . .

Field verification can quickly become tremendously expensive because of the sheer volume of records available for examination. . . . Using several strategies, OEIV hopes to be able to assure accurate total U.S. reserves estimates by making only a small number (probably less than 500 over 3 years) of the very expensive "from scratch" independent estimates of field reserves.

The phrase "from scratch" is unclear. Does it mean making independent measurements? or does it mean using the best available primary data from respondents? If the former, one doubts whether credence will be enhanced, because skeptics may suspect measurements performed by government as strongly as estimates made by industry. And if the government estimator has had significant previous industry employment, a question may arise concerning that estimator's "independence" from industry. If estimation from scratch means that the government takes the best available primary data and computes its own reserve estimate, you are again back where you started, relying ultimately on that suspect source, industry.

Is credibility a mirage? The officially heralded components of credibility are either self-contradictory or at odds with one another. Where mistrust prevails, credibility slips from our grasp, unattainable by the best validation effort.

Is There a User in the Audience?

The picture may brighten if we can find a number of people who consider OGIS data relevant to their work and to decisions they make. The form, the aggregated results, and information on the methodology are available to all potential users. If people welcome the data as useful in decision-making, "credibility" as a major issue may fade into the background. A bleaker hypothesis is that if the data are important and do influence decisions, components of credibility could receive a great deal of attention. Thus, the data "must" be accurate or validated thoroughly or certified as truthful before a user will trust his or her decisions to the data. Who, then, makes up the community of users of OGIS? In what sense are the data relevant to their work? What do they want from the system's reserve data?

First, how specifically were the potential uses of OGIS reserve data spelled out? The legislative justification cited for authorizing Form EIA-23 was extremely broad in nature. Little or no indication of particular congressional requirements could be discerned. While Representatives Moss and Dingell insisted on very detailed reservoir-by-reservoir data, they stated no plans for using the information.

In anticipating uses for OGIS data, EIA wrote (in its justification statement for OMB clearance) that OGIS data would "aid DOE analysts and policy makers in assessing the United States energy position and in formulating energy policy alternatives."[3] And OMB writes, "Reliable oil and gas reserves data, gathered on a uniform basis nationwide by an impartial agent and subject to objective validation, are important to the formulation of our national energy policy" (Morris, 1978). These statements are general to the point of emptiness. No specific explanations are given concerning whom the data will aid or why such material is important to policy-making. Behind these lines there must be some implicit assumption that the writers believe to hold broad acceptance. Let us examine what it may be.

As we have posited before, energy policy has developed under the conflicting forces of two basic, alternative theories—price theory and quantity theory. If the government, following a quantity theory, controls the price of hydrocarbon fuels below the market-clearing price and if the rate of consumption is not decreased, a gap is created. To maintain equity, government must consider allocation of short supplies. More important, government must be concerned with means for narrowing the gap. Therefore, the government has to be sure of the quantity of present and future supply. In addition, if a major policy stand is to become independent of foreign supply, then the quantity of domestic fuel supply becomes even more critical to know. But domestic supply depends on the rate of production, which depends on the quantity of proved reserves, which depends on the quantity of economic indicated reserves, which depends on the quantity of inferred reserves, which depend on economic undiscovered reserves.

Now we can see that—if we assume the quantity theory, apply price control, and aspire for energy independence—the determination of a reliable quantity of reserves becomes very important to policy-making. This figure can indicate what measures would be needed to reduce the gap and when such measures should be implemented to fill the gap created by depleted reserves.

These have to be the implicit assumptions here for using such data. In contrast, if we accept the price theory instead, there can be no gap between supply and demand. Price adjusts supply with demand over time and, as the price rises, the rate of consumption is reduced accordingly. Production, consumption, supply, and demand together become a single quantity at one point in time at that market price.

Thus, there must be a community of potential users of OGIS, at least among those planners and legislators who, implicitly or explicitly, subscribe to the more quantity-oriented school of thought.

When Form 23 was being designed in 1978 in EIA's OGIS office, it was virtually without contribution from any policy makers in DOE. The Federal Energy Reserve Commission did contribute to the design process by attending meetings and reviewing drafts. The FERC had sought reservoir-level natural gas reserve data. In addition, a few staff members of the Moss subcommittee contributed to Form 23 in a sense, to urge the most detailed reserve data possible. The USGS participated briefly in reviewing the survey form. But it is safe to say that virtually no would-be users participated actively in the important design phase. OGIS designers were, for the most part, on their own.

After the first annual survey was printed and distributed, analysts of the Office of Energy Information Validation (OEIV) performed a "requirements review" in June 1979, in order to identify users of OGIS data. Interviews were held with about fifty persons thought to have an interest in the data. The potential community of users, the reviewers determined, could be found in any of five stations:

(1) the Department of Energy and its related agencies, such as the quasi-independent FERC;
(2) other federal and state administrative agencies;
(3) Congress;
(4) industrial trade associations and private companies;
(5) other interest groups and the public in general.

People from every part of the "community"—except Congress, according to instructions the reviewers received from supervisors—were interviewed.

The results? Flatly, there is no community of users inside or outside the Department of Energy. Most potential users interviewed were unable to specify their informational needs for crude oil and natural gas production and reserve data. No users interviewed, including those involved in modeling, could address their requirements in terms of data quality, accuracy, validity, or meaningfulness. Most of those who have anything to say do not need the level of detail OGIS provides. A few users, located in the

FERC, the USGS, the Securities and Exchange Commission, and the Energy Technology branch of DOE, require more detailed or specialized data than those given by OGIS. These bureaus have set up their own systems for collecting such data. In short, the level of detail or aggregation is not quite right for anyone. Whoever keeps asking for this material obviously is not doing so in order to use it. This point is illustrated perfectly by the big to-do made over reservoir-level data by Representatives Moss and Dingell. In a joint letter to John O'Leary, deputy secretary of DOE, the congressmen pressed for data by reservoir:

> The draft form requires that reserve information be reported primarily on a field basis. We question whether this approach would be as useful as reserve reporting on a reservoir basis, which is the basic unit by which industry evaluates reserves, makes economic decisions, and is consistent with the manner in which most companies keep their records.
>
> Collecting the data by reservoirs would have a number of advantages from a regulatory standpoint, including the improved ability to audit producers' submissions, to calculate drilling productivity by more accurately assigning reserve additions and revisions to their appropriate year of discovery, and to better understand the character of reserve additions, either from frontier areas or from extensions of existing reservoirs [Moss and Dingell, 1977].

If reservoir-level data were so important for regulation, why was the FERC not more insistent upon having reservoir-level data for natural gas? There were two probable reasons. In the first place, the FERC was for the most part able to get its general natural gas reserve data from pipeline companies rather than well operators. When the FERC regulators did need reserve or production data for a particular reservoir, the data were collected on a case-by-case basis.

Second, before the Natural Gas Policy Act was passed in October 1978, the OGIS might have had a real client in the FERC. We may remember from Chapter 8 that the formula for setting the ceiling price on natural gas depended on a figure for proved reserves; the lower the reserves, the higher the allowable price might be. Were that formula still in effect, OGIS data could be important. But the Natural Gas Policy Act has legislated a graduated phasing-out of price controls, and the old formula is no longer in effect. Thus, for OGIS, the one certain client for reserve data has been removed.

The real rationale behind the urgency of the Dingell and Moss (1977) request came in their next paragraph:

An equally important consideration, at least in the near term, is that collecting reserve data on a reservoir basis would enable the Congress, the DOE, and the average citizen to go a long way toward understanding, if not resolving, serious questions regarding the possible withholding, under-production, or diversion of significant quantities of natural gas. Indeed, if collection on a field basis were retained, we doubt whether such questions could ever be resolved.

The usefulness of the data, then, was not for policy; data were relevant to mistrust.

If there are no clients inside or outside the Department of Energy, what is the point of having OGIS? The authors of the requirements review tried to salvage the situation with something on the order of a pep rally: "OGIS should undertake efforts to obtain a stronger base of user support for the level of detail being collected by the EIA-23. This is deemed essential to adequately justify continuation of the data collection instrument on the existing basis."[4] These authors suggest also that OGIS should make a concerted effort to determine, possibly from congressional committee staffs, the type of data on oil and gas production and reserves that OGIS believes are necessary to satisfy congressional concerns. The reverse may be more nearly the truth. If members of Congress did know precisely what they wanted, they would already have it. Perhaps in the act of requesting more and better data they have exhausted their interest.

It is not surprising that national policy makers think in generalities and see large aggregates; their perspective is quite different from that of information system designers, data collectors, and those who implement policies. The people in this second grouping must squeeze broadly stated requirements into specific functional units; in paying attention to details and being thorough and comprehensive, they look more at the trees than at the forest. When the information requirements given to data collectors and information system designers are insufficiently specific, these individuals tend to play it safe: When in doubt, include the data in the system; somebody, sometime, might need it, and nobody wants to be accused of omission.

The success of a system relates directly to the degree to which users participate in the design process; this did not take place with OGIS. EIA's isolation from policy-making has been a liability rather than an asset.

This brings us full circle to the tension between the desire for "credibility" and the desire for usefulness. How can data be policy-relevant if data collectors are supposed to be "objective," that is, separated from policy makers?

THE CLEARER THE PURPOSE,
THE LESS STRIFE OVER "CREDIBILITY"

On June 15, 1979, the GAO submitted its third report, "Natural Gas Reserves Estimates: A Good Federal Program Emerging, but Problems and Duplications Persist." Not surprisingly, the report stated that "officials at EIA and FERC continue to encounter problems similar to those outlined in our prior reports." These included duplication, burden on government and industry, and the "need for implementing a credible audit approach." If error keeps repeating itself, though officials change, the causes of error may be embedded in the task itself rather than in its implementation (Majone and Wildavsky, 1978).

Sensing that there may be a defect in the mission as well as in the message, GAO (1979) suggests that EIA put the onus on users:

> We believe EIA should act as an impartial reviewer of energy information requests of Federal agencies, to ensure that the needs and requirements of the agencies are clearly justified and that they are balanced against the burdens they would impose on respondents. . . . Practically speaking, EIA could at least require written justifications for requests for data, with the opportunity for EIA to question data items for which it finds insufficient support.

On the whole, the GAO review is less concerned with the usefulness of the information than with its technical quality and cost. The GAO report states that the Natural Gas Policy Act of 1978 has "superseded" the major FERC justification for reserve data because the natural gas legislation canceled use of FERC recommendations in setting the national gas rate. But the GAO, which uses this important fact only to argue that reporting data on individual reservoirs is unnecessary, ignores the wider implications of this change: Do reserve estimates remain important for government policy-making?

Since the answer would appear to be no, why then should the government invest in collecting this material rather than continuing with or augmenting the AGA and API systems? Those few people within the Department of Energy and on congressional staffs who use, and who do have some interest in reserve data were asked to offer insight. The main uses they cited were:

(1) To watch the supply response over the coming years under the prices set by the Natural Gas Policy Act, and under unregulated prices after 1985; to help decide whether to extend regulation, come 1985. At various times over this period, regulators would ask: If the supply response is small, why? Is there simply not much left? What can be done about it? Those who made this point, however, expressed no strong aversion to using AGA estimates for such a purpose. But the AGA and API have announced that they are going to discontinue their own estimation activity, now that OGIS exists.

(2) To time and plan the shift to other energy sources by encouraging various research and development projects, and by rethinking licensing policies. Again, for this purpose, API and AGA estimates apparently could have served as well as OGIS.

(3) To determine how reasonable is the cost of natural gas from foreign countries. The price the United States pays for imported natural gas would depend partly on estimates of U.S. domestic gas reserves. Producers may have dual incentives to report reserves high or low. Some might report high in the interest of forestalling the need for importing gas. Alternatively, an incentive to report low persists, in anticipation of higher post-1985 prices. Once more, for this use of reserve estimates, the AGA system probably would do as well as OGIS. Indeed, it has, because the price for natural gas from Mexico was negotiated in September, 1979, without benefit of OGIS.

(4) To observe the competitiveness of the producer market. Who controls most of the reserves? OGIS data would allow one to determine market shares for all the largest companies, or for about 85 percent of all proved reserves estimated in the United States. On further questioning, however, an official of FERC who made this point was not sure how OGIS or AGA data could be used to test for competitiveness. As any FTC investigator knows, the steps taken between determining market share and drawing conclusions about competitive behavior are filled with complexities. There is no clear and satisfactory definition of the threshold conditions under which a market becomes competitive; in other words, there is no satisfactory criterion for market competition. A further obstacle to this use of OGIS data lies in the proprietary nature of

the data. EIA may not be empowered to release OGIS data to other agencies.

As for the first use, a low estimate could suggest either further deregulation—or more controls—on grounds that there is apparently little oil and gas left to be found. Prices paid for imported oil and gas, the third use, undoubtedly will be overtaken by events before new domestic reserve data are available. With respect to the fourth use, analytical and legal barriers stand in the way; in addition, almost no one expressed interest in the topic. This leaves us with the second use, timing. In Chapter 10 we argued that the difference in estimates was not relevant to policy in this area. Now we would add that Congress (in considering a major synthetic fuel program) and the President (in proposing it) obviously saw no reason to wait for OGIS, either.

Entirely apart from policy uses, then, participants have reasons for preferring government data collection over that of AGA and API. Most of those interviewed emphasized submission under oath: That respondents are under oath seems to make OGIS results more credible than voluntary trade-association estimates. If the validity of OGIS results ever does come into question, at least the government has something to stand on; government can go in to investigate and double-check, armed with legal sanctions. A major advantage of OGIS is thought to be its visibility, which makes many people in government and Congress more comfortable. At least they will no longer feel dependent on trade-association figures. The prevailing view seems to be: You never know, someday we may need data. Better to have it now than be sorry later. And much better to have independent data than to be forced to use industry figures, which can be subject to manipulation at any time.

The OGIS system was a product of mistrust. It rode in on a strong wave that gathered momentum from the thwarted FPC Form 40, and mounted even higher because of pressure for "credible" data. Who cared about usefulness?

The authors of the OGIS requirements review, recognizing the problem of relevance, recommended acquainting potential users with the system's information details and trying to get user support for the product. Should it not be the other way around? In the middle and long run, everyone would be better off if the line recommended to Congress in the draft requirements review were followed: "OGIS should make a concerted effort to determine, possibly from committee staffs, the type and kind of data they believe is necessary." Although coming late in the process, this advice is never too late to be applied to all user groups. This may mean redesigning Form EIA-23. What it is more likely to mean, in our opinion, is that users will have less to ask for, if they must say why they want data and what will be done with it. In the last chapter, we shall recommend a way to place more responsibility on users themselves.

If enhanced credibility is desired, then coherent policy is needed first—a policy framework that will enable EIA to specify, collect, and validate required information. In the absence of such a framework, data collection is a gamble and validation may become but another example of the triumph of technique over purpose.

NOTES

1. Large: yearly production of 1.5 million barrels of oil or more/15 billion cubic feet of natural gas or more. Intermediate: yearly production of 400,000-1,500,000 barrels of oil/2-15 billion cubic feed of natural gas. Small: yearly production of less 400,000 barrels of oil/less than 2 billion cubic feet of natural gas.

2. From the Fischer letter of December 28, 1977, replying to the congressmen.

3. Supporting statement submitted to OMB for the approval of Form EIA-23, 1978.

4. Requirements Review, internal draft, OEIV, 1979.

REFERENCES

Executive Office of the President (1977) The National Energy Plan. Washington, DC: Government Printing Office.

General Accounting Office (1979) Natural Gas Reserves Estimates: A Good Federal Program Emerging, but Problems and Duplications Persist. Washington, DC: Government Printing Office.

——— (1976) Improvements Still Needed in Federal Energy Data Collection, Analysis, and Reporting. Washington, DC: Government Printing Office.

——— (1974) "Actions needed to improve federal efforts in collecting, analyzing, and reporting energy data," in Energy Information Needs: Study by the General Accounting Office. Washington, DC: Government Printing Office.

MAJONE, G. and A. WILDAVSKY (1978) "Implementation as evolution," pp. 103-117 in H. E. Freeman (ed.) Policy Studies Review Annual, Volume 2. Beverly Hills, CA: Sage.

MORRIS, S. H. (1978) Personal communication to Lincoln Moses, EIA administrator, granting OMB clearance to Form EIA-23, December 22.

MOSS, J. E. and J. D. DINGELL (1977) Personal communication to John O'Leary, Deputy Secretary of the Department of Energy, October 8.

NEWELL, A. (1969) "Heuristic programming: ill-structured problems," in J. Aaron-
ofsky (ed.) Publications in Operations Research. New York: John Wiley.
SCHLESINGER, J. R. (1977) Personal communication to Richard W. Kelley, Chairman of the Professional Audit Review Team (PART), November 7.

12 CONCLUSION

WHAT HAVE WE LEARNED from this selective history of oil and gas estimation? The words of Ecclesiastes—there is nothing new under the sun—ring true. In the language of social inquiry, circumstances do differ but the participants in energy policy and their patterns of behavior do not. Whatever has afflicted energy policy (and its oil and gas reserve and resource estimates) since 1973 has been present throughout this century.

Every decade saw new circumstances. The domestic supply situation of the 1970s was not what it had been in the 1960s. Between the 1930s and the 1940s the United States went from a position of net exporter of oil to the status of a net importer. The remarkable thing is that despite such major changes in circumstance, the positions of the various actors remained consistent and predictable. Under very different situations, and even with different individuals participating in energy policy, the same positions were maintained. People did not passively adjust their perspectives to new circumstances. Rather, a few basic, underlying perspectives were vessels for people's policy positions.

Looking at the situation in 1980 alone, it is evident that the redoubling of oil prices has created vast distributional difficulties among regions that produce and consume energy, among industries differently affected, and among people with various incomes who use energy differently. Distributional conflicts, however, are not the answer to questions about unresponsive energy policies, but the consequences. When the nation subsidized imports after 1973, penalizing domestic production in the process, it left itself vulnerable to huge price increases that greatly worsened conflict over who would pay. The vast consequences of cascading price increases, coupled with increasing dependence on foreign oil, are reasons for agreeing early on protective measures, not rationales for following a course of action that leaves everyone worse off than before with respect to inflation, unemployment, balance of payments, productivity, and more. Since the potential adverse consequences are so much more damaging now than they were in the past, we must ask why post-1973 oil and gas policy, rather than looking to a different future, went back to business as usual. The one consistent element in a turbulent world remains the politics of mistrust.

We have tried to explain this remarkable consistency. What patterns were so strong that they kept surfacing intact through very different circumstances? The patterns we discovered are what we generalize as quantity and price perspectives. Manifested in quantity theory are the consumerist and preservationist models of behavior. The price perspective is reflected somewhat in variable-marketer patterns of behavior (as illustrated by the major producers) and more strongly in constant-marketer practices (as exemplified by the small independent producers).

When one comes to know the participants and the circumstances, positions on energy policy and the (high or low) direction of estimates are predictable. Let us summarize the set of circumstances we have described in the preceding pages.

To understand the direction of policies and estimates historically, we need only envisage two dichotomous sets of circumstances—war or peace, and, during peacetime, upward or downward pressure on prices—that affect the interactions among participants in the energy policy process. The paradox of wartime was that it produced social harmony and agreement among participants. Consequently, estimates were either accepted or, what was tantamount to the same thing, disregarded.

When peace came, however, prices again became points of contention. When prices were low and supplies plentiful, as in the 1930s, the major producers wanted production limited to force prices up and protect their profits. Consumerists wanted prices left unchanged, and preservationists warned about overconsumption of a limited resource. Preservationists found themselves in an uneasy alignment with the major producers, who were calling for supply restrictions in the name of conservation. Both preservationists and industrialists favored low estimates of resources. To preservationists, a low estimate confirmed that the nation was running out of oil and gas. To the industrialists, a low estimate signaled the need for higher prices in order to spur new exploration and discoveries. Consumerists preferred to see high estimates of resources, for this would strengthen their case for keeping prices low.

In periods marked by demand outdistancing supply and an upward pressure on prices, such as the 1970s, the major and independent producers spoke of the sanctity of the market; consumerists believed there was collusive price-rigging among the major integrated oil companies; and preservationists warned against overproduction. Industrialists faced with shortages, government allocation, and rationing sought high resource estimates to stress that new supplies could be brought forth if prices were high enough. But if the estimates of the day were low, industrialists replied similarly: "Higher prices are needed to bring on more supplies. Whatever argument industrialists used to raise prices, consumerists contradicted it, to have prices lowered. With ever-upward pressure on prices, consumerists favored low estimates to show that there is simply very little oil and gas left to find, no matter how high prices go. If estimates were high, consumerists claimed that industrialists had no reason to call for higher prices, for oil and gas were plentiful enough to be made available at reasonable prices. Preservationists, as always, favored low estimates. These relationships appear in schematic form in Table 12.1.

In peacetime there has been no agreement on estimates. On the contrary, the political participants often make a conscious effort to search for and magnify differences that do not strike the technologists of resource estimation as very significant. Even when the experts agree on the figures, policy makers do not.

The differences among estimators arise mainly from variations in their assumptions about the physical and technical aspects of estimation and from variations in the models and the methodologies they employ. Their disagreements have not usually been policy-based. It is what the political world and the policy process do to these scientists' estimates that constitutes our focus of concern. Given a variety of estimates and estimators to choose from, the participants in energy policy pick those that advance their own preferences.

Estimates have thus been servants of policy perspectives. We have been able to find no evidence that estimates exert any dominant or independent influence upon policy decisions. The repeated calls for credibility in data as prerequisite to intelligent policy-making mask this fundamental conclusion to which we have been drawn.

THE MISPLACED QUEST FOR BETTER DATA

The call for "credibility" holds out the illusion that if the data are believable, sound policy will be possible. The GAO, in its 1974 study

TABLE 12.1   Reserves and Resources:
             What the Estimates "Say" to Participants

	When prices are high, participants favor:	When prices are low, participants favor:
Preservationists	Low estimates	Low estimates
	"High prices encourage overproduction."	"Low prices encourage overconsumption."
Consumerists	Low estimates	High estimates
	"There is just not much left to be found, no matter how high prices go."	"There is no need to raise prices."
Industrialists	High estimates	Low estimates
	"Significant new supplies can be found if prices are high."	"Higher prices are needed to bring on more supplies."

prepared for Senator Henry M. Jackson (D-Wash.), chairman of the Senate Interior Committee, called credibility "the single most important problem with energy data." Examining official cries for credibility in the hearings and GAO reports, five attributes are stressed repeatedly as the necessary components of credibility in reserve data: accuracy, objectivity, consistency, transparency, and verity. Looking at these qualities one by one reveals not only that they conflict with one another, but that a single component can also be internally self-contradictory.

Accuracy

> The Congress, in attempting to fashion effective energy policies, has long been concerned with acquiring accurate . . . unbiased . . . information on domestic petroleum reserves [Moss and Dingell, 1977].

A firm figure was wanted, a single number one could count on. As we know all too well, accuracy in a reporting of unseen resources is impossible. Resource estimates are a judgmental balancing of uncertainties, circumstances, expectations of future prices and technologies. The definition of proved reserves, which in magnitude is more certain, is porous and can accommodate many plausible interpretations.

The most we can expect from reserve estimation is for it to show how ambiguous circumstances and uncertainties in making judgments shape these estimates. Thus, the official expectation of "accurate, unbiased information" about reserves is worse than folly. It is dangerous because it suggests the nation must have something that in principle it cannot get.

Objectivity

Objectivity can mean many things. To critics of data from industry, it means independence. The GAO report (1974) claimed that federal energy planners were "unable to demonstrate convincingly the nature and extent of the energy shortage, in large measure because of the lack of independently developed or independently verified data." The chief purpose of the Energy Information Act was to create that hallmark of objectivity, the National Energy Information System. Senator Floyd K. Haskell (D-Colo.), who chaired hearings on the act, stressed his number-one expectation: to establish "an independent and credible permanent agency within the federal government to collect, analyze, and disseminate basic energy-related data and information."[1]

The prerequisite for objectivity was to be a double-edged independence: independence from industry and independence from policy-making.

Senator Howard M. Metzenbaum's (D-Ohio) statement accusing the Federal Power Commission of passively accepting industry reserve estimates was a common cry:

> Are they [the FPC] basing their calculations only on the figures as supplied by the oil and gas industry, or do they have some separate information which has not yet been made available to the American people so we might share those figures with them? We have heard time and again, the only information available comes from the industry, although it is my understanding both the FPC and the FEA do have the authority to make their own independent conclusions [Senate Energy and Natural Resources Committee, 1977: 43-44].

However, no matter how much independent collection the government imagined itself doing, as long as government did not own the industry, industry would remain the ultimate supplier of data.

Those in Congress who pushed for "credibility" expected data collectors to have no previous links with oil or gas companies or with trade associations. But how, without understanding the industry, were those individuals supposed to know what data, in what form, were appropriate to collect? Staff members who tried to fulfill Congress's mandate to "collect everything" were caught in this trap. Hand in hand with the dilemma of expertise went that of the "biased source." Because companies were suspect, their data were suspect; thus, an independent government agency was needed to supply the figures, albeit industry remained the ultimate data source.

Add, then, the demand that data and policy be separate functions within the energy agency. Data gatherers were to have no policy preferences to taint their collection or results. Former Energy Secretary James Schlesinger (1977b) claimed that "the credibility of EIA as a neutral source of energy data and information will be substantially strengthened by the action which separated it from any responsibility for formulating or advocating national energy policy." If data are suspect because they serve policy, sever the link between the two. If data are divorced from policy, however, they will be so "neutral" as to be irrelevant.

Such an arrangement might stand a chance if policy makers had an explicit policy purpose to convey. We know they did not. Discussions between policy people and data people are essential to relate what is produced to what is wanted. Agreement must be reached on purpose, the relevance of data to that purpose, and feasibility of actually producing data in time and with sufficient reliability at the cost contemplated. None of this—policy, data, cost, time, and so on—was agreed upon.

While it is true that one cannot collect data without some purpose in mind, it is not easy to say a priori how specific that purpose ought to be. Data collected with a very specific purpose in mind are not only costly (for they will be useless in other problems), but may even fail to include data that later turn out to be important. The distinction between data and information is also relevant here. The same data can be used to derive different kinds of information (e.g., different kinds of estimates, averages, and the like). It is the information that should be policy-specific, rather than the data themselves. Experience in research for policy analysis, however, suggests that without some initial notion of what use might be made of data, potential users are unlikely to do much, if anything, with what exists. If you do not put it in, you are unlikely to take it out.

Policy thinking on energy has been monumentally ambivalent. Torn between an implicit desire for central management of the energy industry and a deep reluctance to go through with it, Congress stalled with an instruction to "first give us the hard data." Thus, from the Federal Energy Office to today's Department of Energy, great volumes of data on everything are being collected, usually without evident policy purpose. "Maybe someday the data will be useful" or "If we can show them this great information system, it will be the foundation for better policy thinking" may be the only rationales to sustain data collectors.

Like the boy who cried wolf, massive data collection without clear purpose only erodes credence. Suppliers of data, perceiving no purpose, grow annoyed and less willing to fill out yet another form. As numbers are provided more hastily and without "good-faith effort," the quality of data deteriorates.

If policy makers were imbued with purpose and then met with data collectors to agree on what was needed and what was plausible to obtain, the same legislators could suspect "too much communication." Data collectors would appear to be tainted by policy preference. Thus, official cries for "objectivity" in energy-data collection as a requirement for credibility—isolation from industry and isolation from policy—render data collection deaf, dumb, and blind.

Consistency

Consistency meant having a single, centrally coordinated government information system for all aspects of energy. This national energy information system would let energy planners "streamline and consolidate federal energy information functions to reduce the cost of government, to reduce the size of the bureaucracy and limit the burden on the private sector."[2] The Energy Information Administration (EIA) in the new Department of Energy was expected to do this; "by consolidating more than one hundred important energy data collection programs in the federal government, the Department of Energy would provide comprehensive and reliable energy information" (Executive Office of the President, 1977: 85).

This was a tall order, to include standard terms, definitions, codes, units of analysis, levels of aggregation, rules for confidentiality, and more. None of these standards, moreover, was to change over time. Take the concept of reserves. The first obvious drawback was the lack of uniform terms across agencies. Such terms as "measured reserves," "proved reserves," "indicated reserves," and "probable reserves" had no standard definitions. The GAO report said that the absence of uniform definitions would make it impossible to achieve a centralized energy information system. "Reserves" alone, undefined, could make the attempt hopeless.

The definition an agency adopts reflects its particular purpose in collecting the estimate. To force acceptance of a single definition would reduce its usefulness for all purposes. Thus, for example, the regulatory purposes of the Security and Exchange Commission (SEC) differ from those of the Federal Energy Regulatory Commission (FERC).

The SEC is concerned with ownership of oil and gas reserves. Companies file statements with the SEC that include information about reserves owned. The SEC requires only a total figure of reserves owned. It is not interested in field-level or reservoir-level breakdowns. Respondent companies have to divide their reserves into "net proved" and "proved developed," definitions of particular use for the SEC.

The FERC is primarily interested in those reserves controlled (not necessarily owned) by pipeline companies that are adding new pipelines. To add a new line, the pipeline company applies to the FERC for certification. The FERC asks whether the company holds sufficient reserves to justify a new pipeline. The definition of reserves relevant to FERC purposes is quite different from the SEC's definitions. The FERC, unlike the SEC, is interested in field-level breakdowns. Division of reserves into "net proved" and "proved developed" have no meaning for FERC purposes.

A victory for the National Energy Information System—a single term and a single definition for proved reserves—might indeed reduce the cost to government and the burden on respondents. But sacrificed is an understanding of the factors that make for various interpretations of reserves.

One example from the term "proved reserves" is enough to show the futility of consistency: Who should be the respondent? Owners? (Then what about joint owners? Or what if the owner also is owned?) Well operators? Lease operators? One individual may have good reason for reporting the total volumes which relate to properties he physically operates. Another individual may be primarily concerned about accountability for capital expenditures, and may record reserves either on an ownership basis or on a working-interest basis.[3]

In an attempt to make reserve estimates more indicative of profitability, many firms report reserves on a company net basis—after deducting all royalty amounts. Still others, interested in controlled oil for refining operations, deduct only those royalty amounts which can be taken "in kind." In order to avoid double counting (on an economic basis) it is desirable sometimes to deduct from reserves, or to note separately, those reserves for which payment has already been received in advance of production. Finally, those building or controlling processing plants, pipelines, or refineries, may be most interested in the amount of reserves committed to these facilities, regardless of ownership.

On the receiving end, the Federal Trade Commission (FTC) Bureau of Competition and the Securities and Exchange Commission would prefer to see reporting on an ownership basis. But within this category, the two agencies have use for different subcategories. The FTC Bureau of Competition wants certain especially detailed data for investigating industry structure, performance, and market shares. The USGS and FERC strongly prefer reserve data supplied by well operators or lease operators, who know more than do "owner" respondents about the physical determinants of reserves.

Currently the SEC asks for data by ownership, the Oil and Gas Information System (OGIS) wants them by well operator, and the others (including the FTC Bureau of Competition and the Antitrust Division of the Justice Department) are out in the cold, unable to get some data classifications they consider important.

Should a single centralized solution be reached in the name of streamlining? To force "consistency" is to sacrifice a very real diversity in ways of measuring unseen quantities such as reserves and resources. Consistency makes for duller perception on the part of interested publics, and, on the part of the estimators themselves, a disincentive to be discriminating.

Transparency

The majority in Congress who demanded more credibility were most frustrated by the opaque quality of the American Petroleum Institute and American Gas Association's reserve reporting system. No one could see inside to trace or validate the means by which an estimate was reached. Even some people in private industry, to displace some of the mistrust showered upon them, were calling for a show of government validation of industrial estimation processes. According to a 1973 report prepared for the Congressional Research Service,

> based on interviews with industry officials, it is clear that large segments of the petroleum and gas industries are of the opinion the current procedures lack "credibility" and that the federal government should play a greater role in validating API/AGA proved reserve figures. . . .

> What is needed at the minimum is a capability which would permit a responsible federal official to testify before a committee of the Congress that the figures have been reviewed and validated under his supervision and that they can be relied upon [Energy Research, Inc., 1973: 47].

Four years later, with credibility no closer, a report, "The National Energy Plan," urged the federal government virtually to take over reserve estimation in order to secure validity: "The oil and gas industries would be required to open their reserve estimation processes to federal officials, who would supervise the collection and preparation of reserve data" (Executive Office of the President, 1977: 85).

Secretary Schlesinger, under attack from the Professional Audit Review Team of the GAO (and numerous other critics), committed himself in 1977 to a strong validation operation:

> [T]o insure an aggressive and positive effort for verifying the accuracy and validity of energy information, the data validation function [within the Energy Information Administration, the "independent" information arm of the newborn Department of Energy] has been separated and elevated to an Office of Energy Data Validation headed by an EIA Assistant Administrator.... A firm commitment has been made to staff the office with the necessary resources required to carry out a comprehensive validation program [Schlesinger, 1977a].

Alas, 1979 found the GAO still claiming that "although EIA increased attention and resource-to-date validation activities, little progress has been made in the actual assessment of the accuracy and reliability of energy data" (Professional Audit Review Team, 1979).

No quantity of information-gathering resources, however, could ensure valid reserve data. The first barrier for validation is the impossibility of validating an estimate that cannot even be described as accurate or inaccurate. Validators must dissect numerous biases, assumptions, and physical circumstances, and understand their context, and must do this every time they check a number. Moreover, validators face the hopeless task of honoring "consistency"—consistency in conceptualization, in terminology, in statistical procedure, in measurement, in estimators' opinions of the quality of their estimates. Effective validation means being there—not for a day now and then but for some sustained period. This is expensive. Remember that if government validators work that closely with estimators, "independence" from industry goes out the window.

Verification

In addition to the demand for validation, which indicated a technical kind of tracing, officials wanted verification. This meant that respondents be under oath or that forms be "certified" by a company officer, and also that response be mandatory rather than voluntary.

The GAO (1976: 32-35), in a report assessing the state of credibility two years after the first GAO attack on energy data, still gave poor marks to credibility. Lack of verification, the GAO concluded, was a major culprit. Voluntary and unverified reporting never would secure credibility, even if the data were somehow shown to be valid. The GAO wanted legal forms including appropriate punishments for violation.

Verification is even less likely than validation to be attained. A validation effort at least can take issue with an estimator's assumptions and methods. An expert government validator may elevate the quality of estimation through discussion, debate, and sharing insights. Verification, however, is elusive. Examples of proven lying are so rare as to be nonexistent. Swearing under oath or putting a signature on a form might make some people feel better, but it does not guarantee substantive truth.

One by one, the components of "credibility" collapse under examination. Accuracy as a standard is misconceived. Verification is impossible. To verify for accuracy is nonsensical. Consistency walls off diversity. To validate objectively is meaningless. What does all this mean?

Those who demanded credibility, with all its components, did not really want it. What was wanted was a useful number. This was demonstrated in the chapter on natural gas reserve estimates, in which the thing that mattered more than any components of credibility was who you were and what your results were. With political stands divided, and policy rationalized by certain data estimates, whether those numbers were high or low (or even a slight bit higher or lower) mattered greatly to combatants. Under such situations, cries for credibility proliferated.

The same cries are still heard today. One of the latest efforts is a January 1980 report bearing the now-familiar-sounding title, "An Evaluation of the Adequacy and Reliability of Petroleum Information Disseminated by the Department of Energy." This report, prepared for the Department's Office of Consumer Affairs, echoes the old concerns for the components of credibility. The conclusions, nothing new, perpetuate "credibility" as a misleading concept. To restore what the author, David Schwartz, terms "creditability,"

> it is important to develop the report forms and verify the system used to collect information; it is equally important to develop a validation procedure to verify the information received. . . . EIA must develop audit teams to routinely make field investigations of the major petroleum companies, and periodic visits to a sample of small companies, in order to verify the information reported to EIA [Schwartz, 1980: 73-74].

There persists a strong moral and scientific ring to the calls for "accuracy," "objectivity," "consistency," "validity," and "verification." Conversely, when there is a foundation of political agreement, neither estimates nor credibility are likely to be important issues.

Our analysis emphasizes the excessive and misplaced emphasis on defects and distortions in data. No matter how much effort is put into estimating resources, large elements of uncertainty will remain. The best way to improve the utility of estimates is either to reduce the demands placed on data or to encourage drilling. We believe that the concern over data is inordinate given the inherent limits to the accuracy of resource estimates. We believe also that the effort is misplaced, in focusing attention on quantitative questions that cannot be answered—How large are oil and gas resources? How long will they last?—and in deflecting attention from qualitative questions that can be answered—By what processes or policies can uncertainties be minimized and information improved?

Despite all the hullabaloo about data, those in government who purportedly would have to use it display little interest in doing so. There is no avoiding the conclusion to which our evidence leads: It is not agreement on data that will lead to consensus on policy, but agreement on policy that will lead to consensus on data. With prior agreement on policy perspectives, there can be a consensus on how important estimates are and how much uncertainty the users of the data are willing to live with. An underlying settlement on perspectives will reduce the burdens placed on data. Instead of asking, "How can we get data good enough to merit agreement?" we would do better to ask, "How can we organize our thinking and achieve a basic agreement on perspectives?"

DISSENSUS

Data and policy come in sets, each relevant to the other. Our view of the history of resource estimation suggests that more often than not data have prescribed the outer limits of agreement but, within the arena, politics have dominated data. We believe that consensus on political questions makes for more acceptable estimates and can narrow the margins of interpretation. With consensus on core elements common to diverse groups, agreement on the proper questions, and compromises on the fringes, come more appropriate data. With these numbers (whose limits are forged from political consent rather than from clear visions of the natural world), the initial political compromises can be renegotiated. In turn, more data are produced. The iterations are evolutionary rather than teleological.

Why is there no consensus? Robert Stobaugh and Danial Yergin (1980) of the Harvard Business School offer an explanation we think plausible: "The failure to achieve a national consensus on price decontrol has been perhaps the greatest single barrier to a rational energy policy." As Thomas Schelling (1979) might put it, price *is* the problem.

We believe that the bitter fights over oil and natural gas prices are but the latest manifestation of the dissensus that has persisted throughout the century. To develop our argument we can start by observing the growing body of evidence indicating that removing price controls will make us all better off in the long run (e.g., Schelling, 1979; Stobaugh and Yergin, 1979). As Kenneth Arrow and Joseph Kalt (1979: 17) conclude in one of the latest assessments, after weighing the equity-efficiency tradeoffs of decontrol,

> even with standards of social justice that find the prospective trans-fer of income from consumers to producers highly inequitable, the efficiency gains from decontrol are dominant. Consequently, with full cognizance of the distributional implications, we recommend deregulation of domestic petroleum prices. The nation quite simply pays too great a price for trying to maintain income patterns in their pre-OPEC status and trying to forestall the adjustment to a present and future of rising energy prices.

Yet, no matter how many analyses come to the same conclusion, Congress remains deeply divided. A thousand studies cannot bridge the chasm of dissensus. Why not? Edward Mitchell (1969) thinks it is because legislators vote on matters of energy prices on the basis of their ideologies, not on the basis of analytical evidence, and not even on the basis of their constituents' economic interests. Mitchell's appraisal of selected House votes in 1975 and 1976 showed that natural gas deregulation voting was almost totally determined by ideology. Specifically, characterizing the ideology of each member of Congress by the Americans for Democratic Action (ADA) "liberalness" scale, he found that those with low ADA ratings (conservatives) typically supported deregulation, while those with high ratings (liberals) voted against deregulation.

Joseph Kalt (1978) did a similar study of voting behavior in the Senate for oil price deregulation, and he also found ideology a major determinant of how senators voted. Kalt and Peter Navarro (1979-1980) suggest that legislators' ideologies on deregulation refer mainly to their moral stands on income redistribution. "Liberals" vote against price decontrol just as they would oppose any measure they see as hurting the poor. "Conservatives," who find government intervention for income redistribution ideologically loathsome, vote against holding prices down. They are typically joined by representatives of oil-producing states. Kalt and Navarro (1979-1980: 43) claim that

> these observations explain the lack of a national consensus on energy policy and the inability of interminable preaching to generate a wartime sense of common purpose. Indeed, the energy crisis is not the 'moral equivalent of war.' . . . Rather, the war over energy policy is being fought primarily amongst ourselves—a civil war.

The ideology hypothesis advanced by Mitchell and Kalt and Navarro closely complements our own explanation of dissensus as rooted in two fundamentally different perspectives: quantity theory and price theory. Those concerned primarily with the redistribution of income are taking a quantity approach.

But the ideology explanation is not a full explanation. Other issues besides income redistribution brace the chasm of dissensus on energy: The desire for energy independence versus the desire for U.S. integration into the world energy market reflects quantity versus price perspectives. The insistence on preservation of oil and natural gas as precious resources is another expression of a quantity perspective. These examples suggest that even if everyone realized that the distributional goal would make everyone worse off, other elements of dissensus would still loom large.

DATA ACCEPTABLE WITHOUT A CONSENSUS

Cold comfort! We have just told the energy-data community that the only way to win trust in the validity of its information is through external agreement on policy perspectives—but also that such agreement can come only from political settlement, which the energy-data community is in no position to secure. Government data validators can try to transcend mistrust but cannot wish it away. The main unit involved in the Department of Energy is the Energy Information Administration. What can EIA itself do, given the way the world is now, to increase utility and credibility in data and estimates?

The bind in which EIA analysts see themselves can be illustrated by this excerpt from an internal review of the new Oil and Gas Information System (OGIS):

> Interests and needs of DOE organizational elements shift frequently and drastically (for example, through the many and contradictory laws that are passed and given to DOE to implement), making it extremely difficult to maintain any type of user group or to be fully responsive, especially with large complex systems with long lead times. This places a tremendous responsibility on OGIS to recognize possible program impacts resulting from current legislation and world events which affect domestic production and reserves.[4]

Why should EIA have to worry about data every time a new law is passed? If EIA is to be isolated from policy responsibility, should not EIA also be able to transcend the vagaries of legislation? Yet the recommendations at the end of the OGIS review suggested anything but transcendence. The reviewers put the responsibility of puzzling out what Congress wants completely upon EIA, which "should make a concerted effort to determine, possibly from committee staffs, and a review of the *Congressional Record,* the type of data necessary to satisfy congressional concerns." In addition, the reviewers say, EIA must go out and create clients.

> Since most potential users interviewed were unfamiliar with . . . the OGIS program, it is suggested that a synopsis be prepared of data to be collected by the form and routed directly to interested individuals. . . . Such activity would serve to introduce the potential user community to OGIS. It would also provide support and justification to continuing the program. . . . OGIS should undertake efforts to obtain a stronger base of support for the level of detail being collected by the EIA-23. This is deemed essential to adequately justify continuation of the data collection instrument.

Is this how the professionals of the Energy Information Administration should use their talents—in smoke-outs and sales pitches? Ideally, EIA never should have to guess what policy makers want, and should never have to "sell" data. Those who want the data ought to bear responsibility for saying what information is needed and for justifying its collection before EIA designs or approves any form.

What, then, should EIA do? Though they have accepted the restriction against serving a particular policy purpose, EIA people are not hamstrung; they can share their problems with other elements in government, namely, those who claim to need data. What heretofore have been accepted as constraints might be challenged. For instance, often it has been said that the cost of generating genuinely independent oil and gas reserves data would be prohibitive. Government would have to duplicate, and supplement by many physical tests, the estimation effort of the oil and gas industries. But if independence is what is wanted, then the price must be paid. Besides, if the data are as important as proponents in the legislature insist, those in Congress should be willing to sponsor the supporting services. Those who will the ends, goes the old parliamentary adage, also must supply the means.

One response would be to create a professional cadre of estimators permanently devoted to the task. A new career would be created. This Energy Estimation Corps would train and promote its own staff, establishing and maintaining professional standards. It would be genuinely independent, not only from industry and from government, but also from those who set it up.

We definitely do not suggest that the way to improve estimation is just to spend more. Our suggestions are intended, rather, to illuminate the real costs of performing reserve and resource estimation. For example, if one were collecting data within a cost constraint, one would have to choose only those data likely to be desired in some specified future. Suppose, however, mistrust rather than cost is the crucial constraint. If there are no penalties for collecting poor data, but only for failing to have on hand the currently desired figures, overcollection of data might seem the best (if most expensive) way to make sure something unforeseeable today is not missing. Since no one knows today what will be wanted tomorrow, the cost of keeping available any possibly desirable data is high.

Let us suggest a budgeter's approach, one that might reduce EIA's budget. If money means trouble, that too can be shared. Why is money spent to provide data that government clients do not use? Because it is so easy to say things would be better if only there were more or better data, and users themselves need not specify what would be done with it. This is why the General Accounting Office suggested that users be required to justify the purpose for requested data. Justifications divorced from budget discipline, however, tend to be weak. Let us, then, suggest that except for the most basic data—reserves, resources, and holdings—funds should be funneled through user agencies. Agencies that want data collected should justify it in their budgets. Because such requests would have to compete with other parts of user agencies' budgets, potential users would have to ask whether this data trip is worthwhile, compared with other budget items.

Our third suggestion takes a conflict-resolution form. As any sophisticated person in or out of government would say, energy estimation and data validation remain in their infancy. Despite a century of speculation, and serious effort, many of the basic technical questions remain unresolved. The statistical models underlying interpretation of the data, the standards of collection, the relationship between the quality of the data and the assumption of the models in which they are used, are all underdeveloped.

No one who reads the congressional hearings on oil and gas of the past decade could believe that the pure adversary mode, in this instance, served the nation well. Compared, say, to the hearings on airline deregulation—which produced a set of common assumptions about data and policy alternatives—the oil and gas episodes only exacerbated hard feelings. Perhaps it is time, then, to show how much the adversary mode has affected the accuracy, honesty, and validity of data. In recent years, various new mechanisms have arisen with the aim of bringing together antagonistic interests to bargain out agreements on what facts can be certified, as well as what policies can be approved. "Data mediation" has developed to handle community conflict; the Council on Environmental Quality is trying to get interested parties to agree on the scope of (if not always the solution for) issues to be addressed. (For a general discussion of adversary versus bargaining modes, see Schuck, 1979.)

Little harm could come from trying to get the disputants to address issues of data directly and bear (or share) the costs. By attacking the scientific and social issues surrounding oil and gas estimates simultaneously, it may be possible to increase awareness of how much is not known and how much the significance of what is known depends on political agreement sufficient to certify the meaning of diverse data for public policy.

We have suggested a few avenues one might consider in a world without settlement. In the next and final section, we try to imagine how a political settlement might be reached and what one would look like.

TOWARD A POLITICAL SETTLEMENT

Oil and gas policy is like a Becket play. It takes place in a room without furniture. The participants are formally dressed, except that their backsides are bare. Each has gleaming white teeth sunk in another's backside. They must move together, but under the circumstances, they can only shuffle around. Outside the room a cry is heard that energy is in crisis. More shuffling. Another crisis, another cry. Shuffle, shuffle. The participants, the narrator tells us, really have their teeth into the problem. They enjoy what they are doing too much to stop for extraneous external matters. Shuffle. Can we get them to pay attention to the world outside?

It is easy to imagine conflicts over energy diminishing (or even disappearing) through a "technological fix." Water might replace gas or limitless supplies of cheap methane be found, or clean nuclear energy at infinitesimal cost could overcome existing differences. Equally efficacious, a war or a sudden cutoff of supplies from the Persian Gulf might appear so overwhelming as to subsume all other differences. The enormous price increase after 1973 could certainly qualify as some such situation, outside of war. Yet, these events appear to have intensified rather than ameliorated disputes over estimates, prices, profits, equity, distribution, integrated oil companies, multinationals, and all the rest. Instead of unifying against an external opponent, the protagonists pounced on one another. Is there any way they might be brought closer together?

A social settlement is not in the cards. It would require consensus on the perspectives, the values and beliefs that justify social structures. We do not expect agreement on price or quantity perspectives. Indeed, if anything, participants in energy policy appear to be growing further apart on such questions as whether energy should be considered primarily as a contributor to economic development or as a distributor of political power and social status. The argument for solar energy, for example, is not usually economic, considering the demand for substantial subsidies, but is instead largely political—involving devolution of power—and social, concerning lifestyles.

A political settlement, by contrast, would take differing perspectives for granted, seeking a solution to integrate in practice what is irreconcilable in theory. There are three standard approaches to a political settlement: structure, process, and separation. A structural solution alters the organizational arrangements in the oil and gas industries so that its actions are accepted as in the public interest. An approach through process seeks changes in the way decisions are made in the hope that the outcomes will then be deemed legitimate. The separation approach seeks to disaggregate the scope of policy so that one perspective is dominant here and another there, something like parallel play among children. Let us pursue these possibilities.

STRUCTURE

One form of a structural approach, though it is not now on the political agenda, is nationalization of the oil and gas industries. At the stroke of a pen, difficulties over data would be resolved. All the data would belong to all the people. There would be no more charges of withholding or manipulating data for private profit. In exchange, government would be blamed for anything that went wrong. Control of quantities and prices would be the business of government. Government would attempt to distinguish between higher and lower uses and would set prices to balance domestic equity against other considerations, such as the level of imports. No doubt the usual inefficiencies attending governmental allocation would be present. Gaps and shortfalls would be major concerns.

Risk-taking has not been government's strong suit. Losses as well as gains would be subject to public accounting. The inability of government to establish an oil reserve, for example, when it forgot that pumps to get the oil out were missing, would only be a harbinger of things to come. Yet under nationalization, the attention of energy policy to quantities would be consonant with the reality of governmental ownership and operation. Demand and supply would be adjusted by administrative measures.

A considerable step down from nationalization would be the breakup or divestiture of the large, integrated oil companies, which run the gamut from exploration to production to pipelines to refining to strings of gas stations. Ever since Standard Oil was divided in 1911, there have been calls for carrying divestiture further. The advantages, as seen by proponents, are the restoration of competition among many small firms and a decrease in the political power of the major oil companies. The disadvantages, as seen by opponents, are a reduction in the efficiency that comes from scale and a disruption of existing relationships. Even now there are claims that subsidies to small refiners perpetuate inefficiencies, leading to higher prices.

Would divestiture lead to improvement in the quality or validity of oil or gas data? That depends partly on whether one thinks the quality of data is an objective or a subjective phenomenon. Since there would be a larger number of companies, confusion would undoubtedly be greater, especially since comparisons with past patterns would be rendered more difficult. Enhanced competition, moreover, would make companies less rather than more willing to share data. But if validity is indeed in the eye of the beholder, and if divestiture did increase the legitimacy of the industry as a whole, so that the prices its processes produced were considered appropriate, public validity—the credence that relevant others give to data—might well improve. But if divestiture were to be enacted, it would more likely generate conflicts over other data. To monitor and enforce divestiture, the government would require a great deal of new data: What are the indicators of divestiture? of competition in each sector of the industry? Even if all sides agreed to adopt divestiture, its implementation might exacerbate the familiar conflicts over definitions and data.

A more modest basis for a structural settlement would be governmental entry into the oil and gas business on public lands and seas. The old idea of the Tennessee Valley Authority as a "yardstick" could be revived in the form of a federal energy authority. This new authority could drill, produce, and, if necessary, distribute oil and gas. It could not set prices for private parties. The quid pro quo: Industry accepts government as a competitor on public lands; government gives up regulation of prices and profits. The advantages might be acceptance of such structural change as enhancing competition and legitimizing the resulting prices. Consumerists' fears of monopoly and excessive private power might decline. Efforts to add to reserves, and an expanded role for the scientists of the U.S. Geological Survey, might have broad appeal and please even the preservationist.

This third type of structural approach to a political settlement is based on an explicit exchange: Structural change in the energy industry in return for acceptance of market prices. Industry would stop fighting governmental entry into oil and gas exploration and production. Instead of yelling from the sidelines, government would experience its own oil and gas activities directly.

Our purpose is not to argue for or against these alternative political settlements but to tease out their implications for energy data. The advantages of the TVA-type approach for the validity of oil and gas estimates would be considerable. Government itself would have its own reserves and resources to estimate. Government itself would develop a cadre of experienced estimators. Government itself would have data to trade with private industry. Each set of estimators active on public lands and offshore would be influenced by mutual interest in collegial relations, in refining experience, and in exchange of data. Discussion of data would replace exhortation.

Difficulties abound. Government may prove inept, money-wasting, or threatening to industry. Since the best prospects are now on public places, inland or offshore, preferential federal access could be used to freeze out private parties. Cheaper governmental money may yield advantages. Bureaucratic rules may confer disadvantages. Industry might use the occasion to seek subsidies, thus compounding concern over public losses. All this and more is entirely possible.

Most serious, for our purpose, is the possibility that the settlement might not prove politically satisfactory. Consumerists, industrialists, and preservationists may not accept the resulting market conditions. Consumerists would object because the arrangement does not consider equity. Industrialists would object because the new markets would be more risky than they were before the government entered as a new competitor. Add to this the factor of uncertainty: Just how will the new member behave? Preservationists, with yet another competitor in the arena, would fear too-quick development and wasting of precious oil and gas.

The prospects for a structural approach to a political settlement are summarized in Table 12.2. While they hold some promise for the acceptability of data, all three avenues look rather infeasible politically.

At a time of unsteady supply and rising prices, we do not have to persuade variable marketers to love prices. Smaller-scale industry has usually preferred prices. Industry, then, aims to keep what it has. The new windfall profits tax may be regarded as a payment to be allowed to stay in business. Alas, the proceeds themselves are the new burning object of contention. As usual, the government cannot take over the industry, nor is it willing to let private markets operate completely to discover what they would do unaided. This ambivalence is reflected in the windfall-profits-tax solution. Given the record of past practices, turnabout—using government to limit instead of increase profits—may be fair play. For present policy purposes, the seeds of future disputes over profits and taxes have been sown without addressing fundamental issues of energy production or distribution, supply at home or payment abroad. Nevertheless, industrialists are on notice that their present position is precarious. They prefer regulation to nationalization. Divestiture could only be accepted to avoid a worse fate.

Consumerists claim that the lack of competition in the oil and gas industries leads to too high a price and too great a concentration of political power. Let us separate these two consequences. If the concentration of power is the major concern, then changing the structure of the industry—for instance, by divestiture—might lead to a settlement. But if prices remain high even under the restored competition among many small firms, would the principle still dominate? Do consumerists want restored competition even if it means higher prices? If competition is merely a convenient concern to voice, if consumerists' perspectives are grounded in a belief in governmental as opposed to market allocation, or grounded simply in an insistence on low prices, then changing the structure will not be satisfactory.

The rise in prices and the disruption of oil supply have led to the revival of preservationist views that stress limits on the earth's resources and the consequent necessity to preserve them. Where to price theorists the idea of exhaustion is anathema, because at some price, alternatives (coal, nuclear, solar, and the like) are bound to become available, to preservationists this crisis in costs may be an opportunity to advance the cause of frugality. As the costs and risks of importing grow, there are bound to be efforts to increase or at least maintain domestic production. There is also another way to go: conservation. Thus, the quarrel over whether to decrease demand through higher prices or through administrative measures is bound to continue. Later we will ask whether both types of policy could supplement each other.

Can anything be expected to alter the position of quantity theorists? Although much higher prices are evidently in store, they can still argue either that prices should be lower or that profits should be limited. The more consumerists limit profits, the less exploration and production there will be. Few finds then spark the preservationists' argument for raising the price or rationing. All that can confidently be predicted is a continuation of the oil and gas struggle into the newer forms of energy. Old quarrels will be either exacerbated or replaced by new ones no less fierce. Since the stakes will be higher, the conflict may well grow more intense.

TABLE 12.2 Prospects for a Structural Approach

	Nationalist		Divestiture		A Federal Energy Authority	
	Pro	Con	Pro	Con	Pro	Con
Consumerists	No more private monopolies	No more small-firm competition either No assurance of low prices	Restore competition among small firms	Such restoration still could bring high prices	Private monopoly weakened	No assurance of desired prices
Variable marketers: majors		They would no longer exist		Loss of efficiency, disruption, loss of power	Market prices would prevail	Government might use its built-in advantages to squeeze industry
Constant marketers: small firms		They would no longer exist	Chance for survival increased	Doubt among the unaffiliated small firms: would their new competition with past affiliations squeeze them out?	Market prices should prevail	Fear that government would behave like a major, squeezing down small firms

TABLE 12.2 (continued)

	Nationalist		Divestiture		A Federal Energy Authority	
	Pro	Con	Pro	Con	Pro	Con
Preservationists	Opportunity to set quantities and prices so as to conserve	Doubt: private markets sometimes did induce conservation		More competition for scarce resources		Fear of more competitive and wasteful development
Implications for data	All data would belong to all people; no more using data for private profit		More data needed to enforce; could exacerbate conflict over data, but if divestiture increases legitimacy of industry, public acceptance of data could improve		Government would join estimation as a colleague, becoming expert; mistrust would give way to discussion	

PROCESS

The American political process is based not on hiding but on revealing interests. The participants outside of government are supposed to represent themselves. And the clash of interests within agreed-upon rules for aggregating and representing preferences under competitive conditions is counted upon to produce reasonable outcomes. When this does not happen, oil and gas policy being a classic case in point, we are led to look at our political process to see if there is a defect that can be remedied. This book, taking a historical approach through the politics of estimation, has located such a defect in a mistrust so deep and pervasive, in a clash of perspectives so profound, it has stultified all solutions. For behind the clash of private interests was presumed to be a concern for a public interest in democratic procedures and issues that threatened survival that in times of crises would come to the fore. Obviously, there have been failures; the Civil War is the most notable example. Energy is elusive in this respect, because it appears to be much like other important issues. The realization is growing, however, that settling the energy issue stands as a supreme test of the political process to produce outcomes that are both acceptable to citizens and successful in meeting substantive concerns that threaten to throw the country into turmoil, reducing its standard of living, leaving it vulnerable to foreign influence, propelling it into war, and demonstrating that democratic politics cannot cope with a survival issue.

A distinguished group of analysts from Resources for the Future share in our quest for a process approach to settlement. They first draw the following general conclusions in their book, *Energy in America's Future:*

> On a national level, political consensus in regard to energy policy has eluded three successive administrations. Energy issues have absorbed a disproportionate amount of attention, and have fostered suspicion and mistrust among elements of society.... Energy issues have become emotionally charged and discourse on this subject has been dominated by extremes. There has been no generally accepted basis for evaluating alternatives ... and no grand system by which choices can be legitimatized. Governing institutions based on majoritarian principles have bogged down in an issue that has no clear-cut choices. The need here is to specify the *degree* to which national policy should pursue *several* interrelated and potentially conflicting goals [Schurr et al., 1979: 536].

This assessment, indeed, could serve as a summary of our findings from looking at three-quarters of a century of energy estimation.

At this point the analysts turn to an optimism which, though cautious and guarded, we nonetheless think may be misplaced:

Three elements can contribute to lessening the conflict over energy policy:

- The first is improved knowledge about the facts of the energy situation, which includes the frustrating admission that uncertainty about some things is itself an important fact that no amount of shouting and recrimination will change.

- The second element is formulation of a "shared" world view within which energy choices can be made. Conflicting perceptions of energy's role are bound to persist, but there is still room for consensus if we recognize the mutual legitimacy of these perceptions and resolve that the essential core of each must not be violated.

- *Finally, we need a decision process that all contending parties will respect and value sufficiently to protect, even when the outcome requires that original stands be modified* [Schurr et al., 1979: 536-537].

The authors first imply that an end to combat over data is a prerequisite to more fundamental agreement. Our own research has suggested the reverse: that conflict over energy policy has been reflected in, not caused by, controversies over data. Agreement on perspectives about policy is necessary for agreements or estimates.

We agree with the Resources for the Future analysts that there is no "shared view" and no consensus. How can preservation be squared with expansionism, or low prices with high prices, or regulation with competition? The RFF team suggests a sensible if indirect movement toward consensus: agreement on the process of decision so that outcomes will be respected even though all parties do not approve. Exactly. If the participants had *approved* of the process—including the structure of industry, the place of markets, and the role of government—the parties would have *agreed,* or agreed to disagree, long ago.

The two world wars seemed to pull together consensus on process, for the survival of democracy was at stake. Today we do not have a war, popular or otherwise. The evil manifests itself mostly in the form of rising prices and shortages. One would think that the events of 1973 would qualify as a unifying force, a signal for combatants to come together and fashion a consistent energy policy. But the embargo and the price increases had the opposite effect. In the face of those extraordinary external shocks, energy policy-making responded mostly by wishing they would go away, while everyone else took to battling and blaming each other for the crisis.

It is true, of course, that the sudden increase in oil prices made domestic decisions difficult. On one side, the prior limit on oil imports meant, in essence, that the domestic industry was regulated by decisions about how much oil would be imported. Since adjustment was foreign, it proved doubly difficult to modify domestic arrangements. On the other side, the rapid rise in price exacerbated long-standing differences on practically everything—prices, equity, environment, regions, and so on. Nevertheless, notwithstanding all of the above, available alternatives that could have cushioned the blow were disregarded due to distrust. Had the majors and the independent oil companies consistently favored market processes, they would have been in a better position to argue in favor of letting domestic prices go up to increase domestic supply and decrease foreign demand. Instead, due to subsidization of imports, demand for foreign oil increased and domestic production decreased. Alternatively, government could have placed a large tariff on imports and made itself the importer of foreign oil, thus increasing its ability to bargain with outsiders. Distrust of government prevented this. Neither price nor quantity theories were used where and when appropriate. Since everyone who could help was distrusted, the result was no help at all.

The note of hope in RFF's conclusions may be explained by the authors' belief that contemporary events, rather than deep-seated differences, are responsible for the difficulties in deciding energy policy. They point to the huge price increases, vulnerability to disruption of supply from abroad, a shift toward environmental defense, a more activist judiciary, and legislative changes. All this is true. But the inferences drawn from it may not be. Attend carefully to the rationale of the RFF argument:

> If so many shifts had not occurred, adjustment could have taken place within the existing decision system, and it could have retained a continuing legitimacy. In dealing with a multitude of issues that suddenly require simultaneous (and closely shaded) decisions, however, the political circuits have simply become overloaded. Citizens are not sure whom or what to trust, but it appears that they are losing faith in the market processes and other institutions which helped to carry out the necessary adjustments in earlier and less complex days. The skein of energy policies built up from decades of informal compromise and implicit mutual accommodation has come unwound [Schurr et al., 1979: 537].

The phrase "retained a *continuing legitimacy*" is the giveaway, suggesting that the decision-making process has lost something precious it once had. Our view is that legitimacy in oil and gas estimation and policy is not a has-been but a never-was. Circumstances certainly have changed. But why, when external circumstances were kinder in the past and energy supplies were abundant, were bitter battles over estimates the norm rather than the exception? The difference between then and now is not that the participants in oil and gas affairs did not hate one another then, but that now the cost of hostility has become astronomical. In the good old days, the lack of a political settlement meant that instead of "Utopia double-plus," in regard to oil and gas, the United States got "Utopia double-minus"—but it was still Utopia. Now that the supply situation is so unfavorable, failure to legitimize the processes of energy decision-making may take us from Utopia to catastrophe.

Now we are at the nub of the matter: Price and quantity perspectives are unlikely to change, a structural settlement appears unlikely and perhaps insufficient, and failure by making the twin crises of price and supply much worse than they had to be will further exacerbate the political difficulties of allocating losses. The unfortunate messengers who carry energy data may be beheaded for bringing bad news (or no news at all), but that will not help. The politics of decline, a sequel to the politics of mistrust, will be even more unmanageable than the energy issue itself.

SEPARATION

Perhaps political settlement is still possible to embrace by agreeing on a division of spheres. It will not help to have halfhearted governmental operation or shackled markets that cannot function at full effectiveness. It would be better to develop parallel roles so that, in their respective spheres, price and quantity theories, private markets and governmental rules, are able to do their best. The rub is in the revision of responsibilities.

In return for maintenance of markets within the existing industrial structure, taxed at the usual rates, the oil and gas industries would give up existing privileges. Among these would be all abatement of taxes for drilling and depreciation. Multinational oil companies would no longer be able to take the "royalties" or payments to foreign oil producers off their U.S. taxes; they would no longer be tax collectors for OPEC or anyone else except the U.S. government. Industry would be encouraged to make money at home and to develop new sources of supply abroad. No theory of markets is without associated rules for making permissible transactions; these rules can be changed. Instead of telling industry that the losses are all theirs but the gain goes to the government, industry would be rewarded for finding and producing more outside OPEC.

The governmental sphere would be simultaneously enlarged and reduced. Regulation of prices and profits is a halfway house that no longer serves its political function of obtaining consent. Instead, government would directly do the kinds of things it does well.

Government would be the sole importer of oil and gas, striking the best bargain it can. At least in regard to import data, government statistics would be supreme. It could place a substantial tariff and/or tax on gasoline. The proceeds would be used to develop other sources of energy, thus appealing to preservationists. The government could subsidize poorer people, so they would not be hurt disproportionately by higher prices, thus accommodating consumerists. Government could subsidize construction and operation of synthetic fuel plants and even try a few plants on its own. There have been government plants of all kinds, especially in defense, and the record is not all bad. These kinds of vigorous activity by both government and industry may not be ideal, but they are better than inactivity. Suitably separated, government and industry may help solve rather than exacerbate the problem.

Our purpose here is not to argue for a particular political settlement, but to show how such an accord would radically alter the importance accorded to oil and gas estimates. Under a workable separation, uncertainties in estimation, common to public as well as private industry, would be more acceptable. To the extent that results of competitive processes (as in the TVA-type structural approach and in the separation approach) proved acceptable, validity of estimates would be less of an issue.

It may be, of course, that current tenuous compromises on oil and gas policy are all the nation is going to get. Some profess to believe, according to Rich Jaroslovsky of the *Wall Street Journal,* that "for better or worse, the U.S. is finally about to get a national energy policy" (Wall Street Journal, 1980: 1). In order to reduce dependence on foreign oil, prices are being decontrolled. The experience of the past year has convinced some policy makers that demand is sensitive to price. Similarly, by 1985 new gas will be decontrolled so that by the end of the 1980s gas prices should rise to those of oil. Price is supplemented by quantitative measures—auto mileage standards, compulsory conversion of oil to coal by utilities, subsidies for household insulation, and so on. On the supply side, profits are being kept down by the windfall tax on production. Part of the proceeds are to be used to enable poor people to pay higher prices, and part to encourage development of other energy sources ranging from shale to solar. Though Senator Edward Kennedy (D-Mass.) continues to call for recontrol of oil prices "to protect the poor and average-income consumer until the energy economy reaches the point of sufficient supply and genuine competition" (Wall Street Journal, 1980: 18), there is more talk of a "broad consensus."

No one can say whether these understandings will be maintained as higher prices begin to bite in a period of escalating inflation. Consumerists get subsidies for low-income people and reduction of oil and gas industry profits. Preservationists get reduced consumption and subsidies for alternative forms of energy. Industrialists get eventual price decontrol.

Agreement on a policy framework is not necessarily the same as agreement on policy. In fact, as psychologists and statisticians have shown, opinions do tend to merge with increasing information, *provided* the initial opinions are not mutually orthogonal (or polarized, in our language). The interesting question then is, "What is the minimum amount of overlap that is still sufficient to produce convergence by increasing information?" In a sense, both consensus and polarization make information unnecessary, though for different reasons. The interesting cases, from the viewpoint of the providers of data, lie somewhere between the two extremes. Another way of restating our concern in this book is whether the onslaught of external events has finally led to greater receptivity to evidence, or whether polarization of oil and gas issues will continue to drive out consideration of the consequences.

Why could not both price and quantity measures be used to their best advantage? The proceeds of a tariff on oil or a tax on gasoline could be used to offset harm done to the poor and subsidize other energy sources while still allowing industry to do as much as it can. Instead, the cost of consent has been the enactment of measures (notably the windfall profits tax) directed squarely at production by oil companies. Dispute over data, especially data on profits, will only proliferate. And the question of how much oil and gas are yet to be discovered and will be worth extracting will remain both unanswered and a center of contention, since the producing companies will always be able to claim that they could have done better if. . . .

For too long a fundamental problem of political legitimacy has masqueraded as a dispute over data. If there is some sort of a political settlement or if other issues displace energy, the quality of the data will not matter that much. If there is no such settlement and the issue intensifies conflict, disputes over data will loom larger, with less prospect for resolution. If we look to the fault in ourselves and not in vain auguries for reading ultimate truth in the entrails of necessarily uncertain data, we will not be far from wrong.

NOTES

1. Statement regarding an amendment to the Energy Information Act, Congressional Record, February 26, 1976, p. S2499.

2. Statement by Senator Floyd K. Haskell on the proposed Energy Information Act, Congressional Record, February 26, 1976, P. S2499.

3. This paragraph and the one following it are based on Bankston (1975: 39). By a "working interest" is meant total volumes and costs, less deductions for joint venture interest shares of others.

4. Draft review of OGIS review.

REFERENCES

ARROW, K. J. and J. P. KALT (1979) "Why oil prices should be decontrolled." Regulation (September-October).

BANKSTON, G. C. (1975) "Estimating and defining underground hydrocarbon reserves," in Seminar on Reserves and Productive Capacity. Washington, DC: American Petroleum Institute.

Energy Research, Inc. (1973) Analysis of Salient Issues Regarding the Estimation of Proved Oil and Gas Reserve Figures. Washington, DC: Author.

Executive Office of the President (1977) The National Energy Plan. Washington, DC: Government Printing Office.

General Accounting Office (1976) Improvements Still Needed in Federal Energy Data Collection, Analysis, and Reporting. Washington, DC: Government Printing Office.

——— (1974) "Actions needed to improve federal efforts in collecting, analyzing, and reporting energy data," in Energy Information Needs: Study by the General Accounting Office. Washington, DC: Government Printing Office.

KALT, J. P. (1978) "The political economy of federal energy policy: an analysis of voting in the U.S. Senate." Discussion paper 676, Harvard Institute of Economic Research.

——— and P. NAVARRO (1979-1980) "The energy crisis—moral equivalent of civil war." Regulation (September-October/January-February).

MITCHELL, E. J. (1969) "The basis of congressional energy policy." Texas Law Review (March).

MOSS, J. E. and J. D. DINGELL (1977) Personal communication to John O'Leary, Deputy Secretary of the Department of Energy, October 8.

Professional Audit Review Team, General Accounting Office (1979) Activities of the Energy Information Administration, Department of Energy, Report to the President and the Congress. Washington, DC: Author.

SCHELLING, T. C. (1979) Thinking Through the Energy Problem. San Francisco: Committee for Economic Development.

SCHLESINGER, J. R. (1977a) Personal communication to Richard W. Kelley, Chairman of the Professional Audit Review Team, October 3.

——— (1977b) Personal communication to Richard W. Kelley, Chairman of the Professional Audit Review Team, November 7.

SCHUCK, P. H. (1979) "Litigation, bargaining, and regulation." Regulation (July-August): 26-34.

SCHURR, S. H., J. DARMSTADTER, H. PERRY, W. RAMSEY, and M. RUSSELL (1979) Energy in America's Future. Washington, DC: Resources for the Future.

SCHWARTZ, D. (1980) "An evaluation of the adequacy and reliability of petroleum information collected and disseminated by the Department of Energy." Prepared for the U.S. Department of Energy, Office of Consumer Affairs, Washington, D.C.

Senate Energy and Natural Resources Committee (1977) Natural Gas Pricing Proposals of President Carter's Energy Program: Part D of S. 1469. Washington, DC: Government Printing Office.

STOBAUGH, R. and D. YERGIN (1980) "A new look at the energy issue." Washington Star (February 17).

——— [eds.] (1979) Energy Future: Report of the Energy Project at the Harvard Business School. New York: Random House.

Wall Street Journal (1980) February 27.

APPENDIX

Resources

NO. 58   RESOURCES FOR THE FUTURE, MARCH, 1978

SPECIAL ISSUE

From time to time, RFF will publish a special issue of Resources *that focuses on a single, timely topic. This, the first such issue, written by RFF Fellow John J. Schanz, Jr., embodies the results of a series of workshops.*

AUTHORS' NOTE: The authors wish to thank Resources for the Future for permission to reprint this special issue of *Resources*.

Oil and Gas Resources — Welcome to Uncertainty

Until 1973, the American public was accustomed to glad tidings about U.S. oil and gas resources. If you read the business sections of newspapers or followed the trade and professional publications, you were aware that the forecasts became increasingly optimistic over the years (see table 1).

There were some less sanguine estimates from those who looked at the ever-declining curves of oil field production and projected rising costs through time. But these more cautious projections appeared to be overshadowed by the upward path of U.S. oil production. As the world's leading oil producer, the nation passed the 1 billion-barrel level in 1929, 2 billion in 1948, 3 billion in 1966, and reached the 3 and one-half billion level in 1970. The perennial optimism of the wildcatter—"Give us an incentive and we'll go find you some oil and gas"—was well supported by over 100 years of production history. The United States seemed a permanent fixture as the world's number one producer of oil and gas.

The undercurrent of concern during the 1960s over declining exploratory activity in the United States elicited little real attention outside of the oil and gas industry itself and a small circle of petroleum specialists. It was easy for others to treat these worries as merely the customary background noises that accompany an industry's efforts to encourage favorable treatment by Congress on taxation, incentives, or protection from foreign competition. However, the major disturbance caused by the Organization of Petroleum Exporting Countries (OPEC) oil embargo in 1973 brought an immediate end to this lack of public attention.

In 1975, a report by the Committee on Resources and the Environment (COMRATE) of the National Academy of Sciences, based on a review of contemporary estimates, stated that, of the original stock of crude oil and natural gas liquids (249 billion barrels), only 113 remained to be discovered. For natural gas 530 trillion cubic feet (of an original 1,227 trillion) remained.[1] This marked the end of general optimism both in industry and government about the future U.S. oil and gas resource position. For the public and Congress, whose ears are normally more receptive to good news, it was a shocking revelation to learn that instead of over 400 billion barrels of liquid hydrocarbons there might be much less. To have this unwelcome news appear in the midst of the oil and gas industries' post-embargo clamoring for high prices resulted in both public confusion and distrust. With respect to natural gas, the winter crisis of 1976–77 caused renewed

[1] M. King Hubbert, whose work received considerable attention in the press, was among the COMRATE participants. His estimate was reported as 72 billion barrels of oil and 540 trillion cubic feet of gas.

Table 1.

CHANGING PERSPECTIVES OF U.S. OIL AND GAS RESOURCES

Forecast in Year	Original supply of recoverable reserves[a]	
	Oil (billion barrels)	Natural gas (trillion cubic feet)
1948	110	
1952		400
1956	300	856
1965	400	2,000
1969		1,859
1970	432	
1972	458	1,980
1975	249	1,227

[a] Unfortunately, any sampling of estimates encounters variations in the treatment of past production, recoverability, and the inclusion of natural gas liquids. These have been chosen, or adjusted when possible, to make the totals roughly comparable regardless of year of estimate.

doubts and confusion among the public, the media, and members of government.

In the three years since the COM-RATE report, several staff members at Resources for the Future have been looking into questions about oil and gas reserves and resources. It, therefore, seems appropriate at this time to distill from these recent RFF efforts as much understanding about oil and gas resources as possible. We have no intention of producing a new set of resource estimates; there are more than enough of these. Rather, we hope to show why we keep getting different signals about the status of our oil and gas resources. If we can reduce some of the confusion, our efforts will be well rewarded.

Obviously, it will not be possible to explore in these few pages all of the problems in the collection and use of oil and gas statistics. Our attention is directed toward the different methodologies and perspectives employed by the various analysts who produce conflicting estimates.

The following discussion draws heavily upon a number of recent RFF activities, including: a workshop on oil and gas resources sponsored by the National Science Foundation, a study on resource terminology sponsored by the Electric Power Research Institute, a workshop on Maximum Efficient Rate (MER) of oil and gas production sponsored by the U.S. Department of the Interior, and a workshop which reviewed the Federal Energy Administration's *National Energy Outlook, 1976* sponsored by the National Science Foundation. In addition, members of the RFF staff have participated on a regular basis in the work of the committees and boards of the National Academy of Sciences, the Gas Policy Advisory Council of the Federal Power Commission, and the oil and gas resource appraisal groups of the American Association of Petroleum Geologists and the U.S. Geological Survey. The contribution to this summary report of Dr. John C. Calhoun, Jr., Vice-Chancellor of Texas A&M University, who directed the oil and gas resources workshop, is especially acknowledged.

A Matter of Definition and Classification

An oil or gas reservoir is not a subterranean cavern filled with oil and gas, which we empty like a huge storage tank. During geological time, various mixtures of crude oil, natural gas, and salt water were formed and moved about in the interconnected minute pores of certain kinds of rock where they have remained trapped. When the driller's bit penetrates the rock, natural pressures cause a slow migration of the fluids toward the well bore. The well operator may decide initially, or eventually, to give the flow of oil and gas an assist through the application of the sucking action of a pump, or by fracturing the rock around the well, or by injecting water, chemicals, heat, or gases into the rock. To understand this production process, three things must be kept in mind: 1, the flow of fluids through rock pores is a function of the physical forces at work; 2, the quantity resulting from additional effort gradually diminishes, just as wringing a wet rag produces less and less water; and, 3, the only actual measurement that can be made is of the oil and gas produced at the surface—all other information about the reservoir is estimated.

An oil and gas reservoir or pool is basically a hydraulic unit where all the interconnected pores holding the oil and gas in the rock behave as a single fluid system. Theoretically, a well drilled at precisely the right place would be all that would be needed to produce all of the oil or gas the reservoir will ever produce, given sufficient time for the fluids to move through the rock to this one point. In one geographic area, encompassing a few or thousands of acres,

there may be a series of reservoirs or individual traps containing oil and gas that are geologically related but not physically interconnected. To find and produce all of the oil and gas requires additional wells, dispersed either vertically or horizontally. A single isolated reservoir or a group of reservoirs related by physical proximity and geological origin are identified as an oil or gas field. Once the oil and gas exploration teams have found a specific bed of rock that contains oil and gas accumulations, they will tend to follow this "play" by drilling down to that bed or zone over an extended area. A discrete geological environment having a large number of oil and gas fields is known as a basin or province. In the United States, there are over 100 basins found clustered in five major regions. Within the basins there are thousands of fields and many thousands of individual reservoirs. Over 2 million wells have penetrated the earth in the vicinity of these oil and gas traps, and more than 500,000 successful ones are still producing oil and gas. Approximately 10,000 wells are abandoned each year.

Once the physical characteristics of an oil and gas resource system is appreciated, the complexity of the question "how much oil and gas do we have?" becomes more apparent. Any response can be no more than a judgmental estimate. Intelligent communication about oil and gas resources becomes exceed-

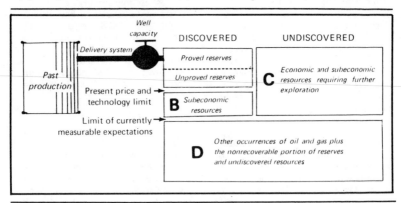

Figure 1: Diagram of Reserves and Resources

ingly difficult unless both the questioner and respondent understand what kind of data they are using. A start in this direction is to use a diagram becoming common in governmental circles (see figure 1).

A complete oil and gas resource diagram is a pictorial representation of all unproduced natural oil and gas hydrocarbons that may exist. We can also visualize a valve attached to the diagram representing the oil and gas wells through which oil and gas is removed from the reservoirs that have already been penetrated by the drill. Beyond this valve there is a conduit which represents the pipelines, tankers, barges, railroad cars, and trucks used to move the oil and gas through processing and on to the final user. It is worth repeating that past production, that is, the quantity already delivered by this system, is *our only actual measurement*. That quantity of oil and gas is gone forever. References to *original oil and gas in place* mean the sum of both the remaining oil and gas plus all that has ever been produced.

The *productivity capacity* of the United States is the amount of oil and gas that can be produced from existing wells during a specified period of time under specified operating conditions. The totality of physical oil and gas in the earth but not yet produced from the continental crust to a depth of perhaps 50,000 feet is sometimes called the *oil and gas resource base*. There are four kinds of oil and gas found in this *resource base*. The first kind (segment A in figure 1) consists of oil and gas which has already been found and is considered producible under present prices using current technology. These quantities are customarily known as *reserves*. The immediately producible portion of these reserves—the oil and gas that will flow from wells in developed reservoirs, the quantity of which can be estimated with considerable accuracy—is classified as *proved reserves*. The balance, or *unproved reserves*, has been discovered but cannot be estimated with as great accuracy and may require additional drilling and development (see figure 2).

In segment B we find oil and gas that has been discovered but in the judgment of the operators cannot be produced under current prices with existing technology. These quantities are known as *subeconomic resources*. There are two kinds of subeconomic resources. First, the unrecoverable, high-cost portion of oil and gas currently left behind in producing reservoirs. Second, oil and gas in other reservoirs that have been found but are not now producing or have been abandoned because they would cost too much to produce due to size or other problems.

Segment C of the resources diagram encompasses the oil and gas that remains to be discovered. Exploratory drilling has not proceeded to a point where there is physical evidence of the actual presence of this oil and gas. There is only expectation, and estimates of undiscovered oil and gas are based solely upon geologic and engineering extrapolation. This requires the use of geological and geophysical data rather than using physical data based upon the actual *existence* of the oil and gas. It is possible to subdivide undiscovered resources into economic and subeconomic quantities, but to do so requires the analyst to make some sort of assumption about prices and technology conditions. Present prices and technology are frequently assumed despite the fact that the oil and gas, when actually discovered, will be produced under future conditions of price and technology.

The final portion is segment D—*other occurrences*. This includes any oil and gas left behind that is not expected under any future circumstances to be worth the effort or cost of production, as well as deposits which are considered too small to either find or produce if found. Finally, this category is a convenient place to account for other forms of oil and gas hydrocarbons about which either little is known, or production technology is so immature that economic and technologic judgments cannot be made, even though large quantities may be involved.

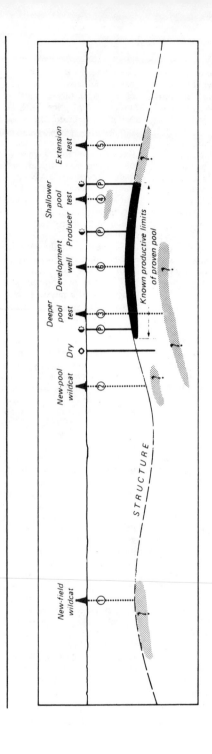

Figure 2: The Classification of Wells by Geologists

NOTE: Proved reserves are established by the producing wells (P). Unproved reserves in the field will require additional drilling by wells 3, 4, 5, and 6. Wildcat exploratory drilling can find undiscovered resources in adjacent pools or in separate fields (1 and 2).

Estimation of Reserves

As the drill bit penetrates a rock reservoir for the first time and finds oil and gas, the first questions asked are how much has been found and can it be produced economically. The initial well provides limited information about the rock strata that have been penetrated and nothing about strata that are below the bottom of the well. Once a layer of rock containing oil and gas has been found, the approximate thickness of the bed at that point—anything from a few to hundreds of feet—is known. A core of rock is usually taken from the bed. Electrical and other measurements are taken inside the hole. All of these data provide information about the porosity and permeability of the rock and the amounts and kinds of fluids it contains. If the reservoir seems to justify production on the basis of this preliminary information, then the drilling equipment is removed, production pipe is put in place, and the well prepared for production: The initial flow of a new well provides information about the production rate, pressure, and other physical data.

At this point, a preliminary judgment on how much oil and gas have been found can be made based on: the flow from a single well; a rock sample a few inches in diameter of a multiacre reservoir; a map of the surface geology; and a seismic "shadow picture" of the structure holding the oil and gas thousands of feet below the surface. Obviously, this first estimate cannot be very precise. Yet based on this one well and past experience with the kind of reservoir that *appears* to have been found, the engineer makes a judgment. This estimate may range from the least amount of oil and gas that appears to have been found to the outer limit of what the reservoir might ultimately produce if the buried structure is entirely filled with oil and gas.

The scientific guesswork about a reservoir hundreds of acres in size is useful but extremely crude. It is akin to going to an unfamiliar supermarket on a foggy night and trying to estimate the total amount of asphalt used in paving the parking lot, with no other data than a cubic inch sample of the blacktop used. How uncertain these judgments about reserves can be was illustrated in a study published by the National Academy of Sciences in 1976.

The study concerned the amount of gas reserves under lease in certain fields in the Gulf of Mexico. Previous estimates had been made by the technical staff of the Federal Power Commission (FPC), but there was disagreement about their accuracy. The Academy suggested that two consulting firms, experienced in the Gulf fields, should make independent estimates using the same geological survey data that was used by the FPC. This was done for a random sample of nineteen (out of a total 168) leases. All the estimates by these firms proved to be lower than those of the FPC staff, but a comparison between the estimates made by the two firms was more interesting. For one lease, the difference between their estimates was only 10 percent. But for nine of the leases, the upper estimate was from two to eleven times higher than the lower estimate.

Even before a well is drilled, companies will appraise the potential of a new region to help them determine whether or not exploratory wells are worth drilling (see figure 3). Once a well has been successful in finding oil and gas, two new estimates can be made: first, an estimate of the minimum amount (the proved reserve) that seems to be producible by that well and, second, a less certain estimate of what might be the ultimate potential of the entire field. As more wells are drilled and additional production data are gathered, the proved reserve estimate may be revised up or down. The expectation of ultimate production can also change upward or· downward, usually over a much wider range than that of the proved reserve figure—several multiples are common. For a typical field it takes approximately five or six years before the proved reserve estimate of remaining oil plus past production begins to approach a true estimate of ultimate production. In other words, it takes a number of years before there emerges a reasonably accurate estimate of what has been discovered *in toto* in a reservoir. The exact amount of producible oil or gas is not known until the field is permanently abandoned and that oil or gas has been measured as past production.

In addition to a company's estimates of proved and ultimate, other appraisals may be made by a producing company during the life of a field for various purposes. Estimates based on well logs and other data are commonly used by banks for making loans. Information is also released to the press about the importance of new discoveries. The Securities and Exchange Commission expects that companies will release information to stockholders about their holdings and expectations. And, finally, the many kinds of information required by government agencies lead to a number of estimates being provided by a variety of federal offices. Considering the array of purposes for which reserve estimates are made and the constant revision of most of these through time, it is not surprising that various reserve reports may appear to be in conflict.

The proved reserves of oil and gas represent only a small portion of the total oil and gas resource base that remains unrecovered in the United States. Yet, these proved reserve data sometimes receive more attention, and in recent years have prompted more controversy, than the more significant resource estimates of undiscovered oil and gas.[2] For crude oil, proved reserves

represent the stock of immediately producible oil from existing wells. The oil producer knows that the amount of oil or gas that can flow in a given year from producing wells is physically linked to the number of wells available and the quantity of oil and gas still remaining in the reservoir. Thus, proved reserves for many years have been the industry's empirical indicator of current capability, not a measure of the total supply of oil and gas left for the future. Equating proved reserves with "years of supply" is particularly misleading.

Since proved reserves plus past production are normally less than we might reasonably expect to produce from known oil and gas fields, do we have any estimates of this undeveloped and less certain, part of our discovered oil and gas reserves? Unfortunately, there are no regular government or industry-wide efforts to report on what is known as *indicated* or *inferred* oil and gas.[3] The American Petroleum Institute (API) does report on additional reserves of oil that could be produced from secondary recovery projects but that are not yet fully evaluated at the time of the proved reserve estimations. An industry-sponsored effort, called the Potential Gas Committee, has included this portion of the gas reserves in its occasional reports on gas resources. The Federal Energy Administration in its 1975 survey of operators had hoped to go beyond merely proved reserves, but its final report only included oil from secondary and tertiary projects not the less certain oil and gas quantities. Currently, the new Department of Energy is again considering how to define and request data on oil and gas reserves that are not reported as proved.

The U.S. Geological Survey in its 1975 Circular 725 relied upon the use of a statistical ratio devised by M. King Hubbert to account for indicated reserves. This ratio is based on the historical relationship of the amount of oil and gas that has been added through

---

[2] Despite the apparent clarity of the generalized concept of proved reserves the actual estimation requires certain judgments to be made concerning the amount of extrapolation to be used, whether to include oil and gas from known reservoirs not actually being produced, or how to account for oil resulting from secondary stimulation. As a consequence, there are at least nine "official" definitions from various professional, industrial, or government agencies. Each one leads to some variation in the estimates made.

[3] The terms probable and possible are also used to describe discovered reserves that cannot qualify as proved or measured.

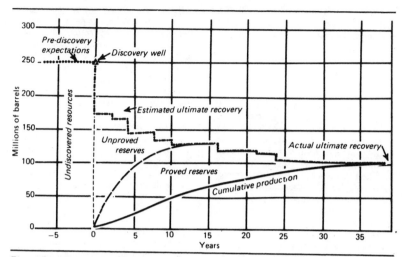

Figure 3: Life Cycle of Oil Reservoir Estimates
(adapted from G. C. Bankston, API Reserves Seminar).

extensions and revisions to proved reserves during the typical life of reservoirs. The relationship shows that approximately 80 percent more oil and gas will be produced from known fields than is currently being reported as proved. Although proved reserves data are considered to be accurate within plus or minus 20 percent, this refers to the oil and gas expected to flow from existing wells. On the average, almost twice as much oil and gas will ultimately be found in these fields once their true size or limits become fully identified. This is not an intentional understating or "hiding" of reserves, but merely a reflection that the definition of "proved" limits the estimators to the drilled portion of the field.

One must be aware that when estimates go beyond proved, accuracy deteriorates rapidly, with errors of perhaps 50 percent or more for indicated reserves (mostly oil and gas resulting from further development of the reservoir) and amounting to perhaps several multiples for inferred reserves (oil and gas resulting from the discovery of additional reservoirs within the same field). Many U.S. professionals and Canadian govern-

ment specialists would prefer, because of the uncertainty, to consider inferred oil and gas as not actually discovered.

To obtain more information on what lies beyond proved reserves in known fields involves a reservoir-by-reservoir examination of considerable magnitude. Considering the range of judgment involved and the unavoidable approximations, the added information obtained may not be worth the cost of acquiring it. In addition, there are problems of handling proprietary data, which, in any event, would be diverse, constantly changing, and of unknown quality and usefulness. It would require combining the personal judgment of the ultimate potential for field A made by a geologist from Company X with estimates for field B from Company Y's geologist, through all of the thousands of fields in the United States. In the final analysis, to know that indicated and inferred U.S. reserves are considered to be 2.4 times our proved reserves instead of 1.8 times has little significance in determining our policies with respect to oil and gas. The more important questions are found in the categories of subeconomic and undiscovered oil and gas resources. It is upon these quantities that our energy future depends most heavily in the medium term.

Estimation of Subeconomic Resources

Subeconomic resources include all of the oil and gas in known reservoirs that is not producible by present technology at present prices, but may become producible in the future with improved technology or higher prices. It should be noted that a simple downward movement in prices or other incentives can cause some reserves to be reclassified, at least temporarily, as subeconomic resources.

As a field is developed, following the drilling of a discovery well, the producer adopts a plan which he hopes will extract all of the oil from the reservoir that can be produced. He then hopes to sell the oil at an anticipated price that will return as much or more than the additional cost of producing it. He hopes that the aggregate return from all wells, over and above the direct costs of production, will pay him not only for production costs but also for the costs of exploration, dry holes, and abandoned wells. To minimize the duration of his exposure to uncertainty, he hopes the pace of production will permit a quick return of his initial investment.

The investment decision in oil production is a balancing of the total quantity to be recovered, the various costs, the rate at which the oil will be recovered, and the price at which it can be sold. Once the decision is made on how many wells to drill and what recovery technology to use, that is, natural flow, pumping, water flooding, injection of steam, or other methods, the amount of oil that will be recovered and the rate at which it will reach the surface are limited within a fairly narrow range. To change that plan, additional investments must be made in drilling additional wells or in altering the production methodology being used. Such a change in the production scheme will be adopted only if the faster production or greater recovery can justify the extra cost.

Thus, an increase in the price of oil or gas may not be adequate to change the plan for the operation of a field already being developed. The only effect of higher prices in that event may be to permit the reservoir to decline to a lower level of daily output per well before it is abandoned because of low oil flow or gas pressure. This additional quantity of oil and gas produced in the later life of a reservoir may only involve a 1 or 2 percent increase in the ultimate recovery because most of the oil or gas left behind is entrapped in the reservoir and could only be recovered by the use of a different technology. However, higher prices which occur before a production plan is fully implemented in a new field can lead not only to later abandonment but to higher recoveries because the prices can be reflected in a timely investment in a modified development scheme.

The appearance of significant improvements in production technology or markedly higher prices can justify modifying the way new reservoirs as well as fully developed fields are being operated. Even an abandoned reservoir can be reopened, although this is less likely because of the expense. It should be noted, however, that new methods of enhancing the recovery of oil and gas should not be viewed as applicable to all kinds of reservoirs. How successfully a new technology can be employed is determined by the kind of structure and natural energies in the reservoir, as well as the kind of rock that is found in it.

There has not been much experience in estimating the size of the national subeconomic resources of oil and gas because in the past the opportunity to discover new and plentiful oil and gas resources has always seemed more attractive to industry. Even for known fields, the estimation of subeconomic resources is complex. First, the estimator must face uncertainty about new and perhaps untested technology. Second, there is need to deal with the effect of price on production using established technology, as well as what price is required to make new technology commercially feasible. Third, there is a lack of information on exactly how much oil or gas is left in the reservoir to be recovered by new technology. Finally, if the data are to have meaning, there is need to deal with the problem of the time over which these prices and technology can be assumed to occur.

It is perhaps surprising that the amount of oil left behind in a reservoir is uncertain. Depending upon the kind of reservoir and the years during which it was exploited, oil recovery from the initial development plan used can vary anywhere from 10 percent to 80 percent of the oil estimated to have been in place originally.[4] In some cases, reservoirs have been reworked with a secondary production technology long after primary methods were begun. More recently, developed fields tend to be exploited by several integrated methods. Since oil in place, recoverable reserves, and a reservoir's recovery factor are all parts of the same equation, it is apparent that estimates for two of them allows the derivation of the third. Thus, if greater production from a reservoir is achieved than originally expected, one is never sure whether the cause is more oil in place, more reserves, or a higher recovery factor.

There is some indication that the overall recovery factor for oil in the United States did not improve very much during the 1960–75 period for several reasons. U.S. production shifted from regions with naturally higher recovery potential to areas with poorer recovery potential. Early estimates of the quantity of oil to be recovered by primary recovery techniques were probably overstated or, conversely, the oil in place may have been understated. Finally, there is a tendency to use a standard recovery factor in relating future production expectations to oil in the reservoir. Each of these tendencies could contribute to the assumption that the U.S. recovery factor has remained near 30 percent for many years. Realistically, it must be concluded that the

[4] Natural gas, because of its physical characteristics, normally has a high recovery factor—on the order of 75 percent. Subeconomic resources and opportunities for enhanced recovery of gas are thus limited for the most part to the fracturing of dense, low-permeability reservoir rock.

true national recovery of oil is an unknown percentage.

The current interest in enhancing petroleum recovery by injecting heat, CO_2, or chemicals has led to more vigorous examination of subeconomic resources than ever before. Our major oil regions have been examined in terms of the amenability of the various kinds of reservoirs to newer methods for increasing recovery. Although some optimistic suggestions have been made that U.S. recovery could be increased from an assumed 32 percent to ultimately 60 percent, more modest near-term goals are now being set for the upgrading of some of our subeconomic resources to reserves. These suggest an overall increase of perhaps 5 to 8 percentage points in the U.S. recovery factor may be possible.

The uncertainty of how much subeconomic oil and gas may be produced is illustrated by the recent report of the National Petroleum Council (NPC). The additional oil from enhanced recovery, according to the NPC, could be as little as 7 billion barrels, under a price assumption of $10 per barrel (1976), but this would increase to 24 billion barrels at $25 per barrel. The effect on the rate of annual production would also vary. At the higher price level, U.S. oil production could be 3.5 million barrels per day greater in 1995. The uncertainty in the estimates is reflected in the judgment that the higher 24 billion barrel amount is merely the central value of an estimate ranging from as little as 12 or as much as 33 billion barrels. In contrast, another study viewed the outer limit of enhanced recovery at 76 billion barrels at $15 per barrel (1974). Despite the fact that enhanced recovery deals with "discovered" oil in known fields, this does not narrow the range of uncertainty. Technological and economic forecasting of recovery is a source of frustration equal to that of estimating the undiscovered (table 2).

Estimation of Undiscovered Resources

If the United States would suddenly cease drilling its customary 25 to 50 thousand new wells each year and would be content with merely producing what it could from existing wells, production would decline progressively by approximately 12 percent per year. After some forty years, production would fall to approximately 1 percent of present production. Since reservoirs do not cease production abruptly, some wells might still be producing a few barrels per day after one hundred years.

Unlike manufacturing, or some kinds of mining operations, the capacity to produce petroleum is not a constant. To avoid a decline in national production, there must be continuous drilling and development. The process of continual annual replacement of what we have produced is heavily dependent upon the magnitude of our undiscovered oil and gas resources.

The potential size of these resources is usually evaluated in one of three ways. There is the geologic or volumetric approach, which attempts to make a direct estimate of the quantity of oil and gas remaining to be discovered and recovered. No attempt is made to show when or if these resources will be produced. The second approach is that of the engineer–manager who makes projections of the drilling, discovery, and production process. These future production profiles implicitly suggest the amount of recoverable oil and gas that is left in the ground. The third methodology is that of the economist who uses the equations in his model to suggest what future supply can be achieved by the oil and gas producers as they respond to price changes. Like the engineer–manager, the econometrician may indicate the quantity of remaining oil and gas resources in his model implicitly rather than explicitly.

The volumetric approach. The geologist's volumetric estimate is essentially what the name suggests. The total volume of sedimentary rock suspected to contain petroleum and natural gas is calculated for the entire United States, region by region. Based upon past geological knowledge, an estimate is made as to the total oil and gas that

may exist in these rock volumes. It is quite apparent that this is a subjective judgment linked to past experience. Underestimates are possible since past experience does not readily account for unknown types of occurrences or future improvement in the ability to detect and produce oil. In contrast, since there is evidence that better areas and larger pools are found first, unexplored regions may prove to be less prolific.

The volumetric determination of the oil and gas that exists in the ground may not be the only calculation. The quantity of oil and gas in place in the rock strata only has economic meaning in terms of the proportion that is both discoverable and producible. The quantity of oil and gas eventually captured depends upon future effort, the effectiveness of the search, the size and depth of the reservoirs, and the economic and technical capacity for producing it.

Considering the many judgmental elements, volumetric estimates, not unexpectedly, have varied widely over the years. Part of this variation reflects the fact that some estimates are the product of extensive study by large groups while others may be the work of a single expert using a relatively simplistic approach to obtain a quick approximation. Moreover, subjective judgments about unknown resources change as more geological information becomes available. These normal divergences are further accentuated by the fact that different analysts have used different assumptions and have estimated different resource elements.

A careful examination of past geologic estimates reveals that it is rare for the same type of resource concept to be involved. Total oil and gas *originally* in place, oil and gas *remaining* in place, *discoverable* oil and gas in place, undiscovered *commercial accumulations* of oil and gas, or *recoverable* oil and gas under given economic and technologic conditions are markedly different quantitative concepts. Unfortunately, the authors of petroleum resource reports all too frequently are obscure about what they have estimated, their methodology, and their assumptions. Yet all

Table 2.

NATIONAL PETROLEUM COUNCIL REPORT ON ESTIMATES OF U.S. ENHANCED OIL RECOVERY POTENTIAL

Source of estimate and price assumption	Potential recovery (billions of barrels)	Production in 1985 (millions of barrels/day)
National Petroleum Council Report		
$ 5	2.2	0.3
$10	7.2	0.4
$15 (1976 dollars)	13.2	0.9
$20	20.5	1.5
$25	24.0	1.7
GURC[a]		
$10 (1974 dollars)	18–36	1.1
$15	51–76	—
FEA/PIR[b]		
business as usual, $11	—	1.8
accelerated development, $11	—	2.3
EPA[c]		
$ 8–12 (1975 dollars)	7	—
$12–16	16	—
FEA/Energy Outlook[d]		
$12	—	0.9
FEA[e]		
$11.28 (1975 dollars)	15.6–30.5	1–2

[a] Gulf Universities Research Consortium Reports, Number 130, November 1973, and Number 148, February 28, 1976.

[b] *Project Independence Report*, Federal Energy Administration, November 1974.

[c] *The Estimated Recovery Potential of Conventional Source Domestic Crude Oil*, Mathematica, Inc., for the U.S. Environmental Protection Agency, May 1975.

[d] *1976 National Energy Outlook*, Federal Energy Administration.

[e] *The Potential and Economics of Enhanced Oil Recovery*, Lewin & Associates, Inc., for the Federal Energy Administration, April 1976.

of these numbers are generally identified as estimates of "the oil and gas resources" of the United States. The unsuspecting recipients of this information must then puzzle over how one expert can say that the oil resources of the United States are 50 billion barrels and another, with seemingly equal confidence, provides an estimate of 1,000 billion barrels.

If one reduces all of these various estimates as best he can to a common base, such as the quantity of undis-covered oil that is discoverable and producible at prices as of a certain date with an assumed 30 percent recovery factor, then the wide differences begin to shrink drastically. An estimate that appeared to be twenty times as large as another sudenly is only twice as large. Once reduced to a common base, there remain understandable differences in judgment between two analysts who possess varying degrees of optimism about what is still to be discovered. But this kind of comparison is not available to the casual reader who cannot know that one geologist has estimated all of the oil in the ground, another has assumed an optimistic 60 percent recovery factor, and another uses the current 30 percent recovery factor.

Geological resource analysis took on a new dimension with the 1975 publication by the U.S. Geological Survey of Circular 725, *Geological Estimates of Undiscovered Recoverable Oil and Gas Resources of the United States*. This was a major scale-up in the Survey's effort and involved a whole team of geologists working for a number of months. It entailed not only the use of traditional volumetric information, but incorporated sophisticated statistical integration of subjective judgments about each of 102 oil and gas provinces. The end product was a probabilistic appraisal of undiscovered, recoverable oil and gas.

Experimentation with this type of delphic approach has been going on for a number of years. Companies and various research groups have searched for a way to combine the various judgments of experienced individuals into a numerical expression of the probability of finding oil and gas. Circular 725 was the first attempt by the federal government to try this approach (see figure 4). Single number estimates that suggested a precision that does not exist have been abandoned. The public and Congress may now have to become used to resource estimates that indicate there is a 95 percent chance there may be a minimal quantity of oil resources but also a 5 percent chance that there could be quite a bit more. For example, the Survey estimates that there is a 95 percent probability that the remaining undiscovered recoverable oil reserves will be at least 50 billion barrels, but only a 5 percent probability that they will be as large as 127 billion barrels. Outside of these ranges there still remain low-level possibilities that a new province may have no oil or gas at all, or that it may contain an undetected Middle East. Only the drill can tell. Some cautious individuals still prefer not to try to attach numbers to what they consider immeasurable quantities.

The Geological Survey recognizes that Circular 725, while a major advancement, was a first effort and must be used with considerable care. Only the portion of the report concerning "undiscovered, economic" resources of crude oil and natural gas are totally new estimates. All other numbers presented were based on other sources of statistics or were derived by simple ratios. Thus the measured and indicated additional reserves are taken from the reports of the American Petroleum Institute and the American Gas Association. The inferred reserves of oil and gas are based not on an evaluation of fields and basins but on the historical trend of extensions and revisions of proved reserves through time. The subeconomic resources are based on simple ratios using two assumptions—that the average U.S. crude oil recovery might reach 60 percent and natural gas 90 percent at some unspecified time in the future.

The additional data provided by Circular 725 has been useful, but it presents problems for many of its users. If the undiscovered oil and gas resources are shown as a probability range,[5] what does one use if one needs a single number? Unfortunately, many seemed to prefer to use the lower limit. In using these data, it has been common to overlook the fact that the subjective judgments behind the estimates were based upon price and technological conditions that prevailed prior to the Arab embargo and the quadrupling of the world price of oil. This leads to the question of how much current prices might alter the estimates. It is believed by many that a recalculation would not make a large difference because the estimates are dominated by large fields which were economic before 1973.

The Survey is now searching out the answers to a number of questions. Can the reserves portion of the estimate, which received modest attention in the first effort, be improved? In estimating

[5] The Survey does provide an average of the most likely and upper and lower estimates. However, the statistical usefulness of this average is uncertain and it only appears in the tables.

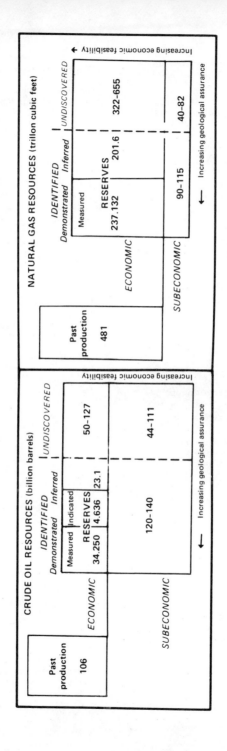

Figure 4: USGS Estimates of Crude Oil and Natural Gas Resources of the United States, December 31, 1974

342 The Politics of Mistrust

subeconomic resources, there is the important question concerning the realism of ever reaching an overall 60 percent recovery. This may now be better understood because of the extensive work just completed in examining enhanced recovery. Since the availability of actual experience by Survey geologists for every oil and gas "play" was naturally somewhat limited, there is an interest in how to tap a broader spectrum of judgment. There is a need to have future appraisals encompass more data on: size distribution of undiscovered fields, depths, reservoir types, and basins found in deep water offshore. These data may be the key to determining actually how "price sensitive" are oil and gas resource estimates. Until these answers are forthcoming, the user of the Survey's Circular 725 must remain fully aware that these are subjective views by a group of government geologists concerning the recoverable amount of pre-1973 "commercial" oil left in the unexplored portions of U.S. basins onshore or to a depth of 200 meters offshore. This recoverable amount is only a portion of the total physical quantity of oil and gas in place remaining beneath the surface in the United States.

Engineering projections. The fact that oil production is a process in which production declines and costs increase became apparent to engineer-managers soon after Colonel Drake, a retired railroad conductor, drilled the first well in Pennsylvania in 1859. Fortunately, many wells do better than Drake's, but a ruler placed on the graph of past production and the cost per barrel of any well or field always provides a dismal picture of a downward trend in the absence of new discoveries and technology. In contrast, projections made by individual companies or industry groups showing increasing future production are illustrations of how additional investment in exploration, drilling, or applications of new technology can cause the aggregate production of oil or gas to increase in the future despite the fact that the older wells are declining and future efforts will face

greater costs per barrel produced per foot drilled.

The best illustrations of this kind of analysis are found in the extensive series of reports by the National Petroleum Council (NPC) to the U.S. Department of the Interior. They contain many examples of how a given number of dollars invested, assuming a specified rate of return to the investor, could generate a required level of geological-geophysical work, leading to the drilling of wildcat wells, and finally the development effort needed to produce the new oil found. Figure 5 from the 1972 NPC study demonstrates how this can lead to various perceptions of the future.

By their very nature, these projections of future production, based on a specified amount of additional effort or investment, are expansive. These speculative futures may or may not incorporate a judgment as to whether the remaining oil and gas resources in the ground are sufficient to provide for these annual flows. In the NPC's extensive study of U.S. energy from 1970 to 1973, projections were coupled to a geologic study of the U.S. petroleum provinces. Since most of the NPC's projections were only to the year 1985, the possibility of a production decline after 1985 due to dwindling resources was not shown.

Many government or industry projections of future production are not primarily designed to deal with the ultimate size of our oil and gas resources. Nonetheless, they still may foster a public belief that resources are adequate in size to meet the projected goals. In addition, there may be only minimal attention paid to the price required to elicit the necessary investment. And whatever that price may be, the accompanying alterations in the demand for oil and gas, given that price, may not be addressed at all.

One specialized form of engineering projection that has been employed by many authors over the years has been to use a production-history profile that will follow the standard pattern observed when minerals or fuels are pro-

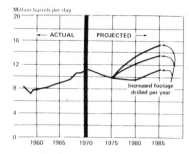

Figure 5: Estimated U.S. Production of Petroleum Liquids at Three Levels of Future Drilling Activity
(from National Petroleum Council, **U.S. Energy Outlook**, 1972)

duced from a finite deposit. The classical configuration is a bell-shaped curve showing an upward sweep, a peaking of production, followed by a decline to final depletion. Not only a specific deposit, but a state, a region, or a nation, as an aggregate of many deposits, often appears to follow this pathway.

If one assumes that this is the general behavior of production, then it becomes possible to estimate when the peak will occur, the quantity that will be produced, and how it will be distributed over time. Customarily this is done by rather simple curve-fitting techniques using an appropriate mathematical formula. One of the most popular production-history curves has been the logistic growth curve, since it is both bell-shaped and symmetrical when fitted to annual data. It can also be used as a long attenuated "S" showing how cumulative production will approach asymptotically a line representing the maximum recoverable resources. In reviewing forecasts between 1948 and the mid-1950s, RFF's Sam Schurr and Bruce Netschert found at least six authors using this kind of approach who expected U.S. petroleum production to peak by 1970.

Among this group, perhaps the greatest amount of attention in recent years has been directed toward the work of M. King Hubbert. Relying heavily on the logistic curve and a family of various statistical series to track the behavior of U.S. oil production, his analysis is both extensive and detailed. Among the family of interrelated curves that he uses are: cumulative proved discoveries, cumulative production, proved reserves, annual production, annual increases and decreases in proved reserves, and discoveries of oil per foot drilled versus total footage drilled. The first three of these, with the appropriate fitted curves, are shown in figure 6.

The logistic curve provides a particularly good fit to any historical series that is approaching or has already reached a plateau. But one must be careful not to assume that the fitting of the curve to the several variations of the same historical series in some way confirms the validity of its use. Despite the vigor with which Hubbert examines past behavior and projects the various patterns of U.S. oil discovery and production into the future, this does not necessarily indicate that the logistic curve is a more reliable predictor of the future than any other curve that might have been chosen.

The use of mathematical formulas to project trends forward provides an aura of precision and objectivity. However, the process of fitting and projecting is a more subjective process than it might appear. The choice of the type of curve to be used preordains in a general way what the future will look like. Then the analyst must exercise further judgment as to the time period to be used and how the curve is fitted to the data. Judgments at this stage of the analysis are particularly critical, because the manner in which the final years are fitted affects the steepness of the expected production decline.

In addition to his decision to use the logistic curve rather than another, Hubbert's case for future decline is bolstered by his assumption that a declining amount of oil will be found per foot drilled. This is a persuasive position to take if one expects that the largest and near-surface fields have been found first. Hubbert supports this hypothesis by another projection involving again the choice of proper data and a mathe-

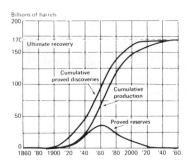

Figure 6: Application of Logistic Curve to U.S. Petroleum Data
(from M. King Hubbert; see References).

matical formula[6] to project the trend of oil found per foot drilled. In this extrapolation he shows that despite extensive drilling the quantity of oil found in the future becomes relatively insignificant and his gloomy expectations for the future are further substantiated.

In mature, densely drilled areas, such as the onshore areas of the lower 48 states, one might be persuaded that it is unlikely that there are many "surprises" left. It does appear unlikely that there are a number of Prudhoe Bays cleverly hidden by nature along the Gulf Coast or in the Rocky Mountains. For these areas it seems to be a question not of new peaks in production but of the duration of the current level of production and the nature of the subsequent decline. But in those areas where drilling has been infrequent—natural gas at greater depths along the Gulf or oil and gas in the Arctic or farther offshore—the future is not as clearly defined. For these regions, most analysts, including Hubbert, do not trust unalterable formulas but turn back to more traditional geologic speculation about the quality of the targets that may be found in these unexplored volumes of rock.

[6] In this case a line representing a constant percentage of decrease each year is used.

Production-history profiles provide for many a sense of "rightness" because they follow the classical pattern of mineral production. Yet they leave a number of questions unanswered. Is it fair to assume that the historical interrelations between the many factors that affect oil exploration and production will continue unchanged into the future? If our production of oil and gas has peaked, has that fact been induced by external institutional factors rather than by a limitation in our hydrocarbon endowment? Might not our technical ingenuity or the new frontiers of exploration once again produce a major surprise? If secondary peaks have been observed in the past for states and nations, why not for the United States?

There are no certain answers to these questions. But for the United States, M. King Hubbert has reminded us of one unavoidable truth—we are not debating whether there will be decline, merely when and how. This does not deter the exploration optimist from reminding us how we drilled for many years in Texas, Saudi Arabia, and the Arctic with little or no success.

Econometric models. The third group to deal with the future supply of oil and gas has been the economists. By professional instinct and training, they initially turn to the marketplace as the starting point for their analysis. Their facility for portraying relationships by mathematical equations, combined with the ability of modern computers to provide rapid and complex calculations, has led to the use of econometric models. Normally found within these models are equations that relate the supply of oil and gas to exploratory and development efforts prompted by changes in price.

Perhaps over the decades more general attention has been directed toward oil rather than gas resources. But more recently, gas supply has demanded considerable attention from the econometrician. This reflects the fact that gas prices have been regulated and there are questions about what would happen if the regulated price were increased or if regulation were to be removed entirely.

Interest has intensified with the recent, rapid decline in proved gas reserves. The occurrence of gas and the search for it are not necessarily linked to oil, so gas supply can be disengaged for separate study. The task is also simplified by the fact that gas supply models are essentially domestic, that is, they need not incorporate, as in the case of oil, the impact of large imports from abroad.

A number of models for gas supply have appeared over the last two decades. Some provide projections and forecasts and a number deal with the supply–price relationships. However, like the engineer–manager projections, the econometric models are not designed to provide estimates of the remaining oil and gas resources of the United States. Nonetheless, in addressing the supply–price question they unavoidably give an impression of resource availability.

An examination of the better-known gas supply models reveals that the inclusion of total U.S. gas resources, or any limit to discoverable and producible resources, tends to be implicit rather than explicit. This is intentional and is not a serious flaw for the intended use of the models. For the most part, econometric equations are not considered particularly reliable beyond short periods of time—of the order of five or ten years. Given these limits, to introduce total resource quantities is an unneeded refinement.

However, many models are designed to indicate that price will trigger an exploration response and the resulting greater production suggests that oil and gas resources are adequate to support higher levels of production than now prevail. The MacAvoy–Pindyck model, developed in the early 1970s to analyze the effects of deregulation policy, suggested the possibility that 34 trillion cubic feet of natural gas could be produced in 1980 at an average wholesale price of 88.3 cents per thousand cubic feet (MCF) with a newly-discovered-field price of 100.3 cents per MCF (see table 3). This result did not hinge upon the total quantity of undiscovered resources required for the United States to achieve that level of production. Nor

was the model constructed to deal with the mechanics of annual investment, the number of wells to be drilled, or the physical ability of the productive system to achieve the required level of effort. The MacAvoy–Pindyck model shares with most of its econometric companions a necessity to simplify the national energy economy. It was designed to answer a specific question—in that process it ignored others.

Econometric models have their own special link to the past. The response, or elasticity, of oil and gas supply to price must be judged in large measure in terms of historical data, despite the realization that in each future year we will deal with a different segment of the original resource. Future resources may very well differ in character and, as a consequence, in cost from those discovered in the past. Economic behavior patterns of operations conducted on vast federal leases in 1,000 feet of water are not the same as those encountered in the private farmlands of Kansas. Nor will the response of gas supply to a doubling in price (in constant dollars) be the same when it starts at 10 cents per MCF as when it starts at $1. A reason to question further the future validity of past experience is to recall that much of the past was characterized by smaller movements in the price of oil and gas relative to other prices, and that for the most part this was downward not upward.

Current efforts. In making resource estimates geologists, engineers, and economists are all to some degree projecting past experience into the future. Insofar as the past does not adequately represent the future, their estimates are likely to be in error. In addition, each profession, starting from its own particular analytical framework, is the victim of a certain amount of tunnel vision. The geologist prefers to perform his task in a price-free, time-free fashion. The engineer may ignore resource constraints and economic reactions in his production model. The econometrician may demonstrate what market price is necessary to reach an equilibrium point but in so

Table 3.

ECONOMETRIC SIMULATIONS OF PHASED DEREGULATION
OF NATURAL GAS

Year	Total reserves (trillion cubic ft)	Production (trillion cubic ft)	Demand (trillion cubic ft)	New contract field price (cents per thousand cubic ft)
1972	233.4	23.3	23.5	31.7
1973	227.8	23.6	24.3	34.7
1974	222.9	24.3	26.3	39.7
1975	222.3	26.4	28.7	64.7
1976	226.1	27.6	30.4	71.7
1977	233.9	28.6	31.9	78.8
1978	245.8	30.2	32.9	85.9
1979	258.6	32.1	33.7	93.1
1980	271.2	34.1	34.2	100.3

From MacAvoy and Pindyck, *Price Controls and the Natural Gas Shortage*, 1975

Table 4.

PIES MODEL NATURAL GAS PRODUCTION REFERENCE SCENARIO

Assumed world oil prices $/bbl	1985 domestic production (trillion cubic ft)			1985 average city gate price (dollars per thousand cubic ft)
	Nonassoc. gas	Assoc. gas	Total	
8	16.3	4.1	20.4	1.79
13	17.4	4.9	22.3	2.03
16	17.4	5.1	22.5	2.07

Note: The Reference Scenario is a market clearing price at which supply and demand
are at equilibrium in an uncontrolled market or deregulated condition.
From FEA's *National Energy Outlook, 1976.*

doing may violate the time sequence or
engineering requirements needed for the
process to be accomplished, given the
magnitude of the remaining resources
and national capabilities.

It is not suggested that the various
analysts are totally unaware of the
limits of their work. More often than
not the problem is the difficulty of trying
to link all dimensions of the resource
system into one model or into one forecast. Moreover, the purposes being
served may not demand a complexity
that exceeds available time and financial
resources.

The Federal Energy Administration
(FEA), in projecting the needs of the
nation by 1985 for Project Independence, initially employed the committee
approach to the problem; so, too, did
the National Petroleum Council. However, subsequent in-house work by the
FEA staff on the *1976 National Energy
Outlook* (NEO) led to the development
of a complex computer model (PIES).
This effort has been an excellent illustration of the long and difficult task of
attempting to introduce the many dimensions of energy into one integrated
analysis. The many scenarios developed

for the *National Energy Outlook* required an analysis of demand, supply, finance, the environment, the national economy, and international aspects.

This should not be construed as suggesting that the ultimate model is now available to the new Department of Energy. A close examination of PIES reveals that the tie between energy and the national economy tends to be one directional. In the 1976 report, environmental and international aspects were not introduced as specifically as one might desire. The model reflects the many imperfections in our understanding of the behavior of energy demand in the marketplace. The resource component of the model is still the familiar 1973 data from the USGS Circular 725. Perhaps most important to the user is the fact that the PIES model does not generate a single forecast, but rather as many forecasts as there are policy combinations that an administration wishes to test (see table 4). It is easy to overlook, in the copious statistics and discussions of the model and its scenarios, that much reliance has been placed on a few key sources of data or relationships. Thus, to whatever extent Circular 725 is limited in its perspective of U.S. oil and gas resources, the *National Energy Outlook* series is equally limited.

Since so many analyses have come to depend upon it, the further work of the USGS has become extremely critical. Currently, the Survey is hoping to refine its presentation of probability data on undiscovered oil and gas resources so that the full range of potential resources within the hypothetical and speculative categories is more apparent. This will allow for an appreciation that beyond the 5 and 95 percent probability boundaries there still remain possibilities for either zero finds or major discoveries for which past experience has not prepared us. Recent interest on the part of the National Petroleum Council and other groups in enhanced recovery will now permit the Survey to be somewhat more specific about the magnitude of subeconomic, discovered resources. In addition, the presentation of data on indicated and inferred reserves (reserves beyond proved) in known fields may be expanded by the Survey.

A number of agencies have joined forces with the Survey in this effort to determine how additional information in economics and technology could be combined with the essentially geological data from the Survey's Resource Appraisal Group. This Inter-Agency Study Group on Oil and Gas Supply is examining not only the amount of the oil and gas resources present but their distribution with respect to size, geography, and depth. An attempt will then be made to define the level of exploratory drilling activity required to find these deposits. This can then be followed with studies that deal with drilling, production, and finding costs, which incorporate considerations of reservoir depth, water depth, and other geological characteristics.

Currently the group is in a testing phase, using three pilot areas to determine the feasibility of performing these various tasks. It is not expected that the current effort will attempt to deal immediately with the time distribution of future oil and gas supplies. But it is hoped that a better appreciation of the magnitude of oil and gas resources at various costs will be obtained, as well as an understanding of the exploratory effort that will be involved.

Other Occurrences

Other occurrences are frequently the source of possible deception about the size of the nation's usable oil and gas supplies. Billions of barrels of oil in low-quality shale, gas locked in impervious shales and sandstones, methane found in coal beds or dissolved in brines under great pressure at depths of 15,000 feet are all a part of our physical resource base. They can and should be accounted for in any total resource inventory, but they cannot and should not be considered comparable to reserves or subeconomic resources. The likelihood of their soon becoming producible under present or near-future prices and technology is small enough that their importance for present generations is uncertain. Thus considerable caution must be taken to avoid giving them too much leverage in current decisions. After fifty years of effort and anticipation, the first commercial barrel of U.S. shale oil has not yet been produced. To be deceived by a too hasty reliance on methane dissolved in the waters of the Gulf of Mexico would be foolish indeed.

Although the oil shales of the West have become the classic example of a "just-around-the-corner" resource, we must somehow account for such a vast quantity of hydrocarbons. Many oil and gas resource appraisals do not include the oil shales because they are restricted to conventional crude oil, natural gas, and natural gas liquids produced from wells. Other analysts do not include them because they are not economically producible at the present time. If, however, a complete accounting is desired, then it is appropriate to at least identify these as other occurrences or noneconomic resources which are currently not produced and are likely to be significantly more costly than other forms of energy now being used. Whether quantification is attempted depends upon the purposes of the inventory.

Hydrocarbons occur in many forms in nature. Just as there are many types of coal (anthracite, bituminous, or lignite) there are heavy oils, tar sands, and kerogens which will not flow to drilled wells. This requires the extraction of the material either through the use of heat and chemicals or physically mining the rock so that it can be processed above ground. Since these are sedimentary deposits, they can be vast in extent but highly variable in recoverable energy content. In effect, they are low-grade deposits requiring expensive processing. As such they must be considered as either subeconomic or probably nonexploitable in any period of time that is of significance to present generations.

A number of largely unexploited sources of methane, the most abundant of the natural gases, have also attracted considerable attention. Among these are natural gas in dense sandstones of the West and the Devonian shales of the East where the rock is relatively impermeable and does not allow the gas to flow freely to a well. As a consequence, the drilling of a well in these formations is not often rewarded with a great quantity of producible gas or a high daily rate of production. Methane in coal is well known as a hazard to mining and is actually recoverable by drilling holes in the coal bed in advance of mining. Another recent discovery has been of the presence of methane in underground salt water found at considerable depth in the Gulf Coast area. The gas is held in the water by the great pressures that exist at the depth.

Relatively simple calculations of the volume of oil shale in the Piceance basin, tarlike substances in Utah, and methane in coal beds or other geological settings yield vast quantities of energy that physically exist. However, like exotic rocks on the moon, the fact of their existence should not be confused with economic and technological accessibility.

In the other occurrence classification, there is also that portion of conventional oil and gas that we do not expect to recover. Similar to low-grade oil shale, it would be physically possible to produce this oil and gas at great cost. One could literally mine an oil reservoir and produce all of the oil, or let a gas well produce until there was no more pressure left. Obviously, long before this, it would be far more sensible to use some other source of energy. Thus, those portions of our oil and gas resources unlikely to ever be recoverable can be accounted for among the other occurrences.

Productive Capacity

It is virtually impossible to determine how much oil and gas can be produced in any given year solely on the basis of knowing the quantity of proved reserves of oil and gas. If the nation finds itself lining up at gas stations or shutting down factories because adequate pressure cannot be maintained in all the utility mains during cold weather, the immediate supply problem is the productive capability of the delivery system, not proved reserves or undiscovered resources.[7]

Over the years little study has been directed toward understanding the limits of the delivery system upon which we depend to move energy from the well to the burner tip. For the fossil fuel group, we have only the American Petroleum Institute's (API) estimate of productive capacity. This is the maximum daily rate of production which could be attained under specific condition on March 31 of any given year. It would require ninety days to reach, starting January 1, and is based upon existing wells, well equipment, and surface facilities. The estimate provides for no reduction in ultimate recovery, and environmental damage or other hazards are not accepted.

Obviously, it is useful to have such a measure of our capability. It is important, however, to be aware that the API definition of national productive capacity does not imply anything about the sustainability of this capacity over any specified period of time beyond the ninety days. Beyond March 31 of the year of estimate, the productive capability would begin to decline. This particular measure of productive capacity does not encompass our capability, or lack of it, for storage, transportation, and processing facilities to handle the oil once produced.

The gas shortage of the winter of 1976–77 was a combination of system limits and the declining deliverability of gas from existing wells. Through emergency measures, such as denying some customers gas and shifting gas between systems on an ad hoc basis, the nation coped with the situation. This does not alter the fact that the gas deliverability from wells in 1977–78 will be different from what it was in the past winter. It is not generally appreciated that ad

hoc plans that worked once may not work as well in another heating season. The fact remains that our oil and gas systems involve thousands of enterprises delivering fuel to millions of households and commercial customers. Exactly how that system works and what its capability might be, given the declining production curves of oil and gas, is only partially understood. As of midwinter, the weather and the amount of natural gas in storage did provide some optimism for the 1977–78 heating season.

The inability to discriminate between reserves and deliverability is the source of considerable confusion in the reporting on the oil and gas situation in the United States. References to the estimated total reserves in a field or resources in a new region are equated with annual production or requirements. Since only approximately 10 to 15 percent of the reserves of a field can be produced in a single year, if connected to a delivery system, billions of barrels of oil reserves or trillions of cubic feet of gas translate into a much smaller amount of oil and gas available even in the early peak years.

To understand oil and gas supply requires more than a realization that estimating reserves is an inexact process; it also involves an appreciation of the limited capability of a well to produce oil and gas upon demand. The time required to explore, find, drill development wells, lay pipe, and provide process facilities is a further restraint on translating reserves into production. To this year's energy consumer the only supply that counts is deliverable oil and gas, not reserves or resources. If that flow is inadequate, periods of five to ten years or more and considerable investment will be required to alter it in any significant way. Considerably more attention to the limits of this process, and perhaps less to reserves, seems warranted.

It is understandable that the productive capacity of the vast oil and gas producing industry and its downstream facilities presents problems in terms of measurement. One would expect, in contrast, that the capability of a known

---

[7] Productive capacity is the more common expression in the oil industry. The gas utility industry's immediate capability is referred to as the "deliverability" of the gas.

producing reservoir would be a reasonably precise number. This has taken
on a new importance in recent years, as
questions have been asked about whether
or not producers holding federal leases
have been producing oil and gas as
diligently as they might if the price for
oil and gas were higher.

This particular question has revived
interest in a measurement that appeared
during World War II called maximum
efficient rate (MER). In concept, MER
can mean the theoretical physical capability of a reservoir to produce oil and
gas over time as a hydraulic unit. To exceed this rate may reduce the amount of
oil and gas recovered. In practice, MER
has come to mean the maximum rate,
in terms of barrels or cubic feet per day,
a reservoir can produce "efficiently"
and "economically" from a fixed number
of wells under actual operating and
market conditions. In effect, this is the
design capacity of the reservoir development plan, and reflects what the operator feels is economically justifiable.
Producing the existing wells too rapidly
could cause oil and gas to be lost in
the reservoirs. Drilling additional wells
could increase the flow from a reservoir
without harm and might even increase
the amount ultimately produced, but
the decision then rests on whether the
extra expense of the well can be justified
by the economic advantage to be gained
by producing more oil or gas or producing it faster. That particular judgment may depend on whether you are the
producer or the federal government
leaseholder.

Even the term efficiency provides its
own share of problems. To the economist, efficiency will tend to be interpreted as determining how recovery
should be distributed over time to arrive
at a maximum value for the oil and
gas produced regardless of the physical
recovery. The reservoir engineer's technical efficiency will be to achieve maximum physical recovery at the lowest cost
under current market conditions. The
government administrator may be interested in a production rate that provides a
maximum quantity of oil and gas to the
public when it needs it, commensurate
with a reasonable return to the producer and acceptable payments to the
Treasury of bonuses and royalties. For
a given reservoir, the annual production
under these three criteria will not necessarily be the same.

A difficult aspect of using MER is
that it is not a constant. Since production of a well or reservoir is from a
declining reserve, the producible quantity actually decreases from day to day.
In practice, MER is determined periodically for most federal leases. It
should be remembered that a reservoir
may include a large number of wells,
and that the maximum efficient rate of
production applies to the whole reservoir and not to any individual well. In
the past, MER was considered a conservation technique to prevent wasting
the natural energies of the reservoir by
moving the various fluids so rapidly
that oil or gas is left behind entrapped
in the reservoir. Even so, in emergencies such as World War II, it is
sometimes considered in the nation's
best interest to produce oil or gas at a
rate that actually causes some loss in
ultimate production.

Offshore operations from costly plat-
forms have introduced new dimensions
to production and transport that have
increased the difficulty of determining
what is both physically and economically possible to accomplish. As a result,
MER, which in the past has been primarily a state conservation regulatory
tool, creates a number of problems
when it is used as a measure of diligence
in exploiting federal leases. The federal
government continues to look for a
means whereby it can properly monitor
operator performance in terms of the
national interest without harming the
entitlement of the leaseholder to serve
and to protect his own interests as a
private enterprise.

Conclusions

The RFF staff has now engaged in over
two years of studying, discussing and
explaining the uncertainties of oil and
resource estimation. That has led not

to better numbers but to perhaps a better understanding of what the existing data can or cannot do for us. By and large, we find that most examinations of oil and gas resources reflect in part the professional background of the estimator but most importantly the purpose for which the work is designed. Many estimates that have been published provide total future quantities of oil and gas that may be produced rather than supply in the economic sense or rates of production over future time. All too frequently, these totals may be translated into years of remaining oil and gas by dividing them by the current or some other assumed rate of production. This leads to the too-simple conclusion that we may be out of oil and gas at the end of that number of years.

Published estimates of total future producible hydrocarbon fluids provide the public with a narrow view of future oil and gas supply. This is compounded by the fact that the public does not know how to interpret the figures. As one RFF workshop participant noted, "the difficulty [in publishing estimates] was the problem and confusion in the public's mind of what all these numbers mean. It has just been an absolute mess. They [the public] have taken undiscovered resources and related them to reserves, and this was not really our intent at all. Suddenly, we find ourselves quoted in the most peculiar ways. And much to our embarrassment."

To the economist, it is important to know how much and for what period of time oil and gas production rates might be increased by a change in the economic structure of the industry or in the cost–price ratios. Or how sensitive future oil and gas production rates are to changes in technology. Answers to these kinds of questions are not contained in the usual published estimates of future oil and gas reserves. As a participant in one RFF workshop said, "Not a single technique, approach, publication, or anything, has yet adequately dealt with what the economists would call the supply schedule. Somehow we have got to get some indication of what different levels of future supply would

be available at different cost–price relationships."

In any given year the production of U.S. crude oil encompasses production from a reservoir that has been newly discovered, along with the production from reservoirs ten to fifty years of age. The important point to note is that the future rate of supply will be a composite of the rates from both old and new reservoirs.

The experts who have appeared in the RFF workshops are agreed that the rates of oil and gas production cannot be increased indefinitely. At some point, the rates must inevitably peak and then continue to decline until the hydrocarbon resources of the earth are exhausted. What the experts cannot agree upon is whether the annual rates of oil and gas supply can still be increased, and over what period of time, before the final decline begins. The extremes are illustrated by proposing different extensions into the future of the past oil production rate curve (see figure 7). The conservative view states that most of our giant fields have been found; the maximum annual rate has already been reached; and that, henceforth, there will be nothing but decline (see Curve A). An optimistic view might be that the annual oil production rate may still rise in response to exploration and new technology to some future maximum from whence it would decline until all reservoirs were exhausted (see Curve B). A moderate view would be a future annual production rate curve somewhat between these two extremes (see Curve C).

Whatever extension is predicted for the future rate of oil supply, the area under the resulting profile of the future can be no greater than the total amount of oil which one estimates can ultimately be recovered. Thus, the estimator of the conservative situation (Curve A) not only envisions a declining rate of production but also a limited amount of total production yet to be achieved. The optimistic estimator (Curve B) sees not only an increased annual rate of supply but also a larger volume of oil yet to be produced. Whether the

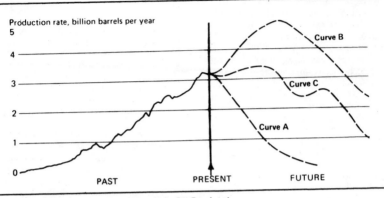

Figure 7: Alternative Futures for U.S. Oil Production

estimator approaches the problem in terms of rates or total future production, the results of the estimate must be internally consistent with respect to the relationship between rates and cumulative production.

Many of the published estimates of future oil and gas supplies have provided a value for the total supply through use of the traditional "volumetric" method. No matter how polished and sophisticated the details may be, the volumetric method still contains two basic perceptions: (1) that the occurrence of hydrocarbons in an unexplored geological region and the parameters that are associated with its occurrence will probably bear a relationship to previously explored regions, and (2) that the searching efficiency for finding oil in new areas will likely resemble what it has been in the past in older regions.

Any resources estimate for future oil and gas production in an unknown region may convey a misleading impression to the nonprofessional. The only thing an estimator can say with absolute accuracy is that he does not know whether there is oil or gas in a given region until wells are drilled to find out. The history of past estimates is rife with situations in which either little oil was found in areas where there was a high expectancy or much oil was found in areas where there was a low

expectancy. Thus the U.S. Geological Survey's probabilistic 2 to 4 billion barrels of undiscovered recoverable oil off the eastern U.S. Atlantic shore may be used by many as a "guaranteed" number. It may become the basis of a political decision either to explore or ignore the area. An individual particularly concerned about environmental protection might be inclined to conclude that this amount of oil does not justify taking the risk of polluting the environment to go after it. The fact is that there may be no oil at all off the Atlantic shore or there may be many times the estimated USGS figure.

If one prefers to approach the future by considering the production rate curve rather than total future production, then the immediate problem is the lack of an established theoretical basis for predicting the future shape of that curve. It appears to be somewhat unwarranted to assume that the curve would be symmetrical. On the contrary, there is reason to suggest that the rising leg of the curve is dominated by one physical and economic process, that is, the discovery of new reservoirs, while the decline will be dominated by a different physical and economic process, that is, the depletion of discovered reservoirs.

The nature of oil and gas reservoirs is such that the highest rates of production occur in the early life of the reservoir. The flow factors of a reservoir taken together generally mean that more than half the production from a particular reservoir will occur after the maximum rate of production is reached. If it is possible to supplement the natural producing energy of the reservoir or to apply technology that will make more of the reservoir oil accessible to production, the history of the reservoir may show additional production-rate peaks after the first one has been reached. This was the case in Pennsylvania and in Illinois.

The best current estimate is that, with present technology and prices, an average of between 30 and 40 percent of the oil known to exist in discovered reservoirs will have been produced at the time the reservoir is considered commercially exhausted. This is an average to be interpreted as we understand expectancy, that is, some people die younger and some live longer. The amount that can be taken from a particular reservoir is dependent upon the nature of the oil itself and the nature of the reservoir. There are known oil reservoirs from which the ultimate production will be as much as 80 percent of the oil contained in the reservoir. In other instances, the amount of oil that can be produced with present technology and prices may be as low as 10 or 15 percent of the oil in the reservoir. If technology improvement or a price rise permitted an abrupt change in recovery factors, a late production rate peak might show in the oil supply curve.

Another approach to examining the future of oil and gas is an examination of the rate at which exploratory drilling finds new oil and gas reservoirs. This approach does not necessarily depend upon prior estimate of whether oil or gas is present. It assumes that, if oil and gas are present, they will be found. The approach requires, however, an estimate of the efficiency for finding in the future. The published graphs which show the manner in which the amount of new oil found in the past related to the total exploratory footage drilled indicate that the finding rate has been decreasing. The reasons generally given

for why less oil is being found per foot of exploratory hole drilled include:

1. We have already found the big reservoirs and those near the surface. Future reservoirs will be found at deeper horizons.

2. The most desirable geological regions have been explored and drilled.

3. The geological areas remaining to be drilled are more inaccessible and more expensive; for example, on the continental shelf.

Whatever the reasons may be for an expected decline in search efficiency, it is relatively easy to see that if one extrapolates this decline into the future, the contribution to production rates due to finding new reservoirs will diminish. Consequently, one would conclude that the maximum production rate probably has been reached, but not all the experts agree that the search efficiency must decline. Both technology and economics could affect the trend.

Disagreement resulting from various methods of estimating future oil and gas supply revolves around whether the volume of oil and gas remaining to be found, or our productive capability, is the primary limiting factor on the domestic production rate in the immediate years ahead. The National Petroleum Council concluded from its inquiry that at least until 1985 the amount remaining to be found is not the limiting factor. NPC visualizes that annual production can increase with appropriate attention to the drilling rates, finding rates, improvements in recovery factor, and economic adjustments.

The straightforward production-history approach of M. King Hubbert and others, which is appealing to many, does appear to be very useful in telling us what is likely to happen in the near future, if we continue doing things more or less the way we have been. It implies that production, drilling, and so on are insensitive to economics and policies. Barring an almost total interruption in exploration, such curves do seem to provide us with what should be our minimum expectation for future U.S. oil and gas output. However, this is not to suggest that any of the other kinds of appraisals are totally free of ties to past reserve and in-place figures and historical, economic, and technological factors.

There is greater satisfaction with recent estimates of future oil and gas supplies because the numbers appear to be converging. Instead of difference in orders of magnitude, two estimates may be within 10 or 25 percent of one another. In part, this merely reflects a greater consistency in methodology and assumptions than previously. Any comfort derived from this apparent consensus can be false. Although two estimators may now agree, even if they have used different methods, this does not necessarily mean that they are both right.

Finally, it is important to emphasize that all oil and gas resource estimates by the many analyses both public and private are dependent upon the same sets of numbers as starting points. Beyond this, there is no right methodology, and estimates are sophisticated guesses at best. All experts are agreed that the usable oil and gas hydrocarbon resources are probably sufficiently limited that the maximum annual rate of production and the decline until reserves are exhausted are events that will fall within a few decades, not much beyond that. The peak in the United States may have already been reached. Yet one must not minimize the importance of capturing the remaining one-half or one-third of our oil and gas.

So basically we are dealing with forecasts of annual production rates for two or three decades, and we must get an idea of the impacts of economic and technological changes on these rates. Cost data should be assembled so that it will be possible to analyze better the responses to economic change. Attention must be directed to the effect of technological change on increasing the recovery factor of existing reservoirs and the lead times needed to accomplish this.

This work will be aided if we can eliminate some of the past disagreements of estimators that stemmed from a lack of consistency in defining recovery factors and other concepts employed. If estimators are agreed on anything, it is that the definitions of terms must be examined closely and more standard definitions accepted for future resolution, if not of the supply question, then at least of why the estimators disagree in fact. Such a resolution would be an important step toward substantive agreement.

This is not as easy as it may seem. Even a seemingly simple term "total oil and gas in place" changes in meaning due to changes in information and the economic or technological perception of the analyst. Gas in tight sands or heavy oils would not have been encompassed within the definition of that term a few years ago. Yet some output from these sources has now joined the production stream.

The realization that there are no measurements in oil and gas resource appraisals is important to impress upon everyone. Even in discovered reservoirs we do not measure the oil in place—it is estimated. Reserves are an estimated value derived from a prior estimate of the oil in place, taking into account economics and technology. If the oil-in-place estimate changes, so will that of the reserves. Reserves and resources are equal to the estimated oil in place multiplied by an assumed recovery factor, substantially less than 100 percent for oil, less the amount of cumulative production. Nothing could be simpler yet so uncertain. There are no hidden formulas for predicting the end of the finite supply of oil and gas in the United States or the world. The definitive study of future oil and gas supply and how it may be altered by economic and technological parameters that have not yet emerged still remains to be done. It is of little comfort that the final, reliable, appraisal of the oil and gas resources of the United States will prove to be historic rather than predictive.

GLOSSARY

A number of oil and gas terms are used differently by different people. Below are some short, nontechnical definitions that may be helpful in reading this issue as well as other reports about oil and gas resources.

Commercial accumulation an occurrence of oil and gas that meets the minimum requirement for size and accessibility to be of commercial interest to a company. The term commercial is frequently synonymous with economic.

Deliverability the amount of natural gas that a well, field, pipeline, or system can supply in a given period of time. Only valid for that period.

Discovered resources that portion of the oil and gas in the earth whose presence has been physically confirmed through actual exploration drilling.

Indicated reserves known oil and gas that is currently producible but cannot be estimated accurately enough to qualify as proved.

Inferred reserves reserves that are producible but the assumption of their presence is based upon limited physical evidence and considerable geologic extrapolation. This places them on the borderline of being undiscovered. The accuracy of the estimate is very poor.

Inplace all of the oil and gas in the reservoir, combining both the recoverable and nonrecoverable portions.

Maximum efficient rate (MER) when used in a practical or operational sense, it is the optimum rate, as of a specific time, at which oil and gas should be drawn from a developed field in order to balance cost, percentage recovery, and speed of withdrawal. To exceed this rate for the reservoir or to produce individual wells too rapidly can lead to loss of oil and gas recovery from the reservoir.

Occurrence a physical accumulation of oil or gas or related hydrocarbons in the earth regardless of size and physical or economic characteristics.

Oil basin a large basin-like geologic structure in which oil and gas fields will be found.

Oil field a geologic unit in which one or more individual, structurally and geologically related, reservoirs are found.

Oil region a large oil-bearing area, often encompassing several states, in which oil basins and fields are found in close proximity.

Production or decline curve (S curve) the annual production of an oil or gas reservoir through time is a dome-shaped profile with its peak usually to the left of center. The progress of the production from its peak toward depletion is called the "decline curve." If this is plotted as cumulative production it follows a gradual S-shape as it approaches the total, or ultimate, production of the reservoir.

Productive capacity the amount of oil that can be withdrawn each day from existing wells with available production facilities. Only valid at one point in time.

Proved reserves an estimate of oil and gas reserves contained primarily in the drilled portion of fields. The data to be employed and the method of estimation are specified so that the average error will normally be less than 20 percent. May also be called measured reserves.

Recoverable that portion of oil and gas resources that can be brought to the surface, as distinct from the oil and gas found in place in the reservoir.

Reserves oil and gas that has been discovered and is producible at the prices and technology that existed when the estimate was made.

Reservoir a continuous, interconnected volume of rock containing oil and gas as a hydraulic unit.

Resource base the total amount of oil and gas that physically exists in a specified volume of the earth's crust.

Resources the total amount of oil and gas, including reserves, that is expected to be produced in the future.

S-curve. See production or decline curve.

Subeconomic resources oil and gas in the ground that are not producible under present prices and technology but may become producible at some future date under higher prices or improved technology.

Undiscovered resources resources which are estimated totally by geologic speculation with no physical evidence through drilling available.

REFERENCES

American Petroleum Institute, *Seminar on Reserves and Productive Capacity* (Washington, D.C., April 1, 1975).

American Petroleum Institute, *Standard Definitions for Petroleum Statistics* Technical Report No. 1, 2nd edition (Washington, D.C., 1976).

American Gas Association and American Petroleum Institute, *Reserves of Crude Oil, Natural Gas Liquids, and Natural Gas in the United States and Canada* (Washington, D.C.) annual.

Eugene Ayres and Charles A. Scarlott, *Energy Sources—The Wealth of the World* (McGraw-Hill, New York, 1952).

Federal Energy Administration, *National Energy Outlook* (Government Printing Office, 1976).

M. King Hubbert, *U.S. Energy Resources: Review as of 1972.* Committee Print: Senate Committee on Interior and Insular Affairs, 93 Cong. 2nd sess.

Hans H. Landsberg, "Review of Federal Energy Administration *National Energy Outlook* (Report to NSF under proposal No. 7680248) (mimeo, Resources for the Future, March 1977).

Mathematica, Inc., *A Comparative State-of-the-Art Assessment of Gas Supply Modeling* (Research Project #436–1) (Electric Power Research Institute, Palo Alto, California, February 1977).

P. W. MacAvoy and R. S. Pindyck, *The Economics of the Natural Gas Shortage (1960–1980)* (North-Holland, Amsterdam and New York, 1975).

James W. McFarland, *MER (Maximum Efficient Rate) Definitions and Calculations Using a Gas-Water Reservoir Model* (LA-6533-MS) (Los Alamos Scientific Laboratory, Los Alamos, New Mexico, October 1976).

National Academy of Sciences, *Gas Reserve Estimation of Offshore Producible Shut-in Leases in the Gulf of Mexico* (Washington, D.C., March 1976).

National Academy of Sciences, *Natural Gas from Unconventional Geologic Sources* (Washington, D.C. 1976).

National Academy of Sciences, Committee on Mineral Resources and the Environment, *Mineral Resources and the Environment* (Washington, D.C., February 1975).

National Petroleum Council, *U.S. Energy Outlook* (Washington, D.C., December 1972).

Potential Gas Committee, Colorado School of Mines, *Potential Supply of Natural Gas in the United States* (Golden, Colorado, November 1973).

John J. Schanz, Jr., *Resource Terminology: An Examination of Concepts and Terms and Recommendations for Improvement* (Springfield, Va., National Technical Information Service, 1975), PB 244–433.

Sam H. Schurr and Bruce C. Netschert, *Energy in the American Economy: 1850–1975* (Baltimore, Johns Hopkins University Press for Resources for the Future, 1960).

Richard P. Sheldon, "Estimates of Undiscovered Petroleum Resources—A Perspective," *United States Geological Survey Annual Report, Fiscal Year 1975,* p. 11ff.

United States Geological Survey, *Geological Estimates of Undiscovered Recoverable Oil and Gas Resources in the United States,* Geological Survey Circular 725 (1975).

RFF WORKSHOP PARTICIPANTS

Resources for the Future wishes to acknowledge the contributions made by participants in the series of workshops held in recent years. These were: the Workshop on Oil and Gas Resources chaired by John C. Calhoun, Texas A&M, and Earl Cook, Texas A&M, rapporteur; the Workshop on Maximum Efficient Rate chaired by John J. Schanz, Jr., Resources for the Future, and Hans H. Landsberg, Resources for the Future, rapporteur; and the Workshop which reviewed the FEA's

1976 National Energy Outlook, chaired by William A. Vogely, Penn State, and Helmut Frank, University of Arizona, rapporteur. The participants, some of whom participated in more than one workshop, are listed alphabetically below with their affiliation at the time of the workshop.

Philip H. Abelson, Carnegie Institution

M. A. Adelman, Massachusetts Institute of Technology

Ralph E. Bailey, Consolidated Coal Company

Daniel Bass, Colorado School of Mines

B. Warren Beebe, Energy Consultant

Harold W. Bertholf, Resources Agency of California

Richard C. Byrd, Interstate Oil Compact Commission

John C. Calhoun, Jr., Texas A&M University

Monte Canfield, Jr., General Accounting Office

Earl Cook, Texas A&M University

Benjamin S. Cooper, Senate Interior Committee

Gordon R. Corey, Commonwealth Edison Company

Ronald G. Cummings, University of New Mexico

Joel Darmstadter, Resources for the Future

John Davidson, Council on Environmental Quality

W. Kenneth Davis, Bechtel Power Corporation

Nicholas G. Dumbros (ret.), Marathon Oil Company

Lloyd D. Elkins, AMOCO Production Company

Herman Enzer, Department of the Interior

Edward W. Erickson, North Carolina State University

Helmut Frank, The University of Arizona

Herman T. Franssen, Congressional Research Service

John H. Gibbons, University of Tennessee

Edwin D. Goebel, Federal Power Commission

Richard L. Gordon, Pennsylvania State University

Bernardo Grossling, U.S. Geological Survey

Marcel Grunspan, Energy Research and Development Administration

Mariano Gurfinkel, International Monetary Fund

DeVerle Harris, University of Arizona

John D. Haun, Colorado School of Mines

Hollis Hedberg, Princeton University

Claude Hocott, University of Texas

Kenneth Hoffman, Brookhaven National Laboratories

William Hogan, Federal Energy Administration

M. King Hubbert, U.S. Geological Survey

Richard L. Jodry, Sun Oil Company

John C. Joers, Continental Oil Company

John M. Kelly, Consultant

Hans H. Landsberg, Resources for the Future

Milton Lipton, W. J. Levy, Inc.

Paul W. MacAvoy, Massachusetts Institute of Technology

Charles S. Matthews, Shell Oil Company

R. G. McCrossan, Institute of Sedimentary & Petroleum Geology

Stephen L. McDonald, The University of Texas

Vincent E. McKelvey, U.S. Geological Survey

Charles Mankin, Oklahoma Geological Survey

Horst Mendershausen, The RAND Corporation

Betty Miller, U.S. Geological Survey

John D. Moody, Petroleum Consultant

Bruce C. Netschert, National Economic Research Associates

David Nissen, Federal Energy Administration

Peter R. Odell, Erasmus University

John F. O'Leary, The MITRE Corporation

Joseph D. Parent, Institute of Gas Technology

Harry Perry, Resources for the Future

James Plummer, National Science Foundation

A. L. Porter (ret.), New Mexico Conservation Commission

William Prast, Continental Oil Company

R. A. Purvis, Energy Resources Conservation

George W. Rathjens, Massachusetts Institute of Technology

Steve Rattien, National Science Foundation

Larry Ruff, The Ford Foundation

Milton Russell, Resources for the Future

W. K. Savage, Scientific Software

John J. Schanz, Jr., Resources for the Future

Walter W. Schroeder, House Subcommittee on Energy and Power

Sam H. Schurr, Resources for the Future

David Schwartz, Michigan State University

Milton F. Searl, Electric Power Research Institute

Mark Sharefkin, Resources for the Future

Marshall B. Standing, Stanford University

Henry B. Steele, University of Houston

James L. Sweeney, Federal Energy Administration

Edward Symonds, Consultant

INDEX

359

ABOUT THE AUTHORS

Aaron Wildavsky is Professor of Political Science at the University of California at Berkeley, and a member of its Survey Research Center. His recent books include the fifth edition of *Presidential Elections* (Scribner's, 1979) with Nelson Polsby, *Speaking Truth to Power* (Little, Brown, 1979; British edition, *The Art and Craft of Policy Analysis,* by Macmillan, 1980), and *How to Limit Government Spending* (University of California Press, 1980).

Ellen Tenenbaum is a research associate with the Institute for Policy and Management Research, and head of the Institute's Washington, D.C., office. She received a Master's degree in public policy from the University of California, Berkeley, in 1976, and then joined the National Institute of Education in Washington, D.C., where she coauthored *High School 77.* In addition to her work with the Institute, she has been evaluating government export development programs for the International Trade Administration of the U.S. Department of Commerce.